Contents

The Chartered
Institute of Marketing

Marketing Environment
2005–2006

Mike Oldroyd

ELSEVIER
BUTTERWORTH
HEINEMANN

AMSTERDAM   BOSTON   HEIDELBERG   LONDON   NEW YORK   OXFORD
PARIS   SAN DIEGO   SAN FRANCISCO   SINGAPORE   SYDNEY   TOKYO

Elsevier Butterworth-Heinemann
Linacre House, Jordan Hill, Oxford OX2 8DP
30 Corporate Drive, Burlington, MA 01803

First published 2005

British Library Cataloguing in Publication Data
A catalogue record for this book is available from the British Library

Library of Congress Cataloguing in Publication Data
A catalogue record for this book is available from the Library of Congress

ISBN 0 7506 6645 5

For information on all Elsevier Butterworth-Heinemann publications
visit our website at http://books.elsevier.com

Typeset by Integra Software Services Pvt. Ltd, Pondicherry, India
www.integra-india.com
Printed and bound in Italy

Preface
welcome to the CIM coursebooks

An introduction from the author

This coursebook provides a student centred framework to help you successfully pass the examination through understanding how organizations and their dynamic marketing environments relate and interact. Social, legislative, economic, political, technological, information and competitive environments affect virtually every organizational function and activity, not least those concerned with marketing.

The Professional Certificate syllabus specifies the knowledge and understanding, skills and application that students are required to demonstrate through the various assessments to achieve the award. It is based on so-called 'Statements of Marketing Practice', which are a set of practical observations defining what tasks marketers typically perform at various stages of their career. In the case of the Marketing Environment these include:

- o Collecting information
- o Interpreting and Presenting Information
- o Contributing Information and Ideas to the Strategy Process
- o Contributing to the production of Marketing Plans and Budgets.

The units that follow will help you to translate theory into application by illustrating how the 'learning' elements of the syllabus can be integrated into active marketing practice. It should be read in conjunction with other Certificate subjects since there are numerous overlaps and synergies to be exploited, particularly with Customer Communications (for exemplars of business format and development of information communication technologies) and Marketing Fundamentals (for stakeholder analysis and marketing applications/implications). For those progressing to Diploma, the concepts form general building blocks that specifically underpin marketing strategy and planning.

This coursebook will also develop what CIM refers to as 'Key Skills for Marketers'. These represent transferable knowledge and competencies common to all business professionals and form an important part of the 'complete' marketer's armoury in future-orientated organizations:

- o Using information communication technologies and the Internet – Units 3, 4, 8 and 9.
- o Using financial information and metrics – see particularly Units 3–9.
- o Presenting information – see activities, examination question debriefs and Units 3, 4 and 9.
- o Improving own learning and performance – see exam hints and later activities.
- o Working with others – see some of the activities.
- o Problem-solving – see questions and activities throughout the text.
- o Applying business law – see particularly Units 3 and 7.

The underlying theme of the syllabus is managing the current and future environment. The content is therefore dynamic, future orientated and action centred with its focus on understanding the nature of an ever-changing environment, applying a toolbox of appropriate methodologies and assessing the significance of emerging environmental challenges.

The main aim of the Marketing Environment syllabus and this coursebook is as follows:

o To explain the nature of the marketing environment and its relevance for organizations and marketing practice (Element 1 see Units 1, 2 and 4).
o To provide knowledge of marketing information and its use in organizations, particularly in its application in the strategy and marketing planning processes (Element 4 see Units 2, 4 and 9).
o To provide participants with a working knowledge of organizations and the various influences of their wider environments (Elements 2 and 3 see Units 3, 4–8).

This coursebook provides you with the means of making sense of the complex relationships that exist between an organization and its environment. It heightens your awareness of changes that are taking place and their implications for your day-to-day work activities. Both the syllabus and the coursebook are revised annually to ensure currency. The emphasis throughout is to reinforce the intention of the CIM that students should develop skills and competency by being given every encouragement to relate their knowledge to understanding, and that understanding to marketing applications.

This coursebook is sufficiently comprehensive to limit the need to consult other sources. Only a few texts are currently available in this area, or provide the necessary breadth and level of coverage required. Appendices are provided covering continuous assessment, guidance on examination preparation, curriculum information as well as answers and debriefings for activities, questions and examination topics set within the text.

The first three units concentrate on the nature of the organization (15 per cent) and its micro-environment (20 per cent). Students will be able to:

o Distinguish between the types of organization within the public, private and voluntary sectors, understand their objectives and the influences on them.
o Demonstrate an understanding of the organization's micro-environment.

The final six study units focus on the wider macro-environments (50 per cent) and environmental information systems (15 per cent). Students will be able to:

o Explain the main elements of an organization's marketing environment and discuss the significance of current and future environmental challenges.
o Describe the interactions between the main elements of the marketing environment.
o Assess the potential impact on an organization of key trends in the social, technical, economic, environmental, political, legal and ethical environments.
o Explain the process for collecting information about the marketing environment from relevant primary and secondary sources. Compare and contrast various techniques for collecting information about the marketing environment.

The units must not, however, be seen as separate compartments of knowledge but rather as interlocked pieces of an intricate jigsaw.

The text is broken up into digestible chunks by definitions, questions and activities. Debriefs are provided to many of these at the end of each unit, but have been purposely limited to encourage maximum contribution from you! All end-of-unit questions are examples from past CIM papers, and you should use them to cement your understanding.

This coursebook will encourage you to think in terms of open systems since as marketers, the organization you work for or compete against, the industries and various economies and societies within which transactions take place, are all interrelated parts of a wider system, the global economy. This and the information communication technologies that are driving its development will be a continuing theme explored throughout. The digital revolution is already transforming much of what we currently take for granted.

One topsy-turvy recommendation I hope you will consider implementing before you progress very far in this coursebook is to read and digest the first few pages of Appendix 1 where guidance on revision and examinations is provided. Waiting until you have completed all nine coursebook units will probably be too late to obtain maximum benefit from this important section, with the examination just around the corner.

Since your next step will be to embark on Unit 1, it is important that you plan your route to examination success in an organized way. A random approach is unlikely to produce the success you are looking for, so consider the following method right from the start:

- Whether you use a paper or computer/laptop-based system, you need a folder containing files of information on the various units and the syllabus that underpins it.
- These files are used to store, process and cross refer your syllabus information.
- Readings and articles can then be scanned, placed in or downloaded to the appropriate file.
- Examples of marketing practice/answers to activities etc. may also be integrated.
- Use your own organization or business college as a source of information and example.
- Remember that collection, interpretation and presentation of information are 'examinable' core skills so start as you mean to go on by developing your own tailor-made Marketing Information System for passing this and all the other units at Certificate level.

To conclude, this coursebook is intended to be a resource; a source of information and explanation as well as a framework for study. It is designed to be a one-stop solution for your professional development in this challenging subject area. Use it systematically and use it well and I am confident you will meet with the examination success you deserve.

Mike Oldroyd

An introduction from the academic development advisor

In the last 2 years we have seen some significant changes to CIM Marketing qualifications. The changes have been introduced on a year-on-year basis, with (Certificate changes implemented in 2002, and the Professional Diploma in Marketing) being launched in 2003. The Professional Postgraduate Diploma in Marketing was launched in 2004. The new qualifications are based on the CIM Professional Marketing Standards, developed through research with employers.

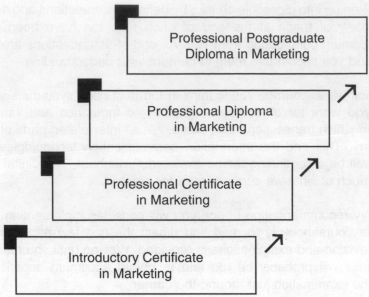

Professional Postgraduate
Diploma in Marketing

Professional Diploma
in Marketing

Professional Certificate
in Marketing

Introductory Certificate
in Marketing

Study note © CIM 2005

As a result the authoring team, Elsevier Butterworth-Heinemann and I have all aimed to rigorously revise and update the coursebook series to make sure that every title is the best possible study aid and accurately reflects the latest CIM syllabus. This has been further enhanced through independent reviews carried out by CIM.

We have aimed to develop the assessment support to include some additional support for the assignment route as well as the examination, so we hope you will find this helpful.

There are a number of new authors and indeed Senior Examiners in the series who have been commissioned for their CIM course teaching and examining experience, as well as their research into specific curriculum-related areas and their wide general knowledge of the latest thinking in marketing.

We are certain that you will find these coursebooks highly beneficial in terms of the content and assessment opportunities and a study tool that will prepare you for both CIM examinations and continuous/integrative assessment opportunities. They will guide you in a logical and structured way through the detail of the syllabus, providing you with the required underpinning knowledge, understanding and application of theory.

The editorial team and authors wish you every success as you embark upon your studies.

Karen Beamish
Academic Development Advisor

How to use these coursebooks

Everyone who has contributed to this series has been careful to structure the books with the exams in mind. Each unit, therefore, covers an essential part of the syllabus. You need to work through the complete coursebook systematically to ensure that you have covered everything you need to know.

This coursebook is divided into units each containing a selection of the following standard elements:

- *Learning objectives* – tell you what you will be expected to know, having read the unit.
- *Syllabus references* – outline what part of the syllabus is covered in the module.
- *Study guides* – tell you how long the unit is and how long its activities take to do.
- *Questions* – are designed to give you practice – they will be similar to those you get in the exam.
- *Answers* (at the end of the book) – give you a suggested format for answering exam questions. Remember there is no such thing as a model answer – you should use these examples only as guidelines.
- *Activities* – give you a chance to put what you have learned into practice.
- *Debriefings* (at the end of the book) – shed light on the methodologies involved in the activities.
- *Hints and tips* – are tips from the senior examiner, examiner or author and are designed to help you avoid common mistakes made by previous candidates and give you guidance on improving your knowledge base.
- *Insights* – encourage you to contextualize your academic knowledge by reference to real-life experience.
- *Key definitions* – highlight and explain the key points relevant to that module.
- *Definitions* – may be used for words you must know to pass the exam.
- *Summaries* – cover what you should have picked up from reading the unit.
- *Further study* – provides details of recommended reading in addition to the coursebook.

While you will find that each section of the syllabus has been covered within this text, you might find that the order of some of the topics has been changed. This is because it sometimes makes more sense to put certain topics together when you are studying, even though they might appear in different sections of the syllabus itself. If you are following the reading and other activities, your coverage of the syllabus will be just fine, but don't forget to follow up with trade press reading!

About MarketingOnline

Elsevier Butterworth-Heinemann offers purchasers of the coursebooks free access to MarketingOnline (www.marketingonline.co.uk), our premier online support engine for the CIM marketing courses. On this site you can benefit from:

- Fully customizable electronic versions of the coursebooks enabling you to annotate, cut and paste sections of text to create your own tailored learning notes
- The capacity to search the coursebook online for instant access to definitions and key concepts
- Useful links to e-marketing articles, provided by Dave Chaffey, Director of Marketing Insights Ltd and a leading UK e marketing consultant, trainer and author
- A glossary providing a comprehensive dictionary of marketing terms
- A Frequently Asked Questions (FAQs) section providing guidance and advice on common problems or queries.

Using MarketingOnline

Logging on

Before you can access MarketingOnline you will first need to get a password. Please go to www.marketingonline.co.uk and click on the registration button where you will then find registration instructions for coursebook purchasers. Once you have got your password, you will need to log on using the on-screen instructions. This will give you access to the various functions of the site.

MarketingOnline provides a range of functions, as outlined in the previous section, that can easily be accessed from the site after you have logged on to the system. Please note the following guidelines detailing how to access the main features:

1. *The coursebooks* – buttons corresponding to the three levels of the CIM marketing qualification are situated on the home page. Select your level and you will be presented with the coursebook title for each module of that level. Click on the desired coursebook to access the full online text (divided up by chapter). On each page of text you have the option to add an electronic bookmark or annotation by following the on-screen instructions. You can also freely cut and paste text into a blank word document to create your own learning notes.
2. *e-Marketing articles* – to access the links to relevant e-marketing articles simply click on the link under the text 'E-marketing Essentials: useful links from Marketing Insights'.
3. *Glossary* – a link to the glossary is provided in the top right hand corner of each page enabling access to this resource at any time.

If you have specific queries about using MarketingOnline then you should consult our fully searchable FAQs section, accessible through the appropriate link in the top right-hand corner of any page of the site. Please also note that a *full user guide* can be downloaded by clicking on the link on the opening page of the website.

unit 1

the nature of the organization and the impact of its environment

Learning outcomes

By the end of this unit you will be able to:

o Distinguish between the types of organization within the public, private and voluntary sectors (1.2/1.3)

o Assess the relative strengths and weaknesses of different types of organization (1.3)

o Understand the diversity of organizational objectives and influences upon them (1.4/1.5)

o Understand the nature of organizations as open systems and the environmental influences that affect them (1.6/1.7).

Study Guide

As may be seen in Table 1.1, which maps the syllabus learning outcomes and units where they are covered, this first unit will provide a framework and organizational setting to explore the dynamic interrelationships between businesses and the various environments in which they operate. The material is relatively straightforward but of critical importance to an understanding of subsequent units, since it provides a foundation upon which the others are built.

The marketing environment is broad and ever changing and it is essential that you work to relate the course material to current developments. Acquire the habit of 'scanning' the quality press for up-to-date articles, reviews and surveys relating business to its environments. Supplement this by tuning in weekly to a serious news analysis programme on TV or radio. Use the Internet, if it is available at work or college, to access various websites with databases related to the environment. As you will see under 'Exam hints' throughout this unit, you will need to be prepared for broad questions which test your grasp and general appreciation of the evolving marketing environment.

1

Table 1.1 Mapping learning outcomes by unit signposting

Learning outcomes	Study units/syllabus reference
Distinguish between the types of organization within the public, private and voluntary sectors, and understand their objectives and the influences upon them	Unit 1
Explain the main elements of an organization's marketing environment and discuss the significance of current and future environmental challenges	Units 2, 9
Describe the interactions between the main elements of the marketing environment	Units 2, 4, 9
Assess the potential impact on an organization of key trends in the social, technical, economic, environmental, political, legal and ethical environments	Units 4–8
Demonstrate an understanding of an organization's micro-environment	Units 2–3
Explain the process of collecting information about the marketing environment from relevant primary and secondary sources	Units 3, 4, 9
Compare and contrast various techniques for collecting information about the marketing environment	Unit 9

This first unit will also help you to familiarize yourself with the approach and style of our coursebooks. It has been developed to ensure that you acquire not only the knowledge necessary for examination success but also the skills to apply that knowledge both in the examination and in your work as a professional marketer. You will find the boxed panels clearly signposted to help you practice, evaluate and extend your knowledge and these will be used throughout so that you can manage your own learning in terms of both pace and depth.

The importance of the marketing environment

Study tip

Start as you mean to go on in the organization of your study materials. From the very beginning of the course it has been a sound advice to:

- Use file dividers to index broad topic area notes.
- Add relevant materials, activity output, articles and clippings.
- Summarize related articles which may provide current examples for illustrating examination answers. The examiner will expect this!
- Cross-reference to other sections of the file since the marketing environment is inter-related and questions may be addressed to more than one part of the syllabus.
- Produce a set of implications for the marketer and/or the organization for every aspect of the syllabus. This is vital since CIM questions generally require you to apply your knowledge in a stated context.
- Incorporate past questions, examiner reports, model answers and revision notes when available.
- Edit and summarize into bullet points for easy memorizing.

In this way, your file sections will be complete and facilitate ease of revision prior to the examination.

The CIM defines marketing as:

> *the management process which identifies, anticipates and supplies customer require-*
> *ments efficiently and profitably.*

This focuses attention on the importance of the marketing environment since identifying and anticipating customer requirements is impossible unless the organization looks outward from itself, to understand its external environment and the implications of changes taking place on its current and future profitability. Few businesses can afford to adopt a 'production orientation', and fail to respond to the evolving opportunities and threats in its marketplace.

Question 1.1

List the elements of the external environment you consider most important to the marketers' understanding of:

1. Its potential customers
2. Its potential profitability.

Provide *four* different examples of external factors where you feel 'change' seems fastest.

Probably your initial thoughts were of existing and potential markets. The changing tastes and preferences of customers, their disposable incomes, and the price and availability of substitutes will clearly be important, as will the size, strength and numbers of competitors. Less obvious are the changes in the broader environment which influence these market conditions. Demographic changes alter the population of various market segments while tax adjustments affect their purchasing power. Cultural and technical developments may exert even more powerful influences on the longer-term supply, demand, profitability and life cycle of different goods and services. Rising concern with the green environment, for example, has caused many businesses to modify their product offerings and methods of production.

No organization, whether small or large, public or private, profit or non-profit making can afford to ignore its environment. As the strategist H.I. Ansoff observed:

> *the firm is a creature of its environment. Its resources, its income, its problems, its*
> *opportunities and its very survival are generated and conditioned by the environment.*

 ## Activity 1.1

Key skills: interpreting information

Interpretation of this quotation formed part of a recent examination paper. Better candidates demonstrated their understanding of each aspect of it in turn. Can you develop the idea of the organization as a creature of its environment? Themes could include:

○ Must exist in an environment full of threats and opportunities
○ Must adapt to the unexpected
○ Environment full of rivals, competitors and allies – How do you relate to them?
○ Pressure to adapt – survival of the fittest
○ Must be constantly aware of surroundings and understand what is going on

    ○ What are your strengths and weaknesses relative to others in the environment?
    ○ Do you rely on size, or speed and flexibility, as your defensive strategy?

Can you brainstorm a list of themes for each of the other elements of the firm conditioned by the environment, that is, resources; income (revenue); problems; opportunities and survival?

How will the analysis vary according to the size and nature of the firm?

(*Note*: This will be discussed in more detail in Unit 2 'The micro-environment'.)

Societal concerns are often translated through the legislative process to impact on the freedom of business to manage. The marketer must be aware of pressures from a range of interested groups to which a positive response may be called for. It is also the domain of actual or potential competitors, and is consequently ignored at the organization's peril.

Large firms, particularly multinationals, may be able to exert greater influence over their business situation, but small firms may have the advantage by responding to the need for change more flexibly.

 ## Definition

Multinationals – Are enterprises engaged in simultaneous manufacture/operations in a number of countries and which take decisions from a global perspective. The worldwide annual turnover of companies such as Exxon (Esso) and Toyota exceeds the gross domestic product of many of the smaller Western European countries.

Important note: Acquire the habit of using the glossary in www.marketingonline.co.uk for definitions of all key terms.

Before exploring the nature of this environment and the marketer's approach to it, we need to study the different forms of business organizations involved in the economy.

The purpose of organizations is to bring together people with common interests in a systematic effort to produce goods and services that they could not readily have produced as individuals. Organization enables specialization and division of labour. This saves time and raises productivity. Organizations are also social in nature providing mutual support and opportunity for development. We all come into contact with organizations when we buy goods, attend lectures, deposit funds or go to the doctors. Your list of examples should reflect this diversity. Whatever the form or purpose of the organization, it will have common characteristics such as:

    ○ A framework of written or tacit rules (e.g. articles of association)
    ○ A decision-making hierarchy (e.g. Board of Directors)
    ○ A record of proceedings (e.g. minutes of meetings)
    ○ A means of coordinating efforts and resources to determine what and how to produce, in what quantities using what channels of distribution (e.g. Chief Executive).

These matters are explored in the CIM coursebook *Marketing Management* while we are concerned with the types of business organizations and their environment.

Business classifications

As marketers, we need to understand the diversity of business both nationally and internationally:

- Each addresses potential customers in different ways due to their differing objectives, strengths and weaknesses.
- Each are buyers and sellers in their own right, but multinationals purchase in bulk using professionals whereas small firms tend to source and sell locally.
- The implications for competition, growth and innovation vary with each.
- Their relative importance is changing with the growth in small businesses and self-employment, a shrinking public sector and the rising importance of entrepreneurial non-profit makers such as charities.

To understand the diversity of business we must first classify the various types and form a framework for understanding their characteristics.

Activity 1.2

Key skills: using information

There are a number of ways in which organizations may be classified. Suggest three examples of each classification approach listed below. By:

- Ownership
- Legal form
- Control
- Sector
- Objectives
- Accountability
- Activity
- Size.

The formal and informal economy

An economy may be thought of as being made up of three parts: the public sector, the private sector and the informal economy.

The public sector

This comprises all those activities involving provision of goods and services by the state. Revenue to finance these is raised by:

- Taxation on the rest of the economy
- Fees and charges
- Government borrowing.

These resources are allocated to the various spending departments who plan provision according to government objectives rather than market forces. These may involve socially desirable objectives embracing some concept of fairness and civil rights achieved through redistribution of income and wealth. The state has taken responsibility in a number of areas where provision by the private sector was not seen as adequate or appropriate. *Public goods* such as defence, law, order and emergency services comprise one major category, while *merit goods* such as health, education and other social services provide the other. A number of other industries might come into the domain of the state for a variety of reasons including: strategic considerations, natural monopolies, job preservation, health and safety (e.g. Network Rail in the UK taking all maintenance work in-house) and national security.

Activity 1.3

Key skills: using information

Match the terms with their correct definitions:

- Contracting out
- Natural monopoly
- Privatization
- Merit goods
- Public goods
- Quango.

— Can be provided by the private sector but concern for equity and whether sufficient would be provided, leads to public provision.

— A good or service which cannot be priced accurately and therefore cannot be efficiently supplied by the private sector. Consumption by one person does not reduce supply for others (e.g. TV signals/street lighting). No consumer can be excluded even if they refuse to pay (e.g. public health) and no one may abstain from consumption (e.g. defence). All consume equally but have no incentive to pay for what must be provided in any case.

— A quasi-autonomous non-government organization is neither an elected nor a private business organization, but has executive or administrative authority to implement or advance government policy. The marketer is likely to encounter large numbers of such bodies (e.g. regulators, standards authorities).

— A firm that can satisfy all the market demand, but still has unexploited cost savings. Competition would duplicate expensive resources.

— The practice by governments (or firms) of employing an outside agent to perform some specific task rather than performing it themselves.

— The transfer of ownership of 51 per cent or more shares from a nationalized concern to private hands.

Government expenditure as a percentage of gross domestic product (GDP) tends to average around 40 per cent. Scandinavian countries, however, have a history of generous social benefit provision and spend closer to 50 per cent of GDP while more free enterprise economies in East Asia opt for low taxes and private provision.

Direct government spending on goods and services has recently been falling in many countries due to the widespread resort to privatization and deregulation. However, transfer payments to fund pensions and health services for ageing populations are on the increase, particularly in developed economies like Japan and Italy. Many developing economies continue to rely on government spending to provide educational and physical infrastructures although international aid agencies favour more reliance on market structures. The rapid introduction of market disciplines in Africa, the former Eastern bloc and Russia has, however, had mixed results.

Market disciplines

Governments in Britain and, to a lesser extent, Europe have also been introducing market disciplines into remaining public sector activities through various actions to make them more acceptable to their users, for example, devolved management and compulsory competitive tendering for central and local government services. This is encouraging a degree of marketing orientation into a wide cross section of public services that were previously producer-orientated. Realization is growing that only by relating their offering to the needs of the client will the necessary contract, budget or funding be forthcoming.

Facilitators versus direct providers

Public organizations of all types are becoming facilitators of services instead of direct providers. Rather than using directly employed labour to provide building, maintenance and waste disposal/refuse services, as in the past, these are now being purchased from private sector contractors. The role of public sector managers is to award the contracts, monitor quality, ensure cost and performance targets are met and above all secure value for money for the rate or taxpayer. Recent examples include commercially run schools following the pattern for privately operated facilities already established in the prison service. This allows the public agencies to concentrate on core services that no other sector can sensibly or willingly supply. Powers are also devolved, through a large number of executive agencies known as quangos, to supervise a wide variety of activities. These are publicly appointed bodies with considerable powers over disposal of resources and important regulatory activities. Their non-elected nature and lack of direct accountability, however, raise concerns over their responsiveness and efficiency.

Exam hint

One of the 'Key Skills for Marketers' is that of 'Improving your own Learning and Performance'. This involves agreeing targets and planning how these will be met, using plans to meet targets and reviewing progress. Your target is probably an 'A' or 'B' grade pass 'first time'. As this key skill makes clear, achievement is a matter of planning within the timescale between now and the examination. Your plan is your 'route map' of intermediate targets (units understood and applied) towards the ultimate goal. The plan must not only be fully implemented but also controlled through regular reviews of your progress against the targets you have set. Any deviation or falling behind (due to work pressures/social commitments, etc.) must be corrected if progress is to be maintained and the desired goal realized.

The processes involved in examination planning and successful marketing planning have much in common. This is the time to draw up your plan of campaign; establish the time constraints; set the milestones; install monthly progress reviews and treat it just like a marketing plan.

Public/private partnerships

This hybrid approach seeks to combine the strengths of private sector management and cost effectiveness with the social concerns and community benefits of the public sector. Local government agencies may sponsor joint construction schemes, for example, that combine the use of government-owned land to develop an integrated dwelling and shopping development, incorporating private businesses, sheltered housing and social amenities. Since most successful economies are a necessary blend of public and private provision, this idea takes the concept of the best of both worlds to its logical conclusion.

The public sector, therefore, owns or controls a complex variety of organizations, but the distinction between these and organizations in other sectors is becoming increasingly blurred, as more and more competition is introduced into their environment.

The private sector

This sector normally accounts for the majority of domestic output, investment goods and exports. Resources are privately owned and businesses compete to satisfy consumer wants and needs. Most are profit motivated and decide on what and how to produce by identifying and anticipating market demands on the one hand, while combining and converting resource inputs efficiently on the other. As you can see in Figure 1.1, a number of different trading organizations may be identified in most countries and we will explore their strengths and weaknesses below. Non-profit-making organizations include trade unions and employer associations, although these would normally be classified as voluntary organizations.

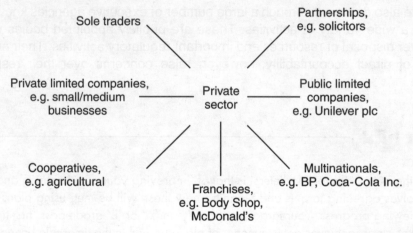

Figure 1.1 Elements of the private sector

Activity 1.4

Before you consider the advantages and drawbacks of these various types of private business organizations, spend a few minutes comparing the relative strengths and weaknesses of the public versus the private sector – use headings and bullet points to set these out.

The informal economy

The activities of the public and private sectors constitute the formal economic activities of a country and their combined output is measured by gross domestic product (GDP). However, three other sectors should be recognized and understood by the marketer.

The *household* economy includes the unpaid domestic services of mainly wives and mothers (e.g. childcare, cooking and cleaning). This economy has undergone significant changes in recent years with women's liberation and increasing employment in the formal economy.

Do-it-yourself activities are also undertaken and include gardening, property improvements, maintenance and repair. Subsistence agriculture is still significant in many developing economies. None of these activities are counted in GDP since no market transactions normally occur.

Marketers are clearly interested in the shifting patterns of this 'economy' because of the demand for goods and services to support activities within it, as well as the implications of the changing lifestyles and tastes of the various household members.

The *voluntary* economy includes those services undertaken by individuals and organizations for which no money payment is normally involved (i.e. non-commercial). It includes the activities of various unions, clubs and associations that act to promote the common interests of their members. Many of these organizations have a special status and services are performed out of friendship or as acts of charity focused on the most needy in the society. As such, they satisfy important needs and generate considerable social welfare, but are not counted in the statistics on national output. Charities such as Oxfam, Help the Aged, and Médecins sans Frontières seek to protect and assist the deprived and disadvantaged within the society or those affected by natural calamity. Many, such as the Red Cross and CARE International have seen their profiles raised, albeit in adverse circumstances, in the post-war strife affecting Iraq.

Often registered and controlled to attract generous tax concessions, they operate on principles very different to the private or public sector, with dedicated staff often working for little or no monetary reward. Rational economic calculation may not be the primary driving force but their performance has, through competition for funding, of necessity become more professional and marketing informed. Effectiveness may be measured in terms of the gross value of the contributions they raise, the degree of suffering they are able to alleviate and their success in raising the public profile of the cause that they represent. Their skill in marketing communications is a key determinant of the latter, while in Britain and America their trading activities have been reflected in the increasing presence of 'charity shops' or 'thrifts'. As such, they constitute an element of choice and competition with established retailers.

The *hidden* or shadow economy involves transactions and activities that are 'undeclared' for tax purposes. Moonlighting workers perform services outside their normal work for cash in hand and no questions asked! The marketer cannot afford to ignore this economy in terms of either hidden purchasing power or as low-cost competition. Small and medium businesses in the formal economy paying tax and insurance, charging sales tax and conforming with legislation may be at a considerable disadvantage compared to the so-called 'cowboy operators'.

Estimated to account for as much as 10–25 per cent of GDP a year, this economy tends to grow with self-employment, high taxation, illegal immigration and unemployment. Other elements of this hidden sector include pilferage, fiddles and outright illegal activities such as drug dealing, smuggling and stolen goods. For example, the huge gap between the minimal factory cost and the 'formal economy' selling price of cigarettes may provide the basis of a massive black marketing racket. Prostitution in Britain is estimated to generate at least £1.2 billion in annual revenues according to *Marketing Week*. Governments regularly announce crackdowns on tax avoidance and evasion targeted on this shadowy economy but with limited success.

Activity 1.5

Key skills: interpreting information

Brainstorm the implications of the trend towards more working wives for:

o Retailers
o Food suppliers
o Household appliance manufacturers.

Why has DIY increased and which businesses are most affected by this 'self-service' trend? Can you think of 'business opportunities' that have arisen from this?

Is the hidden economy growing or shrinking? Justify your answer.

Another important way of classifying business is according to the sector it operates in. Governments normally develop a comprehensive framework that places businesses into classes, groups and activities as part of its annual measurement of national output. Table 1.2 gives an indication of the significant changes in the relative importance, for a developed economy in terms of employment, of different sectors over a comparatively short period of time.

Table 1.2 Percentage sectoral change in employment patterns over time – UK

Sector/Time	1801	1901	1981	2010	2041
Primary	60		4		
Secondary		60		10	
Tertiary			60		
Quaternary					60

The primary sector includes agriculture, fisheries and forestry. Industrialization brings about a dramatic decline in its share of employment as seen in the shift of the 60 per cent across the chart. By the start of the twentieth century the majority were employed in industry which included manufacturing, energy and construction, but again this had fallen considerably by 1981, as service employment became dominant. Manufacturing had already shrunk to 12 per cent of employment in 2003 (3.5 million).

The quaternary sector involves personal rather than business services (e.g. health, education, leisure and other personal services). This may represent the areas where humans have a comparative employment advantage over computer-based technology. Such areas of employment will assume increasing significance as e-business to business developments automate many basic business functions. Even here there is a migration of jobs to developing countries as evidenced by the recent decisions of BT, HSBC and Lloyds TSB to transfer their call centre facilities to India.

The legal form of trading organizations

Sole trader

Characteristics
- Oldest type, simplest to form – self-employment
- Unincorporated – business carried on in its own name
- Ownership and control by a single person
- Individual assumes all rights/duties
- No separate legal existence: the business = the individual
- No disclosure of information bar to tax authorities
- No limit on employees: may employ >100
- Farming/personal services/building/retail
- May originate in the hidden economy.

Merits	Disadvantages
Minimum formalities/privacy	Unlimited liability for any debts
Complete control/no consultation	Raising capital difficult: own funds/plough back/family
Favourable tax treatment	Specialized and risky – banks' view
Highly motivated/single-minded	Jack of all trades/narrow outlook
Least costly to form	Depend on staying healthy so may lack continuity
Close to customers/employees	Self-exploitation – work long hours
Flexible/attend to detail	Competition from large/small
Niches where limit to market	Lack of management skills
Exemption from certain legislation	No one to share burden
Personal satisfactions – status	

Of around 3.75 million enterprises in Britain today (there were 2.5 million in 1979), 97 per cent employ fewer than 20 employees (equivalent to one-third of total employed outside government) and an estimated 80 per cent are sole traders. Small firms and the sole trader are the predominant form in terms of numbers but not in terms of contribution to total output. However, all firms employing fewer than 100, outside government, now account for over 50 per cent of turnover, more than 40 per cent in 1979. This pattern is reproduced in other economies, such as Sri Lanka or Nigeria, where small firms dominate. Large firms, particularly multinationals, tend to prevail in key export and industrialized sectors.

Exam hint

You may have the option of either taking the examination or a Continuous Assessment Assignment (CAA) as your route to successfully completing this and other Certificate Stage Units. While the examination route involves a compulsory mini-case with usually four questions worth 40 per cent of the total marks combined with a choice of three from six optional questions, the CAA involves three parts. These are a compulsory core section worth 45 per cent (2500 words), a choice of two from four options worth 50 per cent (1500 words each) in the elective section and a final reflective statement worth 5 per cent (500 words). These assignments would normally be based on your own organization. This approach can only be undertaken when enrolled at a registered centre.

Found in sectors where entry barriers are low and capital requirements limited, few sole traders could be defined as entrepreneurial. Perhaps 10 per cent of the total might fall into this category and even here their inventiveness is not always sufficient to produce innovation. They will be financially weak compared to well-resourced companies so that even if new product developments make it to market they often face fierce competition and alternative offerings. Limited capital restricts their growth, while excessive competition often requires hard work and long opening hours just to survive. Their social and economic lives tend to merge, and while they are motivated by self-interest they also bear all the risks. They are often under pressure from larger businesses, for example, specialist food retailers have contracted sharply as supermarkets have expanded. Many are self-employed in name only, working exclusively under contract to other organizations.

Partnerships

Characteristics
- Unincorporated
- Two or more in common with a view to profit
- No more than a legally specified maximum number (e.g. 20), bar certain professions
- Form an agreement or bound by legislation
- Unlimited liability and jointly liable
- Share management/profits/losses
- No legal personality.

Merits	Disadvantages
Able to raise more capital	Unlimited liability unless 'Limited' – still must be at least one partner fully liable
Pool expertize/mutual support funds	Lack of legal identity – dissolves if death/disagreement = expense/ trouble
More chance to specialize	Potential disagreements
No company tax on business	Frozen investment

This form is much more attractive to the professions where capital requirements are limited in many cases and codes of conduct limit the risk of financial malpractice. Legal formalities are few and privacy is high. However, recent high profile and costly legal settlements involving poor financial advice given by accountancy firms to corporate clients has caused at least one of the largest (KPMG) to opt for the company form. For most other businesses, the company form is much more attractive.

Registered company

Characteristics
- Incorporated, separate legal entity – enter contracts, and so on
- Formed under relevant legislations, for example, 1985 Companies Act
- Confers various rights and duties
- Members contribute capital and own shares
- Dominant form
- Liability limited to amount invested or guaranteed.

For example, in Britain:

Public company (plc)	Private company (Ltd)
Two or more members	Minimum two/£100 authorized capital
£50 000 and two directors	One director plus a secretary
Offer shares to the public	Offence to offer shares to public – friends OK
Requires business certificate before trading/borrowing	Trade once incorporation certificate is received
Similar legislation elsewhere (e.g. 'inc.' in the USA/Sdn Bhd in Malaysia)	Typical family business
	Raising additional bank funds easier (personal guarantees may be needed)

A registered company has a number of duties and must also submit to the Registrar of Companies:

o *Memorandum of association* – Regulates external affairs/protects investors and suppliers/states name (registered versus business), liability, objectives and scope of business.
o *Articles of association* – Regulate internal administration – issue/transfer of shares, shareholder rights, directors' powers, accounting procedures, and so on.
o *Statutory declaration of compliance* – with the relevant Act.
o *Independently audited annual accounts and directors' report* (smaller firms of fewer than 50 employees provide a summary only).

Note: 'Unlimited liability' companies are exempt from filing accounting data.

Duty of care and trust on all directors

Public companies must also hold an AGM and comply with Stock Exchange regulations.

Merits	Disadvantages
Separate legal entity	Special and double taxation
Limited liability of owners	Complex/costly to form
Greater financial capability	Disclosure requirements
Easy transfer of ownership	Government regulations
Able to fund innovation/new product development	Inflexibility of size
Customers feel reassured	Impersonality

Many companies hold shares in other enterprises which they may have formed or acquired. If these exceed more than 50 per cent of the voting rights, the business is termed a *holding company*. Such holdings may sometimes form a pyramid, with the *ultimate* holding company having overall control. Such structures are common in Japan.

Activity 1.6

Key skills: collecting and using information

Keep your eye on the company section of a quality newspaper (e.g. *Financial Times*) for a company seeking plc status and offering shares for sale to the public. Read the preamble to the offer and list the advantages of this course of action to the business. What are the potential drawbacks?

Ask any friend, colleague or family who owns shares, how often they have attended an AGM. Try to explain the answers they give and draw conclusions as to who exercises the real control.

In undertaking this activity you might reflect on several factors:

o The ability to raise considerable amounts of capital is the main attraction of the public company but what about the 'costs' of raising funds this way?
o What are your feelings about the degree of scrutiny required by the relevant company legislation?
o Does a quotation on the Stock Exchange force the business to think short term rather than long term as some commentators suggest?
o Why have some public companies decided to buy back their shares (e.g. Virgin Group, the Body Shop)?
o Doesn't going public make you vulnerable to a takeover and what if the 'offer' flops (e.g. lastminute.com upset shareholders following their share price collapse)?
o Why have increasing numbers chosen 'unlimited company' status since the law allowed exemption from filing accounts (i.e. financial affairs are kept private)?
o Financial institutions produce pressure to perform, and open trading of shares brings the danger of a hostile takeover bid.
o Negative publicity surrounding so-called 'fat-cat' payments. In the early 1990s Chief Executives in Britain were paid 42 times that of an average worker. A decade later they were earning 411 times that amount. Despite this there is little evidence that higher pay has led to improved performance.

Mini-case – the chips are down?

So called 'blue chip' companies were large organizations making dependable profits with no profit warnings, no scandals and no blunders in basic strategy. Recent experience and an increasingly turbulent environment, however, has brought their continuing existence into question. Certainly companies like Shell, Marks and Spencer and Sainsbury's are no longer the safe stocks they once were. Similarly since the end of 2001 we have seen the collapse of Enron, one of America's most powerful companies with up to an estimated $40 billion of debts while WorldCom, the US's second largest long distance telecoms carrier, admitted to overstating its cash flow by $3.8 billion. In Europe, Italy's worst financial scandal for a decade has centred on Parmalat, a massive agricultural processing concern where false accounting has led to missing billions on its balance sheet. Even the largest of businesses now face much more of a 'roller-coaster' existence than ever before.

Investors might instead have been better advised putting their money in the much smaller Hornby Group, a model railway maker whose profits continue to rise sharply on sales of train sets and model locomotives. This success is partly attributable to demographics (middle-aged men with the income to satisfy their childhood dreams), partly to high-profile media exposure of real-life railway crises and partly to successful new models (e.g. *Hogwarts Castle* loco inspired by Harry Potter). However, in contrast to the $100 billion revenues of Enron at its height, this company could manage only $20 million.

Cooperative

Characteristics

- º Pioneered in mid-nineteenth century – most prevalent in agriculture and retailing
- º Governed by relevant legislation
- º Worker ownership/control but falling numbers/mergers
- º Limited liability but one member, one vote
- º Self-help not profit maximizing via management committee
- º Equitable distribution of dividend *if a surplus is made.*

Comment

A significant but declining force in most sectors, for example, grocery retailing has contracted in the face of competition from the better-managed and more focused multiples, and has been forced to merge and specialize in other niches. Worker cooperatives among farmers and craft workers tend to establish in times of recession or rapid structural decline in the industries concerned. Producer cooperatives doubled in Britain in the 1980s but suffer weaknesses in attracting managers of the right calibre and raising capital for large-scale ventures. The Scott Bader Commonwealth, a chemical concern, is the most-quoted industrial example with an interesting constitution which includes, among other things, a limit of 350 employees per unit, a maximum remuneration spread of 1:7 and no dismissals.

Franchising

Characteristics

- º Franchisor sells the right to market a product under its name to a franchisee
- º Separate entities but interdependent businesses
- º Rapid growth especially retailing (e.g. McDonald's, the Body Shop)
- º Ready-made opportunity for an entrepreneur with capital wishing to minimize risks of a new venture (90 per cent of start-ups survive beyond 3 years).

 Activity 1.7

Key skills: using information

- º Identify a franchise business and a 'manager'-run outlet of a national company in your locality.
- º Observe the quality of service in the two outlets.
- º Assess the relative strengths and weaknesses of the two.
- º Consider *why* franchising has become such an important form of business organization and *what* makes it so customer orientated.

15

In undertaking this activity take account of a 'typical' agreement:

Franchisor agrees to	Franchisee agrees to
Provide business format/initial training	Pay an initial sum to franchisor
Supply product and quality control	Pay a percentage of profit to franchisor
Extend promotional support (e.g. advertising)	Buy supplies of product from franchisor
	Maintain standards laid down

Marketing environment in practice

The case of fast food

McDonald's is probably the most famous name in global franchising and had, until 2002, enjoyed uninterrupted growth. With 30 000 mainly franchised outlets in over 100 countries, it is not surprising that 1 in every 200 people across the globe visits an outlet daily. Yet in 2002, its shares slumped by over a third and the company made the first loss in its history as plans were announced to cut back operations in ten countries. Was the problem some fundamental flaw in the franchise concept or perhaps an environmental explanation? As a marketing analyst at McDonald's what would you do in practice?

o *You would certainly collect information on the situation* Are other fast-food operators similarly affected? Where is the loss of profit concentrated? What is happening to market share and volume sales in different markets? Has anything changed in the wider environment that is impacting on sales? Are franchisees generating the necessary drive and creativity to force sales upward?
o *You would need to interpret the information and then present it effectively to your boss.*
o *This information would then provide an input into the strategy process*, that is find the best solution.

The above are three of the Statements of Marketing Practice that underpin the Marketing Environment syllabus and you may wish to build a case study of such organizations as you work through the units in order to relate theory to practice. For example, in this case you might wish to consider, among others:

o The impact of the war against terror and in Iraq on high-profile US companies
o Changing attitudes towards health and what we eat in the light of rising levels of obesity
o Worries about food safety and the threat of legal action
o The problems of organizational size.

The public services (in Britain)

The public corporations
o Publicly owned, controlled and accountable via ministers to Parliament
o Separate legal entities created by Statute or Royal Charter (e.g. Royal Mint)
o Boards of management appointed by ministers
o Financed from revenue raised or central government funding
o Designed to be commercially independent but subject to ministerial control

- ○ Intended to secure long-term strategic objectives and control of the economy
- ○ Lack of competition and conflicting objectives may lead to inefficiency
- ○ Susceptible to pressure group activity, especially trade unions.

The regulated plcs

- ○ The bulk of the nationalized industries were privatized in the 1980s and 1990s.
- ○ They were sold directly to the public (e.g. BT) or to management/employee buyouts (e.g. National Freight Corporation) or to other companies (e.g. Rover to British Aerospace, subsequently to BMW and then to Ford/Alchemy) or in parts (e.g. British Rail hotels, rolling stock).
- ○ Those remaining are either unprofitable or unsaleable (nuclear) or ideologically difficult (Royal Mail, London Underground – though private investment allowed in 1998).
- ○ The transfer of ownership to private shareholders was justified under:

Political factors	Economic factors
Reduced role of the state	Achieve efficiency improvements
Deregulation of the economy	Increased competition and choice
Encourage shareholding democracy among customers	Pressure on management to become marketing orientated
Enable worker share-ownership	Improve industrial relations
Provide freedom to manage	Exploit new opportunities
Cut borrowing (PSBR) and taxes	Supply side rises in productivity
Cut costs	

- ○ The creation of private monopolies in water, electricity, gas and telecoms was counter-balanced by new regulators with considerable powers to enforce efficiency gains and improvements in service. Recent public concerns that some regulators have become increasingly influenced by the regulated (e.g. OFWAT, OFLOT) have, however, resulted in an enquiry by the Greenbury Committee on public standards and much stricter regulations being applied.

Insight

By comparison of small and medium enterprises (SMEs) and large/global-sized organizations, we observe that both types of organization exist and thrive although this may be dependent on whether the necessary local or global conditions are favourable. The relative strengths of one tend to be weaknesses of the other and vice versa, but either will thrive where the market conditions are appropriate:

The strengths of the global organization

- ○ Economies of scale may be exploited
- ○ Risks may be spread across markets
- ○ Economies in supply and purchase, for example, discounts for volume
- ○ Exploit similarities between markets
- ○ Exploit homogeneity of product, image and advertising messages
- ○ Leverage/bargaining power with suppliers/government, for example, secure subsidies
- ○ Fully utilize skills and other resources

- Exploit best practice and transfer technology, ideas and resources
- Marketing advantages through global brand leadership
- Exploit developments in information technology to the full
- Act as a magnet for suppliers and other key resources
- Access to world financial markets and cheap finance
- Ability to centralize strategy and confront worldwide competition.

The strengths of the SME

- Cater to local consumers
- Cater to local tastes and purchasing habits
- Attention to detail
- Close to the business and its various stakeholders
- Organizationally flexible and adaptable when change is required
- Attracts talent unwilling to work in the confines of the large organization
- Often in a better position to be inventive and innovative.

Conclusions

SMEs will strive to offset the strengths of the larger firms, for example joint purchasing, while global firms will seek to think globally in strategic marketing terms besides thinking locally in operational marketing terms, for example Microsoft amends its Windows and Word software to suit local markets. Going global also carries significant risks as demonstrated by the £20 million loss for Pret A Manager, the sandwich chain now being forced to cut back its outlets.

Local authorities

Services provided by local government include, among others, fire and police, road mainten-ance, consumer protection, recreation, environmental health, education and even airports. They are managed by elected councillors through full-time professional officers. As in the rest of the public sector, they have been subject to radical structural and operational changes over the past decade. Central government control has increased, but authorities have been encouraged to forge mutually beneficial links with local business communities. Exposure to market forces through compulsory competitive tendering has transformed the council officer's role into that of a 'facilitator' rather than a direct provider of local services. Competitive tendering for say, refuse collection, involves the submission of a tender, meeting or exceeding stated service specifications, providing assurance on standards and pricing competitively.

Vision and the organization's mission

It is clear that most economies are composed of a diversity of organizational types, each seeking to achieve their objectives within a challenging environment. Buchanan and Huczynski defined organizations as social arrangements for the controlled performance of collective goals. The marketer needs to understand not only what they are trying to achieve and what is driving their behaviour but also the importance of mobilizing the contribution of all those within the organization towards realizing their achievement.

The need for vision

Every business organization, whether a sole trader or a multinational, requires vision. Business vision may be defined as the ability to imagine or foresee the future prospects and potential for the organization. Effective vision is closely linked to the marketing environment since it requires the ability to discern future conditions in the industry or market concerned. It is a critical requirement at the strategic level of all organizations and is normally the responsibility of the board of directors. Vision, then, involves understanding the future, anticipating how markets, tastes and technologies will evolve and the mobilizing of resources to translate the vision into reality. It is the key to business success and competitive advantage and explains why the marketing environment is so central to the marketer's role and importance. An early example of vision was the declaration by the chairman of Coca-Cola in 1927 that the product should *always be within an arm's length of desire*. The company is now in the global top ten by market capitalization. More recently Bill Gates formulated a vision of a *PC with Windows software on every desk*. In 1999, it became the largest company in the world.

E-vision

The most critical vision at the present time is the future direction of e-commerce. This applies to organizations throughout the supply chain. Retailers, for example, will be deciding whether the future of broadband electronic commerce rests with the currently dominant desktop PC or the digital television allowing armchair shopping. What is your vision for the year 2010? Will you be using your third generation (3G) mobile phone to activate your regular delivery of shopping goods? Will you still be regularly visiting retail outlets? Will such visits tend to be in the nature of social and leisure-related events where you can try out new product and service innovations? If these visits are to themed shopping malls, will you still need the convenience store? The profitable organizations of the year 2010 will be those who today have most actively thought through their own vision of the future and made the necessary investments in technology and marketing to bring it about.

From vision to mission

The Coca-Cola vision was translated into a business mission to make the drink an integral part of consumers' lives. Management set clear objectives – that the brand be available everywhere the consumer seeks liquid refreshment. Converting a vision into a mission statement produces a strong sense of overall purpose and direction. It seeks to establish 'what is our business/what should it be' and distil the fundamental reason for the organization's existence. It encompasses the scope of its core activities and endeavours to distinguish itself from other organizations of its type by clearly defining its uniqueness. Finally, it may provide a set of corporate values intended to unify the various stakeholders in the organization and in effect generate a strong sense of common endeavour.

A business mission statement would normally refer to a number of the following key elements:

- o What is its philosophy, values, priorities and aspirations?
- o What are its key strengths, competencies and competitive edge?
- o What business are we in and what for!
- o Who are its main customers?
- o What are the main products and services offered?
- o What markets does it compete in?
- o What core technology does it use?
- o What are its responsibilities towards society?
- o What is its position regarding key stakeholders?

It is important to make a clear distinction between a vision, a mission and a promotional statement. 'We keep your promise' is the promotional slogan of DHL, the third party carrier, while Nestlé's mission is to become the largest food supplier and to eradicate malnutrition from the world. The Sri Lankan National Bank seeks to promote a 'safe and secure future' while the vision of British Airways (and many other organizations in their own industries) was to become 'the world's favourite airline'. The stated mission of Google, the popular Internet search tool, is 'to organize the world's information'.

Mini case – Mission Impossible

Coca-Cola's decision to recall the entire UK supply of its bottled water, Dasani, is a serious setback to its mission to become an established player in this expanding market. The Food Standards Agency had already launched an investigation when samples of the product had been found to contain bromate (a by-product of the purification process) at higher levels than are legally permitted for either bottled or tap water. It had also emerged that the source for Dasani was mains water supplied to its factory in south London. Both issues clearly impact on the brand prestige of Coca-Cola and the perceived 'purity' of its products.

Important dimensions of the mission statement

o It should be brief, achievable and clear.
o As a clear statement of purpose it allows more specific, relevant and realistic objectives to be formulated.
o It defines a common purpose for the organization, so mobilizing the loyalty and commitment of staff and management.
o It provides a clear statement for external stakeholders of the values and future direction of the business.
o It acts as a control or benchmark for comparison by senior managers in evaluating the success of the business in realizing its purpose.
o It can motivate employees where the stated values of the organization coincide with their own. The mission is part of the corporate culture and this is the glue that unifies contributions.
o With over three-quarters of larger companies having formal mission statements, there is strong evidence of corporate belief in their contribution and importance.
o The mission statement must not, however, be allowed to submerge the arrival of contradictory environmental information which demands immediate decisions in order to amend its purpose, for example, IBM's mainframe dominance in the 1980s blinded it to the emerging reality of distributed computing power.

Exam hint

Key skills: improving your learning and performance

Because of the syllabus emphasis on Marketing Practice and Key Skills, you should recognize that optional questions in the examination will tend to be set in context. For example, you may be asked to discuss mission statements or organizational objectives in the context of a large chemical company or a public sector business college. In other words, you will be required to actively apply your learning to a given situation. Similarly, with the 'presenting information' key skill you will be expected to 'read and synthesize' information in the mini-case in order to answer the questions set.

Objectives are the ends to be achieved in order to fulfil the business mission. Organizations exist to pursue objectives. They are specific and more concrete guideposts by which the organization defines standards to be accomplished in key result areas such as profitability and customer service. Objectives can be classified into strategic, tactical and operational categories and each is linked into a planning process that seeks to identify and implement effective strategies to achieve them:

o *Strategic objectives* – are broad long-term goals set by senior management. Examples include:

– Achieve and maintain a position of leadership in specified markets.
– Automate business-to-business (B2B) transactions with supply chain partners.
– To maintain a product portfolio where those introduced less than 3 years ago account for 25 per cent of sales.
– To earn an average rate of return on capital of 20 per cent and earnings growth of 10 per cent pa.

o *Tactical objectives* – are set by middle managers and relate to functional areas like marketing. They tend to be more measurable, for example:

– Open ten new stores this year
– Develop an informational website for the company
– Reduce operating costs by 5 per cent pa
– Achieve preferred supplier status with designated customers.

o *Operational objectives* – are set by first-line management on a short time horizon:

– Daily production targets
– Reduce customer complaints by 5 per cent per month.

Study tip

It is always effective in examinations to refer directly to academic writers to support the points you wish to make. For example, the renowned management consultant P.F. Drucker argued that there are at least eight key result areas in which a business organization should be judged:

o *Market standing* – Desired share in present/new markets plus service goals to build loyalty
o *Innovation* – In products/services and the skills/processes required to deliver them
o *Human resources* – The supply, skill, development, attitude and performance of staff
o *Financial resources* – Sources of capital and effective utilization
o *Management performance*
o *Productivity* – Efficient use of resources relative to outcomes
o *Social responsibility* – Maintenance of ethical behaviour
o *Profitability* – Indicators of financial well-being.

General organizational objectives

Given the diversity of organizations across the business, public and voluntary sectors it is not surprising that their orientation and objectives vary.

Organization	Primary orientation	Secondary orientation
Private business	Profit	Growth/market share
Cooperative	Members' returns	Democratic processes
Public corporation	Public service + profit	Efficiency
Social services	Public service	Equity
Interest group	Member self-interest	Raise profile
Charitable	Alleviating suffering	Raise contributions

The actual objectives pursued by any one organization, however, may be diverse, complex and subject to considerable influence by the environment.

 Activity 1.8

Key skills: improving your learning and performance

- o List the main objectives you consider would be pursued by a competitive business. Your own organization would be ideal.
- o Now list your own personal and career objectives.
- o How do your objectives relate to those of the business? Do they conflict? or Are they complementary?
- o What are the objectives of the sales or marketing department in the business? Do they conflict with those of the business as a whole?

You probably put profit at the top of your business objectives list, but how many others could you think of? What about the basic survival as a motive, or the desire for growth? Did you think about the personal objectives of those who actually decide the strategies and allocate the resources in business? These might diverge from the interests of the shareholders.

What of your own goals? Do these include such things as a high and rising salary, plenty of perks, training and career development, promotion, job security and a satisfying job? If so, then, perhaps your ambitions would not be best served in a business pursuing cost minimization for maximum profits.

What of your marketing department? Is its inclination to build sales and market share even at the expense of profitability? Should it be constrained by the financial director in this regard or is it the 'right' objective? Clearly, there are a number of difficult questions to be addressed here so we must approach it step by step.

Study tip

Don't just accept at face value what you read in a text or a newspaper. Think through what is said, carefully and logically. Do not be afraid to have your own opinion, but be prepared to justify it to others. Critical awareness of the subject matter is something that is welcomed by the examiner but usually only evident among excellent candidates. Make the investment this needs in 'thinking' and 'discussion' time. It will repay handsome dividends.

Survival

This is a basic drive in all businesses and relates to the needs we have as individuals for security and the satisfaction of our economic wants. The jobs of management and workers depend on it, and this can lead to considerable sacrifices being made in times of economic hardship. The Japanese, in particular, are renowned for their willingness to accept cuts in salary and redouble efforts to restore corporate fortunes.

Many sole proprietors would continue in business even at the cost of exploiting themselves and family workers. The directors of public limited companies will also be aware of the need to avoid the possibility of a hostile takeover bid. These usually lead to the removal of top management, especially where the bid arose due to their underperformance in the eyes of shareholders. The press frequently reports examples, such as the recent successful £8.5 billion bid by Santander Central Hispano, Spain's largest bank, for Abbey or Air France's takeover of Dutch KLM to create Europe's largest airline.

Society is faced with the reality of scarce resources relative to its needs and wants. It requires that these are managed effectively and is prepared to see businesses fail so their resources can be released for use by the more competent managers.

Businesses must justify their use of resources over and over again if they are to survive and avoid possible takeover or liquidation. This means that they must make a profit! K-Mart, for example, the Michigan-based discount chain store, collapsed with debts of $4.7 billion due to its progressive loss of customers to 'bricks and mortar' retailers such as Wal-Mart who were marketing more effectively. In contrast, Amazon, the online bookseller, made its first ever profit of $5 million after 6 years and $3 billion of investment suggesting that it might survive to become a viable long-term Internet business.

Exam hint

The need to survive is a fact of life for all candidates enrolled on professional courses like CIM! Viewed at the outset, the syllabus and the coursebook look like big mountains to climb. So always apply the Chinese proverb – many small steps make a giant stride!

Profit and profit maximization

This is the most-quoted business objective, although, strictly, it is more a motivation than an end in itself. It does, however, provide a *measurement system* for assessing business performance. Profit maximization implies that businesses seek to make not only a profit but the maximum possible profit through time. Profit is the difference between revenue and cost.

Businesses are viewed as rational and self-interested in their decisions, seeking to allocate resources so as to maximize this profit differential by:

o *Supplying those goods that consumers most wish to buy* – through careful research of customer needs, anticipation of their changing preferences and supplying whenever the revenue exceeds the change in costs. As increasing numbers of electronic consumers signal that they prefer the ease and convenience of obtaining their staple groceries, travel/entertainment and increasingly clothes over the Internet, so existing or new e-tailers will respond by developing customer friendly websites to satisfy these needs.
o *Combining resource inputs to produce planned output at minimum possible cost* – Businesses will not satisfy consumer wants to gain revenue irrespective of cost. They will cease to supply further units when additional cost exceeds the price received. At this output they will ensure that factor inputs are combined so as to produce at least cost. For example, e-tailers will weigh the relative costs and benefits of the alternative delivery systems for home shopping, such as own transport, third party carrier, piggy-back local services, post or mail order delivery systems, and select the most efficient now and into the future.
o *Responding quickly to changes in supply and demand conditions* – If consumer tastes change or input prices alter then it will profit the firm to adjust the marketing mix or production methods accordingly. For example, will TV, desktop PC or WAP mobile phone prevail as the order medium, or fibre optics, satellite, aerial, enhanced phone lines or cable as the broadband delivery medium. In either case businesses will respond by reallocating resources and marketing effort accordingly.

Exam hint

Key skills: learning and performance

Maximizing is a principle to apply to your CIM studies and examinations. Aim for maximum understanding from your available study time and then maximize your marks by answering the right questions in a planned and focused way. Be a 'smart' student and use your coursebook to the full!

The pursuit of maximum profit therefore answers two of the basic economic problems arising from scarcity:

1. What to produce and in what quantities and
2. How to produce them efficiently.

It also provides a dynamic growth incentive for the business system (Figure 1.2) to:

o Innovate new and improved products that enhance value for money for consumers and revenue for the firm.
o Invest in research and development of more efficient methods of production to reduce costs.

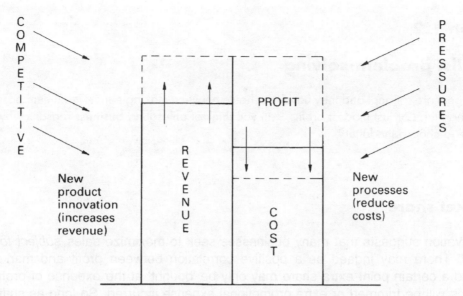

Figure 1.2 The carrot and the stick approach to profit maximization

Maximizing profit would appear to promise an ideal allocation of resources by rewarding those businesses that produce and market the right goods, in the right quantities, using the most efficient methods and ploughing back resources into producing economic growth through new products and better methods.

What if businesses were content with just modest profits or decided to pursue other objectives? What if they are run by salaried managers, who stand to gain nothing from extra profit, rather than the shareholders? What if they are production orientated and are not concerned with the consumers' real needs? These possibilities can only arise in the absence of *full and free competition.*

When competition is very strong, firms must market what consumers demand, otherwise their competitors will, reducing market share and threatening the very survival of the business. Firms must be efficient, otherwise they will be undercut by lower-cost rivals. They must provide excellent service because the consumer is sovereign in such a situation.

No firm, no matter how profitable, can afford to stand still. Much of the profit earned has to be ploughed back into new product development and improved methods if the firm is to retain a competitive edge. Customers will not give a second thought to a badly managed business, which will go bankrupt or be taken over by firms better fitted to manage the resources, for example this is a fate that even the once mighty quality retailer Marks & Spencer (M&S) only narrowly avoided in 2004, following a predatory bid by a rival retailer.

Business therefore appears to be very much a treadmill when competition is strong. Even if an innovative business succeeds in making extra profits, this will merely attract new competitors into the market to erode away the rewards. The scope for pursuing other objectives will only exist where market imperfections exist or large firms dominate.

Question 1.2

Key skills: problem-solving

If managers are rational and they have the choice between making either 'maximum possible profits' in the short term or just modest profits, can you think of any sound business reasons why it might be sensible to choose the latter?

Market share

Observation suggests that many businesses seek to maximize sales *subject to a profit constraint*. There may indeed be a positive correlation between profit and market share, but beyond a certain point extra share may only be 'bought' at the expense of profit. Prices and margins will be trimmed or extra promotional expense incurred. So long as sufficient profit is made to keep shareholders content, management may see an advantage in the stability and security of a dominant position. This objective was until recently at the forefront of cellular telephone companies such as Orange, Cellnet and Vodafone as they have vied to expand 'pay as you talk' sales. A similar picture can be seen in Internet connections and digital TV. Many dot-com business-to-consumer (B2C) companies have invested massively in website advertising and promotion with little short-term prospect of profit. Companies like Amazon.com preferred to expand their customer base and market share rather than earn short-run profits until heavy losses forced a shift of emphasis. On the other hand, Boo.com which budgeted $16 million in advertising to generate $2.7 million in sales revenue no longer exists.

Japanese exporters have been accused of pursuing market share in the short run in order to drive out domestic competitors prior to raising prices and profits in the longer term. *Long-run versus short-run profits* is an important consideration. It is suggested that most American and British companies are under considerable pressure to deliver buoyant short-run profits even at the expense of longer-term investment. Japanese and German companies, by contrast, are able to give greater emphasis to the long run due to the support of shareholding banks.

Business growth

Growth and profits may be positively related but not continuously. The rapid growth in out-of-town grocery superstores appears to be a case in point. Alternatively, growth may require takeovers and acquisitions and these may prove unsuccessful, especially if they represent diversification into unfamiliar areas. It will also put pressure on the scarce management resource.

Growth is, however, attractive for a number of reasons:

o   It is easier to resolve conflicts between stakeholders
o   It provides opportunities for promotion and job satisfaction
o   It increases market power and management status
o   It raises morale in general.

Management objectives

If management is not under severe competitive pressure, it may decide to *satisfice*. That is, it will produce satisfactory performance and profits. Where there is a *separation of ownership from management* there is no automatic incentive for professional managers to maximize profits for shareholders.

The organization may operate with what is termed *organizational slack*. This is the difference between the cost level that would maximize profits and actual costs. These excessive costs would finance a number of 'unnecessary expenditures', for example:

- o Buy market share via lower than profit maximizing prices
- o Excessive director remuneration/Management perks
- o Pet projects and/or excessive staff assistants.

Question 1.3

Can you identify slack in your organization?

How does management respond to a downturn in sales?

The existence of slack enables management to maximize their security, income, status, power and job interest. They can also take in the slack without threatening core activities and programmes in times of adversity. Similarly a lack of competition, the absence of a profit incentive and powerful stakeholder groups led to an accumulation of 'slack' in health, education, local authorities, state-controlled industries and government bureaucracy. This resulted in government efforts to improve productivity across a range of public services through various means:

- o Deregulated markets or introduced internal markets
- o Made services client driven – introduced service charters – set service standards
- o Insisted on compulsory competitive tendering
- o Attracted better-calibre managers while curbing the power of the trades unions
- o Appointed powerful regulators to set price/performance standards.

As the objectives have become more customer orientated in the public sector, so the nature of these organizations has been transformed. The skills of the marketer have also come to the fore in the quest for more focused customer benefits.

Exam hint

Have you given any consideration to the examiner's objectives? Is it to pass only a certain proportion, for example?

In fact, the examiner's objective is to bend over backwards to pass as many students as possible *but only* if they meet the CIM *professional standard*. Employers must have faith in what a CIM qualification stands for, and it is in your long-term career interests to see that this is maintained. So be well prepared, it *pays* to meet the standard required.

How are goals established?

To understand how business goals change, we must understand how they are formed. The board of directors are responsible for deciding objectives and formulating plans and policies to secure their effective achievement. The managing director is appointed to implement policy while non-executive directors are often invited onto the board of public companies to provide an external dimension to formulating objectives.

The key influences may be summarized as internal and external influences.

Internal influences

- The *memorandum of association* or its equivalent sets limits in the objects clause to the powers of a company. Pursuit of purposes outside these limits will be deemed *ultra vires* and therefore legally void. In practice, this clause will be broadly defined to allow the directors to diversify outside their traditional business.
- The *personal values and objectives of senior management* will exert significant influence, particularly where they are represented on the board, for example the marketing director.
- The *expectations* of the internal decision makers and their *degree of aversion to risk*.
- The *limits set by resource availability* – a minimum return on capital may be required in order to attract the necessary internal and external funds to finance other objectives.
- *Key individual and institutional shareholders.*
- The *force of inertia* and past successes may prevent serious internal review of objectives.

External influences

- Successful businesses recognize the importance of matching the capabilities of the organization to its environment. Internal strengths and weaknesses must be set against external threats and opportunities.
- There are a variety of connected and external stakeholders whose interests and attitudes must be considered before objectives are set. Their contribution will often be crucial to the effective implementation of the objectives.
- Conflict between the interests of shareholders and various stakeholders may require compromise to retain their contribution to the achievement of set objectives.
- The competitive environment may constrain what are achievable objectives within a given time frame.
- A change in government will alter the objectives set in local and central government, while changes in legislation will define what is, and is not, achievable for private businesses.
- External interests may be represented on the board, for example worker or consumer directors.

Study tip

You can often fix academic ideas in your own mind by relating the material to your own situation. Consider for a moment your own goals. How frequently do you review them? How have they changed? What are the influences that have brought about the change? Are these influences internally or externally driven? Do you review your objectives frequently enough?

What causes the goals to change?

Virtually, every organization must periodically review its objectives if it is to survive and succeed. There are compelling reasons to regularly consider changes to goals:

- Most organizations operate in a dynamic and constantly changing environment.
- As these environmental forces threaten to throw the business off-course, management must respond proactively by setting a new direction and a renewed focus to unify the organization's efforts.
- Changes in consumer wants must be anticipated and responded to with matching goals.
- Changes in production possibilities transform resource availability and technological options.
- Opportunities and threats from the various environments represent new realities and require new responses.
- Objectives are intended to be achieved and so require renewal as this occurs.
- If control processes show that objectives are not being realized, then a change to more realistic goals will provide more effective motivation for management and staff.
- A change in the chief executive or perhaps a merger or acquisition will tend to change the strategic goals.

Larger organizations may adopt corporate planning to formalize the above process. According to Cole (G.A. Cole, *Management Theory and Practice*, DPP, latest edition):

> *Corporate planning is the continuing process by which the long-term objectives of the organization may be formulated and subsequently attained by means of long-term strategic actions.*

Put more simply (Robbins and Coulter), corporate level strategy seeks to determine what business a corporation should be in.

Strategic objectives are, therefore, the outcome of the above influences and considerations but on, say, a 5- to 10-year rolling basis with ongoing rigorous review and correction.

Exam hint

Key skills: improving performance

Another objective of the examiner is to complete the marking with the minimum headaches. An examiner-friendly script is therefore required, one that is legible, clear, well set out and expressed in an easy-to-understand semi-report style format, that is, bullet points, headings and justification.

The organization as an open system

It is clear from the above section that the objectives of an organization must be reviewed and set by reference to internal and external considerations. Understanding this interplay between internal context and the wider environment has led to the organization being viewed as an open system. This approach focuses on the interrelated activities which enable inputs to be converted into outputs and provides a very useful framework for gaining insight into the relationships that prevail between the organization and its marketing environment.

There are many different systems we could identify: ourselves, the marketing department, our organization, the business system, the marketing environment, wider society, the global economy, the eco-system, our galaxy and the solar system. Each has a boundary that represents its interface with the others. We will be particularly concerned with the interface between the organization and its environment. This is represented in Figure 1.3 and possesses the following common characteristics:

- Productive inputs and energy are received/obtained from the marketing environment.
- The organization adds value by converting these inputs into desired outputs.
- They discharge their outputs into their environment – both positive and negative.
- They apply control by monitoring for feedback on achievement of objectives.

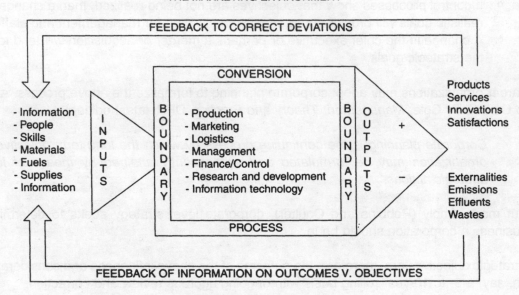

Figure 1.3 Business as an open system

Open systems are interdependent with their marketing environment and must adapt to change if they are to survive and develop. Open systems are vital where the environment is unstable or uncertain. Closed systems do not respond to change and only function well in stable conditions.

Open systems will also scan the external environment for opportunities and threats. When the organization adapts to this external environment it will impact on its *effectiveness*, whereas when it adapts its internal structure and organization it will impact on its *efficiency*.

 Activity 1.9

Key skills: using information

Spend a few moments applying systems thinking to the human body. Think about inputs/ conversion and output and the interface between some of the sub-systems involved, for example, nervous system, memory, digestion and the senses. How adaptive are you to your environment? How effective is your interface with your marketing manager?

The interface between marketing and other functions

Most systems divide into sub-systems. In some organizations, for example, purchasing or sales may be a separate function from marketing while in others they are integrated. Successful adaption requires that relationships are coordinated since individual departments that seek to maximize their own outcomes, inevitably detract from an optimum outcome for the system as a whole. Marketing not only operates over the external boundary with the wider environment but must also establish and maintain effective relationships across the internal boundaries with key departments such as finance, research and development and production. We can identify three fundamental cases of business focus related to the environment:

1. Production orientation
2. Sales orientation
3. Marketing orientation.

Each one has implications for organizational effectiveness and the degree to which it is outward looking. Every business tends to evolve from an inward-looking focus on production efficiency and product quality through greater sales awareness to comprehensive operational emphasis on anticipating and satisfying changing consumer requirements.

Where *production orientation* prevails, the emphasis is on design and operations management. Technical or finance specialists will tend to dominate the hierarchy while the sales function will be minor with no representation on the board. Examples are found in niche markets where demand far exceeds supply (e.g. TVR or Morgan cars) or in the public services like education and health before recent efforts to break their monopoly. The latter tended to be bureaucratic, dominated by professionals with little incentive to inquire into or respond to the real needs of their captive consumers.

In the absence of a seller's market and where competition is increasing, businesses soon learn that producing efficiently is not enough. A natural reaction was to focus on salesmanship and promotion to overcome consumer resistance. The sales director would gain equal status with operations and finance directors to ensure volume and market share.

Exam hint

Key skills: improving performance

What orientation are you going to adopt in the examination?

o A technical orientation, where all your attention goes into getting down the information *you* feel is appropriate?
o A selling orientation with lots of gimmicks to try to convince the examiner that you know what you are talking about but without that ring of confidence?
o A marketing orientation where you focus on what the examiner (i.e. the customer) really wants – a clear answer focused on what the question requires?

A *sales orientation*, however, gave no real thought to the needs and requirements of the final customer. Focusing the efforts of the whole organization to this end was what was required rather than just a cosmetic change of name from sales to marketing department. A marketing

31

orientation is now recognized as a survival condition in a competitive and rapidly changing environment. As T. Levitt observed:

> *Selling focuses on the needs of the seller, marketing on the needs of the buyer. Selling is pre-occupied with the seller's need to convert his product into cash; marketing with the idea of satisfying the needs of the customer by means of the product and the whole cluster of things associated with creating, delivering and finally consuming it.*

Activity 1.10

Key skills: problem-solving

A marketing orientation places the customer at the centre of the whole organization's attention. With this in mind, make a list of desirable organizational characteristics that would achieve this.

Taking an organization of your choice, design an organizational form that would place it close to its customers.

The main difficulty confronting a business wishing to achieve a marketing orientation is the change in organizational culture required. Functional divisions within the business create potential barriers, preventing a cohesive response to customer needs. Unless there is a drive and strong leadership from the top to establish the philosophy throughout the organization, they will fail to pull together, reverting instead to narrow departmental interests. If the organization is unable to get its own internal act together it is unlikely to respond successfully to environmental change.

Managing the marketing environment: a contingency approach

This approach to managing organizations renounces the idea of a universal formula and relies instead on tailoring the response to the specific situation encountered. Research by Lawrence and Lorsch (P.R. Lawrence and J.W. Lorsch, *Organization and Environment: Managing differentiation and integration*, 1969, Irwin) suggests that there is no one best means of managing organizations to meet their current objectives in an environment of uncertain or volatile change. Marketers must therefore identify and then adapt continuously to the conditions that are found to prevail in the present and the future.

A case study in the contingency approach

In the revised 2001 edition of his book *E-shock the New Rules* (publisher Palgrave), Michael de Kare-Silver predicts that e-commerce for retailers and manufacturers will reach a critical mass and this will have significant implications for organizations. Surveys indicate and business leaders agree that their organizations in 2010 will look very different to today. There will be a clear need for greater flexibility in the face of accelerating change combined with faster but better decision-making in response to unavoidable uncertainty.

A comparison of the characteristics of old economy and new economy organizations would include:

Old economy organization	New economy organization
Stable bureaucratic structures	Flexible dynamic structures
Mechanistic and hierarchical	Organic and fluid
Formalized relationships	Lateral, informal, networked relationships
Job and position focused	Task, skills and relationship focused
Permanent 9–5 jobs	Flexitime, as task completion demands
Production orientated	Market and customer orientated
Centralized decision-making	Employee involvement and participation
Salaried	Shared benefits and share ownership

e-Commerce is a challenge that affects the whole organization and will of necessity demand a 'systems' driven response. It will involve radical restructuring for many organizations combined with fundamental shifts in business culture. As de Kare-Silver observes, it comes 'on top of a competitive environment that's already fast changing, becoming more global, consolidating, deregulating and demanding, with customers searching aggressively for greater innovation, more comprehensive service solutions and better value'. Many large organizations are therefore under increasing global competitive pressure to become leaner, meaner and generally more innovative and responsive in the face of multi-faceted environmental change.

Study tip

At the end of each unit you will find a summary of some of the main learning points to be found within it. If you don't fully understand a learning point then return to the relevant part of the unit and re-read it. Be sure to undertake the various activities and questions in the unit and compare your answers with the debrief provided. Not every activity has a debrief since, as you will have realized, some of the questions were intended to get you thinking about the subject matter in the sections that followed.

A number of key trends and responses may be identified that are transforming the organization of such businesses:

Digitalization

Ever more powerful Pentium microprocessors, sophisticated software, broadband delivery and the Internet are working towards the seamless adaption and integration of information technology into our lives. As text, video, sound and vision are digitalized, compressed and transmitted at ever increasing speeds so the potential for fully automated business transactions increases. The mobile phone is fast becoming the critical instrument in marketing at the individual level while, for example, the five major car companies have established an online trade exchange that auctions huge supply contracts for parts and sub-assemblies to ensure the best value for money supplies. Intranet systems allowing the mutual interrogation of customer and supplier computers provide automatic purchasing and stock control and dramatically reduce transactions costs but at the expense of middle managers and clerical staffs. Downsizing is the process by which organizations have stripped middle managers out of the workforce leaving those who remain to take over their duties assisted by the more effective information systems.

Virtual organizations

Digitalization and the Internet make location and physical presence unnecessary. Members of the virtual organization need not necessarily come face to face since they can communicate from any point on the globe by WAP mobile text message, e-mail or video conference. The emphasis will be on flexibility, teamwork and sharing rather than authority and chains of command. Empowerment will be part of this process as decision-making power is delegated to subordinates and task groups with day-to-day tactical matters determined without reference to higher authority. This will bring all organization members and marketers, in particular, much closer to the customer.

Knowledge workers

Peter Drucker first coined the term 'knowledge worker' to describe the processes of employment change in the information society. Knowledge was to become the critical factor of production facilitated through networks of information and contacts. Information is captured, processed, stored and then made available in the right form to the appropriate decision makers and at the right time to achieve maximum competitive advantage. Organizations reinforce this decision quality by de-layering. This involves compressing the hierarchy by reducing the number of reporting levels. This speeds up the flow of information to the decision maker and decisions to those who implement them at the customer interface.

Networks and relationships

In an increasingly complex world, it is argued that organizations should 'stick to the knitting' and focus on their core capabilities where they possess competitive advantage. Other functions should be outsourced to those organizations that are best at what they specialize in. This even includes military commanders in Iraq who have been forced to outsource non-combat roles such as guarding installations or interrogating prisoners. Organizations then become part of a cluster that provide a value chain. This focus on core competencies while contracting third party operations to undertake peripheral activities puts a premium on relationships, accountability and cooperation with business partners. This theme will be developed in the next unit.

Marketing and information communication technologies

We have already seen that the marketer is at the critical interface with the customer. Marketing orientation will become even more organizationally important in future. To facilitate this role the marketer must actively develop information technology capability so that their marketing skills can be applied to maximum effect in the world of electronic commerce. Unless and until the marketer fully appreciates the potential of the e-commerce revolution and its associated technologies, they will never achieve full effectiveness.

Organizational adaptability

The future will belong to the organization that is both focused and able to deploy the resources of the large organization but with the flexibility of the small. Despite multi-billion dollar mergers and amalgamations that bring together the likes of Viacom (cables), Paramount (film/cable), Blockbuster (video) and CBS (TV) the future may lie with organizations on a smaller scale that can attract talented people and unleash their capabilities. The global accessibility provided by the Internet may also serve to break down the formality and remoteness of the big corporation. Transparency, empowerment and informality are more likely to be the style of the new economy dot-coms.

Activity 1.11

Key skills: improving learning and performance

Information and communication technologies and the development of e-commerce are important 'key skills' and themes running throughout this coursebook.

Since mini-cases will be based on this aspect of the syllabus from time to time you should:

- Ensure that you understand and can define all of the information and communication terms used in the above case and elsewhere in the coursebook.
- Consolidate information on e-commerce as you work through the units in this coursebook and others at Certificate level.
- Summarize the impacts and implications of e-commerce.

Large organizations that don't adapt quickly enough to counter threats or exploit opportunities have most to lose due to their large fixed investments. Smaller concerns, freed from the barriers of scale and location, may develop rapidly via the Internet. Marketers must participate in and respond to the challenge posed. Marketing fundamentals and associated skills will still be required, but they will be increasingly information driven in the open systems of global electronic commerce.

Summary

In this unit we have seen that:

- A diversity of organizations exist in a mixed economy.
- The strengths of one form of organization are often the weaknesses of the other.
- An informal economy operates alongside the formally reported one.
- Organizational objectives are stepping stones along the road to achieving the corporate mission.
- Business objectives are varied and reflect different motivations.
- Objectives pursued reflect internal values as well as external influences and constraints.
- There is an important distinction between satisfying and maximizing behaviour.
- Businesses are open systems which rely on interaction with their environment for survival/growth.
- A major part of the work of the marketer is to manage the internal and external boundaries.
- The marketer should respond flexibly to the realities of the changing situation.
- A marketing-oriented structure is the key to effective achievement of objectives.

Further study and examination preparation

The material in this wide-ranging unit covers 15 per cent of the syllabus. It should enable you to attempt any question posed on the organization. There is no guarantee of a question in any particular examination but a full or a part/linked question is normally to be expected. Questions may be set which relate your understanding of organizations to other aspects of the syllabus, for example, Question 7, December 2003, uses the voluntary organization as the context for discussing the macro- and micro-environment. The marking scheme of a CIM examination is flexible to accommodate a variety of teaching approaches and national contexts. Approach each end-of-unit question in a focused manner, that is, consider what the question is asking for; use your understanding of the unit to plan out and answer it within the 30–35 minutes available and then compare the result with the specimen answer provided. Even if you didn't get it 'right first time' don't worry but go back and find out why. The key to success is to immediately put your learning into practice, so always apply the three key words that lead to this: practice, practice and more practice.

The same principle applies to continuous assessment assignments in that success is a direct function of precisely addressing the question brief you are given. This includes staying within the specified word count! Assignments will include assessment criteria that indicate how many marks will accrue to each element. It is important that time and effort are allocated in proportion to the 'mark' payback.

Extending knowledge

To supplement your reading on the organization you may refer to the core text on the Marketing Environment Syllabus. This is the latest edition of Palmer and Hartley, *The Business and Marketing Environment*, published by McGraw-Hill, 1999. Chapter 3 considers the classification of business organizations while Chapter 4 relates to organizational objectives and growth. A similar but more up-to-date text is A. Palmer, *The Business Environment*, McGraw-Hill, 2001. Chapter 2 considers types of business organization while Chapter 3 relates to organizational growth. Case studies are provided in the final chapter. Another more recent text to scan is R. Cartwright, *Mastering the Business Environment*, Palgrave, 2001. These three texts are recommended throughout the units that follow. A number of websites will also be suggested at the end of each unit that you may wish to visit for supplementary information support.

Websites that provide material on marketing environment practice tend to be newspaper-based so they are up to date. These include:

www.ft.com – provides extensive research materials across all industry sectors with links to specialist reports.

www.thetimes.co.uk and www.thetimes100.co.uk for news coverage and the top 100 UK companies.

www.theeconomist.com – holds readily researched archives of articles from back issues.

www.corporateinformation.com/ – worldwide sources listed by country.

www.vlib.org.uk/BusinessEconomics.html is the virtual library for business and economics and holds a catalogue of high quality websites.

Exam question 1.1

Please see Question 2, June 2004. Go to www.cim.co.uk to obtain specimen answers.

Exam question 1.2

Please see Question 3, June 2004. Please go to www.cim.co.uk for specimen answers.

Exam question 1.3

Please see Question 5b, December 2003. Go to www.cim.co.uk for specimen answers.

Exam question 1.4

Please see Question 7a, December 2003. Go to www.cim.co.uk for specimen answers.

unit 2
the micro-environment

Learning objectives

By the end of this unit you will:

o Appreciate the scope and complexity of the marketing environment (1.8/2.1/2.2/3.1)

o Become aware of the important stakeholder interrelationships within the micro-environment (2.2)

o Be able to classify the various external elements and influences (2.1/3.1)

o Recognize the significance of future environmental challenges and their importance for developing marketing strategy and planning (1.8/1.9)

o Assess the marketer's potential for influence in the micro-environment (2.2/2.5)

o Understand the impacts of particular pressure groups such as consumerists and environmentalists (2.4).

Study Guide

This unit introduces the marketing environment, considers the nature and importance of environmental change and identifies some implications for marketing strategy and planning. The micro-environment may be defined as including the groups and organizations that have a two-way operational relationship with the business and which are controlled and influenced by it to some degree. This environment is the work-a-day operational context for the organization. We saw in Unit 1 that the organization is an open system with boundaries to its immediate environment. Relationships must be established across these boundaries if supplies or credit, for example, are to be obtained. Similarly the organization must have effective linkages, through intermediaries, to the marketplace, or directly to the final customers themselves. Competitors also inhabit this environment and the marketer must understand the significance of relationships that prevail within the industry setting. These are examined more fully in the following unit.

Information is critical to understanding and the marketer must draw on a network of intelligence sources, if successful adaption to change is to result. The organization must be proactive if it is to control or at least influence the behaviour of the various stakeholders and pressure groups to be found in the micro-environment.

This is a syllabus area to relate directly to your own experience. You are a consumer; you supply labour services to your employer; you will be aware of the competitors operating in your industry; you may deal directly with distributors or consumers as part of your job description and your functional specialism is marketing, which concerns itself with promoting profitable relationships across the system boundaries. You are in an ideal position to appreciate the micro-environment.

The business as a resource converter

All organizations seek, as Peter Drucker observed, to make resources productive. Every organization, irrespective of its specific objectives, has this as their common goal because resources are scarce and must be competed for and utilized efficiently and effectively. Various inputs (refer to Figure 1.3), are drawn by various means (e.g. paid/volunteer) from the environment and converted in time, place or form to create utility, value and satisfaction for the ultimate consumer.

In modern business, productive inputs are diverse and often complex entities in themselves, drawn from an interrelated global economy. The traditional economic classification of land, labour and capital is therefore simplistic. For example, the human resource which an organization requires may embody numerous skills, enterprise, creativity and an ability to adapt to changing circumstances.

Capital resources are often high technology and very specialized. They include not only buildings, equipment and transportation, but also financial inputs to lubricate the process of resource conversion in advance of actual sales. Business services are important inputs as more and more firms outsource IT services, transport, catering, market research etc. to focus their own resources and attention on their core conversion activities.

 ## Activity 2.1

Select a marketing resource and explain the process of making it productive.

The resource providers may also be viewed as stakeholders in the business./Organizations are, in effect, coalitions of stakeholders and it is the role of management to achieve a workable balance between the claims and interests of these groups./Shareholders, as the owners of the business, would seem to qualify as stakeholders but strictly speaking this term is reserved for the other providers of inputs or recipients of outputs namely:

- o Employees and Management
- o Suppliers and Distributors
- o Customers and Creditors
- o Local community.

The environmental context of the organization

The environment of business has never been so complex and challenging as it is today. Marketers more than ever before are confronted by increasing pressures and demands that they must seek to understand and respond to. At any given point in time, organizations will be confronted by a confusion of environmental factors that may or may not constitute threats to, or opportunities for the marketer (see Figure 2.1).

New government elected	New Euro currency zone	Competitor enters market
Digital network established	Supplier cartel uncovered	Uncertainty in Iraq
£–$ exchange rate rise	Recession in manufacturing	EU expands East
Divorce rate rise		Trade war threat
Japan in recovery	**The organization**	Duty free concessions go
Concerns over GM foods		Congestion charges
Distributors merge	Cheaper credit forecasts	Pledge to meet emission targets
Minimum wage raised	Computer virus fears	WAP mobile sales take off
Life expectancy rises	Congestion hits delivery times	Tax rises

Figure 2.1 Environmental factors

To understand these, a classification is required of the persons, groups, trends and often turbulent events that occur, external to the firm's boundaries. You need a grasp of the big picture, the role of your organization and yourself within it. Systems theory makes clear that every organization operates within an industry setting that in turn interacts with a societal environment that is itself influenced by a global marketplace. The global environment appears very distant to marketers operating on a regional or even a national scale, and yet with information technologies shrinking distances these multinational operations are extending into every corner of the marketplace. These influences may initially seep, but then cascade through into a business. Ryanair, the low-cost airline for example, nearly had its business jeopardised in 2004 when the European Commission unexpectedly demanded repayment of 'illegal subsidies' arising from the cheaper fees it had negotiated with regional airports, such as the one it uses at Charleroi in Belgium. So to set the micro-environment in context we should also classify factors which are relevant to the societal or macro-environment. Within any society all businesses face a common political, economic, social and technological environment, although any one element will often impact differently according to the size and situation of the firm. The key characteristic, however, is the inclusion of forces that impact on the business, creating opportunities and threats, but over which it has no real influence or control.

The macro-environment

The wider environment (Figure 2.2) over which the organization can exert little influence is often referred to by the acronym PEST. The inclusion of a regulatory framework of laws, standards and customs converts the acronym to SLEPT while the addition of ethics and environment (natural) converts it to STEEPLE. These provide compartments into which we can sort the various trends, events, threats and opportunities which occur in the environment.

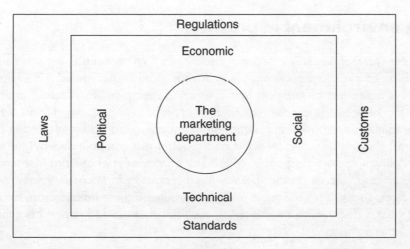

Figure 2.2 PEST factors and the regulatory framework

Units 4–8 will consider each of these macro-environments in some detail, but we may increase our understanding of this unit with just a brief mention of each.

Natural

Confusingly referred to as 'the environment' or 'the green environment', it provides the context in which all other activities take place. It is inevitable that human activity and change, whether economic, political, social or technical, will impact on this natural environment (see Figure 4.1). These can be positive (e.g. transform an arid land into productive land) or more usually negative (e.g. pollution or encroachment on rainforests) impacts. Equally, improvements in technology or forms of organization may transform 'bads' into 'goods', for example, development of non-fossil fuels such as wind power may account over 10 per cent of total needs within a decade. Customers too are increasingly conscious of the quality and sustainability of their living environment and any marketer that fails to take these concerns fully into account will pay a heavy price. Fuller consideration of this important element in the marketing environment will be developed later in this unit as well as in Unit 4.

Political

The role and impact of the State on business extends far beyond the making of laws. The size of the public sector was mentioned earlier and all its organizations affect businesses whether as suppliers, customers, policy makers or regulators. The philosophy of the government in power sets the climate for business and a change of party in office can significantly alter the thrust and direction of all aspects of their policies.

Political strife and uncertainty will also impact on business opportunities. Economic crisis in Argentina has led to an explosion of violent crime, for example, the kidnapping of those driving expensive cars, including marketing executives! Similarly, terrorist attacks in Indonesia and elsewhere may deter direct investment while the Intifada against Israel involving the Holy Places disrupts tourism revenues. Outright war or tribal confrontation, as in parts of Africa, destroys economic resources and infrastructure. On the other hand, reconstruction, as in Iraq, creates significant, if risky, opportunities in the short term. However, business normally needs political stability to thrive so that commercial links may be developed and direct investments made.

Marketing environment in practice

For a marketer working in an international charity, the famine threatening southern Africa must be one of the biggest practical challenges ever faced. With an estimated 13 million people facing starvation, it is a product of turbulent and interacting macro-environmental forces. To address the problem the marketer needs to collect information in order to prioritize and focus responses. Malawi, Zambia, Mozambique, Angola and particularly Zimbabwe are badly affected in a situation where serious harvest shortfalls caused by flood and drought are compounded by the social ravages of HIV/AIDS. Political factors aggravate conditions particularly where grain reserves are corruptly disposed of, or land seizure policies destroy the incentive to farm commercially. Maize production fell by over three-quarters over 2 years in Zimbabwe helping the inflation rate to rise over 100 per cent. This is also a disaster for neighbouring countries that used to import from this former 'bread-basket' of southern Africa.

The marketer, in raising awareness of the massive need for food aid, is confronted by donor countries that appear to be suffering from donor fatigue. This might reflect a growing belief that food crises are brought on primarily by corrupt governments and that any charity aid provided will only prop up repressive regimes. Central government control over distribution often means food aid is either denied to opposition party supporters or directly appropriated. The international charity is largely powerless to control these macro forces but it must still seek to fulfil its mission of helping the vulnerable. Can you contribute any information or ideas to help the marketer in this complex strategy process?

Economic

This is closely linked to the political environment and policies required to achieve government objectives. These impact on the costs, prices, competitiveness and profitability of businesses. The business pages of the quality press and/or the electronic pages of a news website are therefore required reading for the serious marketer since an understanding of the key economic indicators provides the necessary information for anticipating developments in the marketplace. Economic uncertainties also impact negatively on business and consumer confidence. The current rise in the oil price to record levels of over $50 a barrel represent an advance indicator of future inflation and possible economic downturn. The immediate causes of the rise reflected the global not the national economy, that is, terrorist activity in the Middle East, exceptional hurricane activity disruption in US production and rising Chinese demand. The economic horizons of businesses will vary greatly, as seen in Figure 2.3.

Figure 2.3 The four horizons

Many sole traders compete in local convenience markets but the conditions experienced here will often have cascaded down from conditions in the global economy, which in turn influence national economies and regions within them. The importance of international factors has increased in recent years with the development of e-commerce, trading blocks, single markets and the formation of the World Trade Organization (WTO) following the successful conclusion of the GATT talks. Businesses that are reluctant to search out the opportunities presented by these developments may soon find their profitable niche markets exposed to new and often globally distant competitors.

 ## Activity 2.2

Key skills: collecting and presenting information

Prepare a regular business environment brief. Produce a summary of the main events and developments affecting a business of your choice over the past week. Use the elements in your micro- and macro-environment as your headings.

Many companies appoint an executive to collate such information on an ongoing basis in order to build up a moving picture of change in their environment. Perhaps you could organize weekly briefs in your CIM classes.

Social

This is perhaps the most difficult environment for the marketer to identify, evaluate and respond to. It includes changes in population characteristics, educational standards, culture, lifestyles, attitudes and beliefs. The way we think, live and behave is the outcome of complex cultural conditioning by family, friends, school, church, work and the various media. It conditions who decides what we buy, where and when we buy it, and whether we use credit or cash. Social and demographic change may appear to change slowly, yet their impacts are likely to far outweigh any consequences of political decisions over the longer term. The trends towards lower and later births and the corresponding ageing of the population, for example, will generate massive changes over time in patterns of work and spending. Similarly, human migration, whether between continents or within an expanded economic block like the EU, will bring social exposure to different values and outlooks as well as potential conflicts.

Exam hint

Key skills for marketers

Activity 2.2 is an ideal means of developing the key skill of 'presenting information'. Preparing a brief involves reading and synthesizing information. Giving a brief involves making a presentation while group participation involves contribution to discussions. All of these elements together with writing different types of documents constitute the CIM definition of this skill.

Technical

This environment is characterized by accelerating rates of change in the means, methods and knowledge that organizations utilize in the supply chain. It is the primary means by which the production possibilities of society and the productivity of scarce resources can be expanded, enabling more wants to be satisfied. It also constitutes threats to those organizations that fail to innovate new and better products and processes.

The lead time between invention, innovation and market introduction has shrunk significantly with the application of computer technology, while the development of telecommunications has combined to make the global economy a reality. Factors affecting the speed of the diffusion process are dealt with in Unit 8; however, you will personally be experiencing the shortening lead times to critical mass of important innovations such as the fax (20–25 years) the VCR (10–15 years), the basic mobile phone (8–10 years), the Internet (5–8 years), the WAP Internet connected mobile (3–5 years?) and e-commerce (3–5 years?). All businesses face the challenges implied but only the more alert, flexible and proactive, such as Microsoft, 3M, Sony, and some of the more resilient dot-com companies, will translate them into opportunities and profit.

Activity 2.3

Key skills: collecting and interpreting information

Take a typical workday of a marketing executive and log occasions and actions that link your organization to its environment.

Hint: This should include items on news bulletins and in the local papers.

A recurring theme of this coursebook will be that the various environments are in a continuous state of change. Indeed there is evidence to suggest that it is not only ever changing but inherently turbulent. What does this mean, and what is the evidence to support it?

○ The term 'turbulent' suggests an environment in a degree of turmoil, buffeted by uncontrollable forces that continuously disturb any tendency towards stability. Virtually no organization operates in static conditions and interest centres on the degree of turbulence which may vary from industry to industry.

○ Turbulence suggests confusion and a state of flux. The increasingly competitive nature of many markets fits such conditions as could the current outlook for world stock markets, the future price of oil or the value of the once mighty dollar.

○ Turbulence also implies uncertainty and discontinuity, but is not as strong a term as chaos or revolution. One could argue that genetic engineering is potentially transforming or that a gender revolution is currently underway, but the timescale seems sufficiently long to remove much of the uncertainty. On the other hand, the process of invention and innovation is inherently unpredictable along with the extremes of weather and natural disasters that have seemingly increased in frequency over recent years. Hurricanes that swept France at the end of 1999 uprooted over 360 million trees and will take $3 billion and 20 years to replace. By late 2004 it was the Caribbean that suffered its worst hurricane season for a 100 years as Ivan, Frances, Charley and tropical storm Jeanne claimed hundreds of lives and caused tens of billions of dollars' worth of damage. Floods in Haiti were particularly severe due to high levels of deforestation. Earlier in the year the worst drought in 500 years sparked wildfires across the Western USA engulfing 4 million acres and revived memories of the thousands of older people who died of dehydration in the abnormal August 2003 heat wave in Europe. Further turbulence was experienced in Africa as a swarm of 50 million locusts scavenged their way south from Morocco, while the level of the Mekong river fell so low as to threaten the livelihoods of up to 100 million in Southeast Asia. Low rainfall has contributed, but the major cause is the completion of massive dam projects in China. Another is under construction and six more are planned! However, all of these sources of natural turbulence were dwarfed by the December 26th earthquake off the coast of Indonesia registering 8.9 on the Richter scale. The dreadful consequences of the resulting Tsunami on the surrounding coastlines are common knowledge but the marketing consequences for tourism, and the local economies that depend on it, will be both massive and enduring.

○ What is clear is that an array of variable environmental forces are operating to produce a degree of ambiguity for the marketer regarding probable patterns of the future.

○ Apart from technological forces there are other trends including globalization, religious fundamentalism and variable economic growth rates to drive the turbulence. The uncertain state of Russia, China, East Asia and many emerging countries, together with the still unfolding consequences of a post-11 September America provides a basis for current and future volatility.

Exam hint

Key skills: improving your learning and performance

First impressions are important in life and in examinations. How you answer the first question will create an impression and an expectation in the mind of the examiner. It is up to you to ensure that it is a positive impression that will set the tone for the rest of the paper. So don't necessarily answer Question 1a first, but rather the question that you feel most confident with. This will have the added bonus of settling your own nerves and building your confidence in attempting more difficult questions.

Turbulent conditions do not necessarily imply adversity for organizations. Opportunities as well as threats are created and businesses vary in their ability to 'ride' the market rapids. Equally, much of the associated cost may be shared with, or transferred onto, the consumer (in higher prices), the workforce (redundancies), competitors (lower sales), suppliers (lower prices), the government (subsidies/bail-outs) and other stakeholder groups.

Dynamic and complex conditions

These are the two critical dimensions by which marketing environments may be judged, the dynamic and the complex. There is a spectrum of market possibilities ranging from completely static to extremely dynamic conditions in a given environment. Similarly, there is a degree of environmental complexity from the very simple (i.e. a single clear cause and effect), to the extremely complex (with many and varied interdependent causes).

 ## Activity 2.4

Key skills: problem-solving

Locate on a matrix of increasing environmental complexity and dynamism the following organizations: a funeral director; a computer software manufacturer; a university; a biscuit manufacturer; a pop group; an advertising agency; your own organization.

Dynamic conditions – are associated with high energy driving forces within a wider environment with relative few frictions. They suggest markets where significant and potentially powerful environmental forces are in motion, often producing rapid growth, change and development, and these drive the situation in which the organization finds itself. Emerging markets, driven by invention, accelerating innovation and an explosion in information technology, are clear examples of such change. Globalization with its flows of direct investment responding to changing exchange rates, labour market conditions and economic performance is another source of creative energy in the world economy. Dynamic conditions can be unleashed by a catalyst such as deregulation, the burgeoning Internet, new entry into a market or the changing demands of a stakeholder group. Government policy can also lead to the creation of a dynamic economy when red tape is curtailed and incentives for work and enterprise are enhanced. Competition policy may also be sharpened to encourage the process of creative destruction.

Complex conditions – suggest a market context upon which diverse influences are exerted and analysis is complicated. Many variables are involved and these are either interdependent or inter-react through both positive and negative feedback loops. An example of a sustained feedback loop is shown in Figure 2.4. Negative feedback would occur if the process is reversed. Systems theory has demonstrated the intricate complexity of economic and social systems. These are extremely difficult to model. Weather forecasts, despite sophisticated computer analysis and simulation, are frequently criticized for their imperfections, but we are much further away from convincingly modelling societal change. Complexity is very much like a 'black box'; we observe flows in and out, we apply trial and error and make predictions but we don't fully know how it works! We will see later that most markets are not simple and that analysis requires consideration of at least five forces. Alternative outcomes are likely due to the interdependence of rivals. They may seek to manage the complexity through agreements and understandings but the tension created by pursuit of competitive advantage and the potential for a zero sum game (I win/you lose) create options and complex uncertainties.

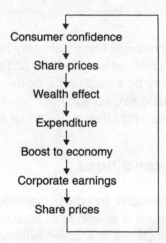

Figure 2.4 Sustained feedback loop

Complexity therefore means that marketers are faced by a succession of non-routine problems and situations demanding action. Few will be simple or repetitive and therefore amendable to standard policy responses. Predictability is likely to be low, the environment dynamic and any action will cause reaction through a highly interconnected system. The fall in retail sales that brought M&S to crisis resulted in positive corporate actions which not only reverberated within internal departments and along the supply chain, but also to downmarket competitors (as prices have been cut) and upmarket designers.

Question 2.1

Have you heard of the 'butterfly effect'? Could a butterfly beating its wings in Outer Mongolia affect the weather sometime later in northern England in a kind of ultimate ripple effect? Can seemingly insignificant events have a transforming impact? Is this a good case for joining a pressure group and starting some ripples?

Adaptability – the proactive response

Exam hint

Key skills: improving your learning and performance

As in undertaking a CAA, achieving a flexible response to change requires the practice of key skills by the marketer. These include:

- ○ *The ability to use the Internet* to search, source and select the required information.
- ○ *The ability to use the information* to cross reference, manipulate and interpret.
- ○ *The ability to solve problem* to identify and explore problems; to compare and select from alternative solutions; to plan, implement and review preferred options.

Some argue that it is people's 'ability to change' that is the critical limiting factor in exploiting the full potential of information and other new technologies. Resistance to change can arise anywhere in the marketing environments. Management can be the countervailing force in reducing resistance or driving change, but may equally form a constraint. What is it that makes for an adaptable organization in the face of dynamic and complex change? Points to consider would include:

- ○ Management must actively confront a difficult environment, not acquiesce or passively accept it.
- ○ Reliance on accumulated experience and perceptions only permits reaction.
- ○ Management must forecast change if it is to act proactively.
- ○ One approach is to 'read the environment' and adapt by making business and marketing changes that resonate with it. This continuous adaption achieves a dynamic equilibrium between internal strengths and capabilities and external opportunities.
- ○ Burns and Stalker argued that dynamic environments required 'organic' organization favouring decentralization of decision-making power and rapid communication up and down the chain of command. Bureaucratic or mechanistic structures were only workable in relatively static conditions.
- ○ Contingency plans are a means of dealing with future uncertainty. This approach could be informed by so-called 'risk analysis' to assess the probability and likely impact of possible environmental changes. Further development could involve executive training in crisis, or shock management, for example, simulate the consequences of an oil tanker running aground or an explosion.
- ○ Adaptability demands flexibility in the redeployment of scarce resources to meet new threats and opportunities.
- ○ Organizations must embrace change and innovation and not wait until the maturity stage of the life cycle. The success of current product lines can create powerful resistance and inhibit necessary adaption to the products of the future. Companies like 3M formalize continuous innovation in their policies.

The marketer may conclude that even the most sophisticated environmental scanning and forecasting techniques will be unable to cost effectively consider more than a very small proportion of the total of potentially useful information available. So many organizations decide that the change is too difficult to manage proactively and choose instead to shadow the actions of competitors as a strategy against being isolated and caught out. An alternative approach is to plan to create your own environment based on your own view or vision of the future. Action is taken to share this vision with stakeholders and build relationships that allow a flexible response to turbulence throughout the micro-environment. The organization sets the market agenda and competitors are left to follow.

The micro-environment

The micro-environment includes key stakeholders that have a close and two-way operational relationship with the business and may be controllable to some degree. The organization must do more than just optimize their own performance, they must optimize the performance of the whole value chain.

Question 2.2

Key skills: problem-solving

Can you allocate the elements in Figure 2.1 to the appropriate global/macro-/micro-environment?

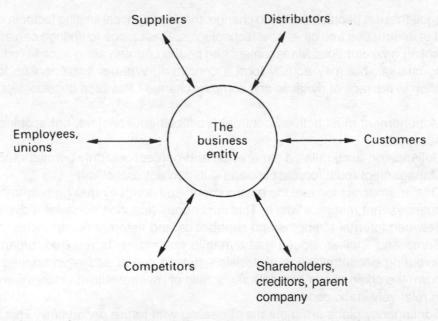

Figure 2.5 The micro-firm environment

Suppliers

No firm can supply all of its own needs. Materials, components, fuel and a host of business services are necessary inputs. Suppliers are a critical link with the environment, a source of cost but also of possible partnership. Vehicle producers may have hundreds of suppliers involving a two-way dependence. They are now streamlining in favour of 'preferred suppliers' in key areas, but demanding in return long-term contracts, total quality, just-in-time delivery, research and design support. Dependence on one or two suppliers, however, has considerable risks, just as it is risky for the smaller business with only one or two customers. Any action or decision may have critical consequences.

Importance to the marketing process:

- Key determinant of availability, delivery times and quality of the product.
- Cost of materials are an important factor in the total cost of many products.
- The supply chain may have many links back to primary producers and be susceptible to disruption.
- The relative power of suppliers is often critical and depends on size, substitutes and degree of actual competition between them.
- The quality of the supplier relationship is a crucial parameter in marketing effectiveness.
- Suppliers can assume the stockholding function, allowing maximum space for selling operations.
- If partnership fails to deliver marketing benefits, backward integration may be considered.

Exam hint

It is essential that you achieve a sound grasp of these basic environmental concepts. As you saw in the examples at the end of Unit 1, they will occur frequently as part of different questions referring to the environment.

Competitors

These are the exceptions in the micro-environment in that normally they continuously threaten rather than contribute to the survival of the business. As we will explore in Unit 3, the reality of competition may be in the form of hundreds of similar rivals, as in catering, or a handful of powerful multinationals, as in pharmaceuticals, or increasingly more likely a number of nimble, technically sophisticated and marketing-focused dot-com competitors.

The relationship is again two way in that while competitors can constrain the achievements of the business, the marketing department can also shape and influence the competitive environment. Business has the discretion to adjust its marketing mix as conditions change. The truly marketing-orientated company will ensure that its strategies, plans, tactics and responses will be decided not in a vacuum but with careful reference to its changing threats and opportunities.

Importance to the marketing process:

- No business can make decisions without reference to its competitive environment
- Even a monopoly must be concerned about potential entrants or effective substitutes
- Pricing must account for what the market will bear and the reactions of competitors
- The more competitors there are and the closer their product offering, the more sensitively sales respond to a relative change in price
- Price wars may erupt from time to time but non-price competition using branding and other product and promotional tactics are the norm.

Customers

All businesses have customers as the final link in the input/output chain. The idea that they are stakeholders is less familiar, although the choice of withdrawing their stake or not will determine the success or otherwise of the enterprise. This might be summed up by the CBI definition of marketing as 'supplying products that don't come back to customers that do'! The marketer will be concerned with all the influences affecting that choice.

Importance to the marketing process:

- o Customers are the only source of revenue for most organizations
- o If they withdraw or transfer their custom to a competitor then survival is threatened
- o A dissatisfied customer tells many more of the experience than does a satisfied one
- o Customer retention is normally more cost effective than recruiting new ones due to the lifetime revenue stream that is often involved
- o Customers are looking for value for money. This is a combination of the broadly defined satisfaction deriving from consumption of the product and its relative price
- o Customer preferences can change very quickly but can be influenced by the marketer
- o Microsoft believes in leading the market but following the customer
- o Customer knowledge and scope for comparison is expanding through use of the Internet.

Intermediaries/distributors

These must also be considered where the firm does not sell directly to the consumer. They are important elements of the marketing channel that makes the product available to the user. They may include wholesalers, retailers, dealers, agents and franchisees. Also included are marketing services such as market research, advertising, media and consultancies. Here creativity and quality must be balanced against service and price. Their power and position may be significant not least in respect of retailer brands that may be promoted aggressively at the expense of manufacturer offerings. Tying in distributors may provide a competitive edge over rivals.

Importance to the marketing process:

- o Distributors who are ineffective in delivering the product to the customer as, where and when they want it will negatively impact on the business. There is a need to balance cost, delivery, speed and safety.
- o Effective partners deliver advantage in the form of transport, stock management, market knowledge, merchandising and display, together with after-sales service. They have a critical impact on availability, timing, quality and price.
- o The marketer must communicate with both the final customer and the distributor(s) delivering the product to this end-user.
- o Distributors have economic leverage arising from their strategic position. They are becoming fewer and more powerful.
- o Distributors have mutual interests in common to form the basis of joint ventures and partnerships.
- o e-Commerce may lead to disintermediation in the value chain as manufacturers consider direct marketing to consumers.

> ## Exam hint
>
> Remember the course you are studying is first and foremost about the environment. Do not be tempted to answer questions in marketing terms alone.

Shareholders and creditors

Shareholders provide the longer-term capital while creditors such as banks and other financial institutions provide short- and medium-term funds. They can affect the business through the sale of shares or withdrawal of credit. Small businesses are particularly vulnerable to the latter in times of recession while institutional shareholders, such as pension funds, are becoming more active in their scrutiny of public company management and remuneration.

Importance to the marketing process:

o These are important constituencies to the organization, so clear and timely communication with them based on an understanding of their needs is required.
o Adverse shareholder perceptions may lead to selling, which drives down the market valuation of the company relative to its net asset value, so risking unwelcome takeover bids.
o Trade and bank credit are critical in maintaining a healthy cash flow. Relationships with both must be nurtured and improved.
o The public image of the business is largely the responsibility of marketing.

Employees and unions

Most businesses have employees who contribute their time and skills for monetary and other rewards. They form part of wider society and reflect its values and beliefs. They are directly affected by company activities, including harmful ones, but again the effects are two way. They can unionize, adversely affect productivity, leave or have equally positive effects on company fortunes. The decline in trade unions has affected the freedom of many firms to manage but so too has increased legislation on health, safety, employment and pollution.

Importance to the marketing process:

o As with customers, retention of skilled staff is normally more cost effective than the uncertainties of recruitment.
o The image of the organization is an important determinant in the quality of applicant attracted.
o The business will attract the calibre of employees it deserves.
o Internal marketing to critical departments and employees is central to the achievement of goals.
o The evolution of virtual companies will make staff much more mobile, forcing organizations to rethink remuneration and training packages.

Activity 2.5

Key skills: interpreting information

Taking a business with which you are familiar, identify and rank its five most important suppliers, distributors, competitors, customers and creditors. What marketing mix does it employ to:

- Retain and motivate its distributors?
- Secure a competitive edge over its rivals?

The micro-environment is of general importance to the marketing process, for the following reasons:

- The marketer can utilize the marketing mix to influence and impact on all the stakeholders.
- The same stakeholders can both damage or advantage the business.
- The micro-environment includes not only actual customers, suppliers, intermediaries and competitors but potential ones as well.
- The marketing mix can also be deployed to convert potential customers into actual ones or to discourage potential competitors from entering the market.
- Successful businesses are often those that are part of larger 'clusters' of collective activity. The Dutch bulb industry is a world-beater because of the concentration of suppliers, research organizations, producers, competitors and intermediaries that complement, strengthen and support one another.
- Such clusters of networked organizations are also the preferred form in e-commerce value chains.
- It generates a tension between competition and cooperation. Businesses compete for customers and sometimes compete for shelf space with distributors, but equally they may cooperate with suppliers over new product development or with intermediaries for joint promotions. The marketer must assess the pay-off associated with both approaches.
- It forms the immediate or operational environment for the marketer and drives tactical responses on a daily basis. Macro-environment changes tend to drive strategic responses.
- The marketer represents the critical interface between key stakeholders and the rest of the organization.

Stakeholder pressures

Stakeholders are defined as any group or individual who can affect or are affected by the achievement of the organization's objectives. Since they have a stake, a legitimate interest in the business, they can influence objectives. Management cannot hope to operate in isolation but must seek to satisfy their stakeholders' legitimate expectations if they are to contribute value in return (Figure 2.6).

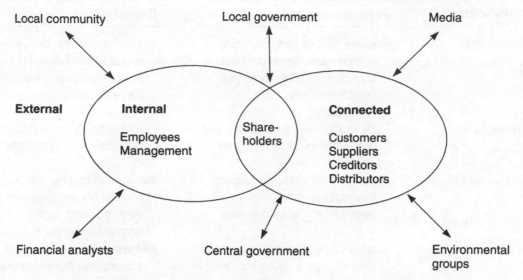

Figure 2.6 Internal, connected and external stakeholders

Direct or connected stakeholders are closely related to the core economic functions of the business. Together with the pressure exerted by competitors, they can change the goals and nature of the organization unless managed effectively.

There is a considerable potential for conflict of interest between the primary stakeholder groups. Higher wages for employees may conflict with shareholder profits or result in higher prices that upset customers. Local community concerns for health and safety may increase costs, reduce competitiveness and jeopardize jobs.

If any stakeholder considers they are not receiving sufficient return they may withdraw their contribution to the organization. For example, if customers no longer feel a product is value for money they will buy elsewhere. If workers consider their remuneration too low they will change jobs and their contribution will be lost.

Balancing these partly conflicting stakeholder expectations while achieving objectives of growth, market share and profitability is not easily achieved, not least in times of rapid change. Internal marketing is now widely recognized as an essential part of any manager's role. Implementation and fulfilment of business strategies requires that managers identify groups of internal as well as external stakeholders and market their plans to them. Further analysis of these critical stakeholder relationships is to be found in the Marketing Fundamentals coursebook.

Stakeholder	Pressure exerted	Expectations
Shareholders	Delegate decision power to board but recent increase in activism over remuneration and appointments. Selling shares is the real threat as a falling share price attracts takeover predators	Above average return on equity, improving return on assets, share value rising
Employees	Absenteeism, turnover, low morale, media leaks, unionization, poor quality worth productivity	Above average remuneration, training and skill development, company growth/promotion, employment security/job satisfaction, improving conditions and wages

Stakeholder	Pressure exerted	Expectations
Customers	Reduce purchases, buy from competitors, organize boycott, complain to other potential customers, press for legislation	Value for money, convenience, product safety/quality assurance, innovation/improved design, better service
Creditors	Limit credit, withdraw credit, cut credit rating, charge higher rates	Regular/timely repayment, early notification of problems
Distributors	Stock and promote competing brands/own label, integrate backwards, delay payment	Reliable supplies, support in promotion, progressive product development, good communications
Suppliers	Supply competitors, reduce priority, limit trade credit, poor-quality service, integrate forward	Reliable payment, regular supply schedules, development support, ability to interrogate stock/ production systems

Exam hint

Key skills: improving your own learning

Any new course of study is hard going at the beginning. You do not know the terminology and you have studied too few pieces of the jigsaw to be able to see the overall picture unfolding.

However, remember that the more pieces you fit together, the easier it gets, not least because you move down your learning curve. Each question and activity you attempt provides experience you can apply to advantage when you address the next. So keep on going and develop some learning momentum!

Indirect or external stakeholder groups are not directly engaged in the business operations but can exert influence on and be seriously affected by their activities. A few of these are listed below for each group. Can you think of others?

- ○ *General public* – This group collectively represents the nation's householders, consumers, workers, pensioners and many other sub-categories of wider society. Their attitudes and expectations are important and reflected in opinion polls. They matter to organizations because public concerns and beliefs impact on their economic decisions. Companies recognize this and the need to market themselves effectively through public relations expenditure. Large companies like IBM and Disney invest considerable time and resources in building and maintaining a positive public image. For example, Walkers Crisps, owned by PepsiCo, is currently sponsoring a 'walking' campaign to encourage healthier lifestyles.
- ○ *Local government* – Interested not only in the investment, jobs, prosperity, tax revenue and prestige the organization generates locally but also in its compliance with relevant legislation, planning requirements etc. One example of this stakeholder power is the anti-smoking law introduced in New York and applied to all workplaces, bars and restaurants.
- ○ *Communities* – Concerned with property values, quality of life, jobs and prosperity, congestion, links with local schools and charitable activities. Can protest, mobilize the

media, obstruct planning applications (Not In My Back Yard), etc. While it is clearly sensible for a potentially hazardous plant in an urban location, with all its attendant risks, to take account of residents and neighbourhood organizations, the same logic applies to service organizations, like banks. Sponsorship and openness will be two of the means deployed to maintain good relations.

o *Financial analysts* – Assess past/future performance in financial and broader terms. They downgrade where suspicious of unethical behaviour and highlight undervalued assets/possible takeover. They have the ear of the shareholders. Public companies, in particular, need to be aware of the information needs of these stakeholders and their influence on the company's ability to raise funds. The organization must market itself effectively to such groups to ensure that their sentiment remains positive.

o *Media* – These include news, articles, features and editorials carried by television, newspapers, radio, journals, magazines and increasingly the Internet. They can seriously enhance or damage the public image of the business. They publicize issues and corporate achievements and form a line of communication from the organization to the local/national community. The marketer must therefore seek to develop good relationships with media representatives to ensure that the organizational case is also heard.

o *Central government* – Governments often hold a controlling influence over many public sector organizations and so are direct stakeholders. They make, interpret and enforce laws, monitor compliance, levy taxes and implement economic policies. They also provide infrastructure, spend, protect, subsidize, rescue and restructure. There is a clear need to establish effective two-way dialogue between relevant central and local agencies and the marketing function. The organization may seek influence through trade associations, lobbying, provision of information, joint projects and even political donations.

o *Environment pressure groups* – Business decisions may be challenged by a variety of action groups concerned over specific causes or interests. They can protest, resist development and generate considerable media attention. Note the interlinkages between the above stakeholders, for example, communities may exert pressure on government to get their case heard or use the media to make their point. Of course, not all stakeholders have the same degree of influence and power. As Brooks and Weatherston point out in their text *The Business Environment*, relevant environmental stakeholders need to be 'mapped' according to their level of interest in the organization's activities on the one hand, and their real power to influence outcomes on the other. Figure 2.7 shows an application of this analytical tool to a college.

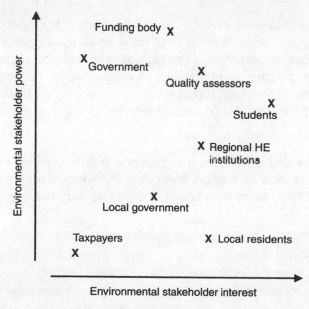

Figure 2.7 Stakeholder mapping: college of higher education

You should actively relate the stakeholders defined above to your own organization or an exemplar so that you can fix their significance in your mind. Multinationals, such as McDonald's, need them all 'on side' if they are to overcome the challenge of market diversity within the global economy.

Marketing environment in practice

McDonald's has felt the full brunt of its external stakeholders in recent years (see 'Cutting the fat at McDonalds' in the December 2003 paper). It misjudged the public surge of sympathy for a protesting local French sheep farmer who 'trashed' their restaurant in Millau. This case was widely reported by the media and compounded a 40 per cent fall in sales of McDonald's as consumer confidence in the safety of French beef all but collapsed following a spate of BSE (mad cow) cases. McDonald's also had to confront religious pressure groups in Italy where it was seeking to double its chain of 272 outlets. A Catholic newspaper attacked fast food as targeting the 'holiness of food' and fit only for other religious groups. Such coverage reflects the hostility of those who view McDonald's as the unacceptable face of American dominated global capitalism. Profits have fallen 70 per cent in the UK and even in the US it faces threats from other fast-food chains such as Subway and lawyers who claim its Big Macs are not only unhealthy but also addictive. There is an increasing resentment that US fast food has usurped local, historic cuisines. Whether this will deflect the general public from the convenience of fast food in the longer term remains to be seen.

 ## Activity 2.6

Key skills: using information

Draw up a stakeholder map for your own organization or a local large employer of your choice.

Consider the criteria you are using in assessing the relative power and influence of each.

The days when organizations could safely 'mind their own business' are clearly no longer!

The behaviour of companies has become everybody's business and organizations must recognize that they are under the watchful gaze of all the above stakeholders from time to time. Pressure groups, for example, exert legislative and ethical pressure in seeking to change business objectives, policies and behaviour in various ways. For example, large firms should pay smaller ones more promptly, top executives should set an example in their remuneration practices and all businesses should employ a higher proportion of women and minority groups in senior positions.

The stakeholders of any organization are unique but may either threaten and challenge its objectives and operations or support them. It is therefore vitally important that the business 'knows its stakeholders', since from knowledge comes the power to deal with them effectively.

Question 2.3

In what sense are you a stakeholder in CIM and how might you seek to influence the organization?

Pressure groups

In this final section we will consider pressure groups as one of the more important elements with an actual or potential interest in, or impact on, the activities of an organization or its ability to achieve its objectives.

Characteristics of pressure groups are as follows:

- They are sub-sections of the population organized on the basis of *specific common interests or attitudes*
- They exert pressure on people, organizations or government for their *own special purpose*
- They seek to *influence* the context of government decisions
- They do not seek election to government office and *are not political parties* (e.g. Green Party)
- They exercise pressure both for the purpose of securing favourable decisions and for preventing undesirable ones.

It is important to make the distinction between a sectional or interest group, whose membership is based on the performance of a specific economic role, and a promotional or cause group, who are bound by shared values or attitudes and seek to promote a particular issue or prevent an adverse outcome. The latter may be formed to fight a specific issue and then disband when it is won or lost.

Activity 2.7

Key skills: use information

List the pressure groups you have belonged to and classify them into the groups described in this section. Do the same for the following: Chambers of Commerce, the Mothers' Union, Campaign for Real Ale (CAMRA), British Medical Association.

Examples of sectional pressure groups include trade unions, consumer associations, trade associations and businesses themselves. Industry bodies such as the Nigerian Chamber of Commerce, the Ceylon National Chamber of Industries or the Trades Union Congress (TUC) are representative organizations. Promotional groups are very numerous and have expanded rapidly in recent years. They fall into several groups and each country will have examples under the various headings:

Welfare	Age Concern, Royal Society for the Prevention of Cruelty to Animals (RSPCA), Action on Smoking & Health (ASH)
Recreation	National Cyclists' Union, Ramblers Association
Cultural	Citizens' Advice Bureau, Lord's Day Observance Society
Environmental	International Fund for Animal Welfare (IFAW), Noise Abatement Society, Greenpeace
Political	Amnesty International, Campaign against Racial Discrimination
International	Oxfam, Médecin sans Frontières, Save the Children Fund, Red Crescent Society

Pressure groups are activists of the stakeholder groups considered so far. They are the means through which the individual can be heard on important issues by joining forces with like-minded people whether locally or nationally. Groups can arise to fight factory or hospital closures, ban hunting with hounds, challenge unacceptable business practices, or fight motorway proposals/airport extentions. They will usually use all means at their disposal to achieve their objectives:

- *Complain* (e.g. to the local media)
- *Inform and persuade* those likely to be affected
- *Debate and challenge* at local meetings
- *Lobby and petition* elected/representatives and state officials
- *Canvass and opinion form* among stakeholder groups
- *March and demonstrate* outside the factory gates
- *Demand and negotiate* action and concessions from the company
- *Take legal action*
- *Other means include alliances, information leaks, infiltration, opinion forming, bribery and misinformation* and blackmailing.

The formal channels through which pressure groups function are:

- *Pressure through government* – Formal pressure may be applied when the group is invited to give evidence to commissions, or committees of inquiry. Government departments will consult directly with recognized and responsible pressure groups to sound out views on proposed legislation. Input at the initial drafting stage is an important advantage. Governments cannot legislate effectively without consultation with interested parties, and these are part of the routine relationships it maintains.
- *Pressure through the legislature* – Pressure groups will seek to recruit sympathetic elected representatives to their cause. Concerned with any matters affecting their constituencies and re-election prospects they are therefore susceptible to particular issues and causes. Businesses often employ professional lobbyists to identify and mobilize such support for their interests. Elected representatives can often introduce proposed legislation and ask questions during debates to publicize a cause, but this is normally much less effective than pressure exerted through government ministers and departments. The need to disclose earnings arising out of representation may also constrain such pressures.
- *Pressure through public campaign* – Educational and propaganda campaigns can be mounted to move public opinion in the longer term. Attention in the short term will tend to focus on raising public and stakeholder awareness and seeking to mobilize them against a specific threat using public meetings, demonstrations, petitions, newspaper advertisements and exposure in the media in general. This now includes the collection of electronic petitions and coordination of protests over the Internet. This may be relatively successful in the case of drink driving, for example, but less certain in a campaign against fast urban driving.

Exam hint

Key skills: improving your performance

Are you able to think of at least one or two more examples for each one cited in the text? The examiner is going to be more impressed with your original examples, rather than re-reading his/her own!

The consumerist movement

The consumerist movement had its origins in America during the late 1950s when commentators like Vance Packard and Ralph Nader began to alert consumers to the fact that businesses were concerned more for their own profits than customer or environmental welfare. Nader's book, Unsafe at any Speed, successfully challenged the might of one of the world's largest multinationals, General Motors, and signalled the birth of consumerism.

In Britain, its development was slower. The publication and interest in the Consumers Association's *Which?* reports, comparing the relative performance and merits of rival brands from the user's point of view, served notice on the ancient maxim 'caveat emptor' (let the buyer beware), replacing it with 'caveat vendictor' (let the seller beware). Such associations are now to be found in most countries and there is little wonder that the reduced willingness of customers to suffer in silence coincided with more proactive companies adopting a marketing orientation towards these increasingly aware stakeholders.

There is no one accepted meaning of the term 'consumerism'. Some of the suggested definitions are as follows:

o The search for getting better value for money
o A social movement seeking to augment the rights and powers of buyers in relation to sellers
o Anything consumers say it is.

Consumerism is clearly a force within the environment designed to aid and protect the consumer by exerting legal, moral and economic pressure on business. It has evolved over time and has embraced a number of issues ranging from unfair pricing and high credit costs through deceptive packaging and product labelling to poor value for money extended warranties. Future causes might include 'excessive choice'. One has only to consider the number of shampoos on supermarket shelves each with its own unique selling proposition. Interestingly psychologists found that shoppers were more likely to buy jams when only six varieties were on display, as when there were twenty four. Other concerns include Internet fraud and junk mail prize fraud.

In 1962 US President J.F. Kennedy laid the foundation to consumerism by proposing four basic rights set out in Figure 2.8

Right of safety	Right to be informed
Right to bo heard	Right to choose

Figure 2.8 Consumer rights

o *Safety* – The right to protection against the marketing of any products which are hazardous to life, especially where hidden dangers may be involved. Products such as pharmaceuticals, cars, tyres, household appliances, insecticides and foods have been the source of many customer-related accidents or diseases and a major spur to consumerism. Current targets for legal actions include the tobacco, gun and drinks industries. Mobile phones constitute a new target due to microwave emissions, interference and in-car usage. The long-term implications of food additives, irradiated and genetically modified foods, *E. coli* bacteria and the transfer of BSE from cattle to humans are four further examples of such concern. Safe alternatives do not always cost more and may provide an edge for companies in the marketplace. However, where extra cost is involved, as in fire-retardant furniture foam, or fully effective air bags and ABS (antilock braking system), competition often prevents concerted action in the interests of greater safety.

○ *Information* – The right to protection from fraudulent, deceitful and grossly misleading information and to be given the necessary facts to enable an informed decision to be taken. This is an important role for consumerists and an area that impacts directly on the ethics of marketing departments. The consumer is a generalist lacking the expertise, the time and often the inclination to acquire the product knowledge necessary to make an informed purchase. Reliance for comprehensive and comprehensible information is therefore placed on the marketer in respect of advertising, promotional copy, personal selling, packaging, guarantees and service contracts. Timeshare, insurance and packaged holiday companies, for example, still seem to inhabit the lower reaches of the pressure sell and 'small print' jungle!

Exam hint

Remember you are a consumer as far as the CIM and your college are concerned. You have a 'right' to expect a relevant syllabus, an applied approach, comprehensive information on examination requirements and feedback on performance.

Make sure you take advantage of your consumer rights and do not forget to regularly access www.cim.co.uk.

○ *Choice* – The right to variety and a competitive service at a fair price. The customer should have the information and opportunity to make an objective selection and be able to distinguish between me-too and 'real' competition in promotional offerings.
○ *A hearing* – The right to express dissatisfaction over poor service and substandard product performance. Consumers should have easy-to-navigate channels for airing their grievances and receive full and sympathetic consideration. The need for legal process and an external policing mechanism will be examined in a later unit.

Consumerist responses have included individual refusal to buy, collective boycotts, lobbying and media campaigns through 'Watch-dog' type consumer affairs television programmes. Consumer groups and individuals can also register their views on company websites or by email. Consumer power has always suffered from diffusion arising from the variety of calls on available buyer purchasing power. Agitating over dissatisfaction with a low value or infrequently purchased good or service is often judged a waste of time and effort. A prime example of 'power diffusion' arises in the Common Agricultural Policy where nearly half of the total EU budget subsidizes farmers. They form a small but concentrated and vociferous pressure group while unorganized households pay higher prices and taxes thought to average £1500 per household in Britain alone.

Business initially viewed the consumerist movement as a threat that created extra costs of compliance and inhibited their freedom of operation. Marketing-orientated organizations, however, soon learnt to listen to what consumers really required. Nissan recently recalled

2.5 million vehicles worldwide to rectify a potential safety fault despite the cost and potential impact on its reliability image.

Consumers vote with their money and, given acceptable choices, will shop elsewhere. Better to accept the challenge of consumerism and address the problems before the competition does it for you!

Marketing environment in practice

Are we being poisoned by our own food?

Read the following extracts from the *Times* and *The Week* and consider how the marketer should respond in practice to scientific studies that suggest a significant range of everyday foods contain potentially dangerous levels of a cancer-causing chemical called acrylamide?

The US Environmental Protection Agency lists the chemical, which is used mainly in the manufacture of plastics, as a 'probable' human carcinogen and has limited the maximum permitted level in American drinking water to 0.5 parts per billion. In Europe, the permitted level for residues left on food from packaging is no more than 10 parts per billion.

Tests suggest that the chemical is produced whenever certain foods are baked, fried, microwaved or grilled at temperatures over 120 °C especially for long periods. Deep-fried and fast foods seem to have the highest levels with chips at 736 ppb and potato crisps at 4000 ppb. It has also been found at relatively high levels in some crackers, breakfast cereals and burnt meat.

The head of food safety at the World Health Organization (WHO) believes that a significant proportion of the 30–40 per cent of cancers linked to diet could be caused by the chemical. Modern food processing and cooking techniques could explain the rising trend of cancer in Western countries.

WHO still maintains that the levels of the chemical that the average person consumes is not life threatening but it may not do too much harm on the precautionary principle to cut back on fatty fried foods and increase our intake of fruit and boiled vegetables.

Summary

Consumerism has provided many customer-orientated businesses with an opportunity to make product strengths and socially responsible marketing a source of competitive advantage. It is a well-established feature of the marketplace and will remain so while ever there is scope for opportunist sellers to mislead and confuse the consumers. Its concerns now extend far beyond consumer protection to issues such as pricing, design obsolescence and, increasingly, ecology to which marketers must positively respond.

Environmentalism

There are an estimated 1400 environmental pressure groups in Britain alone. Demands they are making range over the following:

- ○ Conservation of resources and energy saving
- ○ Reuse, redesign and recycling of products

o Slowing of economic growth and elimination of eco-unfriendly products
o Protection of the natural environment, animal rights and endangered species.

Exam hint

Key skills: improving own performance

You must get as much practice as possible at answering case questions based on extracts and articles. The compulsory question worth 40 per cent of the marks is not testing your specific knowledge of the article in question but your ability to relate it to your overall knowledge of the marketing environment.

Such demands imply economic and financial costs for business, potential redundancies and higher consumer prices. Despite a cyclical pattern to such pressures they are likely to increase rather than diminish with time. Some industries are more likely to be targeted than others but none are immune. Those most recently in the firing line include aerosols, agriculture, airlines, animal testing, chemicals, fertilizers, motorways, oil tankers, plastics, pulp and paper, refrigeration, tobacco, tourism, toxic waste and water. On the other hand, the environment has also been improving in a number of areas. Britain, for example, has more woodland today than it has had for 200 years, the air in London is better than its been for 300 years, plus its rivers and beaches are the cleanest they have been for decades. With entire bureaucracies in the EU devoted to a better environment, the pressure groups have been forced to regroup and refocus.

Question 2.4

Key skills: problem-solving

Take each of the industries listed above and suggest the environmental issue that has placed them in the firing line.

What responses have businesses in these industries made that you are aware of?

What other industries, not mentioned above, would you include as high-profile targets for environmentalists?

A number of possible threats arise if a business ignores its environment:

o The corporate image deteriorates in the eyes of stakeholders
o Customers may prefer alternatives they perceive as less harmful
o Shareholders may prefer to invest in ethically sound companies
o Recruitment and retention of quality staff becomes more difficult
o Unnecessarily strict legislation may be enacted due to failure to act
o Loss of community support, harder attitude from authorities
o Increasing competitive disadvantage to proactive rivals
o Cost penalties – higher energy bill, insurance, legal claims.

Activity 2.8

Key skills: presenting information

In the light of the potential threats outlined here, make a case to your board of directors stating the potential benefits of becoming a more environmentally aware company.

Suppose the board is persuaded by the force of your arguments but asks you for guidelines to ensure that this new philosophy is adopted throughout the company. What would you suggest?

We return to the natural environment in Unit 4 but before concluding, two final aspects should be mentioned: first, the importance of legal form and second, the business response required to such pressure groups.

Sole traders and small limited companies normally face more intense competition and are less likely to have the resources to commit to achieving environmental standards in excess of those required by legislation. On the other hand, they will be owner-managed and do business in localities where they live. Such business people have traditionally filled many civic posts in the local community and may sacrifice profit to maintain their reputation and standing in this and other respects. Public limited companies, in comparison, will be well resourced and have a higher national profile. They will be more aware of developments with regard to the industry and its environment and are more likely to participate in government and other initiatives to bring about improvements.

On the other hand, they are often in a position to relocate production activities to other parts of the world where legislation is less stringent. Small firms will find it less easy to justify the cost of meeting new environmental management standards such as BS 7750, although there are increasing pressures on suppliers to adopt these, irrespective of legal form.

Exam hint

Key skills: metrics

The compulsory question counts for 40 per cent of the total marks on the paper. Given that the paper is 3 hours long, this means you should spend 40 per cent of the time on it, that is, 1 hour 12 minutes. If this compulsory question has four parts to it, then you should be allocating just 18 minutes per part. The question paper will tell you if the parts are worth different mark values, but typically they will be the same.

At 18 minutes per part it is very important that you keep to the time allowed. What examiners find, all too frequently, Is that candidates spend too long on parts they happen to know a lot about at the expense of one or two of the others on which they have time to write very little at all. Do not be tempted to fall into this trap. Spend roughly the same amount of time on each and give the examiner something to mark even in those parts where you are less confident.

The response

The final question is, how should the business respond to pressure from environmentalists, or any of the other pressure groups, for that matter? We have already seen that the organization must prioritize since it has insufficient resources to deal with all pressures. It must assess which pressures are significant and offer the greatest likelihood of impact on the business. The response may be framed in very simple terms, but each option requires considerable management effort and time to make it effective:

- Listen/communicate to them and respond positively
- Consult and liaise with them
- Work with them to make the necessary things happen
- Support them to work for you
- Oppose them if all else fails.

Where a business is sensitive to the interests of relevant pressure groups it is more likely to react more effectively to change in its marketing environment. Similarly, trust built up through a track record of public service is an asset and an investment to protect. Consumers are discouraged by brands where negative publicity arises and insensitivity in one area can cancel out positive progress elsewhere.

Question 2.5

Key skills: collecting information

Can you think of some recent 'negative publicity' for your or any high-profile company? If not, scan the newspapers until you have some examples on file.

The characteristics of the product or service itself provide numerous cues to the various pressure groups and represent the litmus test of an organization's real commitment to its stated corporate values. Similarly the promotional mix raises awareness and reinforces perceptions of a good business image or, alternatively, seeks to ensure that it is not undermined.

The organization must decide its fundamental responsibilities and develop a policy towards each stakeholder group based on the values it considers important. Priorities must be established to ensure that limited resources are not spread too thinly. It should logically focus first on current and prospective legal obligations towards stakeholders.

Due to the slow working of the legislative process and political manifestos, companies have advance warning of such developments. Organizations, or their trade associations, must therefore monitor proposed developments very carefully since they may wish to influence its detailed formulation in their own interests.

Second, the organization will wish to consider its moral responsibilities and where it stands on them (and relative to its competitors). In these, as well as with projected legislation, it will concentrate its attention where the likely impacts on its business are greatest.

Exam hint

Key skills: improving own performance

There is always a strong temptation in a time-constrained examination to start writing as soon as possible, especially when those about you seem to have done so already. It is more than likely, however, that such candidates will be writing unstructured answers which do not address what the question requires, and certainly not in a logical sequence.

As any effective marketer will tell you, it is the planning that goes into a campaign that is the secret of its success. The same is the case with exam questions. Understanding what the customer (i.e. the examiner) wants and then spending 4 or 5 minutes to plan how best to effectively satisfy these wants is what produces the excellent pass. Writing it out in a form the examiner can comprehend is merely the mechanics of the process.

Develop the habit of jotting down *trigger word plans* for all the sample exam questions in this coursebook. Each 'word' represents an idea or factor you will introduce into the essay. Just one word will remind you of the idea and it ensures that you will not omit to include it at the appropriate point in your answer.

Any organization is confronted by a seemingly endless procession of stakeholder or pressure group issues in whose crossfire it threatens to be caught. It is important that the organization does not overreact to these issues since they can be double-edged. Politically correct behaviour, not least in the area of sexual harassment and the promotion of women into senior managerial positions, may also rebound if the result is a steep rise in the turnover of company trained male managers. Performance against intended objectives must be measured and assessed (note the problems facing police forces in raising ethnic group representation to their proportion in the population). Every effort should be made to frame objectives in such a way that progress towards them can be estimated.

Pressures for a positive organizational response

- *More knowledgeable and educated consumers* Aware of their rights and increasingly critical of irresponsible behaviour. They are also more prepared to make legal claims which are costly in terms of time, money and bad publicity for the organization in question.
- *The threat of legislation* may inhibit behaviour that society considers unethical.
- *Rising affluence increases social and environmental concerns.*
- *Competitive pressure* as businesses seek competitive advantage by emphasizing their responsibility towards stakeholders. Customers or investors who value such behaviour will wish to be associated with such companies.
- *Stakeholder pressure* from those concerned with quality or their own corporate image. Many large companies insisted their suppliers were 'millennium compliant' or had implemented codes of good practice.
- *European Union directives* ensure compliance with common standards across the Single Market. This produces a ratchet effect of higher standards in terms of food safety, packaging, recycling, and so on.
- *Pressure group activity* tends to crystallize these pressures and provides support and legal backing.
- *The media* provide focus and attention on many areas of corporate weakness. Recent examples include allegations concerning the use of child labour in the manufacture of

products for socially responsible organizations and the recent furore over genetically modified foods.
  o *Demonstration effects* by high-profile organizations with close link to external stake-holders and responsive to pressure groups.
  o *The power of the Internet* creates open information systems which readily link those with common interest in ethical business behaviour.

Conclusions on pressure groups

We can conclude that pressure group activity and influence are increasing and becoming better organized and more professional in approach to both government and target companies. They are now much more adept at marketing their causes and highlighting the deficiencies of companies towards their stakeholder groups.

Green consumers' guides and the Friends of the Earth green 'con' awards are just two examples of potentially damaging copy for a business's reputation. To minimize such risks, a company must establish and apply values and beliefs conducive to a sustainable business. It must be aware of threats as well as the considerable opportunities of enhancing its reputation in the eyes of stakeholders through effective and well-managed policies towards the environment. Unilever and the World Wildlife Fund for Nature, for example, agreed a sustainable standard for fish products with a special logo if the product was from accredited fishing grounds.

Summary

  o Business ignores its environment at its peril.
  o Marketers have a key role in identifying environmental change.
  o Organizations have a number of primary stakeholders and these make up its micro-environment where influence is two way.
  o Business must also account and respond to opportunities and threats in its wider environment over which it has no control.
  o Pressure groups are increasing in importance and can be classified as interest or cause groups.
  o Pressure groups can employ a number of means and channels through which their pressure may be brought to bear.
  o Consumerism has become a force for companies to reckon with, especially as the causes pursued have broadened out from just narrow consumer protection issues.
  o One of the important current issues for consumers relates to the claims and counterclaims of marketers regarding the eco-friendliness of their offerings.
  o The scope of environmental concerns and the specific threats posed to businesses are potentially serious (e.g. SUV's – emissions, fuel use and road safety concerns; *Exxon Valdez/Sea Empress/ Erica/Jessica (Galapagos Islands)* – tanker spillage; meat products and BSE; genetically modified foods).
  o The constructive response is not necessarily to confront and oppose pressure groups but, where possible, to understand their interests, listen to their point of view and work towards a common solution.

Further study and examination preparation

Since the marketing environment links the organization with external constraints, opportunities and threats, it is unsurprising that questions frequently arise requiring you to explore the relationship between the two. While the syllabus content of this unit is around 10 per cent, its significance extends much wider in terms of questions and part questions appearing at regular intervals on CIM papers. It is also important to note that while the stakeholder concept is treated in more depth in the Marketing Fundamentals syllabus, part or even full questions will continue to appear in the Marketing Environment paper. Pressure groups and how the marketer responds to them in practice remains an important element in examination terms.

Extending knowledge

Palmer and Hartley, *The Business and Marketing Environment*, McGraw-Hill – Chapter 1, Marketing, An Overview and Chapter 2, Nature of the Marketing Environment.

Palmer, A. *The Business Environment*, McGraw-Hill – Chapter 1, What is the Business Environment and Chapter 5 on social responsibility.

Brooks, I. and Weatherston, J. *The Business Environment*, Prentice Hall – Chapters 1 and 2.

Websites would include www.ft.com and www.thetimes.co.uk for general up-to-date coverage of the marketing environment.

www.greenpeace.org for coverage of a host of environmental issues and links with other pressure groups.

http:/www.webdirectory.com/ is a directory of environmental organizations with a search facility.

www.marketingportal.cim.co.uk includes research and reports commissioned for the CIM.

www.tradingstandards.gov.uk take up consumer complaints over bad service.

www.fsa.gov.uk publishes fee and performance comparisons of financial providers.

Exam question 2.1

Please see Question 4, June 2004. Go to www.cim.co.uk for specimen answers.

Exam question 2.2

Please see Question 7, June 2004. Go to www.cim.co.uk for specimen answers.

Exam question 2.3

Please see Question 2, December 2003. Go to www.cim.co.uk for specimen answers.

Exam question 2.4

Please see Question 3a, December 2003. Go to www.cim.co.uk for specimen answers.

unit 3
analysis of the competitive environment

By the end of this unit you will be able to:

o Appreciate the competitive environment and the importance of monitoring rivals (2.6)

o Understand the process of competitor analysis and assess the marketing implications arising for the organization (2.6)

o Identify strategies to improve profitability (2.6)

o Weigh the significance of competition policies and their impact on the market environment (2.7)

o Recognize and access key sources of information relevant to understanding the micro-environment (2.3).

Study Guide

This unit is concerned with the market environment of the organization and deals with the element that impacts continuously on most businesses – *the competition*. The marketer normally confronts this reality on a day-to-day basis.

The balance of the unit is concerned with information, a critical theme throughout this course-book and one explored in detail in Unit 8. Here, and again in Unit 4, we will develop your awareness of internal and particularly external information sources that contribute to greater understanding of the marketing environment.

This unit accounts for around 12 per cent of the syllabus, but it represents a very important segment of the external environment. Subsequent units, which consider other environments, have most of their effects on competitive relationships. The activities should enable you to relate the material to your organization and work experience.

Monitoring competitors

You should re-read the material on actual and potential customers and competitors in Unit 2, where it was made clear that a two-way relationship exists between them and the marketing function. To be fully effective the marketer must appreciate the dynamics of markets, the behaviour of its rivals and the realities of customer preferences and their execution. This need to monitor competitors, however, varies according to the structure of the industry.

Fragmented industries

In fragmented industries the number of participants is very large whereas their average size is relatively small. There is little to be gained by monitoring the competitive behaviour of rivals other than those that represent the closest competitors in terms, perhaps, of location or product/service characteristics. Such industries are characterized by businesses competing for market share based on meeting buyer preferences rather than random selection among identical providers. The market is underlain by a diversity of incomes, attitudes, tastes and preferences so that sellers must discover the qualitative mix which best satisfies the needs of the target customer base. Firms must make the most of their product's unique selling points before the competition arrives, as it inevitably will. Market leaders do not tend to dominate because the scope for cost advantages from greater scale of operation is comparatively small. Advantage goes to those who are flexible and adaptable and such firms will seek to establish a competitive edge over their immediate rivals through innovation or successful differentiation of the marketing mix. Unfortunately, barriers to entry tend to be low into such industries, making new entry into the market likely if high profits are being made by existing firms. The extra supply this represents, combined with imitation of successful trading formulas, drives down margins and profitability over time. Any improvement in general demand conditions due, say, to changing tastes, rising incomes or unfortunate circumstances affecting substitute products will lead to initial improvement in sales and margins. However, subsequent and often rapid erosion of profitability is the characteristic of fragmented industries.

Question 3.1

Key skills: problem-solving

Which of the following would you identify as fragmented industries?

- o Health and fitness centres
- o Restaurants
- o Fast-food outlets
- o Hotels.

What factors account for the fragmentation?

Are there forces leading to consolidation in the fast-food sector?

One familiar situation to marketers, where competition is intense, is where the product has become a so-called 'commodity' as it enters the late maturity stage of the product life cycle. A saturated market dependent on repeat buyers, who are particularly knowledgeable with regard to desirable product and service characteristics, will make successful differentiation extremely difficult or costly to sustain. This produces a price taker situation where the forces of market supply and demand determine the going price, rather than the individual firm. Potential customers will view product offerings as identical and rationally purchase the cheapest. Any attempt to set prices above what the market will bear will lead to drastic loss of sales and market share.

Exam hint

Key skills for marketers

Develop your Internet skills by checking out the price comparison websites that assist the discerning consumer to shop around for the best bargains. It provides you with information on your competitors:

www.pricerunner.com offers perhaps the best price check on products ranging from electric toothbrushes to new cars.

www.kelkoo.co.uk attracts over 2 million hits a month from across Europe for comparisons of holidays, drinks, etc. See also www.lastminute.com for bargain fares and bookings

www.shopsmart.com provides product evaluations and price comparisons on electrical goods, books, etc.

The development of e-commerce might make intense competition the rule rather than the exception due to the greater transparency it creates in pricing. Ready availability of near perfect knowledge will make it difficult for any business to charge more than the going price for standardized products.

Competitors who supply close substitutes are in a strong position to win customers by offering better value for money. Such firms, and particularly new entrants, will strive to win your established customer base by making it attractive to switch allegiance. The marketer, in such circumstances, must first recognize the threat (i.e. monitor close competitors) and then respond by making switching more difficult for existing customers.

Possibilities include:

- Invest in relationship marketing to build long-term mutual benefits
- Build other barriers to protect the market
- Create the equivalent of a habitual or 'monopoly' good by niche marketing, product differentiation and/or effective branding
- Buyout the competitor
- Cut unnecessary costs in order to offer keener prices
- Innovate to continuously distance your product or service offering from rivals.

Exam hint

Key skills: improving own performance

Have you considered the advantages of 'differentiation' for your own examination script? An examiner is faced with marking scripts, literally in hundreds, all answering the same questions. How are you going to make yours stand out?

What you require is a premium product which catches the examiner's eye at the outset.

Product differentiation and branding are the marketer's natural response to competition. If price rivalry is forcing down profit levels, they respond by mobilizing the marketing mix to differentiate the product either by specification or in the minds of the consumer. Branding will be particularly critical in business to consumer selling on the Internet. There will be a premium on established reputations since the easiest purchases for new consumers navigating their way through electronic shopping will be the products they know and trust. The dimensions of possible differentiation are, of course, immense:

o *Product* – Permutations of the *core, tangible* (e.g. design, quality, packaging) and *augmented* product (e.g. brand name, delivery, after-sales service)
o *Price* – Credit and payment terms may vary, as can allowances and trade-in values
o *Promotion* – To support the differentiation (e.g. sales force, advertising)
o *Place* – Offers opportunities through location adopted, coverage and, most importantly, service provided.

Businesses will segment the market in the search for a profitable niche that they will service with a product combining the optimum blend of characteristics that are clearly differentiated from competing products. Those who satisfy customer needs and wants most effectively will earn *excess profits*. The seller, in effect, obtains a monopoly of the branded product and is able to charge a premium price and still retain customers who 'prefer' the product. But what will happen next?

Question 3.2

Can you think of local examples where small firms innovated product or service offerings which were quickly imitated by rivals or new entrants?

Returns associated with successful differentiation will attract imitation from both existing firms (or former employees), wishing to expand sales, and new entrants, seeking profitable opportunities. The customer benefits as the imitation enables rapid diffusion of superior product and service ideas. In addition, the new entrants provide extra choice although there is a tendency to excess capacity in such industries as available customer demand is spread across the increased number of suppliers. There comes a point where attempting to fully utilize available capacity through extra promotion or discounting adds more to cost than to revenue. Hairdressers' and restaurants are therefore seldom full. On the other hand, the publication of the fifth in the planned series of Harry Potter novels underpins a book, film and merchandise business worth £3 billion. Despite JK Rowling being the highest paid woman in Britain with record advance sales in the history of publishing, the book will make little for retailers. This is due to large supermarket groups halving cover prices in feverish competition to the cost of the smaller bookseller.

Concentrated industries

Here, the number of competing firms is generally small but their economic size is large. In economic terms this is known as high seller concentration and is typical in so-called 'oligopolies'.

Activity 3.1

Key skills for marketers (i.e. metrics – carrying out calculations)

Seller concentration is defined as the degree to which production or sales for a particular market is concentrated into the hands of a few large firms. With this definition in mind, calculate a *five-firm concentration ratio* for your own industry (i.e. add up the market shares of the five largest firms). Alternatively, look up a Mintel report on an industry of your choice.

Oligopoly means *competition among the few* and is the typical market structure in mature economies. It arises where the largest four or five firms account for perhaps 70 per cent or more of total sales to the market. Monitoring competitors is of critical importance in this situation because the marketing actions and decisions of any one oligopolist depend crucially on the reactions of its competitors. Their relative strengths and weaknesses must be evaluated and every facet of their marketing behaviour identified and assessed.

Question 3.3

Key skills: using information

Is the company you work for in an oligopoly market structure? Is the college you attend in an oligopoly? Is the bank you use an oligopoly? What about your supermarket or mobile phone operator?

Since each firm accounts for a large slice of the market any substantial change in the market share of one firm, whether achieved by lower prices, product innovation or successful advertising, will adversely affect the shares of competitors. The activities of 'popular' national newspapers often provide an interesting case study of such a market. Firms will watch each other very closely, producing a tension in the market between the *desire to compete* and gain in sales at the expense of competitors on the one hand, and the *desire to collude* in order to limit mutually damaging competitive activity on the other. Similar behaviour may be observed in oligopolies throughout the world, whether it be the four big international oil groups, the five big car groups or Ghana breweries, ABC lager competing head on with Kumasi Club beer.

The key features of this market may be summarized as:

o Economies of scale and entry barriers tend to be significant, for example, car manufacturers
o Customer needs are standardized and integrated through effective marketing and mass distribution systems
o Dominant market leaders may emerge, for example Microsoft, Intel or Nokia
o High concentration with the balance often held by a tail of small firms, for example, grocery retailing
o Demand is uncertain because it is dependent on how rivals react
o The market outcome is not predictable when oligopolists have multiple competitive options available to them.

For example, if one of the oligopolists cuts its prices, another may follow suit, or it may cut its prices more or less than the first firm. Alternatively, it may choose to do nothing, or respond with a large promotional campaign, or launch a new brand. Despite this a number of generalizations are possible:

1. Oligopolists tend to avoid the use of price as a competitive weapon. They are termed 'sticky' because the rivals often face a kinked demand curve. This suggests that the most likely rival reaction would be 'not to follow' a price increase (so gaining market share/sales revenue at your expense), but always 'to follow a price cut' (avoiding any loss of share/sales). Either way the firm will lose profits.
2. Non-price competition, promoting carefully differentiated branded products, is preferred. For example, Procter & Gamble and Unilever market over 50 competing detergents worldwide.
3. There is a tendency to occasional price war when a restructuring of market shares is in progress. For example, low-cost airlines have gained share.
4. Collusion is an attractive option but normally illegal. Argos and Littlewoods were fined £26.5 million in 2003 for fixing the price of toys.
5. Price leadership often occurs to reflect underlying cost changes (e.g. retail petrol, tobacco, car and beer prices). Watch the press for large firms announcing price changes, for example, supermarket petrol prices or bank interest rates, and then look for their competitors' reactions. Do they follow suit or not, and if so, how quickly?

New product development is preferred as the best strategy for achieving a sustainable competitive advantage. One worrying innovation currently being tested by British American Tobacco are flavoured cigarettes (e.g. vanilla or chocolate) which could make the product more attractive to children. The company claims it is not targeting young people and has long added 'undetectable' flavourings to reduce tobacco harshness.

Marketing environment in practice

'The future competitive shape of the UK grocery market'

Despite attempted counterbids by Sainsbury's, Asda and Tesco, Bradford-based Wm Morrison successfully completed its takeover of the much larger Safeway. The resulting four firm concentration ratio will be over 80 per cent. With top-line growth becoming difficult to achieve in the planning constrained and congested south, Safeway represents the last operator that could change hands. After 9 months of deliberation, the Competition Commission ruled out other bids in favour of Morrisons. Its market share should rise over 15 per cent, despite having to dispose of 53 stores, creating a fourth force in the market. The resulting takeover could trigger a supermarket price war as Morrisons have promised price cuts backed by expected cost savings of nearly £300 million from integrating operations.

Summary

We have seen that competitive activity involves more than the price variable. Choice between alternatives is the key as firms compete on service, innovation and non-price variables. Large firms predominate in concentrated industries due to the importance of barriers to entry in which economies of scale figure importantly. Smaller firms are the product of more fragmented structures, although profitable niches can be found in most markets.

Concentrated and fragmented industries also interact. For example, in Britain between 1993 and 2000, an estimated one-fifth of all corner shops, high-street banks and postoffices disappeared and the rate of decline if anything is accelerating.

The need to monitor competitors, while providing some predictions of competitive response, only takes account of rival firms within the market. More complete analysis requires consideration of certain other groups in the micro-environment.

Exam hint

Key skills: improve own performance

An examination question in this area will often state 'in the context of an industry example, explain'. Make sure you know an industry example inside out, preferably your own.

Five-force analysis of competitive structures

Any organization that seeks growth and profitability in its existing market or perhaps is considering diversification into an emerging industry must carefully weigh future prospects. A competitive strategy to shape evolving competitive forces must then be determined to provide achievement of its objectives within a defendable market position.

Businesses earn profit by being more successful than competitors in creating and delivering value to the customer over time. Real success demands that the business:

- o Creates value for money
- o Achieves a competitive edge in delivering that value
- o Operates efficiently.

The profit potential of an industry will be determined by the balance of supply and demand for the product in the short run, and industry structure in the long run. Long-run profitability will vary according to the strength of five basic competitive forces that govern the distribution of the added value created by the firm.

Michael Porter, in his books *Competitive Strategy* (1980) and *Competitive Advantage* (1985), provided the five-forces model of industry structure. This is summarized in Figure 3.1.

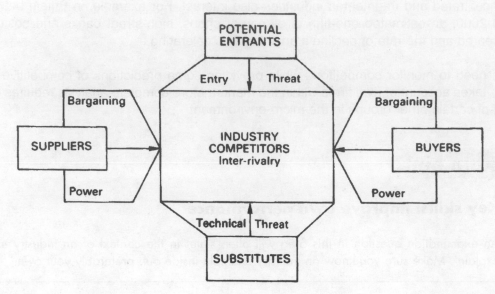

Figure 3.1 The five-forces model
Source: Adapted from M.E. Porter, *Competitive Strategy*, The Free Press, 1980: © The Free Press/Macmillan

Marketers must understand the nature of their competitive environment if they are to profitably exploit it. They must assess what is driving the competition and recognize that the collective strength of these five forces will set the present and future degree of market rivalry. This will determine the profit potential of the industry although each participating firm will seek to position itself so as to exploit maximum competitive advantage.

Question 3.4

Key skills: problem-solving

Use five-force analysis to match fragmented and concentrated industry structures to two of the following combinations:

1. Intense inter-rivalry, high threat of entry, high buyer and supplier bargaining power, strong threat from substitutes
2. Limited inter-rivalry, high threat of entry, low buyer and supplier bargaining power, weak threat of substitutes
3. No inter-rivalry, no threat from substitutes or entry, no buyer or supplier bargaining power
4. Intense inter-rivalry, weak threat from substitutes and entry, low buyer bargaining power, high supplier bargaining power.

Unlike market structure models, this approach provides marketers with a framework for analysing the complexity of their own industry situation. The approach is less rigorous but perhaps more useful in understanding the effect of structural and environmental change over time.

The intensity of inter-rivalry

Rivalry can range along a spectrum from non-existent (e.g. a powerful monopoly position protected by high entry barriers) to a cut-throat price war. In between are found gentlemanly understandings (collusive oligopoly) and normal marketing-based cut and thrust typically involving advertising and promotion, new product development and improvements to customer service.

Rivalry may either succeed in expanding the overall market and its profitability by drawing in new customers or increasing the volumes purchased, or undermine it by reducing margins or increasing marketing costs while serving only to redistribute static sales among the combatants.

Insight

Porter provides additional insight by identifying the variables that help determine the degree of rivalry now and in the future:

The rate of industry growth – Rapid growth reduces rivalry over market shares while in maturity firms battle over stagnant sales.

Other key variables include:

Use of expensive specialized equipment – pressure to fully utilize may lead to price war

Volatility of supply and demand – for example, if a new hotel opens in a locality rivalry will sharpen

The degree of product differentiation and brand loyalty

The significance of switching costs for buyers

The number of firms and their relative size – Divergent corporate cultures, for example, if one firm seeks dominance

What is at stake – if survival is threatened/big investment involved

Misinterpreting competitor's intentions – unintended price wars.

The cost of leaving the industry – may deter exit of weak rivals

The threat of substitutes

An industry is a group of firms producing goods or services that are close substitutes for each other. In practice, the nature of substitutability is complex and a galaxy of widely differing offerings compete for limited discretionary purchasing power which can only be spent once at any point in time. Package holidays compete with conservatories and new computer systems with upgrading the transport fleet.

The threat may materialize in many forms, for example, different materials, an alternative technology or a new distribution channel. Vinyl records, for example, have been partly replaced by cassettes, which in turn have been substituted by compact discs that are now threatened by digital mini discs and the Internet. Despite recent efforts by US record companies to bring law suits against 'pirates' illegally downloading and sharing copyrighted music from the Internet, e-business, for example, is opening up electronic links to a multitude of potential suppliers and intermediaries which may substitute existing relationships within the market. Factors affecting this threat are:

- o *Relative price/performance ratio of the substitute* (e.g. glass/ metal /plastic containers).
- o *Switching costs* for customers to the substitute (e.g. switching from branch to home banking).
- o *Buyer willingness to search out substitutes.*

The rule of thumb to apply here is the higher the price and profitability, the greater the incentive to search for and develop substitutes. One vulnerable sector may be postcards and greeting's cards. Last year, for example, saw 13 million Valentine's cards sent but 57 million text messages. Indeed it is estimated that 70 per cent of all texts pass between romantically connected people.

Question 3.5

Key skills: using information and metrics

You have been asked to make the travel arrangements to Paris for your marketing director, who has an important morning meeting to attend, and a small group of friends who want a weekend of sightseeing. In each case:

What substitutes would you consider?
How close is their current relative price/performance ratio?
Why might the ratios be changing?

The threat of new entry

Long-run profitability and market share will be damaged if significant entry occurs. Supply capacity will tend to increase sharply, putting downward pressure on margins, while extra competition for inputs will bid up costs. Any profitable industry is susceptible to this threat, particularly where a recent improvement in returns has occurred. The dynamics of the competitive process ensures that forces are set in motion to eventually return profitability to levels that no longer attract further entry.

However, as Porter recognized, there are factors that may delay or even prevent this outcome, known collectively as barriers to entry. Their strength will vary from industry to industry. Where barriers are substantial the threat of entry will be weak (e.g. nuclear reprocessing), whereas if they are virtually non-existent the threat will be ever present. The factors to be considered include:

○ *Economies of scale* – The minimum economic scale or break-even point for an entrant will be high either due to capital costs (e.g. a modern microprocessor plant costs $1 billion), research and development expenditure (e.g. drugs) or promotional spending (e.g. branding in detergents). Marketing economies include bulk discounts, spreading fixed costs (e.g. advertising) over large sales volumes and the employment of specialists.

Activity 3.2

Key skills: interpreting information

Examine the grid below and insert in each box an indication of the probable size and stability of returns to be earned, that is, you may designate one box *high and stable returns*, while another you decide on *low and risky returns*.

	Exit barriers	
	Low	*High*
Entry barriers Low	1.	2.
High	3.	4.

○ *Brand loyalty and product differentiation* – Promotional expenditure over time builds goodwill and customer loyalty for incumbent firms. Available product space may also be filled by a proliferation of products. Positioning of a new entrant's brand becomes difficult and heavy spending would be required to establish a new brand image.

○ *Capital requirements* – Risks may deter entrants despite superior prospective rewards.

○ *Switching costs for buyers* – For example, when considering an alternative computer operating system, the customer faces retraining costs, redundancy of equipment and knowledge, inconvenience, time lags as well as the risks inherent in adopting an untried product and supplier relationship. Prospective benefits must offset these costs.

○ *Distribution channel access* – Existing firms may dominate existing channels (e.g. long-term contracts).

○ *Absolute cost advantages* – Entrenched firms have experience and may control prime sites, patents or critical skills.

○ *Expected retaliation* – Potential entrants will weigh the possible responses of existing firms very carefully, for example, an extended price war could quickly remove the attractions of entry into the industry.

○ *Government policies and regulation* – They may provide protection or encourage fair competition.

Potential entrants must carefully weigh this high risk strategy, particularly where start-up losses are high and reactions uncertain. Existing firms may reinforce entry barriers and reduce intensity of rivalry by merging, for example, the £107 billion merger in pharmaceuticals between GlaxoWellcome and SmithKlineBeecham. New entry into concentrated markets is not as frequent as you might think due to the high barriers. The main threat comes from cross-entry by a well-financed business in an adjacent industry or one using similar processes and distribution channels. Takeover by a foreign company of an existing firm, to provide a base for future growth in market share, is another possibility. One entrepreneur has seized an opportunity presented by disaffection with American policies in the Muslim world. An alternative to Coke and Pepsi has been introduced into the French market appealing to its 3 million Muslims. Branded as Mecca cola it has sold over 12 million litres to add to the half a billion litres sold in Islamic countries. Confident of the demand for anti-American goods there are now plans to enter the Italian market and extend the range to 'Muslim up'.

Case history

Glass with attitude

The preciousness of the diamond is perhaps the world's most sophisticated illusion, a feat of marketing more dazzling than the gem itself. De Beers, the pivot of the world diamond cartel, manages to turn the raw, lawless frontier world of diamond digging and dealing into the most smoothly manipulated business in the world. It is not merely gems that De Beers is marketing, but enchanting symbols, myths and magic. The clever slogan that a *diamond is forever* sells two dreams: that diamonds bring eternal love and romance and that diamonds never lose their value.

De Beers' controls of over 75 per cent of the world's rough diamond output. It mines half itself in Africa and buys up the rest through its Central Selling Organization (CSO). Market control or 'stabilization' derives from the monopolist's rule-book: when times are bad support the price; when times are good make excess profits. Control over supply to support the mystique of the diamond is reinforced by clever manipulation of demand. It is easy to forget how much association with Hollywood glamour was the product of professionally designed marketing campaigns. Diamonds were translated into essential middle-class accessories, a statement of aspiration to luxury, yet always just within the reach of their income. Diamonds were associated with romantic rites of passage, such as engagements, weddings and anniversaries. It continues to *sell the dream* with advertising copy such as: 'Is 2 months' salary too much to spend for something that lasts forever?', or 'Show her you would marry her all over again'. The latter campaign led to a fourfold rise in the sale of eternity rings in the USA. The demise of the De Beers cartel continues to be predicted, particularly with accusations of cheating among members such as Russia and Angola. But with vanity, greed, envy, desire and even love, De Beers could scarcely appeal to more common human instincts. The diamond myth lives in a world slightly outside of logic and ordinary economics, and this allows us, the marketing sorcerers, to concoct glamour from carbon and fool us all.

(December 1999 examination case edited from 'The Diamond Business' – *The Economist*, December 1997.)

The bargaining power of suppliers

Where the relative power of suppliers is considerable and their behaviour aggressive, the rate of profit in an industry will be squeezed. However, an ability to establish some corresponding control over supplies will strengthen the hand of businesses in the industry. The main factors determining relative power are as follows:

- o The number and relative size of suppliers.
- o The ability to switch to rival suppliers and the cost involved.
- o The importance of being unimportant – the lower the cost of the supplies as a proportion of total cost, the higher the bargaining power.
- o The threat of forward integration by suppliers, for example, Q8 retail petrol brand of Kuwait.

Exam hint

Key skills: improve own performance

To really understand an examination question *underline the key words*, break it up into the relevant parts, identify the context and establish the precise format required.

The bargaining power of buyers

Buyer power will also tend to reduce profitability and depends on two main factors:

1. *Price responsiveness* – This price elasticity of demand is determined by such things as:

   (a) The importance of the product as a proportion of the total purchases of the buyer
   (b) The emphasis given by the buyer to product differentiation and branding
   (c) The profitability of the buyer, which may dull (or vice versa) their price sensitivity.

2. *Buyer leverage* – A number of factors also affect this:

   (a) Buyer concentration and size
   (b) Volume and the importance of purchases to the seller
   (c) Practicality and costs of switching to alternative suppliers for the buyer
   (d) Knowledge of the market and information available to buyers
   (e) Existence of substitutes and/or threat of backward vertical integration.

Strategic and marketing implications

Five-force analysis is useful to the marketer as:

1. A means of determining the attractiveness of an industry and its ultimate profit potential
2. A framework for examining relationships in their micro-environment
3. An evaluation of the probable degree of rivalry, now and in the future
4. A justification for continuous monitoring of the micro-environment
5. The basis for formulating strategy.

As Kotler suggests 'companies succeed as long as they have matched their products or services to today's marketing environment'.

Strategy is the match an organization makes between its own resources/competences and the risks and opportunities created by its external environment. Competitive strategy is a search for sustainable advantage through a favourable market positioning which achieves above average profitability over time.

Porter saw a choice of generic strategies between the following:

○ *Broad cost leadership* – But with parity or proximity in product features. Such a strategy would emphasize efficient scale of operations and tight control of costs and margins, for example, Ryanair, the largest of Europe's 50+ budget airlines.
○ *Broad differentiation* – With proximity in cost terms. This creates a product or service perceived as unique and desirable by customers in terms of design (e.g. Gucci), brand

image (e.g. Coca-Cola) and/or customer service (e.g. Virgin Airlines). High marketing costs are offset by insulation from rivalry and mitigation of buyer power, while high margins cushion supplier power.

o *Cost or differentiation focus* – On a narrow segment which is least vulnerable to competition. This strategy is vulnerable to imitation or structural decline in demand. Broader-based competitors may overwhelm the segment, for example, in-store specialists within multiple grocers and their pressure on W H Smith/Boots.

Question 3.6

Key skills: presenting and interpreting information

Study the grid in Figure 3.2 and suggest companies that would fit into the strategy boxes for the following industries:

o Multiple groceries
o Travel agents
o Cars.

Competitive advantage

	Lower cost	Differentiation
Broad	Cost leadership e.g. e.g. e.g.	Differentiation e.g. e.g. e.g.
Narrow	Cost focus e.g. e.g. e.g.	Differentiation focus e.g. e.g. e.g.

Competitive scope

Figure 3.2 Strategic grid

One weakness in the above strategies is that they all imply hostile options. In reality there are massive changes taking place in industry as businesses collaborate in partnerships, alliances (e.g. Delta Airlines, Air France, Alitalia and CSA Czech Airlines) and joint ventures (e.g. mobile phones). Another aspect of horizontal collaboration, which we will consider in the next section, is forming cartels. This is an attractive form of collaboration since if successful it would become the sole supplier to the market. Output could be restricted and market price and overall profitability would rise. The existence of restrictive practices legislation (see later) has ruled most forms of collective agreement illegal but cartels still appear to operate clandestinely in some industries (e.g. sugar/concrete/PVC) and internationally (e.g. OPEC (oil), IATA (airlines) and De Beers (diamonds)).

All cartels, however, are subject to instability in the longer term:

o Internal dissension over the allocation of quotas necessary to restrict supply and justify the higher cartel prices
o Incentive for any cartel member to exceed quota for higher profits. This raises supply, making it harder to sustain the price

- ○ Internal policing is essential plus control over market entry
- ○ New producers operate outside the cartel at slightly lower prices, forcing increasing excess capacity on cartel members.

Activity 3.3

Key skills: interpreting information

Consider the gondoliers of Venice. What enables them to charge such high prices, earning around £7000 a month tax-free, for a glorified boat-ride? How do you think they manage to maintain these prices over time? Is clever marketing the explanation?

Insight

e-Commerce impacts on the five forces in grocery retailing

Massive investment in ICT suggests that the driving force of future competitive advantage will be the exploitation of e-knowledge. Home shopping (up 44 per cent in 2003) is more than an alternative channel to access customers, it is the substitute that will cannibalize sales from high-street stores. The bargaining power of the buyers will also increase since the Internet puts the consumer in control. They will be harder to reach, able to compare prices and can, in theory, buy from anywhere in the world. e-Commerce should also provide manufacturers with a unique opportunity to transform their eroded bargaining power with retailers (own brands, massive buying power and powerful EPOS systems that conferred in-depth knowledge of buyer habits) by dealing directly with end users. New entry into grocery retailing would be much easier since only a virtual organization would be required. Credibility and logistical cost would be the key success factors and just as multiple retailers have moved into complementary product groupings, so will any virtual organization with retail competencies offering substitute services, for example, mail order organizations. Strategy demands heavy investment in e-shopping capability and its deployment to service potential customers in areas where its stores are thinly represented. Building and promoting a retailing brand image for quality, choice, value and trust in order to beat off potential entrants is vital as are renegotiated partnerships with key manufacturers to keep them on-board and divert any risk of disintermediation.

The nature of competition policies

Governments formulate competition policies for a number of reasons:

- ○ They fear that market forces may be insufficient to prevent anti-competitive behaviour
- ○ They see a level playing field as fair and just
- ○ They desire efficient and effective use of scarce resources
- ○ Monopoly is seen as the natural outcome of the competitive process and must be controlled
- ○ They do not wish to see economic power abused at the expense of the consumer/ taxpayer.

Making markets more competitive means creating the conditions associated with it. Policies have, therefore, attempted to achieve the following:

o Resist mergers and acquisitions which threaten to reduce the number of sellers to the point where consumer choice is restricted
o Keep entry barriers into markets as low as possible so that supply, through new entrants, can respond
o Deregulation of markets (e.g. domestic energy market and telecommunications)
o Encouragement of small and medium enterprises
o Appointment of regulators in natural monopoly and legislative action against anti-competitive behaviour
o Improve the knowledge of the consumer through prevention of misleading advertising/promotion.

Legislation and competition

Understanding the industry environment in terms of competition and collaboration alone ignores the role of government and the law. Firms facing intense competition may seek to form cartels and associations as a means of restricting output to raise prices and profitability. Equally, firms in concentrated industries may find collaboration and collusion more rewarding than rivalry. Large firms, including those that have monopolized their industry, might also abuse their power and position to discourage potential entrants.

While all these actions would be to the disadvantage of the customer, legislation governing such restraint of trade has been introduced in most countries more with a view to promoting more effective use of resources and to support a belief in the virtues of workable competition.

1. *Restraint of trade* – Most agreements must not involve terms that restrict, or prevent a person from doing business.

Case history

Example

Microsoft, the world's largest software firm, has been the subject of a long running court case arising from its alleged abuse of its market power. The distractions of the legal proceedings and appeal prompted a worrying brain drain from the company while rival start-ups seeking to compete in Microsoft's markets are finding it easier to obtain business partners and raise finance. Microsoft was also frozen out of entire new industries such as smart phones and set-top boxes. The conclusion must be that anti-trust case law was justified because market forces could not have dealt with Microsoft on their own. By shining a spotlight on the company's practices, the case forced it to restrain its behaviour towards customers and competitors on the one hand and emboldened business rivals on the other.

2. *Restrictive practices* – Legislation covers any form of agreement between the majority of firms in the industry that affects their freedom of action in disposing of their output. This is well known as anti-trust legislation in the USA but most countries have similar provision. It strikes a particular chord in Britain where many durable consumer products, such as cars cost significantly more than in America or the EU. Indeed an increasing number of private motorists are personally importing vehicles after scanning the wider market through the Internet, for example, the virtual showroom of Virgin cars

at www.virgin.com/cars or equivalent sites can bypass traditional showrooms at the click of a mouse. However, this particular issue was resolved by the European Commission's decision not to renew exclusive dealerships block exemption after 2002. A summary of the main points arising from UK legislation is outlined below (non-UK readers should consult an intermediate economics text for a summary of your national framework for both restrictive practices and monopolies).

Question 3.7

Key skills: problem-solving

The spectrum of restrictive linkages between firms

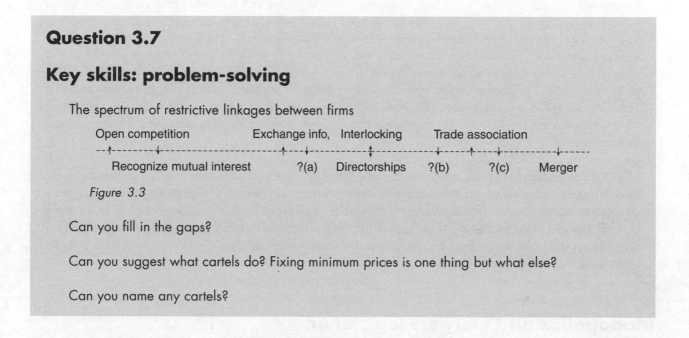

Figure 3.3

Can you fill in the gaps?

Can you suggest what cartels do? Fixing minimum prices is one thing but what else?

Can you name any cartels?

Fair Trading Act 1973

- o A Director General of Fair Trading (DGFT) is in overall control while the Competition Commission (CC) takes operational responsibility.
- o Cover agreements on prices, recommended prices, terms, areas/businesses supplied and so on. The Commission may outlaw the practice of 'recommended retail prices' following investigation of the retail consumer electronics market. This found that the prices of products such as TVs and video recorders varied little between competing stores.
- o Agreements must be registered.
- o Agreements are presumed to be against the public interest unless the parties can justify it to the Restrictive Practices Court.
- o Eight gateways can be used including protection of or benefits to the public, protecting jobs or export earnings or to countervail competition or monopoly.
- o Must not 'on balance' be detrimental to the public.
- o Enforcement of minimum retail prices on distributors and withholding supplies with a view to coerce is also prohibited.

Case history

Example

British supermarkets have lost their long battle to sell cut-price designer goods bought cheaply outside the EU. The European Court ruled that it was illegal for Tesco to sell Levi jeans sourced from the US and East Europe without the supplier's consent. Levi convinced the Court that it needed to ensure that its jeans were sold by trained staff and so justify prices nearly double those being charged by the supermarket. Withholding supplies of perfumes to cut-price multiples was allowed by the British authorities on similar grounds. However, perfumiers in France are now having to close ranks under proposed EU laws that require lists of ingredients to be displayed on product labels. The information is thought necessary to protect consumers against allergies to traditional ingredients. Such information would be commercially sensitive and difficult to implement given the 100 plus ingredients in a perfume. The industry centred on the town of Grasse smell a plot, masterminded by their north European competitors who rely on synthetic ingredients.

The DGFT is empowered to investigate anti-competitive practices by firms with over £5 million turnover. This is defined as a course of conduct that restricts, distorts or prevents competition in the production, acquisition or supply of goods and services. It includes discriminatory and predatory pricing (to force out a rival), vertical price squeezing (e.g. raising prices of controlled inputs to competitors), tie-in sales/full line forcing (buy one item – must buy range) and discriminatory supply.

Monopolies and mergers legislation

The methods adopted in Britain involve:

- A case by case judgemental approach
- A cost–benefit framework to compare good and bad effects
- A loose presumption that monopolies are against the public interest
- A recognition that market dominance might reflect superior efficiency
- Removing barriers to entry – seen as more appropriate than preventing firms getting larger
- Investigating horizontal mergers – more likely to be motivated by the monopoly.

Both the Secretary of State and the DGFT (but not for mergers) have powers to refer a case (for summaries of reports see: www.mmc.gov.uk/report1.htm) to the Competition Commission (CC). The legal definition of a referable monopoly is a 25 per cent market share while proposed mergers involving assets in excess of £30 million, or where they would create a legal monopoly or add to it, may also be referred.

With Vodafone buying America's Airtouch Communications for $62 billion and Exxon's $76 billion takeover of Mobile to create the world's biggest company in revenue terms ($250 billion), these qualifying sums are easily achieved. Despite the apparent scope for cost savings and extra market power, recent research by J.P. Morgan suggests that only 56 per cent of large European merger deals, since 1985, have created value for the acquiring company. A KPMG survey of the largest 700 cross-border mergers suggested only 17 per cent added shareholder value and 53 per cent even destroyed it. Who benefits if employees lose jobs and customers lose choice? Many mergers that appear to offer a $2 + 2 = 5$ synergy opportunity end up as $2 + 2 = 3$! Horizontal mergers of companies in the same line of business, however, tend to achieve better returns, but this may well be at the expense of reduced competition, and the consumer.

In practice, only a very small proportion of qualifying monopolies or mergers are referred and then the CC may just report or will make recommendations. The final decision rests with the Secretary of State, who has been known to overrule CC recommendations. This is particularly likely when the benefits of greater size are thought to offer increased international competitiveness.

The government appears to be adopting a more aggressive approach to competition policy with reviews into high-profile sectors like airports, cross-channel transport and water. These might turn into CC references in due course.

If the Secretary of State decides to act, he or she may ask the DGFT to obtain appropriate undertakings or lay an order before Parliament prohibiting continuation of the practice. Orders are enforced through trading standards officers and offences are punished under criminal law.

Other powers range from regulation of maximum prices to forced sale of controlling interests. The 1998 Competition Act provides no excuse for the authorities not to act and sees much stiffer penalties, with fines of up to 10 per cent of turnover and permission for civil actions to be brought. The Office of Fair Trading (OFT) has been given extra resources and an enhanced role to root out cartels, with attempts at obstruction made a criminal offence. For example, a new regulation has forced mobile phone operators to cut the fees they charge other telecom operators to connect their calls by 15 per cent. The CC estimates this will save consumers up to £700 million. Similarly, BT preferred to pre-empt an Office of Communications Act (Ofcom) inquiry and cut its broadband rental charges to less than a third of the former level. Rather than stifle competition, it calculated that more rapid growth would offset the negative impacts on revenue in the longer term.

Question 3.8

State five ways in which the DGFT is active in the protection of consumers.

1. Receives information on potentially harmful business activities from various sources and can refer them for investigation by the CC or the Consumer Protection Advisory Committee (CPAC) as appropriate.
2. Publicizes consumer rights.
3. Actively encourages industry associations to introduce and progressively improve codes of practice.
4. Obtain assurances from or injunctions against persistent offenders or publishers of misleading advertisements.
5. Propose new laws to the independent CPAC who then reports to the Secretary of State.

The promotion of free competition between member states of the European Union is fundamental to the success of the Single Market. Its legislation therefore overrides the national legislation of member states. Relevant sections include:

○ *Article 85* – prohibits all restrictive agreements affecting trade between member states which prevents or distorts competition
○ *Article 86* – relates to abuse of a dominant market position
○ *Articles 92–94* – forbid government subsidies to firms or industries which distort or threaten to distort competition
○ *Cooperative agreements* – that share facilities, market research and consultancy are acceptable.

Directives have also been introduced governing such matters as ingredients in food and the introduction of sell-by dates. UK law is only now coming into line with EU law and its tough fines of up to 10 per cent of domestic turnover for illegal anti-competitive agreements. Recent examples of EU fines include £95 million against Nintendo and £12 million against Sotherby's for their collusion and price fixing with fellow auctioneers Christies. Their former chief executive was also fined $350 000 in the US and narrowly avoided a prison sentence.

Other areas of legislation and the marketer

1. *Patents* – This is a right given to the inventor to reap all the rewards accruing over a specified period, normally 20 years. To qualify, the invention must be novel and go beyond the current state of the art. A European Patent Office has been established as a cost-effective means of achieving coverage across member states.
2. *Trade marks* – Of considerable importance to the marketer who has invested heavily in a particular brand name, the Trade Marks Act in Britain provides exclusive rights to registered marks (words or symbols). Infringement may lead to an injunction and damages. Winnie the Pooh related sales, for example, account around one-fifth of Disney's $25 billion revenues.

Monitoring the micro-environment

This section concerns sources of information on the micro-environment and should be read in conjunction with the main sources of macro-environmental data in the next unit. Both form the context for consideration of environmental information systems in the final unit. Collecting information is a key statement of marketing practice as is the subsequent 'interpretation and presentation'. It is also one of the key marketing skills that you require to develop. Different types of information are required depending on the decisions to be taken:

○ *Competitors*

   – Prices, discounts, credit terms, and so on
   – Sales volumes by segment, product, region, distribution channel
   – Market shares and key objectives
   – Promotional activities, catalogues, distributor incentives
   – New product development, expansion plans, changes in personnel
   – Financial strength and relationships with key stakeholders.

Similar information is required on suppliers, distributors and potential entrants into the market.

○ *Industry*

   – Sales volumes by product, segment, region and country
   – Sales growth and seasonal/cyclical patterns
   – Production capacities, levels, plans and stock positions
   – Technical change and investment plans.

Information gathered through marketing intelligence and market research needs to be combined with that gathered internally before being classified, processed and analysed. Information databases are central to modern marketing. Collecting information on customers is one thing, but processing and utilizing the massive amounts of data captured by computers is another. This can provide a critical element in the process of:

- Forming or deepening customer relationships and loyalty, for example, one cruise line sends a 'best table' photograph award in a New Year's card to remind recipients of happy times spent on a recent cruise.
- Spotting emerging patterns and trends to provide focus for marketing campaigns.
- Segmenting customers for receipt of tailored offers.

Main sources of information

To complete this unit it would be useful to briefly examine the nature and requirements of an information system for effective competitor analysis. Attempt the following activity before reading on.

Activity 3.4

Key skills: collecting and interpreting information

List at least four sources relevant to a competitor analysis under each of the following headings:

Internal sources (e.g. sales force records); *Company sources* (e.g. company reports)

Industry/market sources (e.g. trade associations); *Government sources* (e.g. censuses)

Commercial sources (e.g. A.C. Nielsen); *Academic sources* (e.g. *Journal of Marketing*)

General sources (e.g. quality press reports); *Internet sources* (e.g. www.strategy-business.com)

Select one source under each heading and explain how it would contribute to the analysis.

Competitor analysis involves the gathering and interpretation of intelligence from a range of sources, regarding key rivals, with the intention of achieving a competitive edge over them by:

- Identifying and exploiting competitor weaknesses
- Avoiding actions that provoke aggressive and possibly damaging responses
- Discovering moves that competitors are unable/unwilling to respond to
- Avoiding any surprises that may give rivals the advantage.

Actual and potential threats must be accounted, for example, firms that could overcome entry barriers; customers or suppliers that could integrate backwards or forwards; possible takeovers of existing rivals or foreign firms benefiting from tariff or regulatory changes.

There are literally hundreds of potential intelligence sources but these are useless unless meaningful information can be extracted. Data mining has been developed as a process of analysing and manipulating data so as to provide new and powerful insights into consumer and competitor behaviour patterns. To understand potential rivals, however, you must understand their goals, capabilities, strategies and view of the future. This drives the spectrum of information needs which includes the following:

o *Financial information* – Successive company annual accounts reveal information on performance and direction of growth. Future borrowing capability can also be ascertained. These may be accessed through websites or the Companies Registration Office. Business reference services and commercial databases provide detailed reports and comparative analyses on hundreds of companies in the form of graphs and ratios. Examples include:

  – Datastream holds 10+ years accounts on all UK quoted companies
  – www.ft.com covers 50 000 listed companies in over 50 countries
  – www.carol.co.uk links to the annual reports of companies in the UK, Europe, Asia and the USA.

These allow you to build a financial health profile of each competitor embracing indices such as turnover, debt, assets, growth and credit rating. Credit reference agencies and your own company's treasury department may provide insight on bill payment habits and credit worthiness.

o *Organizational information* – The trade and quality press are up-to-date sources of such information. A variety of business periodicals often provide in-depth coverage of specific companies. Access is often eased through databases. (For example: see www.europages.com or www.companiesonline.com or asiansources.com or Business Africa online at www.banks-r.demon.co.uk) Monitoring the comments of the chairman and chief executive in consecutive annual reports and responses to questions at AGMs provide strategic background on goals, activities and corporate values. More detailed knowledge may be provided through the salesforce of suppliers or purchasing staff of mutual intermediaries. Stakeholder information networks are of general importance as are local papers and planning application records. To form an organizational profile for a competitor the following might be tracked: key decision makers, new appointments, take-overs, subsidiaries, closures, investments, new ventures and current problems.

o *Production and product information* – Patent application records provide clues to future plans, a rival's research capability as well as technical information. Research networks and the scanning of technical papers give warning of breakthroughs. The Consumers Association provides independent product comparisons and reverse engineering can provide information on attributes and costs. Local chambers of commerce will be a useful source on facilities and employment. Intermediaries are in a good position to contribute product knowledge. Competitors should therefore be monitored in terms of locations/size of facilities; breadth and depth of product line; costs, qualities and performance as well as new product developments.

Question 3.9

Key skills: interpreting information

The darker side of competitor analysis

How would you like to know everything there is to know about your competitors? Wouldn't it make your life as a marketer a lot easier? No, you don't necessarily have to break any laws to get it! There are many ways to find out useful information on troublesome rivals:

o *Milk job applicants* for inside information – they will be keen to impress and probably won't have been warned about divulging secrets
o *Go on plant tours/monitor aerial maps/monitor staff and transport movements*
o *Recruit staff from competitors*
o *Quiz staff at trade shows/conferences/exhibitions* – informal atmosphere and easy conversation
o *Commission 'academic' research among relevant suppliers and intermediaries*
o *Undertake reverse engineering* on competitor products to determine performance/costs
o What about: *examine rubbish, apply pressure, act under false pretences, offer bribes* or *outright espionage?*

Note: Samsung, the world's 3rd largest maker of mobile phones has banned the use of 3G camera phones in its factories, fearing industrial espionage.

Is the marketer failing in their duty, if they don't fully exploit publicly available information?

Some of these practices seem acceptable, some unsavoury – where would (a) you, (b) your organization draw the line that defines ethical behaviour?

Does the line move if corporate survival is threatened?

o *Marketing information* – The field salesforce is a key source of marketing intelligence. Properly trained and with an effective recording and retrieval system they can generate vast amounts of information on new products, comparative prices and discounts, market shares, promotions and packaging. They are at the daily interface with customers who are in the business of comparing product and seller capabilities. Other sources include the Marketing Surveys Index and product research organizations such as Mintel (see world market research abstracts at www.mra.warc.com or www.keynote.co.uk or summary reports).
o With markets often changing so quickly and dramatically, a formalized information system is required. It must incorporate procedures for the coordination and communication of intelligence to relevant decision makers without delay. The existence of a system should encourage participation in the information gathering process by all organization members. This important need for environmental intelligence will be developed further in Units 4 and 8.

Summary

In this unit we have dealt with the following important aspects:

o The nature and implications of competition in fragmented and concentrated industries.
o The importance of monitoring the actions and reactions of competitors.
o An appreciation of the five forces required to undertake a structural analysis of industry profitability.
o A practical framework for assessing the intensity of competition within a market and changes over time.
o Adaption of the five-force framework to allow consideration of collaboration.
o The regulatory framework relating to competition.
o Recognition of the need for an information system and the important sources of information required for a competitor analysis.

Further study and examination preparation

The competitive environment confronts virtually all organizations in some way or another and is the bread-and-butter concern of the marketer. The examiner has a variety of question options available. These range from Porter's analysis, to the competitive/cooperative relationships between a business and its suppliers or distributors, to assessment of the impact of policies relating to competition.

You must demonstrate not just an understanding of theories and analysis discussed in the unit but also an ability to relate to your own or a representative industry. You must be very clear as to the contribution of the marketer to shaping marketing forces and sustaining better than normal profitability over time.

This unit often provides part questions, although a very recent example of a full question is given in Exam question 3.1. Don't bank on a five-force question coming up too frequently. Neither of the specimen papers provided contain one.

Extending knowledge

Palmer and Hartley, *The Business and Marketing Environment*, McGraw-Hill – Chapter 6 on the Competitive Environment.

Palmer, A. *The Business Environment*, McGraw-Hill – Chapter 6 on the Competitive Environment.

Relevant websites would include:

www.ft.com

www.economist.com

www.dtigov.uk/cp/ukpolicy.htm for key aspects of legislation and the 1998 Act

http://europa.eu.int/pol/enter/index_en.htm for EU competition policy

www.strategy-business.com

www.asia-pacific.com/ for news and data from this region. See also www.feer.com/ the Far Eastern Review

www.europages.com

www.companiesonline.com

www.asiansources.com

www.banks-r.demon.co.uk

Exam question 3.1

1. Use examples to compare the competitive environment of a fragmented industry with that of a concentrated industry. (8 marks)
2. As a marketing assistant in a concentrated industry:

   (a) how would you monitor competitors? (6 marks)
   (b) why is it important that you do so? (6 marks)   (December 2004 paper)

Exam question 3.2

Please see Question 3b/c, December 2003. Go to www.cim.co.uk for specimen answers.

Exam question 3.3

Please see Question 3(i), June 2004. Go to www.cim.co.uk for specimen answers.

Exam question 3.4

Explain what is meant by the following concept and theory, outlining how each might contribute to the marketer's understanding of the environment. Use an industry with which you are familiar to illustrate your answer

(a) Open systems   (10 marks)
(b) Porter's five-force analysis.   (10 marks)

unit 4
the macro-environment

Learning objectives

This unit introduces the macro-environment while subsequent units consider the specific economic, legislative, social, technical and informational environments in more depth. By the end of this unit you will be able to:

○ Appreciate the breadth and significance of the external environment (3.1).

○ Undertake an identification and assessment of environmental threats and opportunities facing an organization of your choice (3.1).

○ Appreciate the implications of the natural environment for marketers (3.6).

○ Access and assess relevant data on the environment of business in a time- and cost-effective manner (3.2).

○ Recognize the potential significance of emerging environmental challenges to effective marketing in the present and the future (3.8).

Study Guide

This unit provides the framework for a section of the syllabus accounting for 50 per cent of the total. It is primarily concerned with the importance of monitoring and understanding changes in the wider environment. The main elements of the macro-environment were briefly defined in the first part of Unit 2 and you should refresh your memory of this before reading on.

This introductory unit is also a fertile source of possible examination questions. These may test your general understanding of the macro-environment and its importance in the development of marketing strategy. Another area is that of information sources that underpin the marketer's ability to monitor a changing environment. The natural environment is also of special significance as we saw in the section on environmentalism in Unit 2.

It is vital that you seek to relate your studies to up-to-date and relevant examples and applications. By now you should have acquired the habit of scanning the quality press for these, since the examiner will expect and give credit for your knowledge of current developments.

Understanding the macro-environment

Marketing is actively concerned with anticipating and then responding positively to changes occurring in the external environment. These generally uncontrollable forces in the macro-environment create a succession of potential threats and opportunities.

In Unit 1 we considered the business as an open system interacting with its external environment. Figure 4.1 provides an appreciation of the linkages involved. The business, as an open system, competes for inputs that are privately owned by households. These inputs are converted into outputs of goods and services that are desired and purchased by households using incomes received from selling factor services to the firm. These transactions are not only conducted in the micro-environment of any given business, but also within the wider political, social and economic systems.

The political system, as we will see in Unit 7, provides for the election of a government on the basis of a declared manifesto. Broad policy objectives are set and legislation is enacted to implement it. One important political objective is to secure re-election and this has enhanced the attractiveness of economic growth as the main driving force in the economic system. Households in relative poverty want improved living standards while the rich seem inclined to get richer. If forced to choose they will opt for the political party that offers sustainable growth. Firms also operate within a social and cultural system. The number and structure of households are changing as populations alter. The attitudes and values of those households also change over time and the influence of education and the media. Patterns of consumption reflect evolving lifestyles and societal expectations impact on what is deemed to be acceptable behaviour within businesses.

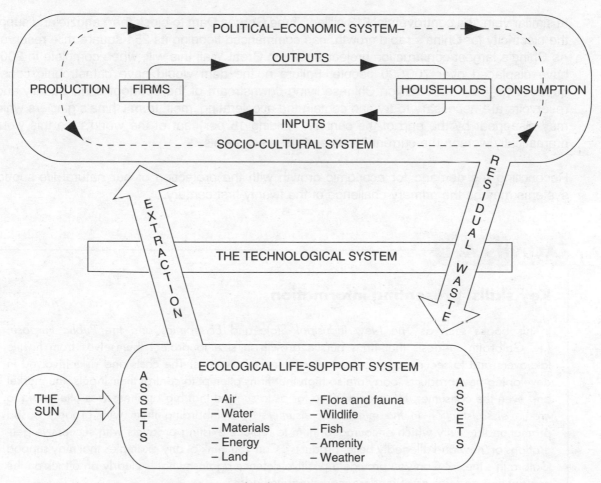

Figure 4.1 Business as open systems within the macro-environment

The natural environment

Figure 4.1 also shows the SLEPT factors as part of a much larger system upon which they depend. This is the natural environment that forms the backdrop to our social and economic lives. A growing economy must draw part of its necessary inputs from this life-supporting system. Some inputs are renewable, as in the case of softwoods or fish stocks, while others, like oil and minerals, are effectively non-renewable assets accumulated through natural processes over very long time periods. Resources do renew, but due to an input of energy from another system, the sun. Similarly, the environment receives discharges from the economic system in the form of residual waste. Waste in excess of the natural assimilative powers of the environment is pollution, which impacts on air, water and land quality as well as the weather. One interesting feedback effect arising from global warming was the near collapse of France's extensive nuclear network due to overheating of the water coolants. Other disruptive power blackouts due to natural causes occurred in North East America and the whole of Italy in late 2003.

The technological system can be double-edged. It can open up the natural world to the ravages of uncontrolled tourism or exploitative cultivation of the rainforests and also facilitate recycling and substitution. For example, scientists have warned that rapidly expanding soya production and a $40 billion development project proposed by the Brazilian government will cause the rainforest to all but disappear by 2020 causing environmental damage that would far outweigh any economic benefits. The Advance Brazil scheme involves the building of new roads, railways and dams. Satellite imaging and computer modelling techniques suggest that eventually only 5 per cent would be left intact. Accounting for 40 per cent of the world's tropical rainforest, 30 per cent of all plant and animal species and generating 20 per cent of the world's oxygen, such an outcome would dramatically affect biodiversity, the carbon cycle, global climate and the greenhouse effect.

In similar vein, the controversial £13 billion Three Gorges Dam to block the Yangzte and supply the electricity for China's rapid growth, has commenced flooding its 254 square mile reservoir. As China's largest construction project since the Great Wall this will, when complete in 2009, have displaced over 700 000 people. Failure of the dam would have catastrophic consequences for the 2–300 million Chinese living downstream of the 600-foot dam. Equally such reservoirs are necessary to try and contain the accelerating 'melt' from China's glaciers which may disappear by the end of the century. Holding 15 per cent of the world's ice this would dramatically worsen the current floods and raise sea levels.

Reconciling the demand for economic growth with the protection of our natural life-support systems may be the primary challenge of the twenty-first century.

Activity 4.1

Key skills: presenting information

In his books such as *The New Industrial State* and *Economics and the Public Purpose*, J.K. Galbraith suggests that firms pursue growth in size to protect themselves from hostile takeovers and to secure some control over their environments. The costs and risks involved in developing new products today are so high that firms attempt to control their inputs, the market and even the consumer. He even went so far as to suggest that big business was attempting to *create dissatisfaction in the minds of consumers* by bombarding them with broadly based promotional activity which encouraged them to replace existing products with successive generations of 'new and allegedly better products'. Can you think of any examples that may support Galbraith's thesis? Can you provide a positive defence against what is clearly an attack on the contribution and values of modern marketing methods?

Decline of the natural environment: the impact of technology

Background

Economic growth has progressively inflicted a significant cost on the natural environment. This has arisen, in part, because of externalities that have been borne by third parties other than the producer or consumer involved. Declining environmental quality has been the unavoidable result, unless the state has intervened to legislate or make the polluter pay.

In this section we will consider the impact of technology and business activity on the environment in future terms. Three fundamental constraints limit the pace and nature of technological change and the continuity of economic growth:

- ○ *Social and institutional* – Reflected in customs and legislation intended to curb the appliance of science in ways felt to be undesirable to society (e.g. a moratorium on nuclear programmes after Chernobyl, bans on animal testing, controls over GM foods, bans on human genetics).

Insight

Cloning the first human embryo

The first small step towards the most fundamental challenge to the natural environment – the world's first cloned human embryo – was announced by the US company Advanced Cell Technology in 2001. They replaced the DNA from a donated female egg with the DNA from the centre of a single adult male cell. The egg cell then divided as in normal development and could have potentially become a human being if implanted in a woman's womb. The Human Fertilisation and Embryology Authority in Britain has now given a limited go-ahead for doctors to create 'designer babies', genetically selected to act as donors for their sick siblings. This is a prime example of the general tension between technology as a force for good or a force for evil in its impacts on the natural environment. Certainly the potential of therapeutic cloning represents amazing promise but there is also the fear that nature is being violated and that a Pandora's box of irrevocable consequences is being opened. It may be well to remember that the so-called 'Black Death' that ravaged over half of Europe's population in the fourteenth century was more likely due to an unknown *E. coli* type virus than the lowly black rat and its fleas.

- ○ *Depletion of non-renewable resources* – This includes fuels, minerals, fertile lands (through overgrazing), tropical rainforests and biological diversity in terms of animal and plant species extinction.
- ○ *Pollution of the ecosystem* – Ecology is the study of plants and animals and their interaction with each other and the environment as a whole. Ecosystems include bio-degradation processes that decompose wastes to provide nutrients for renewed growth.

Problems arise only when their absorptive capabilities are overloaded due to the volume and/or nature of the wastes concerned:

Industrial

Effluents, emissions, solid wastes – for example, sixteen of the world's most polluted cities are in China, while the Scottish salmon industry is threatened by rising levels of carcinogenic residues in the farmed fish. Despite assertions by the Food Standards Agency that levels are within safe levels, the researchers warned that more than three portions a year could increase the cancer risk.

Toxic and chemically complicated wastes – for example, Russia's decaying armaments pose such a threat that Western governments have contributed $20 billion to fund their safe disposal. An estimated 30 000 tons of enriched uranium and 780 tons of arms grade plutonium are stored around the country in often low-security military camps. This does not include abandoned nuclear reactors and submarines.

Plastics and non-degradable materials – for example, *Prestige* sinks with 70 000 tons of oil, Cape Finisterre 2002/3; highly toxic 'ghost ships' cross the Atlantic for dismantling 2003/4.

Consumer

Vehicle emissions – for example, the Airbus380 super-jumbo carrying 800 passengers from 2006.

Urban noise – three times noisier than 30 years ago with mobile phones, traffic and ghetto blasters, the most cited factors.

Disposable packaging – Britons throw away 8 billion plastic bags and 500 million plastic bottles each year although a tax introduced in Eire reduced usage by 90 per cent within 9 months. The government hopes to double the recycling ratio of household rubbish to 25 per cent between 2003 and 2005.

Human wastes – for example, after Christmas, British households throw away an estimated 6 million fir trees, 85 000 miles of wrapping paper and 2.5 billion cards – enough to go around the globe nine times.

Congestion – a survey revealed that the average speed of vehicles in London had fallen to 2.9 mph (slower than walking) although this has improved with the introduction of the congestion charge on vehicles entering central London. Britons spend on average 90 minutes commuting each day and with air and road transport growing out of control ministers concede that gridlock will continue for the next 10 years.

Activity 4.2

Key skills: interpreting information

Match the terms with their correct definitions:

- ○ Effluent
- ○ Emissions
- ○ Acid rain
- ○ Ozone-layer depletion
- ○ Greenhouse effect.

- Carbon dioxide absorbs and radiates back heat which would otherwise escape into space, causing temperature rises.
- Liquid wastes discharged into seas or watercourses.
- Discharges of sulphur dioxide from power stations or vehicle exhaust gases combine with water vapour in the atmosphere.
- Release of gases into the atmosphere.
- Caused by the discharge of CFCs in aerosols, solvents, foam plastics and fridges allowing through dangerous ultraviolet rays.

The source of the decline

The natural environment has found no difficulty in coping with the wastes created by our economic development, at least until recently. Natural disasters have also been relatively easily accommodated (at a cost), be they Californian forest- or Australian bush-fires, Bangladesh floods or Caribbean/Pacific hurricanes, because their impacts have been both localized and reversible. However, the cumulative effects of the nineteenth century's industrial development has involved a different order of 'impact magnitude and irreversibility' in many of the effects created. Figure 4.2 shows the main factors responsible.

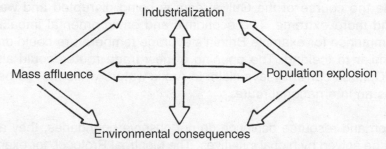

Figure 4.2 Key factors in environmental degradation

While any one of the three elements will cause environmental problems, their combined and interdependent effects are much more serious. Three-quarters of the world's population still live in less-developed countries and should they wish to emulate the high resource-consuming lifestyles of already industrialized countries, the environmental consequences are likely to be unsustainable. If every Chinese or Indian household merely aspires to own a fridge, for example, then the impact on the ozone layer would easily offset current international attempts to reduce CFC emissions. As it is climatologists and NASA have warned that the biggest hole ever in the ozone layer is spreading into South America from Antarctica. The effects of the above are compounded by the pressure of competition, the pursuit of economic gain and the political imperative of economic growth in all countries Many natural resources are neither privately nor corporately owned but are subject to common exploitation with little regard to environmental costs and benefits. Belated recognition of these consequences has mobilized both government and business interests to seek solutions. The immediate reaction of halting or even reversing economic growth has, however, quickly given way to a more pragmatic concern for achieving *sustainable* development.

Exam hint

This is only a very short section, but still a very important aspect of the syllabus. The natural environment will be one of the main business issues of this new century and therefore will recur as a question theme.

This involves meeting the needs of the present generations without compromising the needs and requirements of future generations. In effect, the objective is to achieve a negative relationship between GDP and pollution through the introduction of viable controls for the achievement of sustainable development. One highly specific threat involves the melting of Europe's permafrost due to global warming. Underground temperatures in the Alps are rising five times faster than air temperatures, causing landslides and avalanches. The implications for the Alpine sports industry and its marketing could be dramatic over the coming decades.

Recent developments, such as a mile-wide hole opening up in the North polar ice, an estimated overall shrinkage of 40 per cent within 30 years, the collapse of a vast Antarctic ice shelf and the progressive disappearance of Himalayan glaciers, are creating a sense of alarm and a global 'warning'. If the land-based Arctic ice melts, sea levels will automatically rise threatening to submerge some of the most fertile and densely populated areas of the world, for example Bangladesh and the Netherlands. On the positive side, global warming is opening up a northwest passage from Europe to the Pacific, but on the negative side the course of the Gulf stream is being disrupted and weather is becoming uncertain and more extreme. The economic and environmental impacts of the latter are likely to be immense for example Britain's average temperature could drop by five degrees making it similar to Iceland. The opening of new trade routes could also lead to political disputes as Canada currently lays claim to Arctic waters while the US believes they should be treated as an international route.

Since pollution and resource depletion do not observe boundaries, they are global problems that can only be solved by global initiatives. The Montreal Protocol, for example, agreed to cap CFC production but with reduced targets applying to less-developed countries. Scientists calculate a 70 per cent reduction in greenhouse gases is required to halt global warming but the Americans, who alone are responsible for 20 per cent of world pollution, refuse to implement even token cuts. The Bush Administration did admit that global warming exists and will inflict serious and permanent changes on the global environment, but did not recommend altering current policy. America has not committed to Kyoto targets to reduce greenhouse gas emissions, although Russia's ratification will enable the sale of credits by those exceeding their targets.

Marketing environment in practice

'UN world summit on sustainable development'

A decade after the Rio summit, Johannesburg played host to over a hundred world leaders considering key issues such as biodiversity, agriculture and the unsustainable gap between rich and poor. Unfortunately the one leader that really mattered did not attend – G.W. Bush. Very little was specifically achieved other than the establishment of a network of protected marine areas by 2012 and a target of halving those without basic sanitation by 2015. In general terms, there was a recognition that global action on climate change need not incur massive sacrifices but could even galvanize mature industries, such as vehicles and energy extraction, to the forefront of technical change. Key issues such as protectionist trade policies in agriculture were not on the agenda nor were the environmental consequences of multinational operations in poorer countries. Equally, it could be argued, that what the developing world needs most is peace, stable institutions and effective rule of law. Sustainability may well be synonymous with a society that works.

Case history – nature versus technology: the challenge of GM food

This is food made from crops whose genetic code has been altered or modified in some way. The aim is to develop strains that produce higher yields with more consistent quality, nutritional value and appearance. Further objectives are to enable the crops to grow under hardier conditions with greater resistance to disease and parasites so that fewer chemical-based weedkillers or herbicides need to be applied. In effect, it is a hightech development of what agriculturalists have been doing for centuries through selective use of crop strains/breeding. Genetically Modified (GM) foods are already big business in America where multinational chemical companies, such as Monsanto, supply resistant soya seed. The US Food and Drug Administration has subjected GM crops to unprecedented scrutiny, not least because of fear of litigation over unsafe foods. Millions have eaten GM soya over the past 20 years with no ill effects. However, a 3-year government trial in Britain concluded that commercialization of herbicide resistant oil-seed rape and sugar beet could cause significant damage to wildlife, but found that GM maize was less harmful overall than conventional farming.

GM offers massive potential to the Third World, particularly those affected by soil erosion or unable to afford expensive fertilizers and chemicals. However, despite fewer inorganic additives, there may be long-term side effects arising from artificial gene combinations which, once out of Pandora's box, cannot be contained. Also cross-pollination could produce super resistant weeds. GM foods have won the media label 'Frankenstein food', constituting a marketing nightmare for those promoting its acceptance. Pressure led to hasty and emotive regulations on labelling, but stopped short of an outright ban that would have breached WTO rules, so inviting retaliation from the USA.

GM replaces trial and error with control and systematization. There are risks but there are also substantial rewards from successful drug and genetic developments. Freezing research and development of GM foods may represent a tyranny of pressure groups yet if fears prove unfounded it will be the poor of Africa and Asia who will suffer the consequences. Technology has always generated great benefits which have been partly offset by misuse and misunderstanding. A similar case is the ban imposed on DDT in the 1960s following intense pressure group activity. However, when used in a controlled manner it could help many African countries fight back against the growing threat of malaria. Perhaps there is an important role here, for business and the marketer, in promoting the necessary knowledge and managing the inevitable risk. Our future may depend on it.

Implications of the natural environment for marketers

- Business is central to the problem of environmental decline, but also to the solution.
- Environmental consciousness is rising so monitor the evolving green agenda.
- Few consumers budget on environmental performance alone.
- External stakeholders seek reassurance, improving performance and a risk-free future.

- ○ Agreed objectives need to be set by top management/trading partners. The latter will prefer to deal with a business applying environmental standards it is committed to.
- ○ Seek a competitive edge through ethically sound practices e.g. cleaner technologies.
- ○ Offset resource depletion through technical change, redesign, reduction, reuse, recycling and substitution, linked to quality initiatives.
- ○ An environmental strategy needs to be based on sound ethical principles, an audit, impact assessment (see Unit 9) and action based on benchmarking of best practice.
- ○ Stakeholders must be involved/educated into good environmental practice.
- ○ Pay-off in an increased sense of security, improved image/relationships, lower insurance premiums, avoidance of fines/litigation.

Insight

Mobile phones now pose an environmental threat and marketing challenge. One billion handsets are in use globally, with over 100 million discarded (upgrades average 18 months) each year in Europe alone. Containing lead and beryllium, they represent a threat to health if not disposed of properly. Currently most discards are crudely recycled for sale in less-developed economies but rising ownership suggest a challenge to come.

Conclusions

Heightening concern for society and the natural environment will require that new technology is only introduced with care and foresight as to its likely impacts. Society still divides into technical optimists who see salvation and sustainable development through accelerated research and development and pessimists who view unforeseen threats to the ecosystem as unavoidable, no matter how enlightened the technological intent. For example, it has been suggested that the use of paper in offices has risen by 40 per cent since e-mail was introduced. Society therefore views it as too important to leave to business decisions alone leading to increasing regulation as a result.

From the marketing point of view the natural environment is a potentially valuable but not very consistent market as action-awareness gaps arise between what green consumers profess to want and what they actually buy. Awareness also cuts across segments, with children and women being more environmentally aware than men. On the other hand, with every meat eater consuming the lifetime equivalent of 760 chickens, 20 pigs, 5 cows and half a trawler load of fish there are opportunities and threats a plenty for marketers in the food industry.

Finally, it should not be assumed that environmental impacts are primarily the concern of large firms. A recent OECD study concluded that it was small and medium enterprises (SMEs), accounting for less than 10 per cent of GDP, that were responsible for 70 per cent of pollution. A strategic response is clearly required from such firms with the addition of *packaging* and *people* to the marketing mix as a useful first step!

The challenge of change

Unlike the micro-environment, broad natural, political, economic, social and technical trends and changes do not directly impact on day-to-day operations but are extremely important in shaping the competitive situation and the actions and perceptions of relevant stakeholders.

How many businesses do you know that can afford to be purely production orientated? Ever since the dawn of the industrial era, *change* has been the predominant and enduring feature in both industry and wider society. The marketer is actively involved in the shaping and changing of consumer tastes but such effects are nothing compared to the evolving influences of educational expectations, the media, peer groups and travel.

It is also likely that the twentieth century will be best remembered for technological achievements that have put astronauts on the moon, transformed communication and automated industrial processes. Satellites, computers and supersonic aircraft laid the foundations of a 'global village' where events on the other side of the world are known earlier than those in a nearby town or village. Business must therefore be constantly alert to the challenges of new processes and technology, to possible substitutes and, increasingly, to competitive threats.

Question 4.1

Key skills: problem-solving

Can you think of any businesses that face *static* market conditions? This implies no change in both consumer tastes and the state of technical knowledge.

'But tomorrow always arrives, it is different and then even the mightiest company is in trouble if it has not worked on its future.' This quotation by Peter Drucker underlines the reality of continuous change in modern societies. Size is no automatic defence against the forces of change, indeed, of the companies listed in the *Financial Times Top 100* 25 years ago, only half still remain there today. Those missing failed to meet the challenge and so fell victim to a number of misfortunes such as:

- o 'Old economy' companies replaced by 'new economy' Internet-related businesses
- o Acquisition by another firm, for example, Safeway or Abbey
- o Spectacular failure, for example, Enron or Marconi
- o Poor relative performance, for example, Sabena
- o The state forced to take ownership, for example, Railtrack.

Clearly, the larger business must stay on its toes to survive changing circumstances, although the weight of its bureaucracy may make this difficult. Smaller businesses may have the flexibility to adapt more effectively, but only if given access to sufficient resources. Both must recognize that they are on the equivalent of a moving conveyor, they must move fast just to stand still as tastes, technology and competitive forces alter.

Although *change* is the characteristic feature of industrial and information societies, its pace and complexity appears to have increased. The 1950s and 1960s, for example, while still experiencing change, were relatively stable and predictable. Up to 1970 economic growth and development in many countries was almost continuous and fluctuated within narrow limits. There was no Internet or even calculators, computers or mobile phones. Unemployment and inflation were low in developed countries and a high degree of social consensus prevailed. Political parties had similar agendas and both technological and market changes were manageable. The oil crises of the 1970s replaced this comparative calm with turbulent change that has continued ever since. This was even more the case in Asian economies such as Hong Kong or China, where rapid growth was compounded by critical political uncertainties.

103

In less dynamic economies such change exposed previously sleepy market sectors to considerable threats since familiarity with previously established conditions had led to complacency. Similar effects have been felt more recently with worldwide privatization and deregulation, the introduction of the Euro, international trade disputes, a dot-com collapse, renewed oil price instability, the war on terrorism and in Iraq and so the list goes on. Dynamic and complex market environments demand that the marketer understands the future rather than rely on the patterns of the past and must:

- ○ Scan their environment
- ○ Identify those forces relevant to the organization/its industry
- ○ Forecast political, economic, social and technical change
- ○ Respond to threats and opportunities by implementing strategies
- ○ Monitor the outcome of planned action
- ○ Continue to scan their environment.

Exam hint

Improving own performance

It is sound advice to scan past exam papers for patterns but not to rely on them. There are no 'banker questions' so ensure your future doesn't depend on them! Better to practise relating SLEPT elements to an organization or internationally representative industries, Retailing, transport, financial services, energy generation and tourism.

The response to 'uncontrollable macro forces' in terms of strategies requires more explanation. 'Standing still is the fastest way of moving backwards in a rapidly changing world' is a quotation attributed to Anita Roddick, founder of Body Shop International, businesses cannot afford to passively accept change in the macro-environment but must adapt or suffer the consequences. This requires the marketer not only to scan and analyse threats and opportunities but also develop positive strategic responses.

This might involve lobbying for political change or managing the media in order to influence critical publics. Being proactive, even where scope for direct influence on events is limited, will always have more effect on the outcome of the 'game' than the pure spectator role. However, one of the first steps in effective environmental scanning is to identify the relevant sources of environmental data and it is to this task that we turn next.

Internal and external information systems

There are two main categories of existing information:

1. *Internal data* – gathered in-company as a result of operational activities (e.g. employment, cost and sales figures).
2. *Secondary data* – gathered from external sources (e.g. government statistics, published surveys, etc., see Figure 4.3).

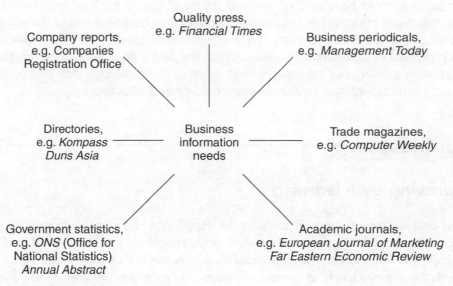

Figure 4.3 Secondary data for a business

A third source of information is *primary data* commissioned specifically to fill knowledge gaps left by the much cheaper alternatives above.

Exam hint

Improving own performance

The examiner will always give credit to candidates who not only make a relevant point in answer to an examination question but can also cite the source. Since sources of information are an explicit part of the CIM syllabus, you would be well advised to link different information sources to different sections in your file, for example, Social Trends linked to population changes.

Key marketing skills: what kind of information is required?

Many different types of information are required, depending on the decisions to be taken. Examples of the more important types include:

Economy

- ○ Main economic indicators – inflation, interest rates, labour market changes, for example vacancies
- ○ Business confidence indicators – capacity utilization, investment
- ○ National income, output and expenditure patterns
- ○ Government taxation and spending plans.

Society

- ○ Demographic indicators – birth/death rates, interregional migration patterns
- ○ Household and working patterns – change in cultural norms
- ○ Leisure activities and ownership ratios for homes, cars, mobiles and so on.

Similar factors could be identified in other areas of the SLEPT environment underlining the diverse nature of information requirements in modern business today. In an environment of rapid change, where time and delay can cost a company dearly, the ability to obtain a clear and accurate picture of developments can provide the firm with a distinct competitive advantage. Information is power, but to achieve this requires a knowledge not just of key sources of information but also of how to access them quickly and effectively.

Exam hint

Improving own learning

News analysis is one means of assessing the importance of current environmental issues. Since editors only have limited space they must make critical choices as to what and what not to include. They will therefore tend to include subjects that are of current and future concern but exclude those they identify as 'yesterday's news'. For example, one method of defining whether an economy is coming out of recession is to track the number of references to it in the quality press over time. As this index declines so the economy must be picking up, since writers and editors no longer see articles on it as 'news', for example,

---

Internal sources

Many questions can only be answered by reference to internal records. The strengths and weaknesses of the business may be identified in this way, although this must be assessed relative to competitors. To be useful records must be gathered in a form that is accessible, accurate and relevant to the forecast or evaluation required. The flow of information through a business should be analysed systematically to achieve these objectives.

Question 4.2

Key skills: collecting information

The marketing department is the primary interface between the business and its customers. What information should it generate? Suggest three key pieces of information from each of the following:

- ○ Management accountant
- ○ Purchasing department
- ○ Operations.

Published material

Such sources are seldom used regularly or systematically by business decision makers. The diffuse nature of many of these sources makes collection, classification and distribution to interested managers an expensive and time-consuming process. The government is one of the main producers of primary data, published through the renamed Office of National Statistics (formerly CSO). Fortunately many of the more important sources have now been produced on CD or the Internet making access almost instantaneous and far more cost effective.

Published business information sources

Some larger organizations delegate a junior executive to undertake this task and circulate a regular summary to appropriate staff. Organizations such as McCarthy and Extel also grew by providing information on specific companies in a readily referenced format. However, whilst the value of such information in informing decisions has been recognized by perceptive marketing executives and planners, their use has been haphazard and on a need-to-know basis only. As we saw in Unit 4, information and communication technologies are now being applied to transform scattered data into quality information available whenever it is required by the appropriate decision maker. The key skill for a marketer to develop is to know *what information* is available on a particular issue and, most importantly where to find it. Published material exists on most topics and is far cheaper than undertaking primary research.

Trade sources

The usual means by which managers keep informed of both internal and external developments, in many cases, is through the grapevine. They establish and build *networks* of information sources which can be drawn on when the need arises. Regular conversations with colleagues, customers and other stakeholder contacts provide a moving tapestry of events supplemented with such things as sales records and consultancy reports. Much of the material gathered from the sources in Figure 4.4 will be sifted, cross-referenced and assimilated on a day-to-day basis.

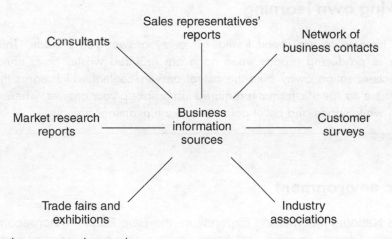

Figure 4.4 Trade sources and networks

Summary of sources of information and assistance in the macro-environment

Social-cultural environment

- ○ *Guide to Official Statistics* – overview of statistics available on the macro-environment.
- ○ *Annual Abstract of Statistics* – all major aspects of government responsibility.
- ○ Office of National Statistics (ONS) Census – population size, distribution, structural change.

- ○ *Social Trends* – annual survey of key societal indicators.
- ○ See www.statistics.gov.uk/onlineproducts/default.asp#social (or economy or population).
- ○ *Family Expenditure Survey* – annual statistical analysis of spending/lifestyle patterns.
- ○ ACORN/Mosaic – classification of local neighbourhoods for segmentation purposes.
- ○ Journals/quality press society sections, for example, *New Society* – changing social patterns.
- ○ British Market Research Bureaux – research cases on lifestyle change.
- ○ UN indicators on population worldwide: www.un.org/depts/unsd/social/population.htm.
- ○ World Bank development data: www.worldbank.org/data/data for example health/ employment.

Political-legislative environment

- ○ Select Committee reports – monitor and report on political issues of the day.
- ○ JUSTIS online legal database – current legislative developments.
- ○ Legal digests – recent case law.
- ○ European Commission – EU directives and implementation timetables.
- ○ Mainstream media and news databases.
- ○ People's Republic of China site: www.moftec.gov.cn.
- ○ Malaysia government: mcsl.mampu.gov.my (gateway to agencies).
- ○ Nigeria law: www.nigeria.law.org.

Exam hint

Improving own learning

Don't be tempted to use report format for every answer you provide. This undifferentiated approach of producing reports when none are required wastes time, annoys the examiner and deflects attention away from the actual answer content which earns the majority of the marks. Where no specific format is required just break-up your answer, where appropriate, with headings, white space and bullet points to make it examiner friendly.

Economic environment

- ○ ONS National Income and Expenditure/the *Blue Book* – macroeconomic analysis
- ○ *Monthly Digest* – most recent figures on the economy, industry and labour market
- ○ *Economic Trends* – changing economic structure and activity patterns
- ○ *Bank of England Quarterly Review* – monitors monetary system/exchange rates
- ○ *Regional Trends* – detailed annual data on social and economic change
- ○ *Employment Gazette* – monthly publication covering wage and price movements
- ○ *CBI Quarterly Survey* – measuring industry confidence and intentions
- ○ *National Institute Economic Review* – quarterly commentary and comparisons. Journals and quality newspapers, for example, *Economist, Financial Times*, various databases
- ○ Bank reviews – articles and economic analysis
- ○ Datastream provides economic data for Asia, Europe and the Americas.

International environment

- ○ Department of Trade and Industry – export credits/advice
- ○ Chambers of commerce – advice/trade/contact networks, for example, www.Srilanka.net/chamber
- ○ Professional bodies, for example, CIM, Institute of Exporters – networks of contacts
- ○ Embassies and trade missions – on-the-spot advice/promotion/contacts
- ○ Eurostat EU database: www.europa.ev.int/comm/eurostat
- ○ Banks, for example, HSBC, provide credit rating/market analysis
- ○ International organizations, e.g. OECD/IMF/WTO/UN World Economic Survey
- ○ International trade centre (UNCTAD/WTO): www.intracen.org
- ○ Trade blocks, for example, EU/ASEAN/NAFTA/Indo-Sri Lanka FTA-research studies/comparisons
- ○ Government departments, for example, customs and excise/planning – specific sectoral data
- ○ World Wide Web
- ○ Quality press, journals and directories, for example, *Kompass, EIU Country Reports/Asia Week*.

Technical environment

- ○ Research journals and conference papers
- ○ Trade press reports
- ○ Channel intermediaries and ultimate customer need surveys
- ○ Technical abstracts and databases
- ○ Professional associations and industry networks.

Summary

In this unit we have seen:

- ○ Why it is crucially important for the organization to monitor change.
- ○ The impacts of change on the natural environment.
- ○ That the marketer should recognize the implications for business being part of larger social, economic and ecological systems.
- ○ The importance of an organization recognizing change in the macro-environment so that scarce management time can be focused on the threats and opportunities.
- ○ Why and how the marketer should draw on internal and external sources of information.

Further study and examination preparation

The importance of this area of the syllabus has been outlined earlier. It is central to the development of your marketing skills particularly with respect to ICT, the use of the Internet and presenting information. Similarly, it relates directly to the statements of marketing practice that are the primary concern of this coursebook, that is, collecting, interpreting and presenting information relevant to marketing strategy and planning processes. The first question is a challenging one and representative of general questions on the environment. Read it very carefully since the examiner requires an example (a charity) and is probing your ability to distinguish the two environments. Focus on why the macro-environment is important from a marketing perspective in the second part. Question 4.2 was referred to in the last unit. Here the focus in on changing macro-environment conditions in the haulage industry. Question 3 provides a very specific question on the natural environment while Question 4 is a part question on sources of information. The latter has been a familiar format in the past, but there is no reason why a full question could not be set on this area in future. It is certainly advisable to know four or five key information sources for each environment and be able to summarize their value to the marketer.

Extending knowledge

Palmer and Hartley, *The Business and Marketing Environment*, McGraw-Hill – Chapter 2, The Nature of the Marketing Environment and Chapter 10 includes a section on the Ecological Environment.

Palmer, A. *The Business Environment*, McGraw-Hill – Chapters 1 and 5.

The best Internet sites for keeping up with the news worldwide include the following:

www.cnn.com for serious international news reports cross-referenced and backed by video clips, photos, audio files and links to relevant websites. It is translated into several languages.

www.news.bbc.co.uk is also translated and offers in-depth reports.

www.washingtonpost.com has won many quality awards and allows you to create a paper customized to a specific region.

www.newsnow.co.uk provides international news updated every 5 minutes with a search facility that covers headlines if you wish to trace the origins of a story.

www.statistics.gov.uk/instantfigures.asp provides data on latest economic indicators.

http://earthtrends.wri.org/ is an environmental information portal.

africa.com is a gateway site to the African continent covering business, news, and so on.

www.allafrica.com provides digests and reviews from 48 national news agencies including special reports on economics, technology and the environment.

www.chinapages.com, MyMalaysia.net.my and lanka.com for business news and information.

asnic.utexas.edu/asnic is a new Asian studies network information centre for the whole of Asia and Asia Pacific.

Exam question 4.1

Please see Question 7, December 2003. Go to www.cim.co.uk for specimen answers.

Exam question 4.2

Please see Question 3(ii) June 2004. Go to www.cim.co.uk.

Exam question 4.3

How might the marketing approach of a fast-food company be influenced by changes in two of the following macro environments?

(a)   The natural environment
(b)   The international environment
(c)   The cultural environment.

(Question 4, December 2002)

Exam question 4.4

You work as Marketing Assistant for a medium sized organization called 'Super Fitness' that is considering expanding its health and fitness clubs into a new area of the country. Produce a brief for your manager that covers the following:

1.   Explanation and justification for the appropriate research methods you would recommend
2.   The information sources that would be most effective in assessing the new area's potential.

(Question 7, December 2002)

unit 5
the demographic, social and cultural environment

Learning objectives

By the end of this unit you will:

o   Have acquired an insight into key demographic changes and their marketing implications (3.3)

o   Have recognized the interrelatedness of the socio-cultural environments (3.3)

o   Appreciate the processes leading to the development of social and cultural values (3.3)

o   Be able to assess the meaning and implications of socio-cultural change (3.3)

o   Understand and apply concepts such as lifestyle, reference groups and social class (3.3)

o   Have considered emerging trends and their potential impact on the marketer (3.3).

Study Guide

A knowledge and understanding of demography and socio-cultural change is vital if the marketer is to truly appreciate the origins of buyer behaviour. Both evolve very slowly but their cumulative impact on market realities over time is considerable. Real living standards in the longer term are more likely to be determined by population changes, for example, than the economic policy making of governments.

Change in this environment is the most difficult to assess, yet the opportunities presented must be grasped and exploited by the marketer. The relevant variables are interrelated, thereby making it difficult to understand the contribution of any one element. As we will see, much that is important in this environment is often unspoken and unwritten, making it one of the greatest challenges to the marketing practitioner.

As a member of society you will be able to identify with much of the content of this unit but you will need to supplement the information provided here. Just as *The Economist* is a useful weekly periodical for the economic, so *New Society* is the equivalent for the social. The Office of National Statistics (ONS) also publishes *Social Trends* (useful articles on current population trends) and the census is available on CD-ROM. International institutions like the World Bank and UN also have extensive comparative coverage on their websites.

Trends in population

Demography is the study of population trends and is important to the marketer because of its concern with the size, structure, composition and characteristics of the population. Segmentation and the assessment of market potential are clearly related to the analysis of such factors but for a specific target population. The ONS publishes detailed population statistics derived from full censuses every 10 years, and updating sample surveys every 5 years. The latest full UK census was in 2001 and businesses may supplement the data obtained with targeted surveys of their own.

The important trends to appreciate include changes in:

- World population and the future size of any given population
- Developed as against less-developed country growth rates
- The age and gender structure and its distribution by region/locality
- Migration within and between national borders
- The demographic impact on world resources and the physical environment.

Activity 5.1

Key skills: collecting and interpreting information

Become familiar with your national population. Use your library to prepare a brief revision on the following:

- Total population, current and trend rate of change
- Age, gender, marital status and location of population
- Occupational structure and ethnic mix
- Significant trends in structure (e.g. ageing, urbanization, etc.).

The implications of population trends to the marketer are felt on the:

- Aggregate demand for goods and services
- Demand side, and its distribution by region/locality/market segment
- Supply side, in the availability of labour
- Mix of public services required and the corresponding tax impact
- Living standards – GDP divided by the total population.

One of the most significant trends in mature industrial economies is the ageing of the population structure. Japan, Europe and, to a lesser extent, the USA are facing a sharp increase in the proportion of over 50s and this is just the leading edge of a global problem that will affect most economies in the next half century. Falling birth rates, greater longevity and the ageing of earlier baby booms are combining to 'grey' the population and shift the centre of gravity of spending power in the economies affected. Development of a new 'super-pill' and advances in genetics imply that even greater longevity may soon be in prospect.

Old, but still fit, healthy and relatively *affluent* pensioners will become the norm in future rather than the old-age pensioner (OAP) image still prevalent today (1 million remain on the poverty line but numbers are falling). Better educated, better off and better informed than their fore-bears, they will command considerable purchasing power. Given current trends, by 2050 the median age in the EU is forecast to rise from 38 to 49 and there will be some 70 million West Europeans aged 65+, representing over 20 per cent of the population. In Italy there are already more over 60s than under 20s, and only greater longevity is preventing declining populations in many parts of Europe.

Marketing environment in practice

The marketing challenge of ageing

Background

Ageing is an increase in the average age of the population and represents a big challenge for the marketer.

Opportunities

There are opportunities with the 'young old', who are fit and healthy and intent on staying that way for as long as possible (note: more than 1 billion Viagra pills have been taken since the 1998 launch). The travel industry will benefit, as will health-related products, security equipment and secure dwellings, quality furniture/other durable replacements, cars, financial services and nostalgia products.

Threats

- o Danger of overlooking other important demographic developments.
- o The dependency ratio will worsen in the UK from the current 3:1 to 2.5:1 by 2015 and 1.5:1 by 2050.
- o Those of working age will have less discretionary income due to the need to repay university loans, purchase expensive housing and provide for private pensions.
- o Labour shortages could develop with a shrinking workforce unless working lives extend.
- o Savings ratios could fall progressively as a rising proportion of elderly dissave.
- o Replacement of final salary with defined contribution schemes, transfers the pension risk to employees.

Significance

- o Emerging economies could gain a competitive edge by virtue of their younger and more energetic age structure – flexibility and a willingness to change should result.
- o US population is forecast to grow by 50 per cent while Europe's declines by 2050 leading to a contraction in the latter's growth rate and economic significance.
- o The centre of gravity of the population is creating a critical mass of the so-called 'third age'. In life-cycle terms it represents an increase in empty nest 1 and 2 as well as single households.
- o The greying of the population may bring about a cultural shift within society, for example, the Dutch are building Senior City in Zeeland, reserved for the over-50s with no schools or discos and motorbikes are banned.
- o Consumer needs and wants change with age and marketers must practise carefully researched age and life-cycle segmentation to exploit it.
- o The over-50s account 44 per cent of the population and own 80 per cent of the wealth. They will form a more dynamic group due to improving health and education. Increasing life expectancy will make them the prime target for the leisure industries.
- o Discretionary spending power will be greatest among the 50–65 year group due to completed families, repaid mortgages, peak earnings and possible inheritance.

- The 2004 Pensions Commission report stated that 9.6 million workers in Britain are not saving enough for a comfortable retirement (12 per cent of income is required if aged 25). Only half of full-time and 15 per cent of part-time workers have a private pension scheme.

- Those approaching retirement will be 'encouraged' by the government to keep working (average retirement age would have to rise from 62 to 70) with promises of larger final pensions or lump sums and a right to retain their jobs at the formal retirement age. Failing this, taxes would have to rise by £57 billion to maintain pensions at current levels up to 2035.

- Responsibility for ageing relatives may increase, reducing both time and income for spending. In 1950 a 65-year-old male could expect to live a further 12 years, compared to 19 years today and 21 years by 2030.

- An ageing market is not a 'maturity' market although the members may be age conscious and smartly dressed.

- Value for money and quality may be important but so is the opinion that they are deserving of a little luxury. If so, then the marketing message must be altered accordingly.

- The advertising slogan 'We'll take good care of you' strikes a valid chord.

Conclusions

Imminent labour shortages are being countered by the use of alternative workforces, such as married women, immigrants and ethnic groups. Numbers of Black and Asian people in England rose 40 per cent during 1991–2001 while the overall population remained static despite substantial immigration from Eastern Europe. New technology, flexible contracts and a developing culture of continuous learning will also help to alleviate any skills gap. Marketers should in any case form partnerships with educational institutions, market attractive recruitment packages while developing a positive image as a responsible employer. As the number of retired people rises sharply from 2010 so will their power as an influential pressure group. More educated and articulate, they will possess the wit, the time and the means to use search and comparison technologies, such as the Internet and teletext and so constitute a demanding and service-orientated customer. Marketers may find the days of fat margins and easy profits become an ever-dimming memory as these 'third ages' flex their latent bargaining power.

Life expectancy rates in the EU are 74 years for males and 80.5 years for females comparing favourably with the USA (72.7m:79.4f) but poorly with Japan (77m:83.3f). Africa fares worst due to the damaging impact of Aids but Russia also faces shrinking population due to low life expectancy and low birth rates. Marketers in these countries face a very different and more depressing population context for their activities.

Question 5.1

Saga, the highly successful family run business catering for the over-50s is being sold for around £1 billion. Founded in 1948 to provide value for money all-inclusive winter packages for older people, it was built upon a customer service ethos. It succeeded in turning 'grey hair into gold' by offering its 8-million customer database everything from travel to insurance, share dealing, credit cards, a website and magazine. In the light of the ageing challenge above, suggest how and why the marketing mix of the new owners may have to be modified to meet its customer needs.

The dependency ratio

This is the ratio of the number of dependents in the population relative to the working population. Workers create the nation's material wealth and so support the non-working population either directly or through tax transfers. The ratio improves in the UK until around 2010, when lower birth rates and retirement of immediate post-war baby boomers combine to reduce it continuously.

Marketing environment in practice

The biggest division in British society may be that between the 'baby boomer's' of the late 1940s and the 'baby buster's' of the 1970s. The boomer's avoided major wars, enjoyed high employment, accumulated wealth nearly continuously, and look forward to a long and comfortable retirement. Baby buster's face a much bleaker future with the combined burden of higher taxes, personal pension contributions, higher education fees and loan/credit debt repayments (particularly in the light of surging house prices). This will tend to depress disposable income among this age group and their attractiveness to marketers for some years to come. Indeed the 35–54 age group have been labelled 'Meldrews' due to their disillusion over politics, disgust over rising crime rates and the quality of public services plus their feeling that there is little to look forward to. The over-55s, by contrast, have become the most satisfied segment of society.

Labour shortages will be good news for the unemployed and those seeking career advancement and promotion, but bad news for tax payers since real resources will need to be diverted to support those no longer contributing productively to society. Health services will need to expand continuously in real terms especially as life expectancies keep on rising. Health expenditure for the over-65s is already four times the average for the under-65s, while for the over-75s it is eight times. A doubling in the US population on retirement benefits by 2030 threatens the solvency of their social security and Medicare budgets. While French plans to raise the pension age from 60 to 65 were met with widespread demonstrations as thousands sought to protect their pension rights. For Austria to meet the levels of pension contributions they are currently committed to, will involve either cutting other spending by 76 per cent or raising tax rates by 50 per cent. This puts them in a quandary since they dare not implement austerity measures but equally the single currency Stability Pact precludes excessive spending or inflating the national debt. This pension time bomb could therefore, in principle, force them out of the Euro.

The fall in the number of births would seem to be a serious development for manufacturers dependent on this segment. The marketers of quality prams, for example, might have been expected to lose sales volume. In practice, married couples, who were now delaying births were more likely to spend extra on their fewer offspring, and with established careers, could afford to do so. On the other hand, rising car ownership was shifting preferences towards a dual purpose carrycot/pram, probably causing the demise of such companies. The marketer must therefore take nothing for granted in this complex area.

World population

Global population has grown exponentially over the last two or three centuries, as Figure 5.1 shows. Stability up to around AD 1000 was replaced with progressively rising rates, especially with industrialization and advances in health care and hygiene.

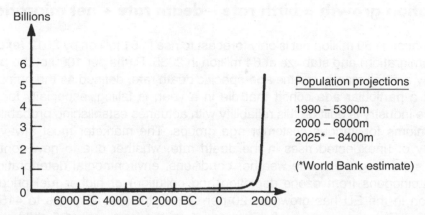

Billions

Population projections

1990 – 5300m
2000 – 6000m
2025* – 8400m

(*World Bank estimate)

6000 BC   4000 BC   2000 BC   0   2000

Figure 5.1 World population growth

As industrial economies matured, however, they enjoyed a *demographic transition* whereby customarily high birth rates fell to levels closer to already-reduced death rates. This process has yet to be completed in many less-developed countries, especially in Africa, meaning that world population will continue to rise, at a reducing rate, at least until the middle of the century. On the other hand, AIDS is reducing life expectancy thereby neutralizing some of this growth.

Malthus predicted a 'dismal' outcome by suggesting that if food production grows arithmetically (i.e. 1-2-3-4) while population grows geometrically (i.e. 2-4-8-16) then population crisis was inevitable. In the absence of voluntary preventative measures to restrict population (e.g. China's one child policy) then equilibrium could only be restored by positive checks such as war, disease, pestilence and famine.

In practice successful economic development has enabled most developing economies to raise living standards and reduce poverty levels. This includes China, although the spectre of population growth still haunts its leaders. With official population well in excess of 1.2 billion, recent surveys by the Family Planning Ministry in Peking suggest at least 200 million children unaccounted for in the official figures. Many poor families in relatively remote rural areas apparently ignored the repressive one child per family laws. India with its growth rate unchecked will see its population grow from 1.03 to 1.46 billion if present trends persist.

Question 5.2

Key skills: problem-solving

How did developed economies avoid Malthus's dismal predictions? Think about factors that shift out the production possibility curve when trying to answer this.

Do the same arguments apply to less-developed economies today and what are the implications for the international marketer? Is there such a thing as an optimum level of population?

Aggregate population

The record in population forecasting in other countries has also been remarkably inaccurate, especially as regards births that tend to fluctuate quite considerably.

Population growth = birth rate – death rate + net migration

UK population is 59 million but is only forecast to rise to 61 million by 2012 (excluding any rise in illegal immigration) and stabilize at 64 million in 2035. Births per 1000 of the population exceed deaths by a small margin but the age-specific death rate, defined as the number of people (per 1000) of a particular age cohort that die in a year, is falling, especially for women. The life insurance industry is built on this reliability with actuaries establishing probabilities to determine risk premiums for various customer age groups. The marketer must always be alert to the possibility of unexpected rises in the death rate, whether due to new contagious illnesses, hospital super-bugs, extreme weather conditions, environmental deterioration (e.g. skin and other carcinogens from ozone depletion and pollution) or higher fuel prices (hypothermia). Population in the EU has grown by 20 per cent in the last 40 years to 415 million, but with the average European woman of childbearing age producing only 1.5 children (2.1 required for replacement), the long-run trend could be downward. EU enlargement will increase the total by 75 million but most immigration will come from Muslim neighbours such as Turkey, Algeria and Egypt where birth rates are twice the EU average. One disturbing development, that may confirm the downward trend of births in countries like Britain is recent research showing average sperm counts among males have declined by a third in the last decade alone. Improved economic performance tends to reduce outward migration but also increases attractiveness for economic migrants fleeing from the world's poverty or trouble spots. Prosperous economies around the world attract such flows but all tend to maintain tight restrictions creating opportunities for illegal trade in human beings whether from East Europe, Vietnam, the Balkans, Afghanistan or conflict affected parts of Africa. However, economies like Sweden and Spain with rapidly ageing populations may soon be anxious to receive rather than restrict such inflows. To preserve the ratio of ageing pensioners to active working population that prevailed in the 1990s would require 130 million immigrants into Europe over the next 50 years. Just as European emigrants were a crucial resource in developing the Americas at the turn of the twentieth century so the Third World could come to its rescue at the turn of the twenty-first century. As a decline in the workforce would have serious implications for economic growth and funding social security programmes, so continued immigration, whether official or illegal, appears inevitable. Statistics now show that 1 in 12 people living in Britain was born overseas, almost double that of 50 years ago, and immigration accounts for 80 per cent of all population growth. Immigrants remit in excess of $50 billion from the rich nations of the West, about the same amount as transferred in aid.

Question 5.3

Did you know?

If the German fertility rate remained at its recent level of only 1.3, its native population would actually become extinct by around 2300. Italy's fertility rate has been even lower!

The average cost of getting married in Britain is £16 000, while raising a child to age 21 is around £165 000!

A couple's decision to have one more or less child to complete the family is a marginal one for them but will have compounded effects if repeated across the age group. Medical and genetic breakthroughs that may provide the ability to both determine sex at conception and eradicate defects may, if legalized, have far-reaching implications for future births.

Population structure

While aggregate population may be stable this can seldom be said for the various dimensions of a population structure that include:

o Age
o Gender
o Marital status
o Region
o Ethnic group
o Occupation.

Activity 5.2

Marketing skills: using information and metrics

What marketing threats/opportunities arising out of age/gender will be faced in your country by:

o A university?
o A cosmetic surgeon?
o Private health insurers?

Many businesses, particularly in services, have responded positively to economic upturn and labour shortages arising out of lower births and ageing by:

o Greater marketing of the business and its prospects to potential recruits
o Building closer links with local educational establishments
o Using the Internet – www.milkround.co.uk
o Tapping alternative workgroups using flexible employment patterns
o Internal marketing for retention, retraining and promotion
o Improving pay and incentives especially for flexibility
o Move to cheaper labour market or use selective immigration.

One important means of compensating for contraction in the under-25s is by increased employment of married women and the older age groups themselves. Women account for 45 per cent of the UK workforce and there is ample scope to raise EU activity rates towards the 66 per cent found in Scandinavia and the US. This solution will also have to be considered by developing economies as they encounter ageing, although there may be significant religious and cultural obstacles to overcome, especially in Muslim countries.

Insight

Fundamentalist Sunni Muslims impose a strict regime which forbids most women to work or study and either forces them to stay at home or cover up using the burqa. The burqa or veil is a cultural phenomenon that will prove resistant to removal, particularly in traditional rural areas. However, religious dress codes that clash with prevailing cultural norms in Western societies are creating tensions and recourse to law to adjudicate on the fine lines between human rights and implicit toleration of female oppression.

Many school-leavers have opted to enter higher education in recent years. There has been a 75 per cent increase in EU students in the last 15 years to 11.8 million, implying a much better qualified and well-informed consumer group in future. The ratio of women in higher education is increasing although males still predominate in engineering, mathematics and computer science. Education is becoming internationalized with most exchanges being officially encouraged. Education for life is another important trend with increasing numbers of larger employers providing some form of continuing vocational training.

The youth-orientated society of the 1960s and 1970s has given way to a more conservative middle-aged culture. With the number of retirees about to boom worldwide to an estimated 600 million, the face of marketing is bound to be affected.

Question 5.4

Key skills: using information and problem-solving

What product values and characteristics will be central to an effective marketing strategy focused on the over-45s?

As the old become more numerous, better educated and live longer, so their political and economic power will increase. Financially well endowed and with a greater propensity to vote, they will exert more pressure on decision makers as well as constituting an important but discerning market segment. The marketer should also recognize that the retired will include among the poorest in society, with nearly 2 million in Britain qualifying for supplementary benefits and a further 1 million qualifying but not taking it up. Many of the supposedly affluent 'empty nesters' also have ageing relatives to support so curtailing their ability to consume. On the other hand, nursing homes may be the grateful beneficiaries.

Marital status and household structure

This is undergoing considerable change in many societies due to later marriage, rising divorce rates and remarriages, making the traditional marketer's assumption of two adults + two children the exception rather than the norm.

Divorce rates of 40 per cent in Britain are the highest in Western Europe especially among those marrying young. The average British marriage now lasts just over 9 years although the greatest increase in divorce rates is among those married over 20 years. Each year 570 000 get married and 300 000 divorce. The divorcees collectively spend an estimated £2 billion mainly on legal fees, maintenance payments and setting up new homes. Earlier marriages have fallen sharply in recent years but cohabitation has increased, as have illegitimate births (one in four are raised by a single parent). Remarriages, already accounting for a third of the annual total, may produce 'composite' family groups, combining different children and ages from previous unions. The increase in single households is accounted for by the rising number of elderly, greater independence among the young, individuals staying single longer and rising divorce rates. This clearly forms a complicated tapestry for marketing analysis, but also a rich seam of potential segmentation.

Insight

The historically low birth rate of 1.64 has been linked to childless career women. Surveys suggest that more are delaying parenthood or forgoing it altogether. Two in five were concerned about its impact on career or finances. Less than one in eight believed that having children was necessary to achieve fulfilment and one third that had children felt no happier and registered a strong loss of independence.

Regional distribution

The marketer should be aware of the shifting distribution of population across regions and localities arising from both natural increase and net migration. The broad movement affecting all industrializing societies has been the steady drift from rural to urban living. Economic decline and depopulation has left a relatively old and poor residue from the south of Italy to the north of Scotland. For example, overall population in the UK has risen 11 per cent over the last 35 years, whereas Scotland's has fallen by 1 per cent.

There has been reverse flow from the inner cities to suburbia and the ribbons of development along the motorway and rail routes radiating away from city centres. As young couples move into these urban fringes to escape either inner-city decay or rural remoteness, so births increase to reinforce the process. However, rising suburban property prices and city centre regeneration have recently put a brake on these flows and the marketer must be careful to identify where the target populations reside, especially the retired. Rising single households in Britain (doubling to a third 1971–2006) and across the EU is also creating opportunities for the construction industry but putting pressure on rural land. Over 4.5 million new homes are projected to be required in the UK alone by 2010.

Question 5.5

Key skills: using information

Many economies are characterized by dense urban conurbations interspersed by relatively sparse local communities. In the light of this or similar disparities in your own country, assess the implications for marketers seeking to serve the needs of these populations.

Ethnic groups

Many populations are diverse in their origins and therefore their buying patterns. Countries like Malaysia and Singapore will have a strong mix of Malay and Chinese, while Britain reflects its European and Commonwealth heritage. Ethnic minorities account for around 9 per cent of the total with Indians, West Indians and Pakistanis comprising the largest groups but with Chinese, Africans, Bangladeshis and Arabs well represented. The US census bureau predicts that the white population will fall from 70 to 50 per cent by 2050 while Hispanics rise from 13 to 25 per cent.

Marketing environment in practice

For the marketer of financial services in Britain, the 2 million Muslim population represents a challenging segment. Shariah law forbids usury making both saving and borrowing difficult. Only the United Bank of Kuwait offers a Shariah-compliant mortgage although ordinary bank accounts may be operated where the interest is given to charity. Again credit cards are ruled as acceptable so long as the monthly balance is cleared thereby avoiding any interest payment. Share dealing is acceptable but not speculation. Permitted investments necessarily exclude shares deriving income from pork products, alcohol, gambling and so forth.

Such groups tend to be younger than the indigenous white population producing a very different pattern of needs to be met by marketers and local authorities alike. Where ethnic concentrations occur the number of births have been more buoyant than elsewhere, although West Indian experience, the oldest New Commonwealth immigrant group, exhibits rates little different to the overall average. Ethnic markets are important as shown by the British Asian food industry. Its annual turnover of £1.5 billion plus is greater than the coal, steel and shipbuilding industries combined. Surveys also an estimated 70 000 wealthy Asians have moved from inner city to prosperous suburbs in recent times.

Question 5.6

Key skills: interpreting information

Why have ethnic minority-owned businesses been able to exploit profitable niche markets among these populations without attracting substantial competition from established businesses?

Occupational structure

At the outset of the industrialization process well over 60 per cent of the employed workforce (and large numbers in subsistence agriculture) are engaged in the primary sectors of agriculture, forestry, fishing, mining and quarrying. This ratio can be as high as 90 per cent in some of the poorest nations of the world, dependent as they are on cash crops for the majority of their exports. Countries such as Malawi rely on foreign aid and traditional migration of the under-employed to the mines of southern Africa.

Industrialization itself is characteristically completed when 60 per cent of the employed population is employed in manufacturing, construction and utilities such as electricity generation. Economies such as Malaysia now generate over 70 per cent of their visible exports from manufacturing in marked contrast to their previous dependence on timber products and rubber. A further transformation into a service-based economy occurs when 60 per cent are employed in the tertiary sector, including transport, financial, retail and personal services. This state is achieved by developed post-industrial societies such as those in North America and Western Europe. It also includes island economies like Singapore and Hong Kong where financial services contribute over 13 per cent of GDP.

The next stage of the development is the full emergence of the information society, when 60 per cent of the workforce will be employed in activities at the interface with the final consumer, be that a customer, an elderly person, a patient, a taxpayer or a student.

The workforce in employment: some important trends

We can identify a number of important and interrelated developments in employment as economies mature and evolve from industrial into service and information societies:

- *The decline in full-time employment* – The cultural 'norm' of a standard workday, work week and work year is progressively ceasing to apply. Whether this is an 8-hour day, 40-hour week and 48-week year as in Northern Europe or a more siesta and festival affected variant as in Southern Europe, the trend is clear. It is partly due to the rise of more focused and flexible organizations wishing to meet the needs and wants of the customer at their convenience, rather than in a time slot favourable only to the producers. More and more organizations operate on a 24-hour, 7-day a week, 52-week a year basis and require a workforce to match. Manufacturers, retailers, transport fleet operators and by implication leisure and catering providers now open all hours and demand a flexible workforce willing to work whatever hours are necessary to get the job done. However, this trend should not be oversold since over 80 per cent of the British workforce remain in a permanent job and average tenure has risen from 6 to 7 years compared to 1984.
- *The corresponding rise in part-time employment* – This has risen in the UK from just under 5 per cent to nearly 30 per cent of all employment in just 25 years. It largely reflects the entry of large numbers of married women into the workforce for whom part-time work is an ideal compromise with domestic responsibilities. It also reflects the growing needs of employers to cover service peaks and holiday periods. Nearly half of all women work part-time, although the percentage of males is also rising as attitudes alter and more seek to supplement income in early retirement. Organizations prefer the adaptability of a part-time workforce and feel better able to adjust to changing economic conditions over the business cycle.
- *Hours are lengthening for full-time workers* – Reflecting the need for flexibility, but also cultural change resulting in more intense and stressful lives for an organization's permanent workforce. An organization dedicated to achieving competitive advantage and more than fully satisfying the needs of its customers needs an equally dedicated workforce to achieve these ends. It also reflects income pressures on employees as they drive to achieve and maintain high consumption affluent lifestyles. This runs counter to the current vogue for achieving a work – life balance, which may be an illusion for most that want to progress in their careers. EU legislation seeks to limit weekly hours to 48 per week, but many managerial and professional staff voluntarily work longer. Over 40 per cent of Britons regularly work more than the national average of 48 hours a week and half are working more hours than 5 years ago. The 35-hour week enacted by France in 1998 has backfired, with unemployment now around 10 per cent. Longer holidays of 5–6 weeks look equally unsustainable when compared to the one or two in Japan and the USA. Americans work hardest, with the exception of South Korea and the Czech Republic. Hours worked have increased in the last 10 years by the equivalent of a full working week and exceed those of Britain by 250 and Germany by 500 hours a year.

Question 5.7

Key skills: interpreting information

What are the attractions of part-time employment to:

o The business?
o The employee?
o The government?

Comment on legal developments and the marketing implications of part-time working.

o *Self-employment is rising* – It is projected to increase by a quarter in the next decade although the incidence varies widely between industries, being especially high in services and construction. Hotels and catering are understandably above average while manufacturing records only half the overall rate. The primary drive is the opportunity created by information technology and e-commerce combined with the desire of organizations to outsource non-core activities. There is no organizational reason why most professional and information workers should not be retained on a self-employed basis.
o *A rise in contractual and temporary employment* – An increasingly competitive environment has forced many businesses to concentrate on core activities. Specialized resources must be fully utilized or it becomes more efficient to contract-out services or contract-in labour as and when required. The convenience of a large directly employed labour force has become a luxury not even the public sector can afford. Transport and distribution may be contracted-out to third-party operators while specialized marketing skills are hired or 'outsourced' through agencies as and when required.
o *The emergence of flexible organizations* – Charles Handy in his book *The Age of Unreason* suggests that more and more organizations employ *a core* of full-time scientific, technical, marketing and managerial employees with company-specific skills and proprietary knowledge to coordinate and direct the fundamental activities of the business. A flexible workforce achieves this, composed of readily adjustable groups including: high turnover semi-skilled full-timers; part-timers; temporary workers; job sharers; staff on temporary contracts; student placements; government trainees; home workers and sub-contractors. For example, call centres, serving banks and insurers through to emergency services and employing an estimated 1 million employees in Britain adopt just such a mix of flexible workers in order to keep the phone, fax and e-mail links operating around the clock.

Marketing environment in practice

McKinsey estimates that the global call centre market will be worth £140 billion by 2008. It already employs 3 per cent of the North American workforce and more than those employed in cars, steel and coal combined in Britain. By receiving calls on behalf of businesses for telemarketing, sales/reservations, technical support or customer relations, they are inextricably linked to marketing. Such services can be readily contracted out to third party companies that might be located anywhere in the world. Indian call centres in Bangalore are growing at a phenomenal rate, serving customers ranging from American Express to Lufthansa. They train their operatives in the language and accents of their customers. They are also familiarized (using TV soaps) to regional accents and keep abreast of local news coverage. With the advent of the Internet potential, customers are much better informed before making a call to buy something. The call centre staff therefore must be equal to this challenge. As the only point of contact between the calling customer and the ultimate product supplier they must be more than just competent and personable.

British banks like HSBC and LloydsTSB have moved their operations to India because of its massive output of well-educated English speaking graduates who, unlike their counterparts in Britain and America, are more than happy to work in the well-appointed centres for one-fifth of the salary. India is on course to win a big slice of the global market but must also bear the risk that fickle Western companies might quickly go elsewhere if the price and service is right.

○ *Employment stress* – A consequence of changing employment patterns is the rise in general stress levels. Increased pressures of competition arising out of environmental changes such as globalization, e-commerce, downsizing and the deregulation of many public services has removed much of the slack in productivity performance. More women have work and domestic economy duties while many men work longer and more intense working hours. Loyalty to the organization is as traditional in Asian economies as hard work and commitment is to the American lifestyle. However, there is a growing segment of 'copers' in many societies and not surprisingly stress and depression are on the increase. Department for Work and Pensions figures state that over 1 million are too stressed to work, 45 per cent more than when Labour came to power in 1997.

Insight

Symptoms of depression now occur in half the population, double the rate of 20 years ago, and are rising fastest among females. Suicide rates in Japan are double those of Britain and mainly affect middle-aged men pushed aside in the economic slump. They have also tripled over 30 years in Britain to become the third largest cause of death among 25–34-year-olds. Three quarters of the workforce also admit to taking up to four 'sickies' per year. An ICM study found a rise in bad temper due to accelerating lives while expectation of instant gratification in modern marketing apparently leads to reduced ability to deal with queues.

Thanks to advances in e-mail technology, even those who work from home will not necessarily avoid the stress of working relationships. Televirtual has developed 3D software that allows the user to generate a high fidelity virtual human who can represent their feelings. The image could then be e-mailed to teleworkers to deliver appropriate motivation! As a result of stress there is now an army of half a million therapists, mentors, grief counsellors, anger managers and lifestyle gurus in Britain alone.

○ *The rise of the knowledge worker* – Well over half the workforce can be designated as knowledge workers including those who produce, process, use and/or distribute knowledge as well as maintain the infrastructure for its transmission. Marketers are clearly knowledge workers because they perform all these functions. Even in manufacturing industry itself, only a third of those employed will normally be manual workers on the shop floor. Since most jobs will require brains rather than brawn in the new century, governments are rapidly expanding vocational and higher education in an effort to avert critical skill shortages from inhibiting high-technology growth opportunities. With the

Japanese pattern of educating virtually all its highly motivated 18-year-olds being emulated by the other emerging countries of East Asia, they appear potentially much better equipped to effect the transition to post-industrial society. The concept of 'lifelong learning' has developed based around computer literacy and the systematic and continuous renewal of knowledge in a rapidly changing world.

o *Flexible work lives* – The need for flexibility to match working hours to operational requirements and produce a more effective work-life balance is producing a kaleidoscope of employment patterns for the marketer to observe. They can all yield higher productivity as well as lower turnover and absence rates:

- *Flexitime* – enabling employees to plan their own time allocation
- *Staggered hours* – lengthening but spreading the 'rush hours'
- *Flexible work years* – match activity patterns to personal circumstances
- *Flexible shifts and rosters* – to effectively cover customer service requirements
- *Longer days but shorter weeks* – to maximize actual working time
- *2 × 12-hour weekend shifts* – to maximize utilization of plant
- *Working from home* – telecommuting through office computer intranet links
- *Planned reduction in hours towards retirement* – In Britain there has been a dramatic decline in labour market participation among over-50s males. The government has demonstrated concern by introducing a tax credit scheme for helping over-50s back into work and offering a £30 000 lump sum for those working 5 years beyond official retirement age. The scale of such initiatives, however, may have to be significantly increased before any sizeable return to the stresses of working life occurs.

Exam hint

Improving own performance

Remember that any question posed on the environment must be answered in context. Regurgitation of academic content alone is insufficient – shape it to fit the question context.

This is why it is inadvisable to prepare model answers to questions you think might be set in the exam. It is highly unlikely that the way the question is posed will match your preparation. Unless you are very careful you will be tempted to make the question fit your prepared answer rather than the other way round! Better to be flexible: read and answer the question precisely.

Increased mobility – Allied to flexibility are lengthened daily travel distances which have risen fivefold in the UK since 1950 from 5 to 28 miles. On present trends they will double again by 2025 although mounting congestion might act as an inhibitor. Organizations require their knowledge workers to be mobile and they are often prepared to travel rather than to move in order to maintain their desired lifestyle or avoid disruption to partner or children.

o *The self-service economy* – Non-standard work patterns imply non-standard leisure patterns with more time being absorbed doing tasks which were previously undertaken by business. Self-service is already well established in most retail outlets while home-shopping cable and satellite systems take the process one step further. Interactive computer systems linked to databases offer dramatic potential to transform the way in which many services are currently marketed, sold and performed. Home banking, direct insurance and distance learning are just a sample of leading-edge applications.

Insight

The ultimate in self-service was the IKEA concept of the self-assembly flatpack. It eliminated the cost of shipping vast quantities of air and redistributed the task of assembly to the final consumer. It also meant that Ingvar Kamprad became one of the richest men in the world as owner of a company with 186 outlets in 31 countries and turnover of £7.6 billion. Employing 76 000 co-workers and visited by 310 million customers in 2003, it is said that 10 per cent of all British births in the early 1990s were conceived on an IKEA bed.

The changing role of women in work and society

The situation of men and women at work differs dramatically across different societies due to varying cultural norms, education levels and stage of development. Nearly three-quarters of Japanese women are university educated yet little more than one in four works after graduation. Frustrated at their failure to find sufficiently challenging jobs in the strong masculine culture of domestic companies, they turn to less discriminating non-Japanese multinationals. A similar pattern prevailed in Spain until its recovery from recession while in the Middle East the almost feudal position and treatment of women has slowly begun to transform. The influence of Islam and its ultra-religious 'mutawah' policy continues to hold sway in requiring conformity to traditional mores of respectable female behaviour.

Britain remains a society where the different genders are employed in different sectors, different industries, different occupations and different levels in the hierarchy. Women usually have family responsibilities yet over half now go out to work, at least part-time. Domestic duties combine to ensure that they often work harder (an estimated 10 hours a week on average) but they are promoted less often and are generally less well paid than male counterparts. Despite improvement the cumulative cost disadvantage of being a woman is calculated as £240 000. Women in Britain now earn, on average, 82 per cent of men's wages, which is improving but still less than in most other European countries. The gap is even greater in terms of weekly pay because men generally work longer hours, attracting overtime rates.

Women are underrepresented in manufacturing but dominate in many of the expanding service industries. Caring occupations such as health and primary education register a ratio of 80:20 in favour of women overall, but men still dominate the top positions.

The rising proportion of women in higher education, to over half by 2001, has contributed to an improvement in their representation in managerial and professional occupations. This is now well over 25 per cent but is not reflected in senior management. Only 10 per cent of the top jobs are taken by women. Women tend to predominate in people- or service-centred staff functions rather than line positions, contributing directly to profitability.

 ## Activity 5.3

Identify the areas, in an organization of your choice, in which women appear to be under-represented.

Investigate the causes of this situation.

Consider the ingredients of a 'positive action plan' to improve the utilization of women in the organization.

Since women already account for half of the educated workforce and form the only credible source of untapped labour potential, how should business respond? Relatively high unemployment may have relieved the pressure in recession, but sustained growth has begun to expose critical shortages. The policy responses have included:

o Targets for employing more women in senior positions
o Workplace nurseries or financial support for private childcare
o Flexible working patterns and career break keep-in-touch schemes
o Women-friendly recruitment, selection, appraisal and promotion procedures
o Attitude retraining and training in 'core' activities
o Common pay and conditions – equal reward for work of equal value.

When the Civil Service adopted similar policies to allow women to mix family and career, it resulted in an actual decline in those prepared to dedicate themselves to getting to the top. One of the main comparative advantages of the male executive is that they normally have the support of a wife, a luxury denied to the latter!

Marketing environment in practice

According to segmentation research by Close Wealth Management, there are 200 000 single, rich and happy (Sarahs) women in Britain. Unfortunately this female affluence has little to do with workplace equity and much to do with failed marriages and associated financial settlements.

One in five women is electing not to have children and this rises to three in five for female executives. In many large companies motherhood is considered a rather furtive activity that interferes with performance and constitutes exclusion from the job. On the other hand do men fare any better? They are expected to be breadwinners, work long hours and face ridicule if they challenge the convention by staying at home. It is the brave man that asks for the flexible working patterns provided to women.

Recognition of so-called 'glass ceilings', preventing women's advancement, has begun to stiffen government resolve for more positive action. Pressure groups are also becoming more active and some shareholders are asking questions at AGMs. However, the most effective catalyst for fundamental change remains a diminishing labour supply that confronts businesses with the choice between hiring more women or lower-quality men.

Exam hint

As you are now over half way through this coursebook have you:

o Developed answer plans to each of the past examination questions set?
o Practised writing a complete answer under timed conditions to at least one of these?
o Obtained feedback on your answer from a tutor or practitioner?

Do not make the mistake of making the actual examination the first opportunity to practise your answering technique. The outcome is likely to be an expensive, time-consuming and confidence-sapping resit. Practice makes perfect, so don't be tempted to skip answering the specimen questions.

Summary of implications for marketers

- Demography is an important demand condition, helping the marketer to predict size and change in target markets by population, age, gender, region, family size or ethnic group.
- Predicting volatile birth rates is more difficult than the relatively stable death rates.
- The original baby boomers in developed countries are approaching retirement age while the more numerous 1960s boomers enter prosperous middle age.
- The scope for demographic segmentation is considerable *and* is a means of adapting marketing approaches and product offerings to match changing needs at the different stages of life. Holiday companies like Club 18–30 or Saga have a clear life-cycle focus.
- The regional dominance of the South East in Britain (with a third of total population/ above average income) creates a marked contrast in consumption patterns and a magnet for luxury producers. Similar patterns are found in other countries, for example SW Malaysia.
- Organizations must market themselves effectively in the face of potential skill shortages, that is, use research and segmentation to target potential employees whose needs must be analysed and matched to those of the organization.
- Greater flexibility is required in recruitment, particularly among married women.
- Marketers must respond to the consequences of demographic trends: flexible finance, mortgages and pension plans to match more flexible but less secure working lives; home-based services to meet the needs of home workers; car dependence in knowledge-worker rural retreats; the demand for 'convenient' and time-saving solutions; flexible opening hours for the cash rich/time poor worker.
- Advertising and promotion should reflect the changing demographic and employment patterns, for example, men sharing household tasks in two-worker households or women pursuing more independent lives.

The social and cultural environment

Difficulties experienced by women in employment are largely a reflection of societal attitudes in general and male-dominated corporate cultures in particular. Culture moulds and regulates daily behaviour through constant conditioning and reinforcement. We learn what is and what is not appropriate behaviour in different social situations. Our attitudes, beliefs, values and language derive from such cultural influences as the family, community, religion and education.

Understanding culture is particularly important to cross-cultural management and marketing in global organizations. Marketers who seek, wittingly or unwittingly, to impose their own behavioural norms on customers or employees with other cultures, will fail. The marketer must recognize that:

1. Culture is built up through a system of values, beliefs and attitudes
2. Culture is specific to one group
3. Culture is not innate but is learned from one generation to the next
4. Culture influences the group in uniform and predictable ways.

Less-developed societies tend to be collectivist cultures and only with economic development and the catalyst of marketing does individualism develop. Private enterprise rewards individual effort and innovative members become tempted into relying on themselves. This allows entrepreneurs to escape the norms of conformity and group consensus. This process is best seen in the Asian tiger economies where development has been associated with a decline in authoritative Confucian values.

Insight

Fox-hunting is a practice that has divided town and country in Britain. Anti-hunt groups profess to be motivated by concern over animal suffering yet there appears to be double standards applied. For example, the cultural practice of Halal (Muslim) butchery and Shechita (Jewish) ritual slaughter account for over half a million animals each year but few concerns are raised. Indeed by law, all animals must be stunned so they are unconscious at the time of slaughter unless they are killed by these two methods. It would seem that some customs are independently powerful in their own right. One parallel to note is the imminent end of bullfighting in Spain. Barcelona has already voted to outlaw the practice and the rest of Catalonia may quickly follow.

Culture, then, is reflected in what we eat, how and where we live, our lifestyles and buying preferences, not to mention our humour, art, religion and music. The international marketer must be especially aware of diverse social mores. When in Rome, do as the Romans do is apt advice since the accepted norms of business behaviour in, say, Japan are very different compared to those in Europe. Bowing one's head is a sign of respect in the East but signals disinterest in the West. Business and general societal customs must also be carefully observed if offence is to be avoided. Language translation is another pitfall to beware of, particularly for global enterprises. Nova does not 'go' as a car brand in Spain but neither would the Spanish 'Bum' snacks do too well in Britain. Nescafés 'blue' pack coffee would receive a 'cold' reception in Russia while in Kuwait it translates into 'death'. Similarly 'Big Macs' are a no-go area as far as the Hindus of India or Sri Lanka are concerned.

 ## Activity 5.4

Key skills: presenting information

The social mores or norms of accepted behaviour in Islamic or East Asian countries are radically different in many ways from those of Europe. Indeed Bin Laden followers are, in effect, conducting a cultural war in the belief that their people are endangered by American morals and values that will take them over, just as Coca-Cola and McDonald's have conquered the globe. Compare the two cultures and suggest behavioural guidelines for an international marketer trading between the two.

The marketer should recognize that while many social mores and customs are deeply rooted, others are in the process of change, for example, the cult of instant gratification and an emerging compensation culture:

o *Role of women* – The primacy of the domestic and maternal role has declined relative to work and career. Smaller families and enhanced parental aspirations have freed resources for girls to pursue higher education. Changing female stereotypes are reflected in advertisements where the subjects are less likely to enthuse about the relative merits of detergents and more prone to be confident and assertive. For the marketer, the working woman provides extra discretionary purchasing power to the household and has increasing influence over its disposal. Demand for property, consumer durables and holidays have been sustained by these incomes while work and domestic pressures have put a premium on time and its effective management.

Convenience foods, time-saving appliances and the combined versatility of the freezer and the microwave have transformed food preparation with many meals being taken separately and 'on the run'. A recent Mintel survey shows that convenience meals now account for the largest slice of the market at over 30 per cent. Traditional roasts are in decline while pizza sales have doubled in a decade. Central heating and instant warmth at the flick of a switch have extracted the drudgery from another basic household function. Lifestyle and mail-order catalogues and one-stop shopping are other necessary innovations to enable the management of enlarging household consumption within the declining non-work time available. The need to be satisfied here is to enable the household to maximize work and leisure by economizing on the non-productive time required to service them.

Exam hint

Many CIM candidates are women, so given that the examiner will wish to appeal to all constituencies of the target candidate market, from time to time, expect an occasional question on the role of women.

---

o *Religious values* – The same religion may be practised across national boundaries, for example, Catholicism is followed by majorities in Eire, Spain, Poland, Chile and the Philippines but culture varies significantly. Religion is also idealistic and prescriptive rather than descriptive of actual living. Buddhism teaches moderation and abhors violence yet Myanmar is 85 per cent Buddhist with Animist, Muslim, Hindu and Christian minorities. In Islamic countries, religious authorities have far greater influence than in, say, the USA. Fundamentalist groups in Egypt, Chechnya and elsewhere, are seeking to assert religious values over economic ones and they challenge the rights of governments to impose and implement a legal system. Such influences would certainly inhibit the effectiveness of the international marketer in the countries concerned. Perhaps the marketer has much to learn from some of the world's more significant religious festivals. The Maha Kumbh Mela attracts an estimated 70 million Hindu pilgrims every 12 years. To bathe in the Ganges on one of the six astrologically auspicious days is said to wipe away the sins of seven lifetimes. This would appear to be a rather powerful and unique selling proposition.

Church attendance in Britain has fallen sharply in the last 25 years to stabilize at around 7 per cent (40 per cent in the USA), reflecting declining religious values among post-war age groups and secularization. The latter supposes continuing belief, but the absence of its formal expression in places of worship and reflects the increasing mobility of households and an array of possible family activities on Sundays have provided alternatives and the means to satisfy them. The rising ownership of cars and television and a parallel decline in the cohesion of many local communities have also contributed to the erosion. Eventual success in the Sunday Opening campaign in late 1993 was the culmination of these forces for change, opening a vast new market for large retailers and do-it-yourself stores. The fact that the IKEA catalogue has a circulation four times that of the Bible (110 million copies) is a telling reflection of these cultural changes. On the other hand, fast-growing membership of new 'religions' may reflect a trend of individualism and diversity in cultural terms.

o *Healthy living and fitness trends* – Natural foods were mainly the realm of eccentric hippies up to 20 years ago. Smoking was also the norm and thought to symbolize maturity and sophistication. Attitudes in high-income societies are markedly different today with widespread concern over heart disease, cancer, obesity and lack of exercise.

Rich countries appear to be dividing into an over-weight majority underclass and a super-healthy minority elite. Children growing up on high calorific diets of fast food and computer-based leisure activities have led the World Health Organization to predict that 50 per cent of British adults will be obese within 20 years.

Insight

The boom in organic food

Organic means that no chemical fertilizers or pesticides have been used in food production, that crops have been rotated and fertilized only with manure and animals are reared without antibiotics or growth hormones. Despite claims there is no conclusive evidence that it is healthier or tastes better and any advantages may be more than offset by the fact that high prices deter consumers from eating sufficient quantities.

With price premiums of over 50 per cent for organically labelled food, it is not surprising that it has become one of the fastest growing segments of the British grocery market. As product lines have expanded so sales have grown from virtually nothing to £1.2 billion in less than 20 years. Four-fifths is imported with only a minimal percentage of domestic farms being certified by the Soil Association as 'organic'.

Its roots may be found in the counterculture to modern agribusiness and the 'evils' of junk food. Organic farming certainly promotes greater biodiversity, but is more land extensive. The concept may also be hijacked by big business, as in the US, due to its profitability. Minimal standards set by the EU have also allowed supermarket groups to exploit organic grey areas (e.g. source eggs from chickens fed with organic grain but in factory farm conditions!). Indeed, such has been the negative publicity that belief in the 'goodness' of such foods is falling especially among the young.

Although jogging as an activity may have waned, fitness clinics and the pseudo-image provided by designer sports wear provide symbolic substitutes. 'Appearances' are increasingly important to all generations and offer complex but profitable marketing opportunities. Note the 30 per cent annual growth rate of cosmetic operations in Brazil, second only to the USA, where 25 per cent of face fixing and stomach tightening occurs among men aged 19–34. The younger age groups, in particular, have a strongly developed image consciousness although children may face lower life expectancy due to their dependence on convenient and trendy junk foods. Similarly Japanese research suggests that figure conscious girls may develop smoking behaviour if they believe it encourages weight loss. Despite heavy advertising fruit and vegetable intake in the age group up to 18 is half that recommended by nutritionists while salt intake is double. Marketers of savoury snacks, oven chips and fizzy drinks should perhaps beware of an eventual backlash.

Marketing environment in practice

A 2004 Commons report suggests obesity has risen 400 per cent in 25 years with 1 in 2 adults currently over-weight and the same proportion in prospect for children by 2020 (worldwide the figure is 300 million obese adults including 25 per cent of the Middle East population). Direct medical costs are £3.5 billion and rising along with the incidence of diabetes and heart disease. Causes range from eating more (junk food) and exercising less (800 less calories burned per day). The marketing of junk foods in supermarkets also stand accused of promoting 'pester power', with up to 75 per cent of spontaneous food purchases being traceable to an insistent child. The average American is ten pounds heavier than a decade ago causing US airlines to spend an estimated $275 million a year extra on fuel.

On the other hand, the number of Americans (11 per cent) on low-carbohydrate diets, such as Atkins, are now so large that sales of eggs in Ohio are enjoying a boom while potato producing Idaho is in crisis. Similarly, world cheese stockpiles are at their lowest since 1971 due largely to Atkins driven consumption doubling the value of output in 2 years to $45 billion. The implications for Pizza companies have been significant.

Cultural change, therefore, equals marketing opportunities. Think of the fortune to be made if you could market a risk-free pill that would make the customer thinner and provide a super suntan into the bargain. Well, a range of so-called 'Barbie pills' have recently been marketed that guarantee to make you 'browner, thinner and friskier!'. They are a synthetic version of a natural hormone called alpha-MSH, originally developed as a protection from skin cancer by inducing an immediate tan. Nature, of course, triggers the production of melatonin when we are naturally exposed to sunlight, but it normally comes too late to protect us from sunburn. By introducing the synthetic version in advance of your holiday you are tanned before you leave. Other potentially important side effects of melatonin are those on the hypothalamus, the part of the brain related to sexual arousal, and also on appetite reduction. As the packaging points out: 'One a day . . . and it works for Ken too'.

Social class

One way of classifying groups within society is according to the class or strata they occupy. A class comprises individuals with a defined status and who share common characteristics including wealth, occupation, income level, educational background and various aspects of lifestyle. For the marketer it is not always the actual social class an individual belongs to that is significant but rather the class they identify with or aspire to.

Open educational access, mobility and rising incomes have facilitated class movement. Even in a class-based society like Britain, studies find that more than 50 per cent had moved class through their lives.

There is, however, an 'underclass' at the bottom of society, from which few escape, especially the one-quarter of all children growing up in the 1990s in families with no adult in employment. Indeed under global capitalism the gap between richest and poorest is getting wider and particularly in the USA where divisions are on ethnic lines. However, 80 per cent of Americans do not resent the rich and believe that people who work hard are likely to succeed.

Class and class aspirations are important since shared values, attitudes and behaviour will be reflected in purchasing preferences and form one of the most widely used methods of segmenting product markets. Examples of widely used categorizations based on class include the JICNAR social grade definitions:

Social class category	Occupation
A (upper middle)	Professional, administrative, top management, for example, directors, barristers
B (middle)	Intermediate professional, managerial, for example, marketing manager, lecturer
C1 (lower middle)	Supervisory, clerical and lower management
C2 (skilled working class)	Skilled manual, for example, crafts
D (working class)	Semi- and unskilled manual
E	State pensioners, long-term unemployed, and so on

An upper class based mainly on wealth is superimposed on this classification. It is important to the marketers of luxuries since a quarter of total wealth is in the hands of 1 per cent of the population. A1 households earning over £100 000 p.a. number 180,000 of which half are foreign according to a credit survey.

Question 5.8

Key skills: interpreting information

- ○ Critically appraise the usefulness of the above classification system.
- ○ Is there an alternative approach to segmenting socioeconomic groups that is more appropriate?
- ○ Is your buying behaviour more related to your income or the social class to which you aspire?
- ○ The classification is based solely on occupation and ignores the fact that changing wage relativities have altered comparative purchasing power. Some C2s are better off than many C1s and Bs, for example, and this is reflected in purchases. Some do not easily fit into the classification (e.g. if living on inherited wealth).
- ○ An alternative classification would be to select specific classes (e.g. upper middle, lower lower, etc.) and define the households concerned in terms of source and size of income, place of residence, type of work, core attitudes and so forth.
- ○ Classes tend to have distinct/symbolic/recognizable product and brand preferences.

In mass urban centres where people are unable to get to know one another with the closer intimacy possible in small communities it is unsurprising that symbols are adopted to signal who we are and where we stand in society's pecking order. We classify those we meet on the type and quality of clothes they wear, the cars they drive, their sports and social activities, the houses and localities they live in as well as their manner, speech and the type of job they do. These are, in effect, badges of class membership and therefore vital pattern indicators for the marketer to recognize and mobilize in focused promotional campaigns.

Reference groups

Related to class is the concept of the reference group whose actions and behaviour influence the attitudes and values of large numbers of others who seek to imitate them. Reference groups may be large or small and include:

- ○ The family
- ○ Student peer group and/or work colleagues
- ○ Club members.

Since most individuals wish to 'belong' to certain preferred groups they will tend to conform to the norms of dress and behaviour laid down by them. Those within the group whose influence over what is and is not acceptable is substantial are known as opinion formers or leaders. Their influence may be based on expertise, knowledge or perhaps a charismatic personality. If a business can persuade such leaders to adopt their product then 'opinion followers' will also tend to purchase. Little wonder that sports equipment manufacturers secure endorsements from top players; use their product and you can be a winner too!

Movie makers are also getting in on the act, although Reebok's legal action arising from an altered film ending suggests potential conflicts between art and commercialism. Potentially more worrying is the assertion that the average American child has by the age of 18, seen 40 000 movie or television murders and 200 000 acts of violence. It may therefore be reassuring to learn that Coca-Cola signed the biggest marketing promotion in history (so far!) when it paid £95 million for the right to use the Harry Potter logo on its cans. Already translated into 47 languages with sales of over £110 million in 200 countries *The Philosopher's Stone* promotes a counterculture of modesty, fair play, sportsmanship and indignation with injustice.

Marketers must identify the relevant reference groups in the segments they have targeted, especially where expensive purchases (relative to the group's income) involving conspicuous consumption are concerned. The need to 'keep up with the Joneses' or emulate members of a reference group to whom the consumer aspires is a powerful basis upon which to charge premium prices, not least to reinforce the implicit snob appeal involved.

Marketing environment in practice

One of the best examples of the power of promotion is that of modern day Santa Claus. Notwithstanding pagan origins and the cult of St Nicholas, his modern-day appearance dates only from 1931. It was then that Coca-Cola Inc. decided to design a new Christmas advertisement campaign. Its inspiration lay in making over Santa in the company's corporate colours of red and white. A plump and bearded former employee was selected as the model for the campaign.

The family

The family is a close and influential reference group. It conditions behaviour and values from birth and continues to influence buying decisions throughout the individual's life. This led to the identification of a *family life cycle* made up of different stages or phases in family life with significant implications for buying behaviour:

- *Young unmarried* – Young and footloose with relatively high disposable income due to limited commitments. Fashion and entertainment orientated.
- *Newly married/no children* – Becoming outdated with a third of all cohabiting couples being unmarried. Dual income with expenditure focused on home building, consumer durables and holidays.
- *Young married/children* – Again 40 per cent of babies are now born out of wedlock in Britain. Home and family expenditure orientated. Limited scope for entertainment/luxury items.
- *Middle-aged married/teenage children* – Approaching maximum dual earnings, high replacement expenditure on quality durables.
- *Older married/children left home* – Disposable income at a peak and focused on retirement planning and luxuries. Well-established tastes and preferences in many cases.
- *Older retired/single* – Reduced disposable income but increasingly numerous and affluent. Conservative tastes and less susceptible to marketing campaigns. Important purchasers of one-off items like cars, holiday homes and expensive garden equipment.

Activity 5.5

Key skills: collecting information

Scan the advertisements in newspapers and magazines and classify their appeal according to (a) reference groups and/or (b) family stages.

In understanding the family and its spending decisions marketers should seek to identify not only who makes the final purchasing decision but also the influence exerted by other family members. Only in this way can they be sure as to whom they should direct their promotional messages. Who is it that decides the type and location of this year's family holiday? Do parents decide on style of dress or their teenage children? Are changes taking place in the distribution of this decision-making power as more married women work and men share the domestic responsibilities?

Stereotyped notions of the male deciding the type of car and home improvements while the female decides the food and furnishings may be increasingly suspect and the business must keep a finger on the changing social pulse if the marketing mix is to remain relevant and effective. That said, a recent edition of *Social Trends* saw little evidence of 'New Man' emerging among younger age groups. The division of roles in households persists, with mothers spending six times as long cooking and cleaning and twice as long shopping.

The Japanese family, once the model of togetherness, is also disintegrating under the weight of multiple TVs, phones, video-recorders, Play Stations and PCs. Surveys suggest that like their European counterparts, Japanese children are no longer eating with their parents nor wish to participate in family activities. The longer-term consequences on culture of such social isolation remain to be seen.

Lifestyle

Lifestyles are defined as the patterns in which people live, spend time and money. They are a function of the individual's motivation and prior learning as well as class, personality and other variables. They are measured by analysts, using *attitude, interests and opinions* (AIO) alongside demographic factors to establish market segments with clusters of common characteristics.

The central idea is to build a picture of how individuals interact with the environment around them by identifying their behavioural patterns. This will then allow marketers to segment the market more effectively and tailor campaigns designed to appeal to particular lifestyle types. The presumption is that these groups will respond to different marketing mixes that can then be exploited to advantage.

Companies such as Laura Ashley and Next have used such analysis to drive their marketing communications and encourage readers of their catalogues to identify with a particular cluster and therefore focus their purchasing behaviour on the products offered. Websites exploiting segmentation opportunities include www.style365.com which specializes in luxury goods with links to 'gold pages' such as Aspreys & Garrard, while www.littleblackdress.co.uk delivers to your door within 24 hours. Selection is by mood or fabric with advisers available for a 'personalized' service. For multi-million celebrities, Dubai are creating by 2008 three hundred man-made island properties designed to look like a map of the world and costing from £3.5 to 20 million each.

The marketer must, however, avoid oversimplified categorization. Individuals may exhibit multiple lifestyle characteristics or evolve from one type to another as time and circumstances alter. Companies may wish to customize their own lifestyle segments or use generic categories such as strivers, aspirers, achievers and succeeders.

 Activity 5.6

Key skills: using information

Consider the realism of the following lifestyle trends and their implications for niche furniture manufacturers and retailers:

Instant gratification	Live now pay later
Easy credit attitudes	To finance the good life now!
Time conservation	Critical resource constraint on consumption
New work ethic	Working to live, not living to work
Consumerism	Concern for price/quality/service/environment
Personal creativity	Desire for self-expression/improvement
Naturalism	Return to nature but retaining material comforts

What other lifestyle trends can you currently identify in society?

A summary of segmentation bases in consumer markets

The main types of segmentation considered so far have been:

- Geographic: Region, climate, density
- Lifestyle
- Demographic: Age, gender, race, nationality and religion; Income and education; Family size and life cycle; Occupation and social class.

The final aspect to consider is geodemographic segmentation based on *neighbourhood and type of dwelling.* As a composite index of factors relevant to buying behaviour this is thought to represent a more accurate assessment than those based solely on one factor such as class or income. A well-used example of this approach is the ACORN system (i.e. A Classification of Residential Neighbourhoods), which classifies households into one of 11 major groups and 36 specific neighbourhood types and is used by companies such as IKEA, the Swedish furniture retailer, to analyse its customer base. Other examples of such databases include PIN (pinpoint identified neighbourhoods) and MOSAIC.

Final thoughts on culture

- Culture is a complex blend of acquired values, beliefs, attitudes and customs that provide context, conditioning and behavioural guidelines for life in society.
- A national culture is usually composed of subcultures based on such considerations as origins, religion or some basis of shared outlook and values.
- Subcultures form important bases for segmentation whether on regional (e.g. Welsh), urban (e.g. Bradford, Pakistani) or locality (e.g. Jewish community, North London) grounds.
- Individuals from different cultures are likely to respond to different imperatives in terms of what, where, when and how they buy goods and services.
- Ample data exist for analysis of purchasing variations related to regional cultural differences. *Regional Trends* is compiled by the ONS and may be supplemented by market research often derived from the regional television companies.
- While the South East with its concentration of higher-income households may provide useful insight into future buying trends in other less prosperous regions, the marketer must also recognize the degree to which purchasing behaviour is culturally driven.

Implications for marketers

- Take care in classifying people into different groups/segments for marketing purposes, since many of the divisions/ behavioural assumptions are generalizations and subject to change.
- If it is an individual's perceptions and aspirations that drive purchasing decisions, rather than their objectively defined status, then prediction is much more hazardous.
- Complex family structures rule out the use of the occupation of the so-called 'head of the family' as an indicator of purchasing potential. Flexible work patterns also compound these difficulties.
- Society is becoming progressively better educated, with lifelong learning the dawning reality. Marketers must adjust their attitudes and communication methods accordingly.
- Social, cultural and demographic factors influence incomes, tastes and preferences, all important demand determinants. Equally they may inhibit purchase decisions.
- Distinguish a customer's beliefs (conclusions based on available objective facts and subjective experience) from their values. Values are more generalized, deep seated and enduring. Greens are good for you may be a belief, but vegetarianism values life itself.
- Products can acquire cultural meaning through the marketing process, for example, designer clothes or a BMW in an achiever's lifestyle.
- The changing role of women is making more promotional spending gender specific, as seen, for example, in car advertisements.

Summary

In this unit we have seen:

- The importance to the marketer of monitoring and understanding the implications of demographic changes. These change slowly over time but their cumulative impact over a period can have immense consequences for buying patterns.
- Relevant factors in population structure and their effects on market supply and demand.

- o Important employment trends, with emphasis on the drive for greater business flexibility.
- o The changing role of women in work and society and the ongoing impacts of this transformation.
- o The meaning of the term 'culture' and its relevance to international/regional marketing.
- o Some of the more important social trends and the marketing lessons to be learnt from them.
- o The significance of social influences such as class, occupation and lifestyle as bases for segmentation, with particular attention to reference groups such as the family.

Further study and examination preparation

Alternative forms of examination question provide ample scope for the examiner to select at least one factor or trend from the social, demographic and cultural environment. Question 5.1 and Question 5.3 provide your first examples of the compulsory cases. The first is based on McDonald's and is relevant to the above discussion of obesity as well as the concept of culture. The second case refers to class and marketing opportunities. Your tutor will have advised you of the importance of the case, reflecting as it does the breadth of the syllabus. I suggest that you read quickly through the case article and then read all four questions carefully. Underline key words and remember you only have, say, 15 minutes for each part after re-reading the case so *stick closely to what the question asks for*! Note that key terms are highlighted in bold for easy reference.

Extending knowledge

Palmer and Hartley, *The Business and Marketing Environment*, McGraw-Hill – Chapter 9, The Social and Demographic Environment. See also A. Palmer, *The Business Environment*, McGraw-Hill – Chapter 11, and C. Handy, *The Age of Unreason*, Hutchinson.

For websites see *Social Trends* at www.statistics.gov/onlineproducts/default.asp#social (and #population)

http://unstats.un.org/unsd/demographic/social/population.htm for UN population data

www.emap.co.uk/cso/ for census information

http://www.worldbank.org/dat/databytopic/population.html for World Bank population data

www.sosig.ac.uk/ is a gateway to the social sciences

www.cec.lu/en/comm/eurostat/eurostat.html for European statistics

Exam question 5.1

Please see Question 1d, December 2003. Go to www.cim.co.uk for specimen answers.

Exam question 5.2

Please see Question 5, June 2004. Go to www.cim.co.uk for specimen answers.

Exam question 5.3

Please see Question 1b, June 2004. Go to www.cim.co.uk for specimen answers.

Exam question 5.4

In the context of the marketing environment, explain the impact and marketing implications of two of the following terms:

(a) Consumerists
(b) New entrants into an industry
(c) Ageing population   (Q7 June 2001)

 (i) Divide your answer equally between impact and marketing implication using a bullet point format with examples from the marketing environment
 (ii) Refer to the Insight on ageing and review your understanding of consumerism from Unit 2 and new entry from Unit 3.

unit 6
the economic and international environment

Learning objectives

By the end of this unit you will be able to:

o   Understand the basic workings of the economy (3.4)

o   Evaluate measures of economic activity and the limitations of economic indicators (3.4)

o   Understand the nature of macroeconomic objectives and the role of government

o   Assess the likely effects of alternative economic and trade policies (3.4)

o   Evaluate economic impacts and implications for marketers in different types of organization

o   Identify the implications of the international environment (3.4).

Study Guide

The economic environment is one area where we all have first-hand experience. Not only do we read the newspapers and listen to items on television or radio, we also feel the direct impact of economic events such as rising taxes at budget time, a falling interest rate or a pay freeze. However, a little knowledge is said to be a dangerous thing, and we need to set our day-to-day experience within a framework of understanding as to how the economy works.

Macroeconomics is about the aggregate behaviour of consumers, businesses and governments. Concern is with the general price level rather than individual product prices, and attention focuses on the total output, income and spending. The rate of economic growth is of central importance as are cyclical fluctuations around this trend.

Businesses must take very careful account of this environment since decisions on capital investment, the timing of a new product launch or hiring and firing, for example, will need to be set against the general economic background. Unanticipated movements in interest or exchange rates can quite literally convert expected profit into crippling loss.

The economy is a complex open system and the marketer who can master the diagnosis of current economic problems and anticipate the direction of policy changes will possess an edge over rivals. An 'economic way of thinking' is a useful attribute for you to develop!

The international environment is also increasingly familiar to us, not only through our travels but also by membership of trade blocks such as the EU, Afta, SAARC and Nafta.

Civilizations through the mists of time have prospered as a result of trade. Recognition of the gains to be made from exchanging surpluses with a relatively low value in the domestic market for scarce and desirable products from foreign lands led, in the seventeenth century, to the development of international trading companies and then colonial empires. International trading networks now form a tightening web of linkages between all corners of the globe with multi-national subsidiaries the nearest modern equivalent of a colonial outpost.

Trade today is more complex with multilateral exchanges facilitated by international finance. Global e-commerce is the current unknown as regards its ultimate significance. Participating nations and businesses are also increasingly vulnerable to global political and economic influences – the fallout from the September 11th attacks is both global and continuing.

The international environment presents the marketer not only with considerable opportunities but also with greater challenges than the domestic market. As with your own economy, it is important you have a clear appreciation of your country's international trade position. Is its balance of payments in surplus or deficit? What is it's pattern of trade with other countries and the composition of its imports and exports? Does it belong to a trading block and, if so, what regulations govern its internal and external relationships? CIM is a qualification undertaken by students from at least 36 countries from around the world. The global environment forms a context common to all and may provide more than its fair share of questions as a result.

This is an area where there is no shortage of information so you will have to be selective in what you file. Your goal is to develop the ability to provide an outline economic assessment of your own country, assess and give examples of economic policy impacts on business and marketers, understand the implications of being an open economy and finally to evaluate how a business should respond in varying economic circumstances.

Government economic objectives

Governments, like businesses, have a number of objectives ranging from social concerns to national security. In the economic realm it has one overriding goal:

- Faster and more sustainable economic growth *plus* three other objectives that might otherwise constrain its achievement.

    - Maintaining higher levels of employment or 'real' jobs.
    - Controlling inflation at very low levels and avoiding deflation.
    - A favourable balance of payments averaged over a period.

Subsidiary goals might include:

- Keeping the aggregate tax burden below 40 per cent of GDP
- Restricting the budget deficit to 3 per cent of GDP (Euro-zone limit for members)
- Balanced regional development, resource conservation and concern for the environment
- Distribution of income reflecting equity, economic contribution, and so on
- A competitive exchange rate.

Exam hint

Improving own learning and performance

To help focus your mind on the syllabus content and pattern of questions posed draw a matrix of syllabus elements and examination series against which you place a tick or number if a question was included. The resulting grid enables you to identify patterns, trends and possible bankers at a glance. Your examiner will be using one to ensure syllabus coverage over a run of papers.

Economic growth and development

This is the fundamental objective because a growing economy allows a government to achieve other goals requiring resources, to resolve allocational conflicts and, most importantly, to win re-election. An electorate that experiences real increases in purchasing power, job opportunities and spending on health, education, defence and pensions is more likely to vote for the return of the party in office. They say that oppositions do not win elections, governments lose them, and failing to deliver improvements in living standards is often the main cause.

Real growth in Britain may have been higher (3.2 per cent in 2004 compared to 1.8 per cent in the EU), and more sustained recently, but has averaged around 2.25 per cent since 1945. This was less than that achieved in France or Germany and significantly below growth averages in East Asia (until the 1997–98 Asian crisis struck) and many developing economies. The primary economic objective is to raise overall performance while limiting fluctuations around the trend. Sustaining continuous growth by better economic management, and so avoiding recessions, should create an atmosphere of investment confidence and more positive expectations for the future. This will be reinforced by encouraging entrepreneurship and innovation through tax incentives.

Growth does not always mean rising consumption even though this accounts for two-thirds of aggregate demand. An export- or investment-led rise in output will do little to raise domestic consumption in the short term but is normally much healthier for longer-run competitiveness. Also distinguish between an increase in GDP, which is achieved by employing spare or unemployed resources and real growth, sustained by rising productivity through investment in skills, infrastructure, capital and new technology. Poorer countries are more concerned with economic development involving a transformation of economy from one based on primary production to one based on manufactures, services and information technology. This will usually require external funds to finance the dramatic improvements required in both the skill base and basic infrastructure.

Economic growth as an objective has attracted growing criticism because of externalities arising from it. Concern has focused on non-renewable resource depletion and greenhouse effects arising from the combustion of carbon fuels in power stations and vehicles. Projected growth, particularly in developing countries, is expected to expand greenhouse gases and raise the temperature of the planet. Melting polar ice caps will raise sea levels and disrupt climatic conditions with potentially damaging side effects on living standards. Acid rain, ozone depletion, oil and chemical spillages, industrial pollution and rising congestion are just some of the other 'bads' associated with economic growth. Adoption of the 1997 Kyoto protocol limiting carbon dioxide emissions has not been helped either by the re-election of President Bush or the observation by the French president that each American emits three times more greenhouse gases than a Frenchman.

Question 6.1

Key skills: problem-solving

Is there a solution to the quandary outlined above? If so, what are the marketing implications?

Key concepts

We will consider the other three macroeconomic objectives once concepts have been defined and basic understanding has been established.

Concept 1 – The circular flow of income

This is a simple model for understanding the workings of the economy.

Think in terms of 'flows' between households and businesses, banks, foreigners and governments. These flows are either incomes or expenditures and circulate around the economic system. We can see in Figure 6.1 that households, as the owners of productive resources, receive a flow of income from firms who employ them to produce goods and services.

Households use this income (i.e. wages, salaries, rents, interest and distributed profit) to purchase goods and services from firms. This flow of expenditure is demand for the products of the firms and the revenue received meets the cost of inputs for the next round of production.

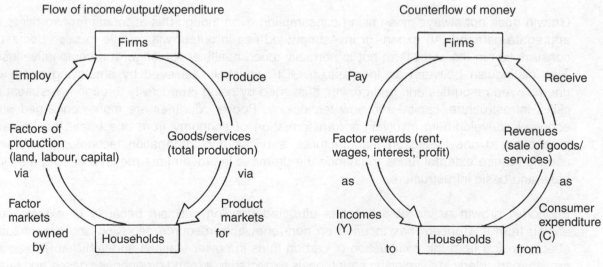

Figure 6.1 The circular flow of economic activity

- ○ Now imagine economic activity as a circulating flow of 'liquid' spending power that can be increased with injections or reduced by leakages of expenditure. If all income received by households is spent then the flow (of activity) continues period after period, but realism suggests that they will normally tend to save. Unless this 'leakage' is re-channelled into the circular flow, the level of the flow will fall because of lower demand for goods and services. Firms cut back on employment and as incomes fall, households will save more as a precaution against unemployment causing activity levels to fall further. The paradox of thrift suggests saving is a good thing and happiness cannot be achieved by spending more than income. Yet saving without corresponding investment leads to lower income and employment and therefore unhappiness.

° In practice, savings are not normally hoarded, but are deposited in financial institutions to earn interest. These funds are lent to households or firms (as investment) and re-injected back into the flow. So long as the investment injection balances the savings leakage, the equilibrium in the flow is maintained. Investment creates additional demand for the producers of plant, equipment and supplies, but is there any guarantee that sufficient aggregate demand will occur to sustain production at the desired level? Unfortunately those who invest are seldom those who decide on what to save.

Question 6.2

Key skills: problem-solving

Can you think of a mechanism that might bring savings and investment to equality at the equilibrium level? Do you think this mechanism will work quickly and effectively?

What is the condition for equilibrium or stability in the circular flow?

To complete our circular flow and make it fully realistic we introduce flows to the government and the rest of the world (Figure 6.2). Households pay taxes on income and expenditure and these are leakages from the flow. Similarly, spending on imported goods and services creates demand for the output of foreign firms. Government spending and exports are injections of purchasing power into the flow, creating demand for domestic firms. Equilibrium is where $S+T+M=I+G+X$, so if injections exceed leakages then income, output and expenditure will rise (until equilibrium is restored) as firms respond to excess demand by producing more and vica versa. It is aggregate demand that drives domestic activity levels (determines employment/income) and is the sum of $C+I+G+X-M$.

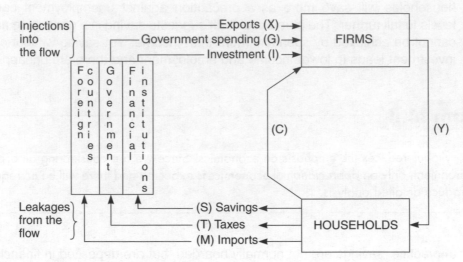

Figure 6.2 The full-economy model of injections and leakages

Concept 2 – The multiplier effect

An extra injection of government or investment spending may actually increase the level of income in the flow by more than the initial expenditure. The injection creates demand for extra output which requires businesses to employ more resources, given they are available. This generates new incomes which are paid to households. Households receiving this income pay taxes, buy imports and save but the rest is spent on domestic consumer goods and services at the second round of the process. Affected businesses produce more output to meet this demand, more resources are brought into employment and incomes are paid out to households and the process repeats.

Leakages determine the ultimate size of the multiplier. The higher these are as a proportion of the circular flow, the lower the multiplier value and vice versa. The multiplier also works in reverse, as falling injections (e.g. reduced exports) cause a cumulative fall in income, output and jobs down the supply chain.

Question 6.3

Key skills: metrics

The multiplier may be defined as:

$$\frac{\text{Change in national income}}{\text{Change in injection}}$$

It may also be expressed as:

$$\frac{1}{\text{Leakage ratios}}$$

If the Italian economy has the following leakage ratios, calculate the value of the *realistic multiplier* for a E5 billion project to build a 3 mile bridge linking Sicily to the mainland:

Taxes 0.4; imports 0.2; savings 0.1

If your government decided to cut the tax bill by $5 billion would the size of the tax multiplier effect be smaller or larger than the investment multiplier?

Concept 3 – The accelerator effect

The *accelerator* reinforces the effect of the multiplier. It arises from the fact that the value of the capital stock (i.e. plant/equipment) is, on average, four or five times as large as the annual value of output. For example, if capital has a useful life of 10 years and total car production of 2 million units is supplied by ten similar-sized plants then average replacement investment, equivalent to one plant, is required each year. Suppose that household demand rises 10 per cent to 2.2 million units. By how much will investment rise?

You may well be surprised at the answer, since a 100 per cent rise in investment spending is substantial and will trigger further multiplier expansions in income.

Study tip

Whether economic news is 'good' or 'bad' depends on the recipient. A rise in interest rates might trigger a media headline *interest rate gloom* and yet savers will be very pleased indeed.

Concept 4 – Inflationary and deflationary gaps

If there is insufficient aggregate demand to enable all businesses to operate profitably using available resources in an economy, a deflationary gap exists putting downward pressure on average prices. Alternatively, if aggregate demand exceeds the amount necessary to secure employment of available resources, an inflationary gap would exist. General prices would tend to rise to ration out the available supply of goods, given sufficient money was in circulation to fuel the process.

Question 6.4

Key skills: problem-solving

If your economy, along with other trading partners, is stuck in a deep recession with activity levels falling and unemployment climbing to disturbingly high rates:

o   Which of the aggregate demand components would you expect to rise, fall or stay unchanged, and why?
o   Which component(s) could be altered?
o   Would falling interest rates, exchange rates and wage rates:

    –   Increase activity levels in the short run?
    –   Increase activity rates in the long term?

Insight

What is the short-term economic future?

Following the Bush re-election and continuing instability of Iraq:

Factors for recession

Oil prices surged to over $55 a barrel due to Middle East uncertainties and adverse weather. This was a record high in money terms and such events are almost always associated with a slowdown in the world economy and a surge in inflation. The US trade deficit continues to widen ($55.5 billion or 5 per cent of GDP). If confidence is shaken in the future value of the dollar then interest rates will have to rise and state spending cut to curtail imports. Rapidly rising consumer borrowing as the main engine of growth is unsustainable (currently 120 per cent of disposable income in Britain). As the property bubble bursts and prices start to fall back (UK at the end of 2004) there will be serious damage to consumer spending confidence.

The economic effects of the Tsunami have yet to be fully assessed but negative impacts on travel and tourism should significantly offset the benefits of reconstruction.

The cost of fighting terrorism is a negative factor for economies causing taxes to rise and investors to be more wary. Making good pension shortfalls will also be a drag on company investment while soaring insurance rates are increasing the cost of doing business.

A recession is long overdue and the trigger may be a wave of redundancies as companies finally face the need to fundamentally restructure to new risks and not least the intensifying competition from India and China.

Factors preventing recession

US and Euro interest rates are very low and an open invitation to consumers and firms to keep spending.

Large tax cuts by the Bush Administration may be made permanent to honour re-election pledges while government spending ($126 billion so far in Iraq) continues unabated. The situation in Iraq may deflect attention from rising debt.

With Indian growth outpacing even China in 2004 at 8 per cent p.a. both are providing the world economy with a major boost. Sales of mobiles have risen in India from 6 to 43 million in 2 years while China, after 25 years of sustained growth is set to overtake Britain as the fifth largest economy. It currently contributes one third of world growth but interest rates are now rising to cool down the economy. Growth is still positive (Germany is the exception) if unspectacular in the Euro-zone and Japan.

The importance of gross domestic product (GDP)

The circular flow represents the value of goods and services produced in an economy, and is measured annually in three ways:

1. *National income* – Incomes created from producing the output, e.g. wages, rent, profit
2. *National output* – Sum of final output or the value added by each domestic firm
3. *National expenditure* – Aggregate spending ($C + I + G + X - M$) on national output.

Gross domestic product (GDP) differs from gross national product (GNP) in that this includes 'net income from abroad', although in Britain's case this only represents about 1–2 per cent of GDP. It is much higher in countries like India and Pakistan due to substantial remittances by nationals working in foreign countries.

Marketing environment in Practice

With oil prices recently at record levels, refining might appear to be a profitable business. Consider, however, the classic perfume, Chanel No. 5. This retails at $246 per fluid ounce. The main ingredient of such a perfume is ethanol, which retails at just $40 a barrel. It appears that the marketers of this popular stocking filler have achieved an astonishing mark-up on their product costs!

Gross domestic product is not adjusted for capital used up in the process of producing annual wealth due to difficulties in agreeing its value. Great care is taken, however, to avoid double-counting output or incomes. Only final output is accounted and transfer incomes such as pensions and student grants are ignored. The three measures are so defined as to be conceptually equal to each other, although in practice a balancing item is required to ensure equality. Errors and omissions in data collection make this necessary. If capital consumption is removed from GNP it is then termed net national income.

Exam hint

Improving your performance

Many economic concepts are of value in revision and examination technique. Time is the scarce resource and you must allocate it efficiently. Opportunity cost means that additional hours spent on one subject means fewer hours to spend on the others. Allocating time between questions in the exam requires the equi-marginal principle. Aim to achieve a position where you could not improve on your overall mark by trading more time on one question for less on another.

The uses of national accounting data

In Britain the Office for National Statistics (ONS) collects and publishes the data in the *Blue Book*. The information provides the basis for forecasts and analysis of the health of an economy. The Treasury has developed a sophisticated computer-based model to predict the future path of the economy and upon which the government will partly base its policy judgements.

GDP figures can provide a measure of the following:

- ○ Gross physical output of goods and services of domestic firms.
- ○ Annual percentage increase or growth in the economy.
- ○ Productivity or GDP per head/capita by dividing GDP by working population.
- ○ Average standard of living by dividing GDP by the general population.
- ○ Comparison of performance between different economies.

Question 6.5

Key skills: metrics

If Sri Lanka's GDP is growing by 3 per cent per annum, and its population is growing by 0.5 per cent while China is growing by 9 per cent and its population by 1.5 per cent, which country is better off?

1. What is the GDP of your economy in local currency terms and how fast is it growing?
2. Does an increase in GDP automatically mean that you are better off?

Care is required when assessing the potential of overseas markets using national income data. Different countries have different values, tastes, needs and proportions spent on armed forces that will affect the amount of available disposable income. Asian economies tend to have higher savings ratios than Europeans, while America's high energy-consuming lifestyle is more than double that of other countries.

The efficiency of governmental statistical agencies also varies widely and exchange rate fluctuations often make comparisons very difficult. In Britain the government recently admitted an £800 million computer related error had warped the statistics. The size of the public sector is also significantly understated due to the failure to include Private Finance Initiative projects worth in excess of £110 billion. Some poorer economies may understate their GDP to attract aid from international agencies while others have very wide disparities in income, making figures on average living standards very misleading. Less-developed economies also tend to have large barter economies, making many transactions difficult to record.

Limitations of the data: are we really better off?

One further reason for caution over the accuracy of the statistics is that GDP data are normally expressed in nominal or current prices terms. If, for example, inflation in China in Question 6.5 was 8 per cent while only 2 per cent in Sri Lanka then the overall position is 0.5 per cent *real* growth for the latter and −0.5 per cent real decline in the former!

Always check if the figures are expressed in nominal or real terms to avoid being misled, that is, GDP at constant prices adjusts for inflation by expressing GDP in terms of prices prevailing in a base year (e.g. at 1997 prices).

Even if all the calculations and estimates were entirely accurate, some problems of interpretation would still remain:

- ○ An increase in exports or investment will not increase *current* living standards.
- ○ An increase in GDP may be due to longer hours or increased female participation rates and involve unaccounted costs in terms of stress, reduced health or less leisure time.
- ○ No account is taken of *externalities* associated with growth such as emissions, effluents and waste. Economic activity to remedy environmental damage (known as defensive expenditures) is actually counted as part of GDP. Measurement of *sustainable* income would also have to take resource depletion into account.
- ○ Gross domestic product increases when people pay for services they would have previously performed themselves. Child-minding, garden maintenance, and laundry are services associated with busy lifestyles but don't represent improvements in living standards.
- ○ No valuation of leisure time or unrecorded activities occurring in the informal economy.
- ○ There is no account of redistribution yet the share of the nation's wealth enjoyed by the richest, 1 per cent, has risen in Britain from a C20th low of 17 per cent in 1991 to 23 per cent.

Gross domestic product is no longer the undisputed measure of economic progress. Although never intended as a measure of welfare its primacy with economists as a tool of analysis tends to obscure its limitations. It does not allow for 'consumption' of non-renewable natural assets or subtract the impact of untreated pollution causing some interest groups to call for an environmentally adjusted measure. Others, like the World Bank, may be leading the way by adopting a single *measure of welfare* that reflects indicators besides income. These might include distribution of income, voluntary leisure time, environmental quality, the standard of health and education, crime levels, employment and informal activities.

You can learn more by logging onto the World Bank website concerned with development economics and the environment (www.worldbank.org/data/wdi/environment.htm).

Exam hint

Improving your performance

The marketing environment provides opportunities to illustrate understanding of the subject by using diagrams or charts. While potentially useful, only provide them if:

- ○ They can be drawn correctly and are relevant to the question.
- ○ Any axes or relationships shown are labelled.

Nothing exposes ignorance of the marketing environment so obviously as an incorrectly drawn relationship!

The business cycle

This refers to the periodic fluctuation in economic activity that occurs in industrialized economies. Left to themselves economies tend to oscillate between periods of high activity, growth in employment and booming confidence as against periods of falling output, rising unemployment and general despondency. This is particularly the case with open economies like Singapore,

Sri Lanka and Britain with a high trade (25–30 per cent) dependency making them especially vulnerable to international shocks. America and Canada, in contrast, have low export and import ratios (10 per cent) and tend to be more stable.

The underlying trend of real GDP growth for the world economy has been firmly upward since the Second World War, particularly in Japan and subsequently in other parts of East Asia. These strongly export-orientated economies have not avoided irregular oscillations particularly during the region's recent crisis. In a global economy part of the fluctuation is due to their interdependence with the main markets they supply. High specialization and focus on a narrow band of products and market segments exposes countries to risks identical to those confronting companies. A downturn in Asian markets or new US trade rules might severely affect German electronic exports or Brazilian textiles.

The business cycle represents the *average* of a multitude of individual industry cycles. Any one business may therefore be in advance or lag the main cycle. The marketer must locate their relative position since published data always refer to the average. The duration of the cycle is also a variable. Up to 1945 it averaged 8 to 9 years in open economies while a less-consistent pattern has prevailed since. Figure 6.3 shows the typical stages of the business cycle.

Recession is defined as at least two successive quarters of *falling* GDP. Unemployment will be rising alongside spare capacity and a widening output gap. Wage and price rises will be difficult to achieve, so inflation will moderate, as will labour militancy. These are difficult times for the marketer since as consumption spending falls, competitive forces will intensify, while budgets come under increasing pressure. Profitability will be declining, business confidence will be low and investment spending depressed. Britain's last recession was as long ago as 1990–92, and the start of 2005 sees unemployment at a 30 year low and inflation at just under 2 per cent. However, we cannot assume the cycle is dead particularly when global unemployment has risen from 0.8 billion to 1 billion since 1995 and factory employment has fallen 15 per cent.

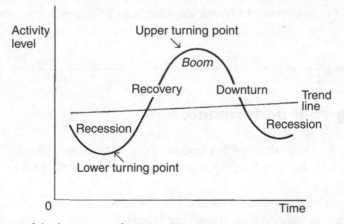

Figure 6.3 The stages of the business cycle

Question 6.6

Key skills: interpreting information

Now identify the key features of the following phases:

○ Recovery
○ Boom
○ Downturn.

The severity and duration of the phases vary from cycle to cycle. Central banks have become more skilled in taming cyclical fluctuations in output and employment but at the price of huge swings in asset prices. There have been a series of 'bubbles' in dot-com stocks, property, commodities and oil as well as unsustainable balance of payments deficits. These may be defined as massive and sustained suspensions of disbelief and if not positively corrected, threaten to end in tears. The best current rule of thumb appears to be the bigger the boom, the bigger the bust with excessive consumer and government spending still threatening a future upper turning point despite recent rises in interest rates.

Marketing environment in practice

Personal debt was, until recently, a taboo for most British families. This is no longer the case with average personal debt of £5300 and rising at 14 per cent per annum. Household debt (credit plus mortgage debt) now averages over £17000, almost equal to total output of £1000 billion. Households typically owe 130 per cent of their annual income, 50 per cent higher than in the unstable boom of 1987–89. Historically low-interest rates have, until recently, kept debt service costs below 10 per cent of disposable income but a series of rate rises have signalled a new reality where such costs will rise very sharply. Many borrowers seemed ignorant of the 40 per cent rise in debt servicing that would occur as interest rates rose, as predicted, towards 5 per cent in early 2005. When the borrowing stops so will the consumer boom and with house prices subsiding it will take an estimated 6 years of sluggish growth or 4 years of zero growth to return debt ratios to a more sustainable 105 per cent of disposable income. Should a 'worst case scenario' of rising taxation, inflation and unemployment combine to explode this unexploded bomb of accumulated debt then expect mortgage arrears and repossessions to rise sharply from their record lows of recent months.

The marketer must anticipate fluctuating economic conditions. Governments tend to underestimate the business cycle and other random influences so the marketer should always be prepared for a shock in either direction that exceeds official forecasts. The upper and lower turning points are the key moments in time to identify since they signal a significant 'sea change' in economic conditions to which the business must actively respond. The upper turning point often occurs more quickly than the lower one. Falling sales and confidence can be contagious in the downturn but slow to ignite in recovery. Once the turning point is passed, the multiplier-accelerator mechanism should progressively move the economy to boom or recession conditions.

 ## Activity 6.1

Key skills: problem-solving

For each phase of the cycle, set out the kind of policies a business should be pursuing. For example, in the *boom* phase, the rate of growth of sales level out as demand bumps along a peak. The firm must remain in stock but all expansion plans should be frozen. Any surplus plant should be sold at this time to realize top prices. New markets may be explored but emphasis should be on controlling costs to meet the gloomier times just around the corner.

If the marketer expects cycles they will not come as a surprise. View them as positive opportunities that can assist new product launches and market penetration if introduced at the right time. The key to success is in timing and the rule of thumb is that the higher and longer the period above the growth trend line, the lower and longer the subsequent period below.

153

Predicting turning points is not easy as demonstrated by the poor performance of highly respected forecasting groups who failed to predict the 1997–98 Asian recession, or its length and then overestimated the speed of recovery! The same may apply in current circumstances but businesses may be able to judge developments more effectively by using two monitoring techniques:

○ *Leading indicators* – Developed in the US these foreshadow change in the pace of the economy by identifying indicators that consistently give advance warning (8–12 months) of upward or downward movement. A composite index is used, normally including the share index, total dwellings started, the rate of interest and the aggregate financial surplus or deficit of all companies. Other less predictable indicators might include the sale of transit vans (a sign of small firm confidence) and commercial vehicles crossing between Malaysia and Singapore. Can you predict real GDP growth in your economy in 2004 using these indicators.

○ *Industry trends survey* – A large representative cross-section of domestic companies is surveyed in depth to measure changes in *business confidence* (e.g. CBI Quarterly Survey of 900 firms). Psychology is important and the famous British economist John Maynard Keynes suggested that the *animal spirits* of capitalism produced alternating phases of optimism and pessimism, both of which tend to feed on themselves! The marketer must always beware of being carried away by such 'herd instincts' that may cause capital spending to fluctuate from over- to under-investment.

Exam hint

Improving your performance

Apply economic thinking to your exam/continuous assessment to focus on the pay-off or marks attached to each part of the question. This is the scoring system that should guide you to the achievement of best allocation of your time. If Part A is worth 5 marks while Part B is worth 10, then economic logic demands nearly double the time and effort be devoted to B.

Investment takes time and is an act of faith in the future. The penalties of a wrong decision are considerable since if the firm commits resources and the market then fails to materialize, or if it does not but demand booms, then market share will be lost to competitors. Environmental changes will often influence expectations and competitive decisions which may be *self-fulfilling* in the short term. If a critical mass of households and businesses *believe* things will improve, and invest and spend on that assumption, then things will, in general, improve, *feeding back* into even more positive expectations. A 'feel good factor' is the expression of such considerations, easy to visualize but economically less easy to achieve. The process can also lead to enormous over-investment, as in the dot-coms and new technology companies up to 2001 and currently in housing.

Having studied the importance of GDP and its tendency to fluctuate around a rising trend, we can now consider the other three major macro objectives. We will then assess the government polices intended to achieve them and their implications for the marketer.

Objectives: higher employment

Full employment was the primary and explicitly stated goal of many governments after 1945. It was seen as a social as well as an important economic objective. Fast growing economies in East and South Asia found it to be an automatic consequence of their developmental process.

This philosophy changed dramatically from the 1970s with the EU suffering over 20 million unemployed by the late 1990s and even Japan accepting its 'inevitability'. Recognition of the need to control inflation was the cause of this loss in priority and unemployment remained high even during periods of economic boom. Fundamental success in the control of inflation has seen a return to near full employment levels in Britain and Eire, but this might be short-lived. The UK rate had fallen to 4.6 per cent by the end of 2004 (compared to 8.9 per cent in the Eurozone) but it had 'lost' 0.75 million manufacturing jobs since 1997 while service employment has risen. However, a record 2.7 million are registered for incapacity benefit. Eire's 'success' has been fuelled by EU subsidies and low-interest rates arising from participation in the single currency but Germany and France have suffered sharply rising unemployment and now lack the freedom to pursue independent vigorous countermeasures.

Unemployment is often referred to as a social and economic evil which can and does impact negatively on businesses:

Economic evil	Social evil
Scarce resources not utilized	Loss of income, status and satisfaction
Tax burden of benefits reduces incentives to work/invest	Relative poverty compared to those in work with affluent lifestyles
Reduces mobility of labour	Alienation from society leading to crime, vandalism and so on.
Reduces purchasing power	Dual society of haves/have-nots
Depresses confidence/risk taking	Young entrants to labour market particularly hard hit

Unemployment is a personal tragedy since work binds us to society and gives meaning to our lives. Not only is our income lost, but also our status, esteem and self-respect. Long-term unemployment affects specific groups such as the young, as employers cease recruitment; the unskilled; ethnic groups and the over-50s; the disabled and those living in inner cities or areas of structural decline. The young are forced to move away from such areas, condemning the latter to unemployment rates double the national average and a downward spiral of decay and producing a marketer's nightmare.

Question 6.7

Key skills: using information

Is unemployment an 'evil' as far as business managers are concerned? Think carefully about this question from the view of your own organization. Think about wage levels, recruitment, discipline and ease of achieving change.

The seeming inability of many governments to achieve permanently lower unemployment and their 'acceptance' of a certain rate as unavoidable was a reflection of a number of factors:

- A rapid rate of technological change – unemployment of those left behind by change.
- Customer orientation, changing tastes, intense competition and shortening life cycles cause rapid structural change that some find it difficult to adjust to.
- Inflow onto the job market exceeding outflow as married women's participation rises.
- The idea of a 'natural' unemployment rate that is consistent with low and stable inflation.
- A more turbulent environment making business focus on job flexibility not security.

These factors can be best understood in terms of 4 main types and causes of unemployment:

1. *Insufficient aggregate demand* – known as cyclical unemployment. Businesses respond to lower orders in recession by cutting overtime, halting recruitment, curtailing the use of contractual labour, layoffs and finally redundancies.

Exam hint

There is no such thing as a 'freebie' in economics and this certainly applies to providing unrequired 'format' or information. Valuable or not the examiner will 'pay' you no marks for them at all!

2. *Imperfect market forces* – prevent labour markets clearing at wage levels where no involuntary unemployment exists. Factors preventing a matching of the supply and demand for different types of labour skill such as lack of qualifications, immobility, discrimination, restrictive employment legislation and poor management. *Frictional* unemployment, for example, arises due to a mismatch between the end of one job and the start of the next for many of the millions of job changers each year. Its duration is short and reflects the mobility of labour in response to vacancies in expanding sectors of the economy.

3. *Relative wages are too high* – if set too high to clear the market due to legal minimum wage levels or union bargaining power then unemployment will result. The productivity associated with the wage paid is also part of this equation. If European wage-for-productivity levels are too high then business will respond by:

   (a) Moving operations to lower-wage countries for example, Dyson.
   (b) Investing in technology as a substitute for relatively expensive labour.

 ## Activity 6.2

Key skills: problem-solving

For each of the types of unemployment being considered, brainstorm possible policies to minimize its occurrence. Ensure each one meets the following requirements:

- The policy will not lead to increased inflation.
- The policy will not lead to inefficiency/uncompetitiveness.
- The policy is consistent with people's needs and wants.

4. *Technological change – new process innovations* typically displaced the tasks performed by semi- and unskilled manual and clerical workers but are now threatening the jobs of middle managers and other knowledge worker groups.

This type of unemployment tends to emerge in the following downturn as obsolete factories are closed. Ever since the Luddites in the early nineteenth century, technology has been viewed by workers as an enemy in the short term even though over time it has created clusters of *new product innovations* that, until recently, have allowed jobs to grow in line with the working population. So long as wants exceed our ability to satisfy them, human resources will be demanded. Machines will specialize in doing what they do best, as will humans.

However, there is now a structural mismatch between those with unwanted skills and abilities in declining industries or where machines have a comparative cost advantage, and skill shortages in high-technology and creative knowledge-based employments. Considerable investment in education and flexible skills will be required if a permanent 'underclass' of the hard-to-employ is not to emerge. Little wonder that education policy is a key issue in election campaigns and one of the top spending priorities. The alternative of large falls in the relative wages of the unskilled will be resisted by unions or prevented by minimum wage legislation as enshrined, for example, in the European Union's social chapter.

Question 6.8

Key skills for marketers: using information

From the point of view of the 'lower-wage economy' assess the positive and negative business impacts of a multinational company transferring its operations there.

Control of inflation

Inflation is a general increase in the average price level that is sustained over a period of time and is usually calculated by changes in a retail price index (RPI). This is measured by a 'basket' of representative goods and services typically consumed by the average household and weighted by their importance in total spending. Some countries distinguish between the so-called 'headline rate' and the 'underlying rate'. The latter excludes exceptional influences such as mortgage interest that tends to inflate the index in times of rising rates.

Inflation has been a persistent problem in many countries for most of the last half century. Governments were often happy to trade off a little more inflation for a little less unemployment. However, from the late 1970s both tended to rise together to unacceptable levels. Known as *stagflation*, this is the worst of both possible economic worlds and one that could once again be threatening some Western economies!

Western leaders like Thatcher and Reagan pledged themselves to control inflation as the central priority even at the expense of sharply rising unemployment. The battle to conquer inflation became a constraint on a government's ability to achieve more growth and jobs. Politically acceptable unemployment became the level that was sustainable without inflation increasing, or rising significantly above levels in the major economies with whom a country competed internationally. The policy was a 'success' in most economies with inflation falling to 30-year lows by 2004. Unfortunately national insurance benefits including pensions are tied to the inflation index in some countries causing politically embarrassing small rises compared to average earnings.

Is inflation a problem from the marketer's point of view?

The answer to this question depends on the rate of inflation involved. If this is slow and predictable then it can be a good thing. *Creeping inflation*, when associated with buoyant high demand, can generate buyer confidence and business investment. Since borrowings are repaid in gently depreciating currency and the value of stocks appreciate, it tends to enhance profitability.

Households experience 'money illusion', whereby they feel better off than they really are as nominal incomes rise. They fail to notice or account for the real value eroding through cost of living rises. This eases the process of change and is preferable to the continuously depressed economic conditions that may be necessary to keep prices from rising at all.

However, once inflation exceeds a critical rate the costs outweigh any possible benefits as:

○ A rapid fall in the value of money hits confidence.
○ Uncertainty over future price levels deters firms from entering long-term contractual commitments and makes future planning very difficult.
○ Arbitrary and unintended redistribution of income occurs:

  – Debtors gain and creditors/savers lose.
  – Fixed income groups like pensioners suffer.
  – Weak bargaining groups are unable to keep pace.

○ Tax allowances erode and rising nominal income means higher tax brackets.
○ Domestic marketers face competitive imports/rising export prices hit foreign sales.
○ Frequent price rises upsets customers with continuous adjustment to lists, packaging, and so on.
○ Prices no longer accurately reflect 'relative' values, confusing the consumer but making them more price sensitive and less responsive to other marketing-mix elements.
○ Investment move to 'unproductive' inflationary hedges for example, gold, antiques, property.
○ Wage groups fight for income shares, disrupting business activity with strikes.
○ It may trigger price wars due to misinterpretation of rival intentions.

Finally, the marketer must remember that what goes up must come down! As inflation accelerates so governments will be forced to drastically reduce demand pressures to restore stability. Curing inflation, with the attendant squeeze on spending, is often worse in its effects than the disease itself! Zero inflationary expectations also make life difficult for marketers being squeezed by cost increases. Price resistance is reinforced by the increasing resort to the 'transparency' of the Internet. Businesses are then left with no option but to raise productivity (and shed jobs) to reduce the cost base. Britain, despite a slowing in the second half is on target for economic growth of nearly 3.4 per cent for 2004, well above its sustainable non-inflationary rate of 2.25 per cent. Given the Chancellors ambitious spending programme, lax monetary policy, oil price increases and rising costs in Iraq, intensifying inflationary pressures seem unavoidable.

Exam hint

Examination questions on the macroeconomic environment frequently test your knowledge and understanding of current economic conditions: changes in growth, employment, inflation, the balance of payments and the *effects* of each on business and the marketer.

The causes of inflation

The marketer needs to appreciate the causes of inflation so that an assessment may be made as to the likely future path of general prices and to avoid being damagingly surprised by sharp changes in their pace or direction. The sources of inflationary pressure originate on both the supply and demand side of an economy:

- ○ *Demand-pull inflation* – Too much spending relative to available productive capacity bids up prices of both inputs and outputs. As wage costs rise these feed into higher prices, prompting further wage demands and creating a wage/price spiral.
- ○ *Monetarist inflation* – Money is the fuel that sustains inflation. If the money supply is not expanded to provide extra cash for higher wages and prices, then interest rates rise, real aggregate demand in the circular flow declines, goods are left unsold and businesses reduce their employment of factors of production. Inflation can only continue at the cost of rising unemployment. Money supply increased by 10 per cent in Britain during 2004.
- ○ *Cost-push inflation* – This occurs when a cost element causes prices to rise but in the absence of any excess demand to justify it. Stakeholders such as employees may push up wages through militant action to increase their real income at the expense of profits. If businesses then raise prices to restore profit margins this reduces the purchasing power of wages and the process repeats, producing a wage/price spiral. Competition between different wage groups to maintain *wage differentials* can also lead to a *wage/wage spiral*.

Marketing environment in practice

Energy shocks

1. Demand for oil had contracted with the 1997 Asian economic crisis causing prices to collapse to $10 a barrel. By the end of 2005 global consumption was rising at its fastest pace for 40 years and prices reached a record $55 a barrel, well above the $30 of the immediate post Iraq war period. Demand was driven by the fast growing Indian and Chinese economies, but consumption was also 25 per cent higher in the slower growing Western economies.

2. Oil is at the centre of the world economy and forms both the lubricant of modern advanced civilization and the means of financing weapons of mass destruction. The attack on a French tanker and threats to interrupt Saudi supplies underlines the vulnerability of Western oil supplies. It is suggested that the current oil price includes a 'terror premium' of up to $8 a barrel.

3. Previous energy shocks had always been good predictors of a global slump to come, that is, recession occurred 12 to 18 months later. The OECD calculates that a $10 rise adds 0.5 per cent to consuming country inflation and reduces growth by a similar margin.

4. It is not in OPEC's interests to provoke a global crisis. High prices trigger recession in the West which feeds back negatively on suppliers (as Sheikh Yamani, the former Saudi oil minister, stated 'the stone age did not end because the cavemen ran out of stone'). Also oil is still a third cheaper in real terms than in 1974.

5. Due to structural shifts from heavy manufacturing industry to services and 'new economy' virtual activities, developed countries use half as much oil per $ of GDP as 30 years ago. However, the more consumers spend on transport, the less they have to spend on other goods and even a weightless 'virtual' economy depends on logistics and just-in-time deliveries.

6. Emerging economies are hit much harder because of their industrialization programmes and increasing ownership of motorized vehicles causing rising oil use per $ of GDP.

7. A low inflation environment makes it difficult to pass on rising fuel costs leading to layoffs and a profits squeeze. Some countries, with very high fuel taxes (e.g. Britain 72 per cent of total price), have witnessed unprecedented demonstrations. However, high fuel prices make sense from an environmental point of view although a blunt instrument. Electronic tolls, as used in Singapore, and now London, offer a more fine tuned result.

8. OPEC is in a price war with Russia and other producers outside the cartel. Russia has sharply increased output to capacity and is currently the world's largest producer ahead of Saudi

Arabia. OPEC knows that any cut in supplies to raise the price will be met by increased supply. History suggests that high prices today produce low ones the day after tomorrow due to greater investment in oil production and energy efficiency. The US government forecasts a doubling in OPEC and a 40 per cent rise in non OPEC oil production by 2025.

9. Energy is a baseline cost for all economies so a 'liberated' Iraq that sought to finance its reconstruction by expanding oil production from its current 2 million barrels to its capacity of 5 million and potential of 8 million would arguably push prices back down.

10. Low prices encourage wasteful consumption (gas guzzling SUVs/pick-ups account over half the US market and add to fuel use/greenhouse gas emissions) and discourage exploration and development for example, drilling in the Alaska National Wildlife refuge (estimated 29 billion barrel reserve) and stimulate the domestic economy by releasing cash to spend elsewhere. They might also de-stabilise countries like Saudi Arabia and Venezuela.

11. Saudi Arabia dominates the world oil market with 25 per cent of global reserves, double that of the second largest producer, Iraq. It is the largest supplier to the US (25 per cent of world oil consumption/imports 60 per cent of its requirements). US oil reserves are just 3 per cent of the total.

12. Over the last 20 years the Saudi economy has suffered generally falling oil prices. A high birth rate has reduced GDP per capita from $28 000 to $7000 and caused unemployment to rise to 18 per cent. It requires a price of $28 per barrel to break even. Discontent is rising among its 14 million people. An estimated 10 000 Saudis have trained at Bin Laden camps and 13 of the 19 hijackers were probably of this origin. Donations of wealthy Muslims, as required under Islam, help finance the Al-Qa'eda network.

13. The world needs a non-nuclear alternative to fossil fuels and the potentially fatal dependence they have created. The Bush Administration, however, refuses to make conservation a part of national policy. Currently they prefer to sustain this central plank of the American dream than break their dangerous addiction to a gas guzzling lifestyle and disarm the oil weapon.

When inflation becomes rapid and uncertain it creates net costs for business and society. It poses difficult marketing-mix problems for the marketer, especially those serving segments most seriously affected. In the extreme, *hyperinflation*, defined as price rises in excess of 50 per cent per month, causes all confidence to be lost in paper money and barter re-emerges.

Consider the recent situation in war-affected Africa or the customer service problems of German café owners in 1923, forced to raise coffee prices while customers sat waiting for their bills. At one stage during the German hyperinflation prices were rising by 5 per cent per hour!

Governments have also learnt that *expectations* adjust as actual inflation is experienced. Any attempt to run an economy at less than the natural or non-accelerating inflation rate of unemployment would cause prices to rise more than expected and compensating wage demands to occur. No permanent trade-off of a little less unemployment for a little more inflation is possible. Inflation would accelerate instead.

Balance of payments

The balance of payments is the systematic annual record of all exchange transactions between the residents of one country and the rest of the world and comprises:

- A *visible* balance of trade – foods/fuels/materials/semi-manufactured/finished goods.
- An *invisible* balance of trade – financial/travel/other services; government transfers; net earnings.

They combine to make the *current* account. A *capital* account reflects net short- and long-term capital movements while a balancing item is included to adjust for data collection errors. The balance of payments must balance, but there is a final balance for official financing which either adds to, or draws from, official currency reserves and borrowing depending on whether a net surplus or deficit arises.

The current account is the best indicator of the long-run health of an economy since it reflects whether an economy is trading successfully. No country can run a persistent current deficit since its reserves would eventually run out, together with the confidence of its foreign creditors. Action would have to be taken well before this point, or, alternatively, be forced on it as condition for a loan from the International Monetary Fund (IMF). However, since the world balance of payments must logically sum to zero, some countries cannot avoid being in deficit at times. What is more important is the cause, whether it is manageable and the direction of change. If a developing country, such as Nigeria, incurs a deficit in order to import investment goods to develop its oil and gas deposits, this will increase productive potential (and exports) in the future (IMF or World Bank loans often support such a rise in productive potential). This is a very different case from a country importing conspicuous consumption goods and living beyond its means. America (5 per cent of GDP) and Britain's (nearly £5 billion) current balances deteriorated sharply in 1999–2004. Britain's trade deficit is a record £34 billion due partly to the loss of the oil surplus, as the UK became a net importer for the first time in 11 years. The balance of payments is not a desirable objective in itself, but rather, as a deficit worsens, it will become a tightening constraint on the government's ability to achieve other macroeconomic objectives. In the short term a deficit can be financed by willing foreign creditors, currency reserves or by raising interest rates to attract foreign capital flows. This will only succeed if creditors believe an offsetting fall in the exchange rate is not imminent. Higher rates will also tend to depress consumer and investment spending, reducing aggregate demand and therefore sales.

Exam hint

Make sure that you know and memorize the current values of the main economic indicators in your own country. Macroeconomic questions frequently ask you to discuss the current or future situations.

Economic indicators

Governments use a wide range of economic indicators to decide on policy changes and monitor their effectiveness as will an independent central bank before deciding interest rate policy. Stock markets react quite strongly to publication of such figures when they diverge from expectations and may cause a fundamental reassessment of the underlying health of the economy. Such indices are equally important for businesses in determining their future marketing plans and policies. Governments have a number of objectives and find that achievement of one goal may conflict with realizing the others, making it necessary to have as many policies as objectives if they are to be mutually accomplished.

Key indicators to monitor include the following:

- o Activity, growth and unemployment rates
- o Inflation and interest rates
- o Trade figures and exchange rates.

161

Activity 6.3

Key skills: collecting and presenting information

State 3 specific indicators you would monitor under each of the key indicator headings.

Economic policies

The main types of policy available for use by a government are

- o   Fiscal and budgetary
- o   Money and credit control
- o   Physical policies – wage and price controls
- o   Supply side
- o   Trade and exchange rate.

The syllabus requires an appreciation, not an in-depth understanding of these policies, so our concern is with their influence on business and the implications for marketing.

Exam hint

Start giving serious thought to the forthcoming examination. One important key to planning a revision schedule is to try to determine possible topics. Note that your paper is set up to a year previously due to the administration required in approving it and ensuring efficient distribution to centres around the world.

What questions would you choose if you were setting an exam paper based on the syllabus and relating it to a dynamic environment? Why don't you brainstorm some possibilities with your tutor? Look at previous papers and think about 'topical' issues when the paper was prepared (and still be relevant 12 months later).

Fiscal and budgetary

Taxation is the main source of revenue for government to finance its budgeted expenditures. Often accounting for 40–50 per cent of national expenditure, the government has an important impact, although if tax revenues are at similar levels the overall effect is broadly neutral. Both are decided in an annual budget and the marketer should monitor this event closely, together with the pre-budget statements.

Government spending and taxation offers a relatively quick and effective means of changing the pressure of demand and therefore activity levels. Extra spending on health and education, for example, impact on demand for a whole range of goods and services so marketers should carefully consider the implications of spending plans as well as actual policy changes because:

- They review performance/set out government economic forecasts/objectives/plans
- Policy actions may be inferred from the objectives set
- Tax and spending changes impact on the circular flow at different points in time
- Targeted tax changes affect specific segments, e.g. child tax credits
- Tax on specific product groups can have serious and selective consequences, e.g. tobacco duties on retailers
- The scope for lobbying activity by special interests e.g. incentives for N Sea exploration
- Measures have ramifications for trends in other macro-environments, e.g labour force participation.

The key requirement of fiscal policy is that it produces sound public finances and so avoids any danger of the government sector being a source of adverse shocks in the economy. Government borrowing has risen by £10 billion more than expected to 35 per cent of GDP, for example, and to remain within the Chancellors 'golden rule' may require higher taxes and spending cuts against a background of slower growth in 2005/06. It can also support monetary policy in containing inflationary pressures or providing the scope for interest rates to fall. The marketer must appreciate the broad intention of these policies while recognizing that projections involve considerable uncertainty.

Marketing environment in practice

- Britain by 2005 has enjoyed its longest period of sustained growth since records began in 1870. It has averaged close to 3 per cent in recent years, well above its long-term average of 2.4 per cent. It has the lowest unemployment, the steadiest inflation and the smallest national debt of the world's major economies. Every 1 per cent growth more or less than the long-term average of 2.4 per cent tends to cause unemployment to rise or fall by 0.3 per cent.
- Plans to increase government spending/pledges not to raise income tax or VAT depend on such growth. Each 1 per cent shortfall in growth represents an £8 billion drop in tax revenues.
- To meet its golden rules that government borrowing should only be for investment and that the budget should balance over the economic cycle suggests that, taxes/national insurance will have to rise in 2005/06.
- Britain cannot afford to lose its 'reputation' for having the most flexible labour markets or being most tax competitive yet business has suffered most of the recent tax increases.
- Germany is radically cutting income taxes by 10 per cent in an effort to 'kick-start' its ailing economy.

Money and credit

This involves control of the supply of money and the credit-creating power of the retail banks. The central bank may seek to control this capability, if it fears that its target for inflation will not be met, by means of:

- Controlling the supply of new money and changing base rates of interest
- Controlling existing money supply by open market operations – selling/buying government securities injects/withdraws money from the banking system
- Cash/liquidity ratio requirements – limit the size of the credit multiplier effect
- Quantitative controls to ration credit
- Lender of the last resort power to enforce base rates.

Such measures can be used to expand or contract money and credit as required, but with a long time lag of up to 2 years. The marketer must estimate the full impact of successive interest rate changes since it takes time for consumers to react in terms of demand for housing or durables and the strength of the reaction is often unpredictable. Indeed monetary policy was once compared to trying to draw a brick across a table using only a piece of elastic. Either the brick remains stationary or it tends to fly across the table and hit you in the face!

Anything that might affect the stability of money needs to be carefully monitored. As Milton Friedman observed, following a massive research study, 'inflation is always and everywhere a monetary phenomena'. Success in reducing inflation to very low levels in recent years suggests that monetary stability has now been achieved. The key is to make intermediate targets for money supply growth, government borrowing and exchange rates consistent with growth desired in nominal GDP and inflation, and then stick to them. The marketer must learn to interpret signals, for example:

o Why are base rates reduced on fears of recession or negative shocks like stock market crashes?
o Why are UK interest rates higher than those in the EU?
o Why are rates tending to converge towards the average of your main trading partners?
o What, then, is the link between interest rate changes and the exchange rate?

Question 6.9

Which type of firms are most affected by a credit squeeze?

Prices and incomes policy

Such policies were mainly used during the 1960s and 1970s in an attempt to achieve lower unemployment without incurring higher inflation and consequent balance of payments problems. If wage groups could be forced or persuaded to moderate their pay settlements and firms their price increases, despite demand pressure to justify them, then employment and output would rise.

Governments are still prone, particularly in boom times, to introduce public sector pay restraint as a means of controlling public spending and to set a 'good example' for the private sector to follow (e.g. Argentina). In practice, such policies normally prove counterproductive or short-lived due to shortages or pay explosions. The appropriate analogy was a boiling pot with the heat (demand pressure) turned up and the lid tightly on.

Question 6.10

Are you clear as to the difference between a slow-down, a soft landing, a recession, a deflation, a slump and a depression in an economy – or is it just 'economist jargon' to keep us guessing?

Supply-side policies

These grew out of disillusion with demand management policies to achieve the macroeconomic objectives. The standard response to low growth and rising unemployment had been to stimulate consumer, government and investment spending on the assumption that domestic firms would raise production and resource use. Multiplier and accelerator reactions would then stimulate businesses to invest in extra capacity and productivity improvements. The business response in practice was:

- o To improve margins and profits instead of raising output
- o A reluctance to invest due to stop-go patterns of demand
- o Marked by an inability to respond quickly enough leading to import penetration.

Resulting inflation and payments deficits would then force a policy reversal. Supply-side policies aimed instead to promote higher growth and employment, without triggering inflation, by relaxing constraints on productive capacity and efficiency. The policies involved:

- o Reform of trade unions to ensure that their reduced power was used responsibly and democratically (with strikes at a minimum).
- o Removal of tax distortions and disincentives to work and invest.
- o Measures to improve the quality, quantity and relevance of training.
- o Improved job, career and training information.
- o Measures to encourage mobility and flexibility.
- o Encouraging employee share-ownership and self-employment.
- o Reducing red tape and regulations inhibiting business.
- o Greater competition and removal of minimum wages.
- o Privatization and the opening up of state services to private competition or internal markets.
- o Deregulation of markets to reduce entry barriers and increase competition.

Some countries have specific economic problems they need to confront. For example, Singapore faced chronic labour shortages but resisted the obvious solution of an influx of immigrants. Instead it has used technology to equip the whole island with an optical fibre network that reaches every home and business. Being wired for the electronic age is viewed as the best route to productivity growth and resolving labour scarcity.

Exam hint

Improving your learning and performance

Undertake a SWOT analysis of your economy.

Draw up a balance sheet of its strengths and weaknesses and then identify opportunities and threats. This formed the basis of a recent case question on China.

Trade and exchange rate policies

Many open economies operate a flexible exchange rate system that acts as an automatic two-way adjustment mechanism to keep the balance of payments in approximate balance. Should the payments position worsen then the exchange rate should fall relative to trading rivals making exports cheaper in foreign currency terms and therefore more competitive. Imports become relatively more expensive so favouring home-produced products. Export receipts rise, import payments fall and the balance of payments position is restored. Unfortunately, this process is just a little too good to be true otherwise Britain would not currently have record deficits. The marketer should recognize one or two qualifications:

o Short-term and speculative capital movements can occur on a massive scale in the global economy and this can drive exchange rates rather than fundamentals like supply/ demand for products. Relatively high interest rates will tend to maintain an uncompetitive rate.

o The exchange rate is probably the most important 'price' there is but takes time to work through. A lower rate causes a deficit that worsens before it improves since imported materials are now more expensive, but must be paid for before extra exports can be produced and shipped.

o The strength of reaction to a falling exchange rate may be uncertain. How big will the demand increase be in foreign markets? How will foreign competitors react? Can we meet the extra demand? Won't costs rise due to higher import prices? Will businesses gear up for extra production or merely raise export prices and make higher profit?

o Unplanned exchange rate movements create risk. A transaction negotiated at one exchange rate may become unprofitable by the time it is fulfilled. Foreign assets purchased at one point in time may later become a balance sheet liability due to currency appreciation.

o Currency appreciation is a serious threat to foreign sales (and domestic markets), as many international marketers have found to their cost. Is the solution to cut export prices in foreign currency terms, reinforce product and promotional policies to reduce price sensitivity, or source overseas? For example, Marks & Spencer's sourcing policy had to change as the rising pound has forced them to turn their back on long-standing domestic suppliers while Dyson was forced to relocate vacuum manufacture to Malaysia.

Many governments prefer to aim for exchange rate stability given the uncertainties and costs associated with exchange rate fluctuations. This may cause it to manage its exchange rate or shadow the value of a critical currency such as the £ or the $. Another alternative is to join that currency block and accept the disciplines of an exchange rate set collectively. The danger in this approach is that the economy must be managed with this sole objective in mind. Any tendency towards a persistently expanding deficit or surplus would be unsustainable. The latter would draw criticism from trading partners, while the former leads to a progressive drain on reserves and national economic confidence. A lasting policy response would be required but correction of the problem may be painful because only two policy options exist:

o *Expenditure reduction* – Higher taxes reduce household incomes causing consumer demand, including demand for imports, to fall. Falling domestic sales encourage firms to export more as well as putting downward pressure on wages and prices, so improving general competitiveness.

o *Expenditure switching* – Resources and expenditure are switched away from imports to domestically produced goods. Policies include various types of protectionism and incentives for exporters. The other means is devaluation which implies sacrificing the stable exchange rate (or leaving the currency block). The first two policies deal with symptoms of a deficit at the expense of trading partners, rather than with the basic cause. International trade agreements also limit their scope. All governments seek to promote exports by providing information, advice, assistance and often insurance against bad debts. Aggressive use of hidden subsidies to obtain unfair trade advantage, however, is not internationally acceptable.

The impact of international trade

All countries are open systems and must deal with the realities of the international environment. Some economies, such as the USA, are so large that the domestic economy is the dominant influence. Most, however, are like the UK (accounting for just 5–6 per cent of global output), export orientated and always susceptible to outside shocks. So why are so many countries so eager to expand their international exposure? World trade brings diversity of choice – as seen in any sizeable supermarket at any season.

- National differences in culture, human skills, resource availability, ingenuity and technology lead to product, cost and price differences.
- A global market rewards specialization and allows exploitation of comparative advantage.
- International trade curbs monopoly power, increases competition, lowers consumer prices.
- World markets offer scope for economies of scale and significantly reduced costs.
- Access to world markets spreads risks and can counter-balance domestic activity.
- Trade/distribution networks encourage/enable rapid diffusion of new ideas/inventions.
- Trade brings contact, mutual interest, cultural understanding, interdependence and cooperation.
- Coca-Cola in Beijing and McDonald's in Moscow fosters world peace and security.
- Liberalization of planned economies allows their integration into the world trading system.
- Growth in world trade has been continuous offering expanding opportunities.
- Trade liberalization agreements encouraged emerging economies to open their markets. In 1946 only 5 per cent of world GDP was traded internationally, today it is 25 per cent.
- The World Trade Organization (WTO) was established in 1995 with a mandate to enforce world trade laws.
- Unimpeded development of Internet, travel and trade links are producing a global culture.
- Continued expansion of multinational enterprises and development of global companies.

Marketing in practice

The challenge of globalization

Background

This is a process by which the world economy is becoming a unified interdependent system based on ICT and progressive lowering of trade barriers. It involves multinational businesses adopting world-wide strategies that apply the same or similar marketing mixes in all markets. The process is facilitated by the progressive development of electronic commerce and enabled by mass media and travel creating similar patterns of consumption in otherwise diverse cultures.

Global growth accelerated sharply in 2004 due to unprecedented 6 per cent growth in the poorest countries. Living standards have increased rapidly, reflected in the fall from 472 million people living on under $1 a day in Asia-Pacific in 1991 to a projected 19 million by 2015 (the impact of the Tsunami has yet to be factored in). Sub-Saharan Africa is the exception to this trend, a situation unlikely to improve given continuing atrocities in Darfur and the Congo.

Globalization is characterized by international flows of capital, information and increasingly mobile labour. The key agents in the process are international firms, who conduct a significant proportion of their business in foreign countries. A global marketing perspective implies a centrally coordinated plan directed towards a worldwide audience rather than the usual decentralized focus on local or regional markets. Global products include the likes of Rolex, Coca-Cola, Sony, Nike, McDonald's, Airbus, Xerox, Virgin and Microsoft.

Dramatic growth in the last half century means that large multinationals now account for a staggering one-fifth of world output and 70 per cent of total global trade, with Britain now the leading foreign investor spending $132 billion or 25 per cent of the global total. Global revenues of the largest multinational exceed the GDP of all but the largest country. Other factors accounting for this trend include:

o Continuous progress in reducing tariff barriers through trade rounds and the formation of the WTO.
o 146 countries in membership and a new system for settling disputes.
o Development of regional free-trade zones representing attempts by countries with similar interests to obtain the benefits of free trade while retaining the advantage of some protection against the outside world. These may represent the building blocks to eventual global free trade. Examples include the EU, Nafta, APEC and SADC.
o Many emerging countries in Africa, Latin America and Asia now see open economies and direct investment as the better route to development than protectionism.
o An infrastructure of international institutions is in place to support sustainable global growth.

  – *International Monetary Fund* – responsible for supervision of the world financial system and provides lending support and structural reform programmes for countries in difficulty, as recently in the case of Argentina, Russia, Indonesia and Brazil.
  – *World Bank* – provides long-term capital for development purposes.
  – *Organization for Economic Co-operation and Development* – represents the richest and most powerful governments whose main role is to coordinate economic policies to avert any mutually reinforcing inflation or deflation that would damage trade.
  – *World Trade Organization* – encourages multilateral trade and seeks to resolve trade disputes.

Others include the Arab League, the Organization of African Unity, the Organization of American States and the Commonwealth of Independent States.

Advantages

o Enhanced scope for specialization and standardization of production and distribution.
o Cost effective R&D, product design and promotion – attractions of universal image advertising combined with the scope to adapt to suit local conditions.
o Shorter new product planning cycle via learning/comparison/feedback from global experience.
o Faster reaction to customer preferences and superior marketing potential.
o Transport cost savings, improved supply chain efficiency and leverage.
o Direct investment gives tariff-free access to trade blocks given that local content requirements are met.
o Direct access increases local market knowledge and customer confidence.
o Rivals derive competitive advantage out of their network of global activities.
o Greater political stability: web of multinational subsidiaries and 'common' commercial interests.
o Pressure on governments to conform to stable economic management as a condition for continued direct investment and favourable reaction from global financial markets.

Disadvantages

- Cultural sensitivities force changes to 'global products', for example, Big Macs in India.
- Divergence in language and stage of economic development implies differentiation.
- Concern over the American/Western cultural domination undermining national identity.
- Risk of strategic dependence on multinationals whose strategy is globally not nationally driven.
- Powerful companies can play one country off against another to secure incentive packages.
- Multinationals may use their leverage to obtain favourable treatment and avoid profits tax via transfer pricing (i.e. by varying internally set prices on components transferred between subsidiaries).
- Political tensions between the developed and developing countries, for example, over debt relief or write-offs making slow progress while rich nations refuse to cut their massive subsidies ($47 billion EU) that distort world markets and destroy Third-World farming through unfair competition.
- The gap between the world's richest and poorest has doubled since 1960.

Significance

- The marketer must monitor a worldwide marketplace and the global environment.
- The threat of competition in domestic markets is significantly increased.
- Interdependence creates the potential for rapid communication of shocks through the system.
- Slower growth may produce protectionist responses since governments are concerned with national competitive advantage and face pressure from affected interest groups.

Conclusions

No marketer can remain insulated from this dynamic global economic system. It represents a major arena for profitable opportunity but equally a significant source of potential volatility and threat. Either way, the international environment cannot be ignored but must be closely monitored and carefully assessed. Fortunately, the international institutions mentioned above collect a wealth of information on the evolving state of the world economy and its constituent blocks, providing a database for marketing research on both trade potential and competitive risk.

The basis for trade: at the micro level

Although the principle of comparative advantage holds across a range of commodities, in practice equivalent consumer and industrial goods are imported and exported by many countries. Traded goods like cars and computers are differentiated products and the consumer desires a wide choice. Households do not want identical telephones or saloon cars and each manufacturer gains economies by producing one main brand for an international market rather than lots of brands in low volumes for a purely domestic one. Gains from trade in this case do not necessarily derive from relative cost differences but rather from brand diversity and effective marketing.

Although large numbers of small and medium companies either do not participate in international trade or engage in only a peripheral way, the advantages for them can be substantial:

1. Providing a wider market for specialist niche producers.
2. Additional volume to reduce the cost base and secure economies.
3. Escape from a saturated or threatened domestic market.
4. One possible means of extending the product life cycle.
5. As a source of volume growth to support expensive R&D.
6. To counter a depressed home market and maintain capacity.
7. As a competitive strategy to counter and deter foreign rival entry into the home market.
8. As a means of spreading risks.
9. To exploit the scope for e-commerce.

Entry into foreign markets requires a serious commitment. It is a strategic decision since the implications of subsequent withdrawal due to lack of preparation would be expensive in terms of cost, image and credibility.

Marketing environment in practice

EU enlargement

o Hungary, Poland, Slovakia, Slovenia, Estonia, Latvia, Lithuania, Malta, Cyprus and the Czech Republic joined the EU in 2004 to be followed by Bulgaria and Romania in 2007. This expands the Single Market 40 per cent by area, and 75 million by population to open up new marketing opportunities for new and existing members alike. Stability and rising prosperity for former Soviet bloc members is seen as a political gain. Studies suggest a modest economic benefit of around £6 billion for existing members and two to three times that for new members. This is due to a regional aid package for the poorest regions of only £23 billion over the first 3 years and farm aid to new members just 25 per cent of the normal level in 2004 rising to 100 per cent in 2013. There is also a 'transition' period (e.g. 7 years for Poland) before freedom to travel and work is allowed.

New members had to demonstrate economic and environmental stability together with a fully functioning democratic market economy. Compliance with 80 000 pages of EU legislation including the Social Chapter, was required and in the first 2 years after entry the EU reserves the right to take purposeful measures if it feels that new entrants are distorting the Single Market.

EU growth is currently just over 2 per cent but much is government spending driven. The Euro has risen 15 per cent putting severe strains on the Stability Pact. The Commission, on behalf of smaller member countries, is taking the Council of Ministers to the European Court of Justice for breaching this pact by not punishing France and Germany for their excessive deficits incurred to stave of recession.

Frictions in the international environment

Notwithstanding the powerful forces encouraging ever greater participation in the emergent global marketplace, there are numerous reasons for sparks to fly in international trade. These can appear arbitrary to the marketer and yet be extremely damaging. Producers threatened by imports are organized, concentrated, supported by their unions and very vocal compared to the exporters or consumers who stand to lose from such controls. Developed country farm protection, for example, is estimated to cost poorer countries over $100 billion a year (double their aid receipts).

Russia and Taiwan are especially vulnerable to US trade sanctions because they are not members of the WTO. China, has recently joined although it has had to agree to a number of reforms to open its economy to fairer trade. Another recent friction involved a 20 per cent drop in French exports to the US following the Iraq war due to a 'shoppers boycott'.

Exam hint

By now you should know the meaning of the many acronyms used in this subject. These might arise in the examination paper, so make sure you revise the meaning of GAT T, WTO, GDP, ICT, SWOT and SLEPT.

Activity 6.4

Key skills: using information

Match the terms with their correct definitions:

o Tariff
o Quota
o Embargo
o Non-tariff barriers
o Terms of trade
o Customs duty.

– Taxes on imported goods aimed at reducing their competitiveness with domestic equivalents.
– Various standards and regulations to which imports must conform.
– Tax imposed on imports in order to raise revenue.
– The index of average export prices compared to average import prices.
– A quantitative limit on the volume of imports per time period.
– Export prohibition on a particular good to certain countries, usually for political reasons.

Dumping involves goods sold in foreign markets at below cost of production and are viewed as an unfair trading practice under WTO rules. However, interpretation is difficult and lower prices might reflect superior efficiency. The US recently responded to a surge in imports of bras, evening gowns and knitted fabrics by imposing quotas on Chinese textiles. Unfortunately such actions can trigger trade wars and China is hugely important to the global economy. Its trade surplus with America is massive ($150 bn) and needs to be addressed if a calamitous fall in the dollar is to be avoided. Hence the so-called 'bra wars'. More recently the US has initiated another dispute with Europe by lodging a complaint with the WTO over subsidies for the Airbus A380 super jumbo. The EU has responded alleging massive illegal US subsidies in the form of tax breaks and government contracts to Boeing.

Marketing environment in practice

Implications for marketers

- o Marketers must monitor the international environment for advance warning of impending threats.
- o A deflationary scenario encourages protectionist instincts and threatens global prosperity.
- o A tension exists between free trade advantages to the world as a whole and self-interest – one country can always gain from controls if all others continue to trade freely.
- o Successive trade talks have ended in recrimination and accusation over multinational influence and rich nation protection of its farmers.
- o Fear of international retaliation is often the main force against protectionism.
- o Protection of infant industries is frequently used as a defence in developing nations.
- o International marketers still face tariffs and quotas, for example, protecting domestic interests.
- o Non-tariff barriers involve environmental, quality, health or safety standards and so may require expensive product modification.
- o The marketer may also find a far from level playing field as domestic producers receive preferential assistance, for example, tax breaks, supports and patriotic attitudes.
- o The failure to agree an agenda for future trade liberalization might harden attitudes.
- o Many charities promote the cause of 'fair trade' for poor producers by encouraging consumers to purchase only products produced according to certain criteria such as grown on family run farms, without the use of pesticides and at higher prices.

Case history

Case in point – the future of the global economy

Global economic performance in 2004 was the best in 30 years. Growth forecasts for 2005 have had to be trimmed from 5 to 4.3 per cent due to high oil prices, but this is still above the long term trend rate. The real risk is if the Americans stop spending. Consumer spending has outstripped salary growth threefold since 2001 financed by rising debt, falling savings (to just 1 per cent) and property appreciation. It has also led to widening current account imbalances. It presents a clear danger that America will retreat into protectionism and thereby threaten global growth. It is currently experiencing jobless growth due to above average productivity growth and fears a loss of jobs through outsourcing to India and other developing countries.

Exam hint

The international environment has global candidate appeal. Remember, the examiner will be influenced by current events as well as syllabus content and its coverage over a run of papers. If anything of major global importance happened recently, it *could* be the basis of a question in *your* examination.

Summary

In this important unit we have analysed key aspects of the macroeconomic and international environment and focused on the need for marketers to appreciate the meaning of economic indicators. A grasp of future economic conditions will provide an important edge over rivals. To achieve this we have:

- Assessed each of the main macroeconomic objectives.
- Investigated the circular flow to understand changes in income, output and expenditure.
- Examined concepts such as the multiplier and the accelerator.
- Looked at the meaning and measurement of GDP.
- Identified the phases of the business cycle and how it might be managed to advantage.
- Focused on the key indicators for marketers to monitor.
- Outlined the impact of the main policy weapons on business and the marketer.
- Examined the benefits and implications of expanding world trade.
- Considered frictions in the international trade process.

Further study and examination preparation

The economy is always going to be an important part of the macro-environment and the origin of major impacts on the business. Given its day-to-day importance for the marketer it would be surprising if questions based on the content of this unit did not occur with some frequency.

A sound knowledge of your own national economy is therefore very important and should be summarized under headings such as: inflation, unemployment, balance of payments, economic growth, phase of the cycle, investment activity and the economic policy stance. The use of a variety of broad statistics, drawn from some of the mentioned sources would be expected by the examiner.

Extending knowledge

Palmer and Hartley, *The Business and Marketing Environment*, McGraw-Hill – Chapter 7, The National Economic Environment and Chapter 13, The International Marketing Environment.

Websites include: Economic Trends

www.statistics.gov.uk

www.feer.com for Far Eastern Economic Review

www.ft.com

www.economist.com

www.worldbank.org

www.wto.org/index.htm

www.oecd.org

www.adb.org for the Asian Development Bank

http://europa.eu.int/euro/html/entry.html for the Euro site

Exam question 6.1

Please see Question 1, June 2004. For specimen answers please go to www.cim.co.uk.

Exam question 6.2

Please see Question 4, December 2003. For specimen answers please go to www.cim.co.uk.

Exam question 6.3

Please see Question 7b, December 2003. For specimen answers please go to www.cim.co.uk.

Exam question 6.4

(a) Illustrate the concept of the business cycle and explain why the marketer should have an understanding of its various phases. (10 marks)
(b) Explain the economic policies that might be introduced after the upper turning point and their significance for the marketer. (10 marks)

Question 3, June 2003.

Exam question 6.5

Your company is seeking a major expansion inforeign markets and you have been asked to prepare a brief guide on the international environment.

Using headings and bullet points, produce a draft for this guide that considers the following: the nature of the international environment; information needs; information sources and key success factors.

Question 6, June 2003.

Provide the 'brief guide draft/headings/bullet' format but not a discussion of entry strategies.

unit 7
the political and legislative environment

Learning objectives

In this important unit, we will explore the interface between two significant and closely interlinked aspects of the macro-environment. The societal agenda is set within the political environment and enacted and applied within the legislative environment. By the end of this challenging unit you will have:

○ Consolidated your understanding of the political environment/its organizational impacts

○ Reinforced your grasp of the points of political pressure and influence (3.5)

○ Distinguished between different forms of regulation (3.5)

○ Appreciated the essential features of a complex legislative framework (3.5)

○ Assessed the significance of legislation for marketers and key stakeholders (3.5).

Study Guide

This unit considers a political environment that embraces institutions, agencies, laws and pressure groups. These elements may influence and constrain both organizations and individuals in society. They also define freedom in terms of what can and, can not legally be done in business today. Pressure groups were explored in Unit 2 and are now considered with lobbyists and the media. If marketers are influenced by the political dimension, in general, they are most certainly influenced by the legislative environment in particular. General issues concerning the legal framework will be considered involving the role and objectives of law and regulation; the methods available; an outline of the legal system; the costs and benefits of compliance as well as the impacts involved on business and society.

A brief appreciation of relevant areas of the law will be provided using British statutes as examples. Students from Asia, Africa, Europe and the Caribbean should understand that they may refer to their own legal system when examples are cited in examinations. Different countries have different legal traditions and systems. Even in Britain the law applying to England and Wales is different in many respects from that applying in Scotland.

The examiner will definitely not expect a detailed knowledge of the law. Legal issues are, however, becoming increasingly important, not least in the area of marketing. A marketer must know when to seek legal advice and understand it sufficiently to ensure that the right questions are posed. Lawyers are primarily concerned with the finer points of the law and are in an advisory capacity. Final decisions balancing commercial as well as legal considerations rest with the marketing and other directors.

The political environment

The political environment might produce a variety of emotions ranging from apathy to outright cynicism, but it is one that marketers ignore at their peril. Its impacts on business activity and international trade are both numerous and potentially damaging, as seen most vividly on 2 November 2004 when the world's most powerful democracy confirmed a second Republican victory. Both contenders had 10 000 lawyers on standby in 'swing' states to contest close results following the last election 'debacle' in Florida but were not required. The Bush second term will have very different policy outcomes for key interest groups both within and outside America. Similarly, the narrow, and some would say unexpected, victory of Zanu PF over the challenge of Zimbabwe's main opposition party, the Movement for Democratic Change presaged the progressive occupation of white-owned farms by the war veterans and nation-wide turbulence leading directly to Mugabe retaining power in the presidential elections. EU, though not Commonwealth, sanctions were initially imposed when independent observers highlighted electoral malpractices, but the election result stood. Elsewhere political elite's have been responsible for considerable corruption as seen in the transfer of a staggering $60 billion to foreign bank accounts from 1996–99 in Brazil. This represented a quarter of the country's national debt and compares to the 9 per cent of GDP thought to have been 'stolen' by the dos Santos government in oil rich Angola between 1997 and 2002. A new political dimension to account for is the potential magnitude of the threat posed by terrorism and suicide attacks. Bloody bombings on the Madrid rail system appeared to 'swing' the Spanish elections in March 2004 although the impact of the Bin Laden video on the eve of the American election was less conclusive. Hostage taking in Iraq has similarly been used as an attempted lever on Italian and British political decision-making. Smallpox scares have led to immunization of critical workers and the stockpiling of vaccines for the general public should it become necessary while numerous flights have been diverted. Disruption caused by such threats is as damaging as incidents themselves. Also worrying was the precedent set by the damage to the tanker *Limburg* off the coast of Yemen allegedly caused by a terrorist attack.

The role and significance of government in a market economy is considerable:

o The government has full political power and executive authority to pursue the policies of its choice.
o The public sector, including executive agencies, normally accounts for a significant percentage of jobs, direct spending and total expenditure when transfer payments are accounted for.
o As a 'swing sector' in terms of its ability to influence overall economic activity levels.
o It influences most key decisions, for example, to work, save, spend, invest via tax/interest rates.
o It enacts legal and regulatory frameworks that limit business freedom in the wider interests of society – well-conceived regulation is accepted as a key role of the state and most aspects of marketing activity are covered by some form of control.
o Governments help to shape standards of public behaviour and conduct.
o Democratic governments must present their executive and legislative record for electoral scrutiny at prescribed intervals.
o Day-to-day practice of government relies on gathering feedback from interest groups within the environment and as such is susceptible to pressure and influence.

177

○ Present-day governments operate in an open global system that may constrain its freedom of action. Governments must recognize the power of the markets; the need to keep national performance in line with competitor benchmarks; the influence of trading partners and the rules of international club membership, for example, the WTO, UN, IMF, and so on.

○ They must also recognize the latent power of the Internet reflected in the ability of individuals and groups to circumvent political control over the media and coordinate activities. The Miss World riots in Nigeria were organized using mobiles and laptops as are so-called 'flash mobs'.

Exam hint

It is politically expedient to regularly consult the Syllabus, Examination reports and the CIM Code of Conduct (see www.cim.co.uk/learningzone) since these define and comment upon the rules applying to your examination.

There are still exceptions, but the trend towards international 'acceptability' of political outcomes has strengthened since the collapse of Communism. Examples include:

○ Cuba and North Korea continue to operate in relative isolation (*Note*: recent tensions over reopening of nuclear weapons programme).

○ China, as a communist one-party state. Power is formally held by a Central Committee elected by the Party Congress. The Committee in turn elects a seven-member Politburo headed by a supreme authority. However, China is emerging from relative isolation and has gradually improved relationships despite Tiananmen Square and other human rights criticisms. It has encouraged foreign investment in special economic zones, introduced market forces and joined the WTO. Its recent economic growth has been rapid and sustained (it could out-grow the US by 2025 and already has a $100 billion trade surplus) but it has unresolved political contradictions such as high unemployment and widening inequality of income. It clashed with America over refusal to free its exchange rate but recently increased it.

○ In Russia, President Putin, elected by a massive majority, has consolidated his position. He accurately describes Russia as 'a rich country full of poor people' since it controls 13 per cent of the world's oil and 36 per cent of its natural gas yet has seen its GDP halve since the fall of Communism, with many until recently living below the poverty line even in the capital Moscow. However, Russia too is recovering strongly, since the collapse of the rouble in 1998, due partly to improved relations with the West. Putin promises to create a strong state and a 'dictatorship of law' to confront those previously above or beyond its powers. One marketing consequence of his attempt to foster family values and the belief that Russia can regain its former greatness is a ban on the sale of Barbie dolls and other Western toys for encouraging consumerism in children. There are some who worry that Russia might return to the kind of system that has taken hold in parts of the Third World, namely an elected autocracy with the power to stifle the independent media and enforce change.

Insight

American Democracy?

The House of Representatives is the key policy maker, yet the majority of biannual elections are foregone conclusions. As in the last three elections when 98 per cent of Congress was re-elected, the incumbent nearly always wins. This arises from the long established practice of 'gerrymandering' where in most state's politicians fix the boundaries of electoral districts (In Britain it is the non-political Boundary Commission that adjusts for population change). California with 53 districts has only one contest where the outcome isn't taken as inevitable. Despite a sharp rise in turnout to 60 per cent in the latest election, the overall trend is downward as voters conclude they have no influence. Although constituencies can't be manipulated for senatorial (2 per State) and presidential elections the situation is still polarized with only 17 or 18 'swing' states. As good marketers the presidential contenders (brands?) concentrate time and resource on these states and ignore the rest. The candidate who wins the popular vote in a state wins all it's electoral college votes. This 'winner take all' system can, however, result in the one who loses the popular vote winning the presidency as was the case with Bush in 2000 but not 2004.

Legislation and the decisions of public authorities clearly have a continuing influence on business activities and must be monitored carefully to:

o   Alert management to impending legislation
o   Mobilize efforts to represent stakeholder interests to the legislators
o   Develop awareness of public agency intentions/decisions affecting business
o   Identify likely changes arising out of electoral shifts
o   Assess political manifesto implications/philosophy of ministers.

The government also controls the macroeconomic framework and its decisions affect both its position as a major customer of the private sector and the political distribution of the tax burden. Business has a collective interest in the relative burden of business taxes and rates as well as trends in the size and composition of government spending on goods and services. Governments now aim to create overall stability and this is usually reflected in spending despite the pressures exerted by the demands of social security, health and education. In Britain, the government has added 50 000 public sector jobs, boosted spending by over 60 per cent and raised average civil service pay by 20 per cent over 4 years. Public spending has risen from 39.8 per cent to 43 per cent and will converge with the EU average of 49 per cent by 2009 on current trends.

The public sector itself has undergone a fundamental transformation in recent years with policies of privatization, deregulation and the contracting-out to private tender of more and more local authority and civil service functions. Much investment in Britain's public services (£110 billion) is undertaken through the Private Finance Initiative while economies like Sri Lanka have adopted liberalization and privatization policies to promote growth and the re-emergence of the vital tourism industry.

The market solution or pure capitalist policies of the political right, based on the values of private ownership and an enterprise culture have, however, been blunted and moderated in social democracies, like the EU, by counterforces promoting 'responsible' capitalism and its attendant codes of good conduct. The middle way is a partnership of private initiative and responsible public enterprise to promote the welfare of all members of society, not just the rich and economically successful.

Activity 7.1

Key skills: interpreting information

Match the terms with their correct definitions:

o Privatization
o Deregulation
o Enterprise culture
o Party manifesto
o First-past-the-post.

- The candidate with the most votes cast is the election winner, irrespective of the distribution of votes to other contenders.
- Removal of rules and requirements restricting competition.
- A programme of intended policies if successfully elected.
- A climate that encourages self-reliance, entrepreneurship, individual wealth creation.
- Transfer of 50 per cent or more of the voting shares to private hands.

The political framework

Political systems are located along a spectrum ranging from totalitarianism to popular democracy. The main features of these two systems are outlined below:

Totalitarianism/Autocracy	Democracy
Single leader	Universal suffrage
One ruling party	Periodic free elections
Official ideology rules	Freedom of speech/media
Opposition parties repressed	Open political competition
Power is concentrated	Pluralistic – power spread throughout society
Central direction/command Government controls media	Majority rule/minorities are protected and equal under the law
Minorities persecuted	Pressure groups free to lobby between elections

Political power is the ability to bring about change through influencing the behaviour of others. All organizations are affected by politics because people have different views, ideals and interests. Disagreements naturally arise over such matters as objectives to be pursued, decisions to be made and, perhaps most importantly, resources to be allocated. These must be resolved, otherwise conflict would result and organizations and indeed society would cease to function effectively. Political stability arises out of the identification and effective resolution of disputes through a mixture of authority, enforcement and compromise.

Political stability is important, not least to investors who wish to minimize their risks. Multinationals, for example, are reluctant to invest in any economy experiencing political or labour unrest. For example, the Tiananmen Square incident in Beijing in 1989 had serious and long-lasting repercussions not only in China itself but also in Hong Kong and the wider East Asia region. Similarly, Mugabe's seizure of white farms caused the IMF and World Bank to suspend lending and frightened much foreign investment away.

Question 7.1

What are the areas and issues where 'politics' are involved in:

- The marketing department?
- Relationships between marketing and finance?

What sources of information should the marketer consult to keep a finger on the political environment pulse? Are there more cost-effective means of keeping abreast of national and supra-national legislative developments?

The inputs into the political system originate in wider society and arise out of their changing attitudes, values, perceptions and demands. These will be diverse and conflicting and tend to coalesce around support for alternative party manifestos at election time (between elections they will be channelled and given focus by pressure groups and lobbyists) for example, lower taxes, devolution of power to the regions, more education spending, and so on. Political parties seek to differentiate themselves from their rivals, but also appeal to a sufficiently wide constituency as to gain election to government.

Elections are the ultimate democratic control over government and provide the electorate with an opportunity to pass judgement on performance. It is also an opportunity to judge the 'promises and proposals' of the opposition. Fear of defeat at the next general election, or a very strong wish for a second term, should encourage account of the public wishes.

Question 7.2

Key skills: using information

Since voters are very much like customers as far as political parties are concerned, what advice would the marketer offer to the election campaign manager of:

- The party currently in office?
- The main opposition party?
- A Green party looking to establish a base in Parliament?

Britain has a first-past-the-post electoral system that produces a number of characteristics:

- A simple majority of seats gives one party the power to form a strong government.
- Governments seldom win a 'majority' of votes cast – opposition vote gets split.
- Fewer smaller parties – do not see their proportion of the vote reflected in seats won.
- Avoids the compromises/vulnerability to interest groups found in coalition government.

This appears unfair but elections are held to produce governments and avoid the uncertainties of an indefinite outcome. There is always considerable resistance to change in political systems because of the uncertainties involved and disruption of established vested interests. Adoption of the new EU constitution with its changed voting patterns to accommodate new members may prove to be a case in point. Alternatives exist, as in Europe and Australasia, but these involve proportional voting systems. These produce a more 'representative' electoral outcome but potentially at the expense of strong and effective government. A succession of weak coalitions has, for example, created a frequent absence of government in Italy and one susceptible to bribery and corruption. It remains to be seen if Mwai Kibaki, as leader of a coalition of disparate opposition parties, will consolidate the overthrow of one-party rule that has prevailed in Kenya since 1963.

The politics of coalition are important to the stability of most economies, not least those with a strong ethnic mix to their societies. The consequences of civil war are all too clear in countries like Sri Lanka and many African states. Sectarian violence can flare along many fault lines as seen most recently in the Sudan. The list of similar ethnic or religious flash points in Israel, Nigeria, Iraq or Indonesia goes on and on.

The main concern for business is for stability from political decision-making, a dependable planning horizon and a positive climate in which to operate. This is not possible if corruption is draining the strength out of the country's development process or civil war is squandering its critical resources. The political environment is of vital importance to effective marketing and one that can easily be taken for granted in times of stability and continuity. Witness the plunge in the Russian stock market when hardliners arrested Khodorkovsky, the country's wealthiest businessman on corruption charges.

Changes in government in a polarized system can cause serious discontinuity as established policies are reversed, institutions abolished and legislation amended to reflect the new political philosophy. At election time, as in Britain in 2005, business must carefully ponder the implications of alternative policies and pledges being implemented.

Discontinuity can create uncertainty for business, especially if the party in power is changed frequently. Similar discontinuity faced the people of Hong Kong after June 1997 although much political energy had been invested in assuring smooth transference of power, so limiting adverse business and popular reaction. After 8 years of Chinese rule, Hong Kong is still a long way from true democracy. The island's executive is entirely appointed by Peking and only 24 of the 60 legislators are elected democratically. Gibraltar is another case in point. After a succession of votes, its community has once again voted decisively (99 per cent on an 88 per cent turnout) to reject joint sovereignty with Spain. The legitimacy of the vote was rejected by Spain who are in turn refusing an arguably more legitimate demand to return Olivenca to Portugal.

Activity 7.2

Key skills: using information and problem-solving

With Tony Blair winning a record third term, why not check out its pledges and key policies. Assess the marketing implications, arising from both achievement/non-achievement, as appropriate (or apply a similar analysis to your own political environment).

The electoral cycle

The other source of political instability is the tendency for elections to 'influence' business cycles. Governments know that reducing taxes and increasing spending, as an election approaches, will create a temporary sense of well being. Disposable income rises, as does employment and business activity. This will be short-lived if prices and imports also tend to rise, since action will have to be taken to reverse the resulting inflation and trade deficit. However, since there will be a lag before such effects are felt, the government may well win re-election and be in a position to apply the economic brakes. These can then be released as the next general election approaches. The American election in late 2004 provides a case in point with rapid growth of over 3.5 per cent generated by massive tax cuts, increases in spending and a weaker dollar. Given the possible consequences of the record debts and deficits now faced by a re-elected Bush, it might turn out to be a good election to lose for the Democrats. One final point to note is that an adversarial two- or three-party system does tend to widen the credibility gap between politically nurtured expectations, on the one hand, and actual performance of the economy, on the other. It is as well that the marketer takes with a pinch of salt the ideals and objectives advertised and promoted by the various parties in general and the government in particular. Politics is said to be the 'art of the possible' but this sometimes has a habit of being less than expected!

Central and local government

Parliament is the supreme legislative authority in Britain. Although private members (of Parliament) can propose bills the vast majority that become law are government sponsored or supported, whatever the actual make-up and workings of the legislature. The marketer should appreciate the origins of new laws and how businesses might influence their form and content:

Stages	Influence
1. *Origin* – Popular issue, committee of inquiry recommendation, election pledge, pressure group, government initiative, to close loopholes.	Trade association may press for legislation.
2. *Green Paper* – Government puts ideas on paper for discussion.	Monitor and contribute if industry interests are to be affected.
3. *White paper* – Government sets out definite proposals.	Comments from parties affected will be accounted/included.
4. *Draft bill – first reading.*	
5. *Main debate – second reading.*	MPs can be lobbied to speak in support.
6. *Committee stage* – studies the detail.	
7. *Report stage – to full House of Commons.*	
8. *Final debate and amendments – third reading.*	Last opportunity to lobby support.
9. *To House of Lords – process repeated.*	
10. *Possible reference back to Commons.*	For example, restrictions on right to trial by jury.
11. *Royal Assent – the law is enacted.*	

Note: It is vitally important that business views on proposed laws are made clearly and persuasively at this time. If legislation is inevitable, then business must ensure that it is workable and no unintended disadvantageous side-effects result. Emotional legislation in response to a public outcry is to be avoided through active lobbying.

The process is long and complicated, placing a limit on how much legislative business can be completed. Virtually all government-sponsored bills become law although the opposition can use delaying tactics. Case law, in contrast, evolves through independent judicial decisions and is not susceptible to influence by business, although the right of appeal exists.

Activity 7.3

Marketing environment in practice

The ability of business lobbies to influence legislation that affects them is considerable. The transport industry lobby campaigns successfully against carbon taxes and cuts in greenhouse gases. The farm and defence lobbies are other notable examples.

Select a topical bill (e.g. gaming or pensions) affecting a strong business lobby and assess their effectiveness.

Pressure groups, as discussed in Unit 2, represent a channel through which individuals and groups can make their views known to governments between elections. They are much more important than political parties in terms of membership and represent numerous, overlapping and competing influences within society.

Pressure groups effectiveness requires *commitment, cohesion, organization, resources and strategic positioning*. Those who decide government policies need pressure groups. They often have a statutory duty to consult and require advice, information and feedback of views and reactions from those affected. They favour those groups with the ability to deliver on bargains and compromises made and who provide support in return. They also need cooperation in the implementation and administration of new laws.

Exam hint

Marketing skills: working with others

The marketing environment is a large diverse syllabus so, why don't you pool resources with a fellow student and actively compare notes and ideas? Your combined strengths will produce synergy (1 + 1 = 3) and help to reduce the overall workload.

Businesses are strategically well positioned to obtain political support when right-wing governments are in office but not always as successful when left-of-centre governments rule. However, effective pressure group activity tends to stimulate the development of counter-pressure, that is, the countervailing action between rival coalitions limits the influence of any one grouping. Ministers will also be in a position to play one group off against another!

Government through devolved powers

Brief mention should be made of other dimensions of government with which the marketer might interact. Very close to home are local or city authorities whose political representatives are often protective of their independence and may even represent opposition parties and policies. The appropriate decision-making authority has therefore to be identified and lobbied, as in the case of central government.

Local government in Britain has undergone radical change in the last 10 years. Their powers to set business rates, raise taxes independently and decide expenditure totals have all been constrained by central government actions such as spending caps. Setting of national standards in education and other social services have also limited local autonomy.

Local government officers are now service facilitators rather than direct providers because of the requirement on them to offer contracts out to competitive bidding. This has made them more marketing orientated in pursuing value for money services for ratepayers although formerly 'free' services, such as libraries and leisure centres, are now often run on a more commercial basis. Consumer needs are identified and services provided, priced and promoted in order to cover costs and make a contribution to council funds.

Apart from bidding for council contracts in street cleaning, parks maintenance, refuse disposal, and so on, there are also opportunities for working jointly on projects combining civic improvement and commercial development. Local authorities are important stakeholders since they undertake urban planning and redevelopment, decide planning applications, control the supply of school-leavers, maintain local roads and infrastructure and provide a variety of inspectorates that impact on local business. It is an aspect of the environment, therefore, where the business should build positive and mutually beneficial relationships.

While some local government authorities have had to adapt to centralizing tendencies others, such as the Swiss cantons, Scotland and Wales enjoy a devolution of powers. Marketers serving these populations must in future recognize the implications of the transfer of legislative authority and react accordingly.

One final area to note is that of government agencies and other quasi-government bodies. The intention of many governments is to raise productivity and accountability by transforming government departments into executive agencies. These are free from day-to-day control from the centre and therefore able to focus on the achievement of long-term performance objectives. Such agencies are unelected, however, and this raises questions over their independence and accountability especially given the potential spending power and influence some of these organizations command.

Supranational bodies – the European Union (EU)

The EU is the most integrated and economically powerful bloc of countries in the world. Its members represent a combined market of over 400 million affluent consumers. As such, it is a magnet for marketers from around the world.

The Single European Market (SEM) initiative originated over concern with Europe's declining competitiveness relative to America and the emerging nations of the Pacific Rim. Despite the Common Market, Europe remained fragmented into culturally differentiated markets protected by an array of non-tariff barriers to trade. A common desire for increased competitiveness and employment opportunities was the driving force behind the idea of a truly free market, which, it was hoped, would release a dynamic and revived spirit of enterprise within European businesses.

Activity 7.4

Key skills: collecting information and problem-solving

Use CD-ROM databases or newspaper summaries to locate any surveys assessing progress to date in implementation of the SEM and the new Constitution.

Membership of the SEM, the European Monetary System, the Euro and the acceptance of a new Constitution creates economic and legal obligations that imply a progressive loss of national sovereignty. The institutions relevant to the exercise of this transferred legislative authority include:

○ *The European Parliament* – is an elected body (MEPs) with widening powers. Originally it was primarily consultative, supplying advice through the workings of various standing committees. More recently it has acquired and flexed its powers to reject proposals, veto the budget and even vote out the entire incoming commission, for example, over the Buttiglione appointment. In May 2005 it voted against Britain's Working Hours Directive opt out.

○ *The Council of Ministers* – is where the real decision-making power lies. It is composed of representative ministers, according to the issue under discussion. To speed up the process, the Nice treaty proposed increasing the voting power of the larger countries but ending the national veto in 39 new policy areas. More and more of the voting is on a 'qualified majority' basis implying that marketers wishing to influence outcomes must broaden their lobbying base and/or cooperate with other sympathetic interest groups.

○ *The European Commission* – as the executive body of the Union it has drafted regulations and directives to promote the SEM and achieve a level competitive playing field. It has the power to impose punitive fines for contravening competition rules. Membership is decided by 25 governments and its role is to coordinate national policies and secure the adoption and execution of the EU policies. The outcome has been a large number of measures and directives to facilitate the evolution of an integrated market. Compliance costs have arisen for business in the process, but so too have the opportunities for greater trade. One recent regulation (still requiring assent) requires local authorities to collect, strip down and recycle all electrical devices. Presently, 90 per cent of this waste is either dumped in landfill or incinerated. The cost will be borne by electrical manufacturers. Another regulation might require the re-labelling of most British yoghurt as 'mild alternate-culture heat treated fermented milk' since it does not conform to their standardised definition of a Euro-pudding.

○ *The European Court of Justice* – deals with any actions a business may wish to bring against EU institutions. It also provides a means of individual redress where member states are not fully complying with their legal obligations. Both national governments and organizations have learnt to their cost the consequences of referral to this final court of appeal.

The main issues currently confronting the EU are the future of the single currency (Sweden and Britain remain outside), breaches of the stability pact (France/Germany), implementation of enlargement and confirmation of the Constitution to streamline decision-making. Enlargement raises real concerns, not least over pressures on the budget and endemic corruption in much of Eastern Europe. It is also linked to the far-reaching Constitution, creating as it does a European president, foreign minister and justice department. Economic policy, foreign affairs, trade, agriculture, fisheries, immigration, employment policy, environmental protection, home affairs and space exploration would all be primarily EU governed. However, 19 countries will hold referendums with the first vote (in favour) taken in Spain during February 2005. The British vote if required, is not scheduled until early 2006.

Marketing environment in practice

The marketing challenge of a single currency

Background

The Euro became the major transaction currency for the 13 participating countries on 1 January 1999. Six hundred billion Euro notes and coins entered circulation from 1 January 2002 and displaced existing national coinage 6 months later. A massive marketing campaign accompanied the launch to persuade the Euro users to feel, look at and tilt their notes to appreciate its security features and so minimize the impact of forgery. The single currency complements the Single European Market, introduced to facilitate and encourage open and free intra-EU trade. As such it is a political rather than an economic currency being designed to further European unity.

The UK ruled out joining until a clear case could be made. The government supports entry into the Euro 'in principle' but faces many uncertainties in practice.

Uncertainties

- o The government will only recommend monetary union if five economic tests are passed. Following 'exhaustive' Treasury assessment only one test was passed by mid-2003 – *that the City and financial institutions were ready to adjust.* The tests are very broad and open to interpretation but failed tests included: *business cycles and economic structures are insufficiently compatible;* insufficient *flexibility for adjustment to shocks; creation of better conditions for making long-term decisions to invest in Britain not assured and insufficient convergence to assure higher growth and a lasting rise in jobs.*
- o Public opinion, the Conservatives and the media are currently against, the CBI are ambivalent while the TUC are for. A positive government recommendation could move the balance of public opinion closer to acceptance.
- o The EU 'one policy fits all' only works if convergence is achieved.
- o If the pound is overvalued on entry it will impact negatively.
- o The political tone remains pro-Euro with a commitment to work towards further convergence (e.g. raise stamp duty and bring VAT into line) and continuing review of the 5 tests.

Advantages

- o Currency uncertainty and transaction costs reduced.
- o The most powerful trading block with over 400 million largely well-off consumers.
- o Independent European Central Bank (ECB) should stabilize inflation/assure low-interest rates.
- o Members will be forced into deregulation/structural changes to put their economies in order.
- o Competition should improve productivity, reduce costs and expand trade.

Disadvantages

- o Lack of adjustment mechanisms for individual countries may cause tensions.
- o The introduction of the Euro did cause sharp price rises in Germany and Greece.
- o A unified monetary policy cannot meet the needs of up to 25 separate countries.
- o Europe's not as open, mobile or flexible as the US (limited fund transfers to poor regions).
- o Unresolved structural problems, for example state ownership, subsidies, rigid labour markets.
- o Pressure is developing to unify other aspects of policy, for example taxation.
- o There is no mechanism for leaving the Euro and the stability pact is suspended.

Significance

- Few small companies have planned for the Euro or its cost (est. 2.5 per cent of turnover).
- Cumulative loss of foreign direct investment if we don't join, for example warnings from multinationals.
- Winners are businesses with high cross-border revenues.
- Losers are those pricing above EU levels – Euro 'transparency' allows comparisons.
- Winners are those who adapt most successfully. Relocation and restructuring will be required.
- Local markets will become Euro-wide markets and marketers in small firms must face up to more competition. Market extension strategies must be considered to exploit niches.
- Marketers should review price lists, competitor reactions and promotional lead time.
- Marketers need to review training and adjust business systems for currency conversion.
- The hidden economy will have to convert from sterling into the Euro – the tax man cometh?
- The Euro has become a world reserve currency so creating the potential for volatility.

Conclusion

There is continued uncertainty regarding UK entry and the ultimate prospects for the Euro. The Euro presents a marketing challenge whether the UK enters or not. Turbulence will continue in Europe while the financial markets judge the resolve of the authorities. Benefits should flow in the longer run but uncertainties continue over enlargement, referendum and continuing fraud and mismanagement.

Lobbyists and the media

Lobbying may be defined as influencing members of a relevant legislature and soliciting their votes. This important activity has attracted adverse publicity but most lobbying activity comes within accepted definitions of ethical behaviour. To be effective it must be exerted *where and when the decisions are being made*.

The value of professional lobbyists to a business are as follows:

Monitoring	an early-warning service on forthcoming legislation
Interpreting	the implications of proposed legislation
Identify	political figures with a special interest in your issue
Inform	political decision makers about (your) industry developments
Prepare	background briefs and cases for busy legislators
Coordinate	constituency 'protest' letters to political representatives
Advise	the business on strategy and tactics to adopt

While there is little likelihood of stopping proposed legislation, the lobbyist will be seeking to persuade those with political power to think again on details, clarify ambiguity, gain assurances and secure legislation the industry can live with!

Exam hint

The mini-case is a critical aspect of the examination. Avoid the temptation to write out blocks of the text as answers to questions. The case often provides themes, clues, hints and/or examples but you must process and re-express the information in the light of your syllabus knowledge.

The pre-budget period is a busy one for lobby groups. Business, union, consumer, heritage, environment and an array of other interest groups wish to make their presence felt. However, public perceptions and public opinion are also important inputs into the political process. The climate the government seeks to create through its policies and laws is an output intended to positively influence these opinions. Putting a positive 'spin' on events will, if successful, make the public more likely to re-elect the government concerned.

The mass media, including press, radio and television, are important influences on these perceptions and opinions. They supply awareness of political issues and scrutiny of government behaviour and performance. As with pressure groups, they can influence decision makers and their policies through their campaigns. Investigative journalism in particular can have serious impacts on business as well as politicians. Exposure of malpractice can lead to loss of sales, resignations and policy changes.

Public relations (PR) is an another important aspect of marketing management and special skills are required to create and maintain mutually beneficial relationships with the media. It is a two-way relationship based on principles similar to those between a minister and a pressure group. PR aims to influence both the media agenda as well as the tenor of any debate that results. Issues and outcomes must be monitored through market research to assess shifts in public opinion.

Question 7.3

Key skills: working with others

If you were contacted by the local media requesting an interview regarding an issue arising over the marketing of a new product, how would you respond and what would you say?

Case history

The most important issue confronting southern Africa?

The politics of AIDS

1. Of 42 million people with HIV worldwide, 28 million live in sub-Saharan Africa.
2. An estimated 25 million have died so far worldwide but 'only' 15 000 in Britain (MRSA, the hospital 'superbug', kills 5000).
3. Russia has the fastest growth rate but India may have most cases by 2010.
4. Unlike other epidemic diseases that affect the old and young, AIDS mainly hits those aged 15–49.
5. There are more teachers in Zambia and Swaziland being killed of AIDS than are being trained to replace them.

6. A US census report suggested that life expectancy in 'relatively rich' Botswana should be 74.4 but is likely to fall to 26.7.
7. Senegal, Kenya and Uganda have avoided the general trend through intensive education campaigns and strong advocacy of condoms.
8. The spread of AIDS from high- to low-risk groups in many parts of Africa is facilitated by poverty, ignorance, cultural mores and lack of treatment.
9. Some epidemiologists are suggesting that 100 million could become infected in the next decade as HIV spreads across India and China. There are also fears regarding a similar virus passed to humans from apes as a result of eating or handling bushmeat. This flesh of wild animals is eaten by many people in Central Africa and has been smuggled illegally to the British market.

Questions

1. How important is an understanding of the environment to an understanding of the AIDS crisis?
2. How can the political environment make a positive contribution to a solution?
3. What could the marketer contribute to defeat the spread of AIDS?

Conclusions

The marketer should continuously reassess the political landscape surrounding the business. Inertia ensures that much of the political environment remains constant but pressure to set and implement a policy agenda means there will always be shifts in direction and corresponding impacts, particularly in the medium to long term.

A pluralistic society ensures that political change is often the product of compromise and consensus. Business interest groups can influence decisions but only if they understand the real nature of the political agenda. This may be driven by considerations of tactical or party advantage especially approaching election time.

The legal framework

Legal issues and cases involving businesses are regularly in the news. Seldom a week goes by without mention of such things as a music copyright infringement, an advert being withdrawn, an out-of-court settlement for negligence, a new law governing video nasties, a case of insider dealing, an accusation of sexual harassment or a fine imposed by a government inspectorate. Law was initially based on a concept of natural justice and parties to a transaction were treated as equals. Each party looked to their own best interest and suffered the consequences of their own poor judgement. Consumers were faced with the reality of 'caveat emptor' (let the buyer beware) but the growing power and size of businesses relative to individual consumers made this untenable. Pressure grew for legal protection which tilted the scales by increasing the rights of buyers and the duties of sellers. Similar principles will apply to those organizations that thought the Internet would allow unlimited, inexpensive access to consumers without regulatory restrictions. A French court order has required Yahoo to block access for French users to Nazi memorabilia on its US website while China employs literally thousands to 'police' the web. The

Internet is no more a borderless medium than the telephone and a country has every right within its territory to check and redress harm. It can, however, only act against companies with assets in its territory and those that find local regulations repressive can choose not to do business there.

Question 7.4

Key skills: collecting information

How does the law influence or affect you during a typical working day? This may not be directly, unless you get a speeding ticket! But how does it affect your day indirectly?

The framework of law is the product of both legal and political influences. An independent judiciary is normally responsible for the interpretation of common law. These are broad, comprehensive principles based on ideals of justice, fairness and common sense. The term 'common' means that it applies to all subjects. The way that common law is interpreted and applied changes over time through the effect of legal judgements made in higher courts. They then become precedents that must be applied by lower courts. Such judgements adapt the law to reflect current attitudes and values within society. One recent judgement awarded damages to asbestosis sufferers who had grown up in close proximity to the plant manufacturing the product. This exposed the company to substantial liabilities arising from potential claims from other victims. In another judgement, a woman dying of lung cancer was awarded $28 billion by a Los Angeles jury, the biggest individual settlement in US legal history. Philip Morris was found guilty of fraud, negligence and product liability but will appeal.

Governments introduce new laws in the form of statutes in order to implement their political manifestos. These acts reflect political philosophy as well as a growing pressure from society and pressure groups on government to regulate undesired activity or behaviour. New York businesses are required to implement a no-smoking ban in bars, restaurants (as with Ireland and Norway to protect catering workers) and public places. Meanwhile, the EU has introduced new laws that put the onus on employers to protect employees from a wide range of harassment on pain of heavy fines. This was designed to combat the macho culture of the Mediterranean but also has the side-effect of making companies think twice about organizing 'office' parties.

As society becomes increasingly complex so the resulting rise in workload forces governments to concentrate on 'enabling legislation', delegating authority to government departments, agencies or local authorities to fill in and administer the details. These are issued in the form of statutory instruments, regulations and bye-laws.

These authorities are normally responsible for the following roles:

- o Rule making and their interpretation (i.e. regulations)
- o Standards setting (e.g. emissions, food and hygiene)
- o Inspections – usually unannounced spot checks due to complaints
- o Enforcement – various sanctions from fines to closure.

Entry into economic unions also makes member countries subject to its regulations and legal provisions. Directives from the EU require implementation by member states, superseding national laws. They affect business, particularly in the area of competition policy, where fines of up to 10 per cent of turnover may be levied.

Role and objectives of legislation

Legislation involves a delicate process of balancing the diverse and often conflicting interests of the various stakeholders involved. Some of these may be summarized as follows:

- Governs exchanges between parties – the foundation stone of the market economy
- Ensures a level playing field between individuals and companies
- Counterbalances the economic power of business
- Settles disputes between stakeholders
- Denies market access to certain groups (e.g. alcohol to children)
- Balances the rights of the individual company with the collective rights of wider society
- Prohibits certain goods or activities (e.g. hard drugs/pornography)
- Seeks to prevent abuse without imposing excessive regulation
- Governs what business can and cannot do.

Unfortunately the law is a relatively blunt weapon in the achievement of such objectives, not least because society's attitudes and concerns can often change rapidly whereas the law tends to lag behind. There is a limit to what the legislature can amend or enact each year and many worthy legal bills fail to become law because of lack of parliamentary time. The activities of the media and community pressure groups such as the consumers associations have, however, made buyers more aware of their rights and more willing to initiate action to seek redress. Attitudes have changed dramatically in recent years with much more demanding expectations of the 'service' consumers believe they have a right to expect from business. A hardening compensation culture (though Britain still has the lowest tort costs at 0.6 per cent of GDP – one third the US level) also demonstrates a stronger willingness to seek redress. Not all this pressure on business to deliver the 'proper' goods comes from the law alone as Figure 7.1 shows.

Activity 7.5

Key skills: applying business law

Match the terms with their correct definitions:

- Caveat emptor and Caveat vendictor
- Standards Institute
- Code of practice
- Legislation
- Statute
- Ombudsman
- Seal of approval.

    - Let the buyer beware (no legal obligation to notify defects) and let the seller beware.
    - The process of making laws.
    - Voluntary guidelines to encourage desirable modes of behaviour.
    - A quango established to set product safety/quality standards.
    - An official appointed to investigate individual complaints of maladministration.
    - Law laid down by government legislation.
    - A mark, given by an expert, to confirm or guarantee a product.

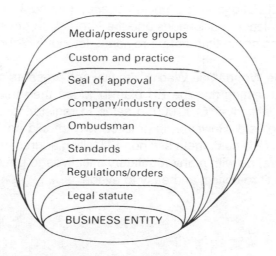

Figure 7.1 Regulatory pressures on business – a broader view

The government then has primary responsibility for the establishment, updating and operation of the legal framework. The law provides a means by which it can constrain business activities by defining the powers and responsibilities of owners and management. Many governments have sought to curtail the amount of regulation in recent years. They have launched successive campaigns to reduce bureaucracy and red tape especially where it impacts on smaller businesses. The Dutch government have calculated that red tape costs them over £11 billion of which half originates from the EU. They have targeted 2500 of the estimated 100 000 EU directives for removal and also deregulated a number of industries, such as telecommunications and transport services, in order to increase competition and release the latent potential for productivity improvements where slack and inefficiency had accumulated. On the other hand, they have had to establish a large number of quangos to regulate and oversee these operations. One notable regulation that the Singapore government has recently relaxed is their ban on chewing gum (also lap-dancing and bungee jumping). They have allowed some imports as part of a free trade deal with America.

Exam hint

Improving your performance

Don't be a 'DAQ' whether you are undertaking continuous assessment assignments or struggling to answer examination questions. What is a DAQ? Well it's a candidate who doesn't answer the question that's been set. A DAQ might decide to answer the question they hoped would be set or discuss a related topic because they had invested a lot of time in revising it. Whatever the reason a DAQ only ever gets one mark for their work and that's, you've guessed it – zero!

One area of marketing in which such extra legal bodies operate is in advertising and promotion. With the development of online interactive multimedia using digital broadband technology, not to mention e-commerce, more and more advertising is or will become cross-border. This raises the question of compliance with different national regulations. In Britain the Advertising Standards Authority was set up by the industry to counter the need for legislation by ensuring that all who commission, prepare and publish advertisements comply with the codes of advertising and sales promotion. It adjudicates complaints from the public and other interested parties. However, other bodies, like the Broadcasting Standards Council, govern specific media like TV. The Independent Television Commission, however, licences commercial services, whether terrestrial, cable or satellite, and regulates advertising and other standards through its code of practice. If nations lack a unified agency (although a single regulator, Ofcom will cover broadcasting, telecommunications and the Internet) to govern the content of advertising on its media, it may be some time before regional, let alone global, standards can be agreed.

On the other hand, the World Wide Web is a reality and presents a very real challenge in terms of regulation. It is interesting that the EU plan to widen their tax taken from e-commerce by requiring companies with over €100 000 in sales to register for value added tax in order to ensure a level playing field. However, in practice why should an online trader from, say, East Asia register and won't EU customers use non-EU billing addresses to avoid payment? In effect the new tax may prove, as with many regulatory initiatives to govern the Internet, to be unfair, costly to police, difficult to collect and easy to evade.

Question 7.5

Key skills: applying the law

What do you understand by the term 'red tape'? Survey your organization for examples.

Impacts and influences on business

There is something of a pendulum effect operating with regulation since fresh societal concerns regarding certain business activities will bring calls for the government to *do something about it!* The costs of regulation and ensuring compliance must be balanced with the benefits to stakeholders and society of the legislation in question. Some of the drawbacks of legislation and regulation include:

- ○ The extra costs of purchasing and installing required equipment; training staff to conform to standards; recording, reporting and taking action where deviations arise.
- ○ Conforming to legal requirements (e.g. tighter emission standards) adds to business costs and reduces competitiveness with overseas rivals.
- ○ Conforming to safety standards (e.g. testing required on new pharmaceutical products) delays introduction and returns so deterring investment and innovation.
- ○ Complicated regulatory procedures may be an entry barrier to small companies.
- ○ Legal and insurance costs – fines and adverse publicity.
- ○ Reduced consumer choice – loss of the right to buy as we wish.
- ○ Employment or environmental legislation may drive businesses to locate in Third World countries, taking jobs, investment and potential exports with them.

Note 1: Environmental laws and regulations vary widely across the global economy. Predictably it is the affluent economies which are most concerned for the quality of their environment. Poorer countries, such as China, India, Russia and Brazil, give more priority to the developmental process. Multinationals therefore find it difficult to develop standard environmental policies and are forced to tailor their general aspirations to local regulations. This creates scope for double standards and media exploitation to the disadvantage of the business.

Note 2: Small companies are harder hit by regulations. Compliance costs will be a higher proportion of total cost, they lack form-filling expertise and the time involved is a diversion from real business. Since small firms tend to be single-product or single-market operations, regulation is more likely to affect the whole business than in a large multi-product concern.

Note 3: Virtually all marketing activity is subject to a wide range of laws and regulation and these may originate from or even overlap at supranational, national, state or local levels. They are often in a state of flux and may change unexpectedly at the whim of public pressure or a change in government thinking. It is therefore hard work to keep up with important changes and the marketer might have to outsource this information role.

Note 4: Compensation culture is the corrupting notion that someone must be financially liable for anything that goes wrong. Originating in America, it has resulted in hospital lawsuits becoming commonplace. Firing incompetent teachers has become a legal nightmare while many professional workers are ceasing to practise due to high insurance premiums. When pharmaceutical companies halt research into potentially life-saving drugs (e.g. new antibiotics made quickly obsolete by 'smart bacteria') because liability has become disproportionate to economic return then only one thing suffers, society at large. President Bush has blamed the high cost of healthcare on this culture and will presumably fulfil his campaign pledge to cap damages for pain and suffering at $250 000.

Exam hint

Improving your performance

Questions will focus at least in part on the impact of the law on the activities of the marketer so refer to Figure 7.2 for examples from recent legislation to demonstrate your awareness.

While many businesses complain that they cannot compete fairly or profitably with current or proposed legislation, others cannot seem to compete without it, pressing the government for tariffs and quotas or longer periods of patent protection for the products they develop. Suppliers of branded goods, such as Coca-Cola and Nescafé for example, are seeking stricter regulations to stop retailers using 'me-too' packaging for their own-label products or selling their grey product through normal retail channels (Levi).

In fact the law is there to achieve three primary goals:

1. To protect businesses from one another (see Unit 3)
2. To protect consumers from business exploitation and
3. To protect the interests of wider society against damaging business behaviour (see Unit 3).

Clearly, legislation can be double-edged, in some cases making markets more competitive while in others creating new entry barriers. Industry will be well advised, therefore, to actively lobby for workable legislation when the government proposes change.

Some of the positive impacts on the marketing environment

- *Facilitates desirable social change* – Regulation sets norms of acceptable behaviour, alters behaviour, promotes change and can influence attitudes and perceptions. Legislation in the areas of equal pay, equal opportunities and sex discrimination have underpinned increasing female participation rates in the labour force and rising proportions in higher managerial positions.
- *Corrects market failures and ensures fair markets* – Legislation to deter restrictive practices and the exercise of monopoly power produces workable competition to the benefit of consumers in the form of lower prices and wider choice. It provides a framework of control that accounts externalities and acts on the structure of incentives to limit choices or protect certain interests.

     ○ *Encourages further knowledge* – New environmental standards provide opportunities and rewards and so encourages research into problems like the greenhouse and ozone effects. Regulation can provide leverage on the pace of change and influences the direction of effort by promoting or prohibiting certain technologies.

     ○ *Reassurance of the public at large* – The introduction of more stringent vehicle tests, for example, reduces safety concerns and improves emission standards. Complex regulations cover food safety and new product development encouraging greater consumption.

It should be noted that the beneficial impacts of regulation are both difficult to measure and more likely to be understated. Business will also be more inclined to measure the costs of compliance and to a much greater degree than society will be inclined to calculate the benefits.

One critical area of future legislation or industry self-regulation will be the Internet given the rising concern over fraud, cyber junkmail and the potential intrusion to privacy. This will also need to address cyber crime given the recent theft of one of the world's most guarded secrets – the Microsoft source code, that is its blueprint for its Windows program. The vulnerability of Microsoft to such industrial espionage gives every company with electronically coded intellectual property cause for real concern. This ranges from theft of customer lists to outright economic warfare. So while the Internet offers almost unimaginable potential as a global marketing channel it must also be tamed within acceptable codes of conduct that apply worldwide. Failing such supranational action (e.g. by the WTO) the full benefits of the Internet may not be achieved if negative customer and corporate attitudes build up.

Appropriate action

The relevant legislation which impacts on the business in general and the marketer in particular may be seen in Figure 7.2.

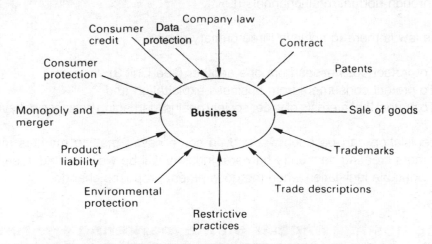

Figure 7.2 The potential impact of legislation on a business

Management needs to formulate a coherent policy in respect of legal matters. Primarily, it must seek to avoid liability under the various laws and regulations that affect it. This means establishing policy guidelines to ensure that at least minimum standards are attained. It also requires a policy regarding whether to take legal action against others and if so in what circumstances. This may involve competitors infringing patents (as in the case of multimedia products where adequate copies are available at a fraction of the cover price very soon after release), or bad debts, or even a libel action against environmental activists maligning the company product, as in the case of McDonald's.

In all but the simplest of cases a business should hire professional legal advice and representation. The law is extremely complex, not least where precedents are involved. Lawyers may deal with out-of-court advice and small claims, such as recovery of bad debts, and specialists will probably be retained where highly technical matters are concerned.

Exam hint

Improving your performance

You have now undertaken over three-quarters of the syllabus. Are you attempting the end-of-unit questions while the material is fresh in your mind? You can then come back and review your effort later as your knowledge, ideas and confidence in the subject grows.

A number of considerations need to be accounted here:

- The expensive nature of legal actions.
- The effect of actions on the company image.
- Longer-run interest in ongoing business relationships may incline companies to live and let live rather than resort to law.
- Business contracts may therefore include the means of resolving disputes arising, for example, use of mediators or arbitrators.
- Regulatory agencies may be content with assurances over future standards.
- Voluntary codes may be preferred to regulation and legal processes. These are standards of practice all businesses in the industry are expected to follow. They are difficult to enforce and may be replaced by law if widely ignored or flouted. UK retailers have agreed on a code to promote Internet retailing.
- Industrial tribunals are quasi-judicial bodies used for cases of unfair dismissal, discrimination and related matters. To avoid liability in such cases a business must ensure that it meets all its obligations by establishing the required internal policies and procedures and monitor their operating effectiveness (e.g. verbal and written warnings prior to dismissal of employees).
- Smaller companies are often exempted from certain legislation because of the high costs of compliance (e.g. employee protection).

Fair trading and the consumer

The syllabus wants you to achieve a general understanding of the influence of legislation on marketing. Detailed and specific knowledge of statutes or cases is not required, but a broad grasp of implications for marketing is expected. There will not be specific questions on, say, the finer points of contract law, but there may be general questions on the current legal position of the consumer and the possible scope for future legislation. The remaining section of this unit provides a brief appreciation of the main English legal areas impacting on the marketer. Non-UK readers should relate points to their own national legal context.

Contractual relationships

Contract law is the legal cornerstone regulating exchanges between buyers and sellers. Without a contract there is no direct relationship between the parties and hence no rights and obligations. A contract, in effect, exchanges promises. The buyer may promise to pay a certain sum of money in exchange for a specified product or service.

Activity 7.6

Key skills: interpreting information

Make time to study the 'terms and conditions' attached to goods or services supplied by your company and compare them to the elements outlined here. Alternatively, study those you have to sign when making a major purchase.

A contract comprises a number of elements, including:

○ *Offer* – Whether by word or deed, it is legally binding on the stated terms.
○ *Acceptance* – Must be voluntary and genuine on both sides.
○ *Intent to create a legally binding contract* – Most commercial contracts assume this.
○ *Consideration* – Something of value (e.g. cash) is exchanged for it to be enforceable.
○ *Capacity* – Parties must have the capacity to make a contract for it to be binding.
○ *Legality* – Contracts are deemed illegal if contravene existing law (e.g. restraint of trade).

Exam hint

If you are a non-UK candidate for the CIM examination you have the option of relating answers concerning legislative environment questions either to UK legislation, as outlined in this unit, or to that of your own country. It is important in the latter case to familiarize yourself in general terms with the equivalent legislation in your own country.

Remedies for breach of contract include injunctions and award of damages. Any award will only be to compensate the injured party for damages incurred (no actual loss = nominal damages) and all reasonable steps must be taken to mitigate (minimize) the extent of the damage sustained.

A small painting and decorating company, for example, is confronted by difficult judgements where a customer challenges an invoice by claiming that the work done was not performed as specified or agreed. If the sums involved are small, is it worth the time and effort involved to take the case to court? Given the highly technical issues in judging whether a contract has been satisfactorily completed, is the risk of an adverse judgement worth the considerable legal costs involved? Finally, what of the impact on the image of the company if it is seen to be taking its customers to court over relatively trifling amounts, not to mention the need to retain the goodwill of large customers in the longer run?

Activity 7.7

Key skills: collecting information

An effective method of extending your knowledge of the special difficulties confronting the sole proprietor or small business is to talk to them directly. Undertake a personal survey of a cross section of such businesses that you have dealings with and ask them to outline their three greatest legal headaches.

Protecting the consumer

This area of the law has grown incrementally in recent decades.

Since the Fair Trading Act 1973 the British consumer has enjoyed the protection afforded by the Director-General of Fair Trading (DGFT), in effect a 'consumer watchdog'. His or her role is to gather information on the activities of suppliers, identify those detrimental to consumers and recommend action to be taken. This covers terms and conditions of sale, selling and promotional methods, packaging and supply as well as payment methods.

A permanent Office of Fair Trading (OFT) provides a pool of expertise and experience in consumer affairs and represents a considerable deterrent to dishonest traders. As a statutory body it can deal with suspected abuses as they arise and prosecute actions against persistent offenders on behalf of the public. It has recently been given new powers to clamp down on loan sharks and the advertising of charge rates. Local authorities are responsible for most of the day-to-day enforcement of consumer protection legislation and their knowledge in areas such as weights and measures, trade descriptions and trading standards are complementary.

The areas where consumers require positive assurance of the good faith of suppliers are outlined below:

Assurance on labelling and description of goods

It is a criminal offence to falsely describe goods or services offered for sale. This applies to physical features and fitness for purpose. Similarly, prices must not be misleadingly stated. Acts govern how food can be stored, described and sold. Quantities and contents in prepackaged foods must comply with the stated amount (a current issue in this area is the labelling of genetically modified foods).

Assurance on quality and expected performance

Goods supplied must be as described by the vendor and of merchantable quality. This means fit for the purpose for which it was bought with due regard to price, description and any other factor. Any consumer contract clauses intended to limit liability in this respect are void.

Similar protection is extended to services whereby consumers have a right to expect that these will be carried out with reasonable care and skill, within a reasonable time and at the agreed price, or at a reasonable charge where none was previously agreed.

Assurance of safety

Acts regulate the sale of dangerous goods in terms of availability, packaging and labelling. Retail chemists, for example, must be under the supervision of a registered pharmacist.

Product liability is where a manufacturer can be shown to be under a duty of care to the customer, that is to avoid acts or omissions that could reasonably be expected to harm.

A 1985 EU directive makes producers, including importers into the European Union, liable for product defects. One important defence is where the state of scientific and technical knowledge at the time was such that the producer might not have been expected to discover the defect.

Restraint of objectionable sales promotion

False statements in adverts are an offence under the Trade Descriptions Act while 'voluntary' codes have evolved as a means of more flexible regulation. Health warnings on cigarettes are the result of voluntary agreements between the government and the industry concerned. The DGFT may seek an injunction (i.e. court order) from the High Court to prohibit false or misleading advertisements.

Assurance on fair payment terms

Acts provide comprehensive protection and enforcement on consumer credit and hire agreements including disclosure of the real interest rate (the per cent APR) and total to be paid plus full awareness of transaction rights and liabilities (e.g. the right to repay debt early). A 'cooling-off' or cancellation period also applies if the credit agreement is drawn up away from the business (e.g. at home) so reducing the effectiveness of high pressure sales techniques.

Question 7.6

Key skills: applying business law

In the light of recent scandals over misleading selling of pension policies and endowments, up-front commissions and so on, what is the appropriate response to recent surveys suggesting that 30 per cent of life insurance policies are *terminated within 2 years* at considerable financial loss to the consumer?

Implications for the marketer

Since the customer now has the option of settling a dispute with the supplier concerned or going directly to the authorities, it has forced even reputable companies to review and formalize their trading standards. Companies who have prospered by guaranteeing quality, no-quibble exchanges and refunds must now codify their excellence in practice.

They may also be forced to increasingly resort to law to counter the damage of adverse media coverage to their brand image. Individuals, often supported by pressure groups, are now bringing more civil suits on a no win-no fee basis. The State of New York has filed a lawsuit against major gun manufacturers accusing them of 'public nuisance' because of failure to introduce safety controls. Smith & Wesson was absent from the suit because it had voluntarily agreed to subscribe to a new code of conduct.

Clearly, one way forward for businesses are therefore voluntary industry codes. These are both encouraged and monitored by the authorities. Tailor-made to the needs of the industry concerned, they can be effective if gaining membership is conditional on compliance. Normally, such codes include a means of resolving disputes with customers through a process of arbitration. They may also provide a marketing edge to participating companies where the customer looks for a mark of service or quality assurance.

We can summarize some of the more important implications of this legislative environment as follows:

- ○ Failing to comply with at least the minimum legal requirements is bad business.
- ○ As in the case of individuals, prosecution leads to a bad public image and damage to credibility, for example, Firestone, one of the world's major tyre manufacturers, faced crippling lawsuits over alleged use of corroded steel in its products. A 1.4 million tyre recall was instituted by the company following highly critical reports by government safety inspectors. Defects allegedly caused the tread to wear out rapidly at high speed and one unlawful death suit already filed blames poor safety procedures at its factories. The company share price fell heavily. Jarvis, once Britain's largest construction firm and capitalised at £1 billion in 1998, suffered even more after being implicated in fatal rail crashes. At the end of 2004 it was worth under £20 million.
- ○ Being forced to resort to law is potentially costly and time consuming.
- ○ Systems must be in place plus staff suitably trained, to ensure compliance with legislation.
- ○ Proposed legislation should be monitored and a proactive approach to implementation adopted.
- ○ Employee legislation must also reduce marketers' flexibility and freedom of action.
- ○ Voluntary codes, if perceived as fair to stakeholders, can be cost-effective options.
- ○ The marketer can use superior legal standards as a source of potential competitive advantage. Compliance with exacting consumer legislation may put foreign competitors at a disadvantage and help create an image of 'best practice'.

While legislation is unlikely to be reversed it can be viewed *positively* in defining the areas within the boundaries of the law and voluntary good practice where the firm has 'freedom to market':

- ○ It has the right to market any good or service given compliance with health and safety requirements.
- ○ It has the freedom to price products provided it does not conspire or discriminate.
- ○ It has discretion in the marketing and promotional mix adopted providing it does not mislead or misrepresent.

Laws therefore represent freedoms as well as constraints; rights as well as obligations.

Question 7.7

Key skills: using information

The tobacco industry has been under considerable pressure in recent years arising out of the habitual nature of consumption and its links to cancer, heart and respiratory diseases. The Canadian health authorities introduced a hard-hitting advertising campaign depicting images of diseased hearts and cancerous tumours on cigarette packets and a written warning that they lead to sexual impotence. Despite premature death for one of every two users, the tobacco industry has vowed to fight them in court:

- ○ If there is a proven link to these diseases why, given a rising trend of consumption among younger age groups, has smoking not been made illegal?
- ○ Why do major retailers, who profess to be socially responsible, continue to sell such products?

Summary

In this unit we have dealt with important aspects of the closely linked political and legal environments for marketers. They have included recognition that:

o The political process is complex but pressure points are available to business lobbies.
o The political environment is a source of uncertainty especially around elections.
o The authority of supranational bodies, like the EU, must now be accounted for and monitored.
o The media play an important part in setting the political agenda. The influence of lobbyists is less readily detected but of greater potential importance to business interests.
o The law represents an evolving framework to reflect societal concerns and enable commercial activities to take place in a fair but effective manner.
o There is an underlying tension between the needs of business to innovate and deploy resources efficiently over time, and the health, safety and equitable treatment of various stakeholders.
o Quasi-legal means of regulation, such as codes of practice, serve an important function.
o There are many considerations to weigh before an organization initiates legal proceedings.

Further study and examination preparation

Given the number of questions on the paper as a whole, you cannot guarantee that a full question will always come up on this environment. There is a strong likelihood, however, that it would form at least part of a question, particularly within a section A case as seen below. The examiner will be aware that candidates come from different national backgrounds and will set questions accordingly. The focus is much more likely to be on the impact of this environment on marketing than on political or legal specifics.

Extending knowledge

Palmer and Hartley, *The Business and Marketing Environment*, McGraw-Hill – Chapter 11, The Legal Environment. See also A. Palmer, *The Business Environment*, McGraw-Hill – Chapter 9.

Websites to scan include:

www.gold.net/ifl is an index of legal resources

www.open.gov.uk is a gateway to a diversity of government information

www.ft.com

www.economist.com

www.the-times.co.uk

www.Europa.Eu.Int for information on the EU

www.poptel.org.uk/labour-party/index-t.html

www.conservative-party.org.uk

www.parliamentlive.tv.co.uk features political debates

www.C.Span.org covers the Senate and House of Representatives

Exam question 7.1

Please see Question 1d, June 2004. For specimen answers go to www.cim.co.uk.

Exam question 7.2

Please see Question 1c, December 2003. For specimen answers go to www.cim.co.uk.

Exam question 7.3

Please see Question 6d, December 2003. For specimen answers go to www.cim.co.uk.

Exam question 7.4

Please see Question 2, June 2004. For specimen answers go to www.cim.co.uk.

unit 8 the technical/ information environments

Learning objectives

This unit examines the all-embracing effects of the technological and information environments, as well as the dynamic and complex nature of change itself. By the end of this unit you will have:

- Understood the role of business in the development and diffusion of new technology (3.7)

- Appreciated the factors driving and limiting change in the technical and information environments

- Recognized the importance of monitoring and forecasting technical change

- Explored the role of information, and the significance of the information revolution.

Study Guide

We live in a technological society whose effects impact on all aspects of our life. Our work is particularly subject to such influences and major transformations have occurred in recent years in the majority of industries and occupations. So too have our means of transport, how we shop, the ways we spend our leisure time, how we learn, the houses we live in and the way our health is monitored. Only our sleeping habits seem relatively unaffected, although even here new drugs, insulation, bed designs and environment control are affecting the lives of many. As one example, Internet-based UK retail sales tripled to £40 billion during 2002–03 and 40 per cent growth is expected for 2004 according to the ONS.

The marketer must strive to understand the changes taking place and be sensitive to new developments. The necessary skills must be acquired and continuously updated so that change is prepared for and promoted. Individual and organizational survival may depend on it.

With regard to the technological environment it is an area which can generate a diversity of examples as context for examining its impacts. Much of marketing is underpinned by technology:

- Advertising relies on communication technology
- Logistics on transport technology
- Market research on information systems.

This unit will therefore concentrate on general themes and leave you the responsibility of finding relevant applications from your own experience and reading.

The examiner may require you to select technologies of your own choice and discuss their effects. Relevant applications from your own working environment are more likely to interest and impress the examiner, as it shows you are seeking to relate your studies to your work situation. Do make sure, however, that you have a working knowledge of technical terms affecting the work of marketers.

Definition of terms

The successful development of new technology comprises a number of distinct stages:

KNOWLEDGE – RESEARCH – INVENTION – DEVELOPMENT – INNOVATION – DIFFUSION – REFINEMENT

New technology represents new production possibilities and therefore the means of satisfying consumer needs and wants, more efficiently and effectively. It allows more and better value-for-money goods to be produced with given resources.

The state of technology is a function of resources and the knowledge and skills to use them while technical change is the result of changing resources, increased product and process knowledge and the accumulation of applications experience. Knowledge of the current state of technology is the foundation upon which research takes place. New ideas and developments in sciences often form the basis of advance and synthesis in others. Research and invention is the generation of new ideas, or improvement of existing ones, while development is their useful application to specific products or processes.

Innovation relates to the actual commercial exploitation of a development or new idea while diffusion refers to the rate of its adoption through the potential target population concerned. Refinement exploits the full potential of the technology and often forms the basis of product differentiation in the growth and early maturity stages of the life cycle.

Continuous innovation provides the fundamental drive and dynamic in capitalism. It is probably the only strategy that, if successfully implemented, will ensure a firm earns excess profits over time. New products that more effectively satisfy customer needs and wants will increase profits as will cost-saving processes and technologies. However, only by ploughing back profit into maintaining technological or design leadership can long-term profits be ensured. Competitors will seek to enter the market and imitate the innovations, but they will always be aiming for a moving target. Similarly, anything that inhibits this creative process may threaten the economic growth and development of the system.

Examples of such innovation include: a new Volvo designed by an all-female team with lift up door and an 'autopark' function that sizes up a potential space and steers itself into the spot: a vehicle that automatically obeys the speed limit through a satellite linked system; supermarket scanners that value an entire trolley in seconds and automatically deduct the cost from a compatible credit card; and a Wakamaru robot that is programmed to watch over elderly people.

Characteristics of technology

This environment is not just about hi-tech and computers but is all-pervasive. Some advances are relatively simple, such as 3M's adhesive message pads, the Durex Performa condom or Wrigley's non-stick chewing gum, while others are more complex, as in new packaging technologies. Others, like the Dyson computer controlled vacuum cleaner or dual tub environmentally friendly washing machine, may transform aspects of housework.

Question 8.1

Key skills: problem-solving

○ Give six examples of industries with big cost-saving innovations over the last 5 years.
○ Can you think of any industry that had no significant cost-saving innovations?

As one of the major macro-environment variables it has a breadth of impact that affects all the others. Stock market crashes, for example, can be triggered by automatic computer sell signals. Increased employment of married women has been facilitated by the development of labour-saving, controllable and convenient technologies in the home which will culminate in 'intelligent domestic environments' controlled by information and communication technologies (ICT). The political complexion of Eastern Europe and China has altered beyond recognition, with exposure of their material expectations to the telecommunication broadcasts of Western democracies.

Perhaps the biggest potential impact of all arises from our increasing dependence on technology in general and programmable chips in particular. The millennium bug may not have been materialized but computers are susceptible to viruses and glitches that may involve significant specific or worldwide costs. Over six and a half thousand viruses were detected in the first half of 2004 alone. One e-mail virus was unleashed in the Philippines and within hours had swept through Europe and America attacking 5 million machines and causing an estimated $1.5 billion of damage. More recently the Sasser and SoBigF variant of the Blaster virus each infected almost one in five computers causing serious damage to many companies. The e-mail, entitled ILOVEYOU, had an irresistible selling proposition that paralysed thousands of organizations. Disrupting both US and UK legislatures, it demonstrated the vulnerability of open electronic systems to cyber warfare. Sasser was developed by an 18 year old German computer nerd, but managed to disrupt hospitals in Hong Kong, the rail network in Australia and the coastguard in Britain. Only a few incidents come to light because companies are anxious to protect their image and share prices. The first mobile phone virus called Cabir detected in 2004 was able to steal phone numbers and text messages. Computer problems have also plagued government agencies. For example, £500 million IT system installed at the Child Support Agency is still not providing payments to thousands of single parents 1 year after installation. Similar fears surround a similar £4 billion project for centralising NHS patient records.

With most of the world's essential systems controlled by computer software, such vulnerability brings the risk of critical failures in air traffic control, nuclear plant, medical facilities, defence and the financial system. System breakdown would lead to economic disruption and probable public disorder. It is clearly important that organizations plan for such contingencies since the potential commercial damage arising from some form of computer breakdown is almost inestimable for businesses such as travel companies or financial institutions. As we saw with Microsoft, hackers continue, almost as a matter of course, to gain access to 'secure' facilities despite massive investments to improve systems effectiveness. How long will it be before their services are coordinated by revolutionaries or rogue governments? Such thoughts should at least prompt the marketer to audit their information systems, ensure back-up (Note businesses affected by September 11th attacks) is in place and that manually based contingency plans are potentially operational. Similar actions should be encouraged in the value chain.

Other threats arise out of the unregulated development of genetic modification which could allow the spread of even more deadly viruses than that of the species jumping AIDS contagion. Even global air travel poses threats as demonstrated by the in-flight spread of infectious diseases and cases of malaria reported near British airports caused by mosquitoes 'hitching a lift'. Severe acute respiratory syndrome (SARS) was spread by this means leading to wide-spread panic and disruption especially in Hong Kong where retail sales fell by 50 per cent as shoppers stayed at home. The final official death toll of 800 was statistically insignificant compared to the millions who die each year from 'common diseases' yet it produced reaction out of all proportion to the probable risk. It signals global vulnerability to a modern plague, which like Spanish flu in 1918, could kill millions while paralysing commercial activity.

Marketing environment in practice

The human genome project

Background

1. One of the greatest scientific breakthroughs in human history
2. A collaboration of scientists from Britain, China, France, Germany, Japan and the US achieved understanding of the precise genetic code that makes us human
3. It heralds the era of biomedicine that corporate biotech giants can exploit
4. Genomics may open up enormous commercial opportunities for biotechnology companies but investment is even riskier and more volatile than Internet stocks.

Potential advantages

1. More rapid development of treatments for cancer, birth defects and common ailments. This includes development of Delta 32, the so-called 'survival gene', which is one of ten mutant genes carried by those who are resistant to AIDS
2. Life expectancy could be doubled by curing the previously incurable with personalized body repair kits and through the recent discovery of the 'Methuselah gene'
3. Freely available to everyone despite private sector involvement
4. Genetically based antidotes to Spanish flu-like viruses are now being developed
5. Age of personalized health care with gene therapy revolutionizing medicine
6. Appetite-suppressing drugs in development that have reduced food intake in mice to one-tenth without any reduction in metabolic rate.

Potential drawbacks

1. Its use to 'engineer' human beings, i.e. designer babies (sex can already be predetermined)
2. Discrimination against the genetically disadvantaged
3. Insurance and loan restrictions on individuals known to be susceptible to disease
4. Companies may demand genetic tests before taking on new employees
5. Possible invasion of privacy
6. Lack of current ethical guidelines, e.g. human cloning using harvested embryo stem cells
7. No guarantee that genetic testing will be affordable by the poor – increasing healthcare gap
8. Excessive control over life-saving diagnosis/treatment by firms patenting specific genes
9. Fear eventual development of 'white plague' diseases genetically engineered to kill specific biological groups
10. Pressure groups will view the development of GM primates (monkeys share 98 per cent of our DNA) for medical research as totally unacceptable.

Exam hint

Remember to turn your mobile off before the examination starts and resist any temptation to use it as a flexible aid to problem-solving or 'picturing' the answer!

Technology progressed in phases until industrialization, when a marked acceleration occurred. Technology has always extended human capabilities and industrialization massively extended human musculature. Just three or four lifetimes have seen transformation from agricultural through industrial to service economy and the pace is not slackening as developed countries enter a post-industrial 'information/communication' society. This is based on:

○ Technology as the primary driving force for social change
○ Convergence of computer/telecommunications media technologies
○ A high and rising proportion of communications/information technology ownership e.g. by 2007, 2 billion people, or a third of the world's population will own a mobile. This is expected to double by 2015
○ Extension of the powers of the human nervous systems of sight and sound via TV, telephone, mobile telephone, fax and other information systems such as the Internet
○ Development of digital superhighways unifying information, communication and multi-media Mobiles are becoming integral to our lives with location software, multimedia messaging and Internet access freeing us from our PC's. Linking wirelessly to the Internet will transform the mobile into a device that is always on, always connected and with the speed and applications of a laptop
○ Credit transfer rather than cash-based society, e.g. Switch/Visa cards are already a global currency
○ A diverse, decentralized and differentiated society composed of knowledge workers.

Question 8.2

Key skills: using information

What was the typical lifestyle 30 years ago? What products and services that are taken for granted today did not exist then?

The role of business

Business is the main conduit by which science and technology impacts on society. Most change is incremental and progressive in nature but breakthroughs can and do bring sudden and dramatic change requiring organizations to monitor their technological environment more closely than others. If a rival succeeds in achieving a technological advantage it is a much more significant competitive edge than any other, due to the time, difficulty and resource commitments required to counter it. You may recall the damage inflicted on the Swiss watch industry by Japanese microprocessor-controlled timepieces, or more recently the impacts on traditional booksellers of Amazon.com or Direct Line on insurance brokers. There are also potentially survival threatening risks as discovered by the successful bidders who gambled €110 billion on 3G licences to develop high-speed mobile networks with Internet access. It has been calculated that recouping start-up costs would require revenues of €500 from each individual in Europe.

With competition from rival technologies such as wireless LAN, the gamblers are already beginning to write off a large part of their investment.

Exam hint

Have a look at Exam question 8.1 posed at the end of this unit. Plan out an answer as you work through the remainder of this section.

The drive to innovate depends on a number of factors:

1. *Stage of the product or technology life cycle* – The introduction and growth stages of any new invention will be characterized by creative product innovation which will continue until the technology matures.
2. *Size of the firm* – Studies suggest that small firms provide a more productive climate for invention but lack the resources and organization to diffuse it quickly and effectively. Small firms tend to specialize and the risk of failure is high. Even large firms must beware of over-commitment (e.g. 3G mobiles).
3. *Nature of competition in the market* – The drive is powerful in fragmented markets but the resources and size to exploit them successfully is often lacking. Financial resources and control of the market exist in monopoly but innovation would make obsolete previous investments. The ideal combination is in concentrated industries, where size and market share is combined with considerable rewards if innovation can undermine rival product offerings. Interdependence, therefore, ensures that each company will maintain considerable research and development capability as a precaution against rivals obtaining such an edge
4. *The pace of change in consumer tastes* – If the existing market is static then new products supplied to new consumers in new ways may be the only strategy for growth.

Activity 8.1

Scan advertisements in magazines and the trade press for products or services which are being marketed on the basis of their technical sophistication or innovativeness (e.g. space hotel holidays planned for late 2004 by the Russian Space Agency at around £13.6 million for a 3 week stay). Would-be space tourists already on the waiting list (following Dennis Tito's footsteps in May 2001) will be accompanied by a professional cosmonaut and must train extensively and learn Russian. Another example is Echonet, being developed by Panasonic, a new generation mobile that gives their owners control over virtually every household electrical appliance (each fitted with tiny transponders). It will also warn in the event of breakdowns or break-ins.

Examine how they are promoted (particularly in the light of the Columbia space shuttle tragedy).

What are the technical imperatives?

We live in a technological era where knowledge and expertise confers status and societal approval. The Japanese and other Asian economies are admired for their ability to emulate and improve on Western technology. In their turn, European and American companies such as

General Motors, Fiat and Volkswagen have invested staggering sums in robotization and computer integrated manufacturing in an effort to counter the lower wage costs and team-based productivity of Asian competitors. *Global competition* is clearly one of the imperatives forcing technological change.

Technology can also be viewed as a Pandora's box which, once opened, can never again be closed. Advances in one sphere of science provide the catalyst for a dozen others in adjacent fields where time, money and human expertise provide the only limits to the expanding frontiers of knowledge.

International trade has developed through time by the opening up of new and superior trade routes. As Bloor observes in his book *The Electronic B @ zaar*, the Silk Road ran through China and central Asia to the empires of Athens and Rome. For 18 centuries it was the premier Eurasian trade route with silks and spices bartered for precious metals. It was displaced by Magellan, as the merchant states of Europe established a global highway across the seven seas which, like the Silk Road, spawned a web of feeder trade routes policed by their navies. Trade in primary products soon gave way to manufactures with the Industrial Revolution. Technological developments in transportation ensured that people and goods could move ever faster around the world.

At the end of the twentieth century Tim Berners-Lee invented an unexpected and potentially powerful new trade route that grew at breathtaking speed from the West coast of America to connect the developed economies of Europe and East Asia. The Internet is a global information highway with electronic strands extending to every human nook and cranny of the world. It has existed for only a decade but is destined to be the trade route to the future either supplanting existing trading arrangements or transforming them beyond recognition.

Key marketing skills: using ICT and the Internet

With wireless connections to the Internet taking off, an estimate of over 1 billion Internet users worldwide does not look unreasonable. America's 200 million online consumers alone spent £120 billion on the web. Access in some developing countries is inhibited by limited Internet service provision or unreliable and costly phone links (although China has more mobile phones than the USA). Depending on the competence of the user and the power and speed of the recipient's computer, the potential uses of this driving technology are as:

○ *An international source of information* – most constraints of national boundaries are eliminated allowing students, researchers and companies of all sizes to access vast databases. (The amount of information stored on computers has doubled since 1999.) Seventy-five per cent of US car buyers are said to consult the Internet for information before deciding what to buy, while Gucci provides a sophisticated information-only fashion site whose high definition pictures make it one of the most elegant virtual arcades. Users can click onto highlights of the latest collection and essential accessories.
○ *A communication tool* – offering a value added and cost saving means of promoting corporate or brand image as well as managing the supply chain by linking subsidiaries and stakeholders to a private intranet.
○ *A channel for e-commerce* – speed, convenience and interactivity are driving the development of digital information super-highways capable of delivering a myriad of business services using text, sound and vision (business to business and business to consumer).
○ *A major engine of potential future job growth.*
○ *A potential legal threat* – if the precedent set by an Australian court in a recent libel case becomes an international standard. The trial was allowed there on the grounds that 'libel material' while originating in more liberal America could be downloaded on the Internet and read anywhere.

Insight

Is the Web getting smaller?

Following massive growth from under 20 000 websites in 1996 to over 35 million at the end of 2001 there has been a modest fall. This is probably due to a fall in registered domain names that speculators had hoped would be bought up by businesses looking for a stylish Internet identity. These can only be registered for 2 years at a time and are being abandoned particularly as new suffixes, such as .info, come along to relieve the pressure on the dot-com domain.

Recession may also be giving a fillip to e-commerce as businesses strive to reduce costs while continuing to meet demand. Large firms are pushing smaller suppliers to adopt e-commerce systems while post-11 September the use of mobile Internet access is booming. Reduced inclination to travel has also promoted videoconferencing.

The initial dynamic of e-commerce has found its focus on business to business applications (80 per cent of global revenues) where the scope for savings through electronically driven purchasing, stock management and logistics is greatest. Business to consumer growth is fastest in product or service groups where e-commerce produces comparative advantage in ease of transactions and value added online service, for example book extracts and CD demos. The customer's familiarity with a certain product or website is another critical determinant.

Despite ongoing concerns over the security of e-transactions and more realistically priced dot-com stocks, the future still looks very positive. It should be remembered that there were as many as a thousand US car producers in the 1920s yet only a handful survived. Of the Internet companies launched since 1995 precedent would suggest that over 90 per cent will end up as nearly worthless. Only the fittest survive in the competitive process, but initial diversity normally ensures that all alternative approaches to the market are explored. e-Commerce transfers key functions to the customer who must access the site and complete online ordering procedures whereas the website must passively wait for a customer to click on. Traditional marketing therefore has a critical role in organizations like Amazon and AOL, since millions must be spent in advertising and sales promotion to get their sites and services known. It is not sufficient for traditional companies to add a website as an electronic equivalent of their sales brochure. The whole business must be redesigned to exploit the cost saving and communication-easing properties of this forcing technology.

Fifty-year innovation cycle

Another technology imperative may be provided by this long-wave cycle. It has been observed that economic development since the Industrial Revolution has progressed in 50-year cycles based on successive clusters of critical innovations, for example textiles, steam power, railways, and so on.

Businesses initially responded to downturns by cost cutting and retrenchment but as depression continued were forced to consider more radical solutions to declining sales and profitability. A new wave of innovations was created as businesses became prepared to risk resources on new or existing inventions, for example, digital communications, biotechnology, lasers and nanotechnology are currently state of the art.

Activity 8.2

Key skills: collecting information

Taking these state-of-the-art technologies, brainstorm as many product innovations based on them as possible. Can you think of any product or process innovations that represent fusions of these separate technologies?

Creative destruction

Schumpeter viewed innovation as the source of creative destruction whereby dominant established firms and industries based on mature technology are challenged by new firms, using substitute products or processes, often from a different industry. Such entrepreneurial initiatives constantly threaten to shake up monopoly and oligopoly market situations, keeping them on their toes (e.g. IBM and Compaq in PCs). The joint venture between Mercedes-Benz and Swatch provided an interesting example of this in the urban electric car market until the latter's stake was bought out in 1999.

Technological change is part of the *dynamic of capitalism*. The expectation of new and improved products is part of the culture and businesses are rewarded when these needs are satisfied. Businesses are motivated by the need to survive and make profits, governments to promote growth and people to improve and change. This produces a drive for technology that feeds on itself, rippling through society as one advance triggers another in a technological *multiplier-accelerator effect*.

New generations of products are introduced with progressively reducing lead times, stimulating the planned obsolescence of current offerings. The power of snob appeal conferred on pioneer consumers and the requirement for followers to 'keep up with the Joneses' through emulation reinforces the treadmill of constant novelty and change. A case in point would be videos. Dixons, Britain's largest electrical store, is already planning to phase out the VCR since DVD sales currently outstrip VCR's by 40 to 1.

Question 8.3

Key skills: using information to contribute to the strategy process

What are the opportunities and threats of technological change as far as the business organization is concerned? What steps can the business take to minimize the threats and maximize the opportunities?

Microprocessors: a metatechnology with universal applications

This has become by far the most important technology of the late twentieth century. Despite a progression from valves and transistors, it represents a 'technological leap' innovation. This has allowed the enhancement of design and performance in a wide diversity of products and services.

The technology has also significantly contributed to the efficiency and effectiveness of communication systems, information services and other infrastructures (e.g. computerized traffic signals and electronic-based road-pricing systems to relieve congestion).

Microprocessors both extend and increasingly displace a wide range of intellectual and intuitive skills. In effect it constitutes the most rapid and dramatic industrial change in history and is still proceeding rapidly with the latest generation chips manufactured by Intel.

Question 8.4

Marketing skills: interpreting information

Suppose that an unusual electrical storm unaccountably disrupted the workings of all microprocessors that have ever been produced. What would be the immediate effects on the following:

- ○ The motorist?
- ○ The household?
- ○ The marketing department?

Characteristics include reliability, robustness, speed, cost economy, dependability and accuracy. When applied to manufacturing processes these characteristics have led rapidly towards the development of computer-integrated semi-automated plants. These are small, self-organizing systems that learn from their environments as well as from their experience and adapt accordingly. The limits of power and performance that can be packed on a chip are, however, being approached although alternatives include parallel processing and even DNA-based 'living' computers.

Exam hint

Working with others

As the examination or assessment deadline approaches you must manage time effectively and use your marketing skills of working with others. You will probably need the help and support of your family, your partner and your boss in these critical days. Don't leave the preparatory work until too late thus creating overload on you and those around you.

The technological diffusion process

The rate at which firms adopt innovations is the rate of diffusion and involves cost and risk as well as the prospect of return.

As can be seen in Figure 8.1, the process is similar to the product life cycle. Factors that determine whether the rate is rapid or slow include:

- ○ *Profitability* – Depends on a number of cost and revenue factors. The larger the innovation's impact on these relative to what is currently in use, the more rapid the diffusion.
- ○ *Deterrence* – This measures the consequences of *not adopting* the new technology. If a serious loss of sales is likely due to the superiority of the new technology then

diffusion will be rapid as producers are forced to jump on the bandwagon or go out of business.

○ *Scale of investment* – Hi-tech generally means large financial outlays on both hardware and software aspects of operations. Businesses have limited internal resources and access to external risk capital, causing diffusion to be slower in such cases.

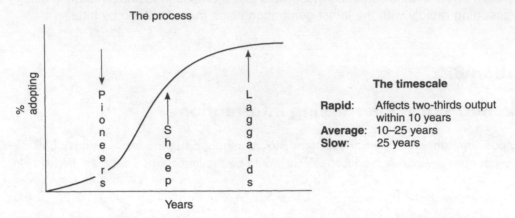

Figure 8.1 The diffusion process

○ *Market structure* – Oligopoly is probably the most effective structure for rapid diffusion. Multinationals have the organizational ability and resources to effect this globally.
○ *Characteristics of the new product or process*.
○ *Potential range of applications* – More means greater profitability and sales potential for the technology.
○ *Environmental acceptability* – Actual/perceived impacts of a new technology affects diffusion due to legislation/liabilities that arise, for example, rising cost of verifying drugs has halved R&D spend in 20 years.
○ *Change agents* – For a new idea to succeed in a business it needs a champion to challenge the status quo and persuade decision makers of the need for change. Much is invested in the current way of doing things and resistance to change occurs among management, customers and the workforce. The government is often a change agent through initiatives to support innovation or willingness to place orders.

Case history

The case of the Internet

According to Timmins in his book *Electronic Commerce*, this is diffusing so fast primarily because of the following factors:

○ *Low entry cost* – for a web presence compared to other business to business solutions such as electronic data interchange (EDI).
○ *Rapid return on investment* – in months by eliminating paperwork/providing customer support.
○ *Investment is flexible* – open networks and standards support trading relationships with a multitude of business partners. Switching costs are minimized compared to specific EDI systems.
○ *Connectivity and ultra-rapid communication* – e-mail links save time and cost in communication, order and delivery confirmation, and so on.
○ *Meets information needs* – use a browser to identify market trends, competitors or opportunities.

- ○ *Critical mass* – attracts more users/providers of business solutions. Stakeholders are increasingly connected and international participation by governments reinforces user confidence.
- ○ *Technology driven innovation cycle* – established companies/start-ups create new opportunities through information communication technologies (ICT), so attracting new entrepreneurs/reinforcing the virtuous circle of development.
- ○ *Spin-off from other applications* – Internet monitoring services indicate that 95 of the top 100 sites are concerned with pornography and users spent over £2 billion worldwide at 400 000 sites sounding the death knell for the adult magazine industry.

Technological transfer

Another aspect of diffusion is the transfer of technology from:

- ○ Basic research to practical applications
- ○ Military/aerospace applications to industrial products
- ○ Hi-tech to consumer goods and services
- ○ Developed to less-developed countries.

Fundamental new technologies originate from a number of sources, including universities and research institutes, military establishments, government agencies as well as businesses. Technology may be licensed from the inventor, or leading-edge multinationals encouraged to locate high-technology subsidiaries and transfer expertise into an economy. For example, American and Japanese computer companies were attracted into central Scotland, providing opportunities for third generation indigenous companies to prosper.

Many developing countries rely on foreign multinationals in banking, oil, textiles or food processing to provide a similar driving force to their industrialization process. Such companies often form an integral part of a dual economy that brings much-needed exposure to cutting-edge technologies, management methods and information technology.

Question 8.5

If your firm has invested large sums in developing a revolutionary new product or service idea, what actions would you advise it to take in order to generate maximum returns?

Technological forecasting

Successful management's have always kept a cautious eye on the pace of change in both their own and adjacent industries. However, this has tended to be a 'defensive' eye to the danger of being overtaken by substitute technology rather than with a proactive intention to achieve competitive advantage. Governments can be significant catalysts in kick-starting the research process through grants, subsidies and tax allowances, particularly in pursuit of external security or national competitive advantage.

A technological forecast should be the foundation block of long-term plans, based on effective collusion between the technologist, designer and marketer. This is necessary to achieve the essential balance between creating and satisfying the needs of the customer. Alternative or substitute product or process technology is more difficult to forecast than core technology, and requires a more qualitative analysis. Forecasts of technologies are therefore of three types:

Exam hint

Improving your performance

Make short notes on other technological developments in each element of the marketing mix:

- o *Product* – CAD/CAM and design cycles
- o *Place* – EDI with intermediaries, satellite tracking of vehicles
- o *Promotion* – Interactive TV, computer-designed samples, database marketing
- o *Price* – Barcode scanning, electronic pricing.

1. *Evolution of the current technology* – existing trends in key technologies are identified and then extrapolated.
2. *Morphological* – analysis explores technological opportunities by systematically defining the basic features of current technology, identifying the known alternatives to each and then looking for feasible alternative combinations.

A car, for example, can have alternative fuels: petrol, diesel, battery, gas, solar, hydrogen fuel cell, and so on; alternative body materials: steel, plastic, aluminium, fibreglass, and so on; alternative braking systems: friction disk, air, cable, and so on. These can then be combined in different formulas to produce alternative concept cars (hybrids are also possible, e.g. diesel/battery). This provides a fresh perspective on customary technologies and a fruitful basis for brainstorming feasible product alternatives. One recently developed example is Glasphalt, that resembles traditional road resurfacing materials but contains 30 per cent crushed glass. This conveniently combines recycling, reduced extraction of new materials and diminished pressure on landfill sites.

3. *Scenarios* – provide broader views of the future and insight into more diverse developments. Alternative personal transportation systems, for example, might include microlight aircraft systems but equally developments in interactive video, teleworking and virtual reality might make many such journeys unnecessary in future.

Insight

Google and Spam?

Google, the Internet search engine floated onto the stock exchange in 2004, was valued at $27 billion despite profits of only around $150 million. Responsible for half of all web searches, the company was only formed in 1998. Used by over 100 million customers per month and processing 3000 searches a second, it generates its revenue from ads placed on the website. Launched with a higher rating than even Microsoft, the company does not, however, have an equivalent monopoly so any rival with a better search engine will cause its customers to switch. Accordingly the company has unveiled plans for a 'free' e-mail service that offers 100 times more storage space than rivals. A key attraction of Gmail is its powerful 'spam' filters for removing unwanted promotional material. However, users e-mails will be used for targeted advertising, which means that any reference to say a sporting fixture is likely to prompt a ticketing agency link.

Potential impacts must be identified, not only for the industry itself but also for channel intermediaries and end users. Feasible technologies are then screened to remove improbable options due to considerations of cost, environmental safety and so forth and a timescale determined for the remainder. This might be done by the use of Delphi techniques, drawing on the expertise of practitioners in the field.

Possible technologies must, however, be set against marketing forecasts of what the demand will be. Timing is also critical in achieving innovative success and avoiding technological failure. An innovation which is right for its time must not only have all the requisite technical building blocks in place but also receptive users, with the need, income and strength of preference to demand it in profitable volumes.

Unanticipated consequences should also be considered. These include impacts on current methods (e.g. the Indian police's carrier pigeon service, as the world's last messenger bird service, is now obsolete due to improved radio technology and the Internet) as well as complementary effects, such as the estimated 700 billion sheets of paper used in Britain's photocopiers every year. Similarly the average Briton is estimated to waste up to 18 working days a year waiting for e-mails and Internet pages to download.

Question 8.6

Key skills: using information and problem-solving

These were all in the future 5 years ago – Where are they now?

- A chequeless society
- Virtual reality holidays
- Fifty per cent of residences with interactive access to databases
- Videophones in everyday use
- Drive-by-wire electronic systems for congestion-free 'intelligent' motorways
- Speech-responsive computers
- Windscreen maps in cars
- Digital signatures for transactions.

Information technology and marketing applications

In this section we will briefly summarize the main applications for marketers arising out of information technology. You should keep abreast of any developments that potentially improve the marketer's performance. The logical order to consider this is from product conception through to after-sales service and eventual disposal. German companies like Mercedes, for example, must now maintain computerized records of all vehicles sold so they may be tracked and accounted for in compliance with recycling legislation.

○ *Product development* – This is based on forecasting and the use of various databases to assess customer requirements and tastes. Marketing research is facilitated through computerized analysis packages, for example SPSS.

○ *Product design* – Product development times are falling sharply through the flexibility, versatility and time saving involved in computer-aided design, manufacture and engineering (CAD/CAM/CAE). New cars which once took 7 years from drawing board to production line now take much less than half that. The main implication is a shrinking maturity and decline stage for many products combined with a geometric expansion in models and parts numbers. Virtual reality offers further possibilities in terms of computer stimulation.

Marketing environment in practice

A microscopic speck of dandruff recently led to the arrest and conviction of a violent armed robber 10 years after the incident. The case, which relied on advances in DNA technology, prompted a national advertising campaign featuring the case by shampoo makers Head and Shoulders using the slogan 'Don't get caught with dandruff'.

○ *Mass customization* – is enabled by computer integrated manufacture (CIM) and presents an opportunity for marketers to deal not with population segments but with individuals. Technology now allows for marketing solutions tailored to the needs of the specific customer. The car buyer can specify the precise design components they wish to be incorporated into their new vehicle and the computer will do the rest. The ultimate expression of the marketing concept is to provide a bundle of benefits honed to the complete satisfaction of a customer's wants but until information communication technologies allowed it this was only economically feasible for high value business to business transactions. e-Commerce businesses do not have to content themselves with product differentiation in broadly segmented markets. Tesco, the world's largest online retailer, is able to customize its grocery deliveries to specific households while Levi Strauss utilize in-store booths to yield a three-dimensional laser measurement that can be downloaded to the computer controlled cutting machines for a 'perfect fit'.

○ *Database marketing/management* – is a necessary corollary to mass customization. Information communication technologies, like the Internet, and applications such as e-commerce allow the marketer to capture, store, communicate, process and mine vast amounts of information in customer databases. This opens up massive opportunities for the far-sighted marketer to anticipate and identify their changing needs and build and maintain effective relationships. Database marketing involves the fusion of information gathered on actual and potential customers and competitors as well as internal cost and sales data. This can be used to screen then select target customers and fine-tune the marketing mix offered, in order to achieve maximum profit contribution in the light of operational and financial constraints. Significant benefits accrue from the ability to use previous purchasing history to identify requirements and target promotional messages accordingly. Such cost efficiency and targeted effectiveness is essential to the direct marketers using mail shots, telesales, personal selling or e-shopping. Database analysis is more versatile in identifying new or pre-existing lifestyle segments. Profiles of cruise customers or sun worshippers can be used to identify and target the like-minded for mail shot purposes.

○ *Manufacturing operations* – Integrated computer control has enabled production to become increasingly versatile through the use of flexible manufacturing systems (FMS). Whereas cost efficiency used to demand large production runs due to long set-up times, these can now be altered in seconds. Waiting time is eliminated and small batches produced at near-equivalent speed and cost. As seen above this is of great significance to the marketer in terms of product availability and the ability to respond to increased demand arising from promotional initiatives. The spread of the just-in-time (JIT) stock control concept from Toyota has also transformed volume production and distribution systems. Responsibility for delivery of parts onto the shop-floor, as they are required for assembly or processing, is transferred to suppliers. Work in progress is therefore minimized. Similar systems have been adopted by retailers, in order to extend range, maximize selling areas and sales per square metre.

o *Warehousing and logistics* – Service levels for fast moving consumer goods are improving through the automation of storage and handling facilities. Maximum availability and rapid response to changing tastes and preferences now require a system which can instantly capture changing sales trends and translate them into the necessary supply and stock adjustments. Electronic point of sale (EPOS) systems using product barcodes and increasingly sensitive laser readers provide the sales data for stock control, sales analysis, automatic replenishment or new-order placement. More and more businesses are linked through electronic data interchange (EDI) systems to facilitate such automatic computer linkage. Linked systems allow interrogation of stock and order status together with the transmission of marketing mix details. Delivery now often takes place around the clock to avoid traffic congestion and conform to JIT requirements. Computerized transportation programmes plan optimal routes while satellite beacon systems and radio links allow flexible redeployment. Digital technology similarly eases the delivery of a wide array of 'home' services and offers opportunities for targeting customer segments.

o *Point of sale* – Electronic funds transfer at the point of sale (EFTPOS), from the customer's to the retailer's account (e.g. Switch), has transformed the potential of retail outlets not only in terms of additional sales area and frequently replenished demand-related stock ranges, but also speedier and more accurate customer transactions, shorter queues, improved cash flow and enhanced security. Some supermarkets have introduced trolleys with mini-scanners, enabling customers to process their own transactions as they shop and avoiding the need for checkouts. E-shopping orders will be picked in-store and either delivered directly to the home in an agreed time frame or collected from the store. The Internet is transforming direct marketing as well as improving customer relationships through accessible websites.

Exam hint

Improving your performance

Information communication technology has been an area of weakness for some candidates. Since the CIM explicitly require candidates to develop ICT skills, every effort must be made to be as up to date as possible.

Future applications of technology

e-Commerce to e-business

This application of information communication technology has captured the media if not the public imagination. It operates through the World Wide Web which is an open global system that allows access to anyone in the world with a computer, modem and telephone line. Companies initially provided informational and promotional web pages that users could 'hit' for information and advice. These soon became interactive allowing the marketing and purchase of goods and services using a credit card. One of the most popular is eBay, the auction site, which has seen a 20-fold rise in trade over 3 years and is set to expand more rapidly as TV advertising contributes to its appeal. With online sales rising sharply (UK doubled to £1 billion in 2002), many traditional retailers are seeking to establish websites to offset any decline in traditional channels of distribution.

Case history

The marketing challenge of e-business to business

Few challenges have received more attention than the growth of business to business exchanges on the Internet. The pace was set by Covisint, the consortium of car producers led by GM, Ford and Daimler Chrysler and followed by a succession of other industries including aerospace, chemicals, energy and food. The three automotive manufacturers alone annually purchase nearly $250 billion of supplies. The WorldWide Retail Exchange has attracted The Gap (US), Auchan (France) and Tesco (UK) among others.

Horizontal trading exchanges cater for buyers and sellers across different industries with common requirements, for example paper, printers and office furniture, with savings averaging 20 per cent. Vertical exchanges, incorporating all potential contributors to the supply chain, are far more important and offer dramatic scope (savings of 20–40 per cent) for rationalizing procurement in fragmented industries such as construction. Predictions suggest these will grow exponentially until virtually all chains are covered.

Business to business trading exchanges are as old as commerce itself, but online globally organized trading exchanges between buyers and sellers using tenders, auctions and combined buying on the Internet is revolutionary and can massively improve procurement for organizations of any size. E-procurement through trading exchanges uses technology but is still founded on relationships between suppliers, intermediaries, market makers and buyers. Software compatibility is obviously important but trading standards are critical particularly given the dramatic collapse of online energy traders like Enron. Intermediaries are emerging to provide assurance on the identity and trustworthiness of global Internet partners but fees and possibly costly experience may be required before such networks can be established.

Despite the high rate of diffusion associated with this development, not least due to the deterrence factor of not taking it on board, there is considerable resistance where staff have established procedures and relationships. Its introduction requires a cultural change of some proportions due the high risks of displacing existing supply relationships with electronic trade for materials and components crucial to the quality and success of its product offering. Yet these supplies offer the greatest potential for savings.

Significance to buyers and seller:

1. It is 'p' for profitable as well as being 'e' for efficient.
2. Collaboration with business partners becomes more effective and flexible.
3. It can provide competitive advantage for the whole supply chain.
4. It provides an underlying strategy to enable the whole business to exploit the opportunities.
5. Information capture/analysis of organization spend to improve buying power.
6. Small firms can secure deeper discounts from pooled purchasing.
7. Operational efficiencies reduce transaction costs in the move from paper-based to web-based transactions – minimum administrative effort and more effective use of staff time.
8. Improved feedback makes suppliers more responsive to customers' needs/improves ability to meet their expectations: it takes a clever question to turn data into information, but it needs intelligence to effectively use the result.

9. Potentially global network of suppliers widens choice and reduces cost.
10. Smaller suppliers can be integrated into electronic supply chains at minimal cost, that is a PC.
11. A shift in the balance of power from suppliers to buyers with persistent downward price pressure through transparency.

As with every business challenge there will be winners and losers as the e-business to business concept diffuses and matures across a succession of industries. The marketer must strive to ensure that their organization harnesses the potential benefits of this new form of electronic collaboration between business partners. The era of global electronic trading is upon us and many businesses will succeed or fail according to their competence in exploiting its potential.

Internet share trading is rapidly increasing its share of the overall market along with travel bookings, banking and other financial services. These are rational rather than personal purchases and so well suited to the Internet. Many organizations are offering incentives to encourage online usage, for example high interest Internet accounts or zero postage on goods supplied. Employment in the area of digital media, including home shopping and other Internet-based services are predicted to expand exponentially over the next few years. One less recognized benefit is the recent development of Universal Network Language by the UN which provides intelligible translations for the first time. This software will soon allow users to surf websites written in any language (currently 80 per cent are English) thereby encouraging the global dissemination of languages such as Mandarin Chinese, Swahili, Bhasa, Urdu and Russian.

On the downside, there are concerns regarding confidentiality, consumer protection and the fact that the Internet potentially puts children at risk and spreads bugs and viruses very rapidly. Successful attacks on large US websites, by flooding targeted companies like Yahoo and Amazon with fake messages, undermines trust in the Internet. If such hackers can close down key sites, what might become of the e-commerce revolution? This has increased interest in open source software such as Linux, which unlike proprietary architecture such as Microsoft, allows anyone to get involved in removing bugs and improving the system. Governments are also increasingly concerned over the global diversity of legal regimes where goods may be bought and the corresponding evasion of sales taxes. These issues may only be resolved by international agreements.

Question 8.7

Marketing skills: presenting information

Identify four product areas where restructuring due to the rise of Internet sales will be greatest.

Identify four product/service areas where the impact of the Internet sales will be least.

Explain your reasoning.

e-Commerce may, however, by eclipsed in potential scale by 'closed system' electronic business to business. Developments in telecommunications (digitalization) and the ability to overcome the problems of incompatible computer systems opened the way for electronic data interchange (EDI) on a dramatic scale. While final consumers may still prefer the impulsive attractions of the high street store, business to business sales and service should expand without limit. Legal difficulties over the status of electronic documents have also now been resolved through the development of trading data communications standards. Benefits of automated systems arise in terms of improved accuracy, lower stockholding, accessibility and lower costs when transmitting credit/delivery notes, price/product information, availability status, and so on. Expansion in such networks offers scope for improved relationships and customer service levels and most industry supply chains are expected to follow the example of banking and vehicles in automating a high proportion of total transactions in order to keep downward pressure on costs and prices.

Teleworking

Alternatively known as telecommuting or the electronic cottage, this involves working from home using telecommunications and computing equipment. The most frequently cited occupations expected to figure in future expansion plans are data entry, sales or marketing work and computer-based activities.

The main benefits of teleworking include:

○ Flexibility and reduced cost
○ Convenience and a solution to travel problems
○ Retain skilled staff and employ those with care responsibilities
○ Space saving and ability to work in preferred locations.

Other benefits include savings in travel time, greater productivity due to fewer distractions and reduced stress levels. The falling cost of technology and increasingly versatile broadband equipment that is available makes this an attractive option as office and non-labour costs soar in urban centres. Global telecommunications also allows teleworkers from less-developed countries to compete with high-wage equivalents in affluent nations. Telework may be processed in India or Pakistan at one-tenth the cost of London.

There are, however, a number of drawbacks to teleworking:

○ Management and communication difficulties, for example lack of face-to-face meetings.
○ Social isolation and losing touch with the organization.

Technical and security problems may also arise as well as difficulties in ensuring quality control. Many workers find work discipline a difficulty and miss the creative spark provided by fellow workers. Employers have therefore often taken steps to increase social integration by providing more communication with colleagues, managers and customers.

Question 8.8

Key skills: problem-solving

Technology now allows a vehicle to be fitted with the equivalent of the electronic office (i.e. laptop, fax, carphone, etc.). With regard to marketing, do you think the future lies with mobile or residential teleworkers?

Teleconferencing/electronic meetings

Meetings can take up to two-thirds of a manager's time. It is therefore essential that such time is used productively, especially where clients are involved. If, say, ten people meet for an hour then the average contribution of each is just six minutes. Since 20 per cent of those present tend to speak 80 per cent of the time the contributions of the majority are actually restricted much further.

Technology cannot substitute for brain power and human interaction but it can vastly increase contributions. Given appropriate technology (an ISDN line can support broadcast video conferencing, text and graphics), participants can type their ideas and contributions onto a network of screens and react to those provided by the others. Brainstorming and evaluation can take place quickly and anonymously if necessary. Videoconferencing using broadband technology allows participants to see one another while videophone developments will enable the customer to see its telesales operator and vice versa! Texting and e-mails also appears to be transforming the nature of personal relationships with actual 'dating' taking a back-seat to the mobile phone.

Virtual companies

These organizations have few or no assets but provide services through the use of third-party contractors. They will use computers to coordinate activities and will become increasingly successful in the future.

Database marketing

Digital (broadband) television

This development is likely to transform the nature of advertising and promotion and possibly supplant the PC for e-shopping. This technology is interactive, enables e-mail and home shopping, allows significantly more programmes, more on-screen peripheral information and much more flexibility (e.g. click an advert icon for more information). Access will be by customer choice given the ability to view in real time or to customize viewing. This will lead to more audience fragmentation on the one hand, but enhanced ability to target audience segments with adverts and direct response promotions on the other. The ability to filter out adverts may lead to more programme sponsorship, for example, shopsmart.com sponsored mid-evening movies.

Automated customer handling

Customer relations management has been transformed through personalized mass communications that facilitates the building of trust and long-term relationships with stakeholders. Touch-tone phones and automated exchanges direct customer contacts through a series of prompts (and classical music) to the right person in the right department or an automated message. FAQ is a convention used in such systems and on the Internet, to compile a list of 'frequently asked questions' and responses typically encountered by an organization. Basic information can be acquired quickly providing savings for both parties. The technology brings the customer stakeholder closer to the organization, increases their participation and improves service levels, However, as with most information technologies, care must be taken to minimize or avoid alienation arising from the lack of human interface and other potential frustrations. It remains to be seen whether the development of videophone technology, with pleasing digitalized 'human' images, will resolve some of these problems. Such an image has already been programmed for potential use in news-casting and weather reports. Similar developments for direct marketing and customer care cannot be far behind!

Resistance to change

Technology has been the major engine in the development of mass affluence yet it has always been resisted. From the Luddites, who smashed the knitting frames that threatened their livelihoods at the outset of the Industrial Revolution, to the print workers displaced by computer typesetting (and more recently coal miners made redundant by cheaper alternate fuels), the outcome has always been the same: beneficial advance may have been delayed but never prevented.

The short-term impact of technologically induced unemployment has frequently been considerable, not least on communities dependent on the industry in structural decline. In the long run, however, there has been a growth in demand for labour that has broadly paralleled the growth in the labour force.

Process technology has substituted machines for labour to minimize costs but new *product technology* has created employment opportunities in so-called 'sunrise' industries. The eBay site, for example, has created employment for an estimated 10 000 on-line traders, Adaption has been difficult, however, because the new jobs have generally required higher-order skills than the ones they replaced.

It is not only employees who resist change, but also consumers, distributors and managers themselves. Changes in method and organization are as readily resisted as in technical processes, although change in one normally requires change in the others.

Question 8.9

Key skills: problem-solving

Management is about the efficient allocation of resources to match changing consumer needs and wants, yet British management has frequently been criticized for its reluctance or inability to bring about change. Identify factors that may account for this weakness. Identify conditions that enable management in your own country to become effective change agents.

Customers may resist product changes out of force of habit, prejudice or conservatism born of age. Product revivals may succeed on similar grounds as adults relive their youth or bring their children up consuming equivalent goods and services. Market understandings may also make the business reconsider introducing changes that disrupt competitive relationships.

Change may also be resisted by external forces, for example, pressure groups, concerned with the impact on the environment. Laws and regulations also constrain what is possible. The Data Protection Act, for example, required that mailing list organizations register and abide with its provisions, so limiting the scope for use by direct marketing businesses. Provisional EU legislation will forbid unsolicited fax transmissions unless prior permission is obtained. This will inhibit the activities of many direct marketers and limit the growth in corporate junk mail.

The symptoms of resistance to change

The marketer should be aware of why people resist change and take steps to minimize it. This applies as much to marketing staff as to affected stakeholders in the micro-environment. An important first step is in the identification of resistance to change as evidenced by:

- o Increased turnover rates, illness and absenteeism
- o Reduced productivity or operational effectiveness
- o Failure to cooperate or communicate – head-in-the-sand attitudes
- o General loss of morale
- o Increased membership of unions or staff associations
- o Action up to and including actual sabotage of operations.

Question 8.10

Key skills: problem-solving

What would be the symptoms to look for among the customer base as evidence of an adverse reaction to a change in order-processing procedures initiated by your organization? What steps might you have taken to reduce this resistance?

All the forces that contribute to stability in personality may also contribute to resisting change. Such forces work to the advantage of established brands, for example, since consumer behaviour is also governed by:

o *Habit* – In purchasing patterns.
o *Primacy* – The first successful means we find of solving a problem or meeting a need is used again in future. Hence a firm keeps using the same advertising agency.
o *Selective perception* – Evidence that conflicts with preconceptions is ignored (e.g. buy British despite the fact that some foreign alternatives are now superior in quality).
o *Dependence* – This relates to buying patterns to maintain our sense of belonging to a group or a class.

Change is also resisted if it is against our best interests. Indeed, it is not the change itself but the results and consequences of it that are often the cause of the problem. The interests of both individuals and stakeholders do not always coincide with those of the organization. Other factors increasing resistance to change might include:

o *The nature of past experience of change* – If this has been negative and prejudicial then resistance will be stronger.
o *If apprehensions are unanswered* – If people mistakenly fear that they will not be able to cope with change then misapprehensions arise, producing unnecessary resistance.
o *The manner of the change* – Resented if autocratic.
o *Lack of consultation or participation* – For example, if a supermarket alters its layout without reference to its customers.
o *Where change is infrequent* – Experience and confidence are therefore lacking.

Conclusion

Technological change is very much a double-edged phenomenon. It has so far prevented the dismal predictions of both Malthus and Marx by enabling rising productivity and real living standards but at the cost of high transitional unemployment. Its accelerating pace has enabled a sharply rising population to be accommodated but has produced 'future shock' among many seeking to cope with the myriad changes involved. It has provided convenience through increasingly intelligent products and services but also unforeseen consequences as the effects have rippled through society. Genetic technology, for example, may cure inherited diseases and enhance crop quality and consistency, but might equally release uncontrollable mutations and sterilize wildlife.

Question 8.11

Key skills: problem-solving

Identify some unintended consequences of the following product developments:

- o The car, for example, the RAC claims that the average motorist spends 5 days per annum stuck in traffic – this could rise to 14 days by 2005!
- o The telephone, for example, the *Daily Mail* claimed the average Briton spends 45 hours a year waiting on the telephone.
- o The television.
- o The CCTV camera, for example, catches the average person 300 times a day in Britain.

How have they changed the nature of marketing?

Summary

In this unit concerning the technological environment:

- o Some of the main characteristics of technology and its main phases were identified, culminating in the information or communications era which developed economies are currently entering.
- o The critical role of business was examined and the factors encouraging innovativeness.
- o Technical imperatives driving the pace and diversity of technological change were identified and explained. The capitalist dynamic and the source of 50-year-long wave cycles were studied.
- o The microprocessor, as the key enabling technology in the information revolution, was described in terms which accounted for the all-inclusive impact it has had on all aspects of contemporary society.
- o The diffusion process was explained and the need for technological forecasting emphasized. Sources of information by which a business can keep track of potential developments were outlined.
- o Various applications to sales and marketing were discussed with reference to the supply chain. Some future applications were assessed including telecommuting and marketing databases.
- o The symptoms and sources of resistance to change of the customer and employee were explored.

Further study and examination preparation

Technology is an all-pervasive aspect of a business environment that knows no boundaries. Companies of every nationality will be seeking to exploit its potential for competitive advantage. It is therefore likely to be a popular aspect of the macro-environment for examination questions, given its general applicability to all CIM international centres. Expect a compulsory question on the technology area from time to time (e.g. December 2001).

Extending knowledge

Palmer and Hartley, *The Business and Marketing Environment*, McGraw-Hill – Chapter 5, The Information Environment, Chapter 12, The Technological Environment. See also A. Palmer, *The Business Environment*, McGraw-Hill – Chapter 4, The Internet Environment, Chapter 12, The Technical and Information Environment; M. de Kare-Silver, *E-shock, the New Rules*, Palgrave and A. Toffler, *Future Shock*, Bantam Books.

For websites see: www.amazon.co.uk as an example of how internet technology may be harnessed to the provision of innovative customer service

www.what is.com is a directory of internet terminology

www.cyberatlas.com for a business perspective on internet developments

www.fpmg.co.uk and www.eyuk.com are consultancy company sites often offering free reports

For e-business see: http://www.brint.com/Elecomm.htm as a portal and http://www.ebusiness forum.com as an Economist Intelligence Unit forum for news, issues, etc. Also http://www1. oecd.org/dsti/sti/it/ec for OECD reports.

Exam question 8.1

Please see Question 6a, December 2003. For specimen answers go to www.cim.co.uk.

Exam question 8.2

Please see Question 6c, June 2004. For specimen answers go to www.cim.co.uk.

Exam question 8.3

Technical innovation in the world car industry has accelerated in recent years with the application of electronics and ICT. These innovations have impacted on all aspects of the supply chain and are viewed as a source of potential competitive advantage. In this context answer and two of the following:

(a) Suggest areas where ICT is impacting on the world car industry and assess the implications for the final customer
(b) Consider the factors that drive the diffusion of new technologies and the implications of this for competition in the industry
(c) What do you understand by the term competitive advantage? Discuss how it might be established in a highly competitive marketplace using technological innovation.

(Question 4, June 2003)

Exam question 8.4

A popular definition of distribution management is that it involves 'getting the right goods to the right people at the right time and the proper price'.

(a) With examples from grocery distribution, discuss the influence of current changes in technology on the fulfilment of this activity. (10 marks)

(Question 2a, June 2002)

unit 9

environmental information systems – coping with the challenge of environmental change

Study Guide

This concluding study unit focuses on the effective management of the future marketing environment. It is concerned with element 4 of the syllabus, environmental information systems, accounting for 15 per cent of the total. We have already dealt with Sections 4.4 and 4.5 in Units 2 and 4 so this unit will consider the remaining aspects of coping with environmental change.

The first aspect is concerned with the importance of information and the need for organizations to develop an effective marketing information system. The second introduces a concept that is much more fully developed in the Marketing Research and Information module at Stage 2, that is marketing research and the benefits it can provide. The third considers key problems in dealing with the dynamism and uncertainty of future change. The fourth surveys the tools and techniques available to the marketer in establishing the nature and significance of the environmental challenge. The final aspect considers the continuing impact of information communication technologies on environmental information systems.

We also consider the all-embracing nature of change. Multi-faceted and in most cases interactive, change in one part of the system causes reactions elsewhere. It is both complicated and turbulent in nature requiring marketers to understand the complex processes at work and if possible be part of the change itself rather than merely responding belatedly to its confusing effects.

This unit draws together the various strands of the marketing environment syllabus and provides focus on all the relevant statements of marketing practice. It is very much concerned not only with the collection, presentation and effective interpretation of important marketing information, but also with the creative manipulation of that information into a form that is useful for the strategy and planning processes of the organization.

Monitoring the marketing environment

Systems thinking, you will recall from Unit 1, helps to provide an integrated view of the world. Organizations compete and collaborate with a variety of primary stakeholders and interact as interrelated parts of the wider marketing environment. This environment is subject to continuous change but organizations are also adaptive. This causes them to seek greater understanding of their environment in order to plan or react more effectively. To be effective the business organization must possess the following sub-systems:

- A *sensing system* – to access sources of information and appraise developments (see information sources in Units 2 and 4). However, if secondary sources provide insufficient market understanding then market research may have to be considered.
- An *information classification system* – to convert raw data (i.e. unanalysed facts and figures) into potentially usable information.
- An *information processing system* – involving feedback and two-way exchanges.
- An *information database and retrieval system*.
- A *control system* – to establish any deviations from established objectives.
- A *planning and policy-making system* – with decisions based on choices identified and evaluated by the marketing information system.
- A *communication system* – to receive information from internal and external sources and to distribute information to relevant decision makers and stakeholders.

The importance of information

To be useful to marketers the collected facts and figures, for example, sales data from the point of sale have to be collated, ordered, processed and then analysed into a form that is helpful to marketing decisions, for example, to produce sales trends to inform future ordering, delivery and stock control.

Information, like communication, is said to be the lifeblood of the modern organization. One implication of the proliferation of information communication technologies is the need to learn continuously about marketing information systems and their potential to provide marketers with more and better information at their fingertips. One type of information to avoid is 'junk mail'. Of so billion daily emails worldwide 88% are junk of which only one-third is ever read. It is growing at such a rate as to threaten the viability of the e-mail system. One offsetting development here is that of 'self-destructing' e-mails after a prescribed time elapse.

Activity 9.1

Key skills: using ICT and the Internet

Brainstorm a list of information communication technologies of relevance to the marketer that you think have already been mentioned in the coursebook so far. Then check to see how many, if any, you missed or weren't actually there!

Information is also power but only when certain conditions are met. The focus is not information gathering, since competitors can do that equally well, but rather on ensuring it is utilized effectively in order to achieve competitive advantage. Information is of limited value unless it is:

- collected from the right sources
- accurate enough to form the basis of effective decision-making (varies with risk)
- collected at a time relevant to decisions to be taken
- processed into market intelligence and distributed to the right business level/location
- made available to the appropriate people to discuss and act upon as required
- accessible to key internal and external stakeholders and partners
- collected, processed, stored and distributed in a timely and cost-effective manner
- concise, in providing the level of detail appropriate to the decision needs (avoids *overload*).

Exam hint

Key skill: improving your own learning and performance

Now is the time to consider brainstorming a list of 'must dos' regarding your forthcoming assessment deadline or examination. Have you visited the various CIM websites, for example, and consulted past papers/examples of assessment? Have you studied the Senior Examiner's comments on these and been attempting sample questions under examination conditions? Are you applying feedback control to understand where you went wrong and then put it right in time for the real thing.

'Quality information' therefore needs to be collected, processed and communicated for four important marketing purposes: *planning, strategy formulation, decision-making and control*.

Information from the marketing environment is clearly an important input into the assessment of strengths and weaknesses, opportunities and threats in the strategy process. This requires communication with, and interrogation of external systems as the preliminary to decision-making. Control, on the other hand, relies on the comparison of feedback on actual performance to planned performance using internally and externally generated information.

Information communication technologies are the primary mechanisms through which change can be managed and the means of providing the 'necessary' information to relevant decision makers, so ensuring more effective outcomes compared to competitors. Through dynamic technological developments such as the Internet, teleconferencing, e-mail, extranets, digital TV, WAP technologies and the rest there are numerous advances to be realized:

- ○ Improving connection, dialogue and relationships with important stakeholders.
- ○ Improving your ability to learn from others and past trends.
- ○ A strengthening bridge of open communication between the organization/its environment.
- ○ An online picture of a changing environment through an explosion of secondary sources.
- ○ Perhaps a new element in the marketing mix, P for processing quality information.
- ○ Allowing instantaneous customer-focused response to complaints, and so on.
- ○ Increased speed and cost-effectiveness of research.

Question 9.1

Key skills: presenting information

In Activity 9.1 you brainstormed a number of information communication technologies and some have been referred to in this section. What others can you think of and can you arrange them into a classification?

Marketing skills: information at your fingertips

Keeping an ear to the ground (or, more likely, to the mobile phone or the Internet!) in an informal way may have been the traditional means for the marketer to keep informed, but it will not always be effective in times of rapid change. The information may either come too late or not become available to the decision maker who requires it. The volume of potentially useful data often appears boundless, and as it expands from year to year, the need to manage it more effectively becomes more pressing. It takes a clever question to turn data into information, but it takes marketing intelligence to profitably use the result. Excellent companies must work more smartly if they are to survive, and this raises demand for better-quality information to support decisions.

Marketers need information at their fingertips to manipulate and add value to. This implies that just as professionally managed organizations now need marketing information systems, so marketers should invest, not only in the development of a personal information system, but also in a network of business contacts. Building a matrix of stakeholder and organizational contacts is one of the keys to working effectiveness.

A changing economic structure has shifted the emphasis in favour of knowledge workers and knowledge-intensive sectors such as financial and public services. We live in an increasingly information-based society where even small firms add to the demand for value-added information services from government and consultancies. Mass markets are fragmenting into specialist niches as tastes become less standardized and predictable, so sophisticated marketing information and analysis is required to take advantage of the opportunities presented.

The explosion in business-focused information is a reflection of these forces. There are 3500 business to business magazines in the UK and similar diversity exists in other countries. Collectively, such sources are termed the 'business press'.

231

The marketing information system (MIS)

Kotler defines a marketing information system as the people, equipment and procedures to gather, sort, analyse, evaluate and distribute needed, timely and accurate information to marketing decision makers. This very neatly summarizes the above discussion of the importance of information. Information is now too important to be left to chance and the marketer must ensure that information needs are identified, anticipated and assessed as the basis for systematic provision through well-designed systems.

Question 9.2

Key skills: working with others and collecting information

List the roles of the marketer in formulating an effective MIS.

The information that comprises the MkIS comes from the following three sources:

1. *Internal data* – day-to-day company activities generate masses of operational and control data that can be manipulated and processed to provide assessment of ongoing marketing performance as well as help identify strengths and weaknesses. You need only consider the significance of revenue flows, orders and sales records to the 'Price' variable or customer service data to 'Product and Promotion'. Such data have the attractions of easy accessibility and availability as well as cheapness but are likely to be in a form best suited to accountants rather than the needs of marketers.
2. *Marketing intelligence* – This is information gathered on the environment through personal information networks and trade sources. The marketer distils the information gathered by all strata of organization employees from a diverse range of stakeholders. This should be complemented by competitor research using secondary sources then cross-referenced to provide understanding of the evolving and normally competitive environment. Intelligence may also be purchased from specialist suppliers such as Nielson but at a cost. Distilling value from such intelligence is a time-intensive but potentially rewarding activity.
3. *Marketing research* – Marketing decision makers cannot always wait for the right information to turn up and should take positive steps to identify what they require. Kotler defines this as linking the customer and public to the marketer through information used to:

    (a) Identify and define marketing opportunities and problems
    (b) Generate, refine and evaluate marketing actions
    (c) Monitor marketing performance
    (d) Improve understanding of the marketing process.

Organizations that have the ability to sense environmental change and be proactive in their response tend to perform better than those that lack it. It often signals the need for organizational change and reformulation of marketing strategy, but there is no guarantee of the appropriate response being made in time. This vitally depends on the quality of the information systems available to the business and the extent of management's understanding of the complex and often interacting changes taking place in the external environment.

'To manage a business well is to manage its future, and to manage its future is to manage information' (M. Harper, Jr).

Exam hint

Improving your performance

To manage your future you must manage your information! How is your folder shaping up? Have you been processing information unit to unit or does it just contain unprocessed inputs? More importantly have you tested out your 'outputs' on your tutor/boss/colleague, etc. and used their feedback to fill any gaps.

As Figure 9.1 shows, any business needs an integrated internal and external information system to provide the means for dovetailing organizational and marketing developments with environmental change.

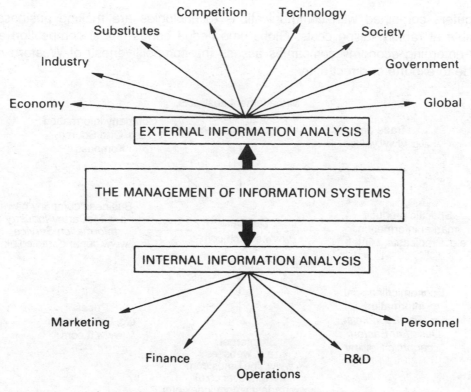

Figure 9.1 An integrated internal and external information system

An efficient information system must be able to programme information into the 'corporate memory' of organization members in much the same way as a computer. The objective is to make the information accessible and usable by the relevant decision maker when required. The power and flexibility of state-of-the-art networked computer database systems now offer this capability and can support the more 'human' networks mentioned above.

Online business information

Databases are revolutionizing management information systems. A database is simply a file of information in electronic form providing ease and speed of access and manipulation. Online means that the database is stored on a remote computer but can be accessed directly by business users through phone lines. Real-time systems mean that they are constantly being updated with new inputs of information while CD-ROM systems are millions of pieces of information stored on compact discs, updated on a regular basis (see Waterlow Directory: Multimedia and CD-ROM) and accessed flexibly by the computer. The rapid development and take-up by business of fax machines, scanners and intelligent printers is also expanding the potential of such information sources by providing hard copies to remote locations when required.

Some of the main types of databases currently available include those shown in Figure 9.2. By keying in a competitor's name, for example, such systems can search out all available published material. Search engines provide the largest databases with websites such as Google processing over 200 million search requests each day and scanning 3 billion web pages in an average of 0.2 seconds. This involves a system embracing 54 000 servers, yet it only covers half the World Wide Web. Despite a doubling of information stored on computers since 1999, the majority of human knowledge continues to be stored in books. It also should be remembered that a search engine 'records' what you searched for, and when, so revealing possible motives. Under America's Patriot Act the US government can compel access if it is deemed part of a terrorist investigation.

Computers combined with communications technologies are making business information available at rapidly falling costs. Global knowledge brings global competition as Asian and other emerging economy companies assess the competitiveness of Western markets as a prelude to exports or direct entry.

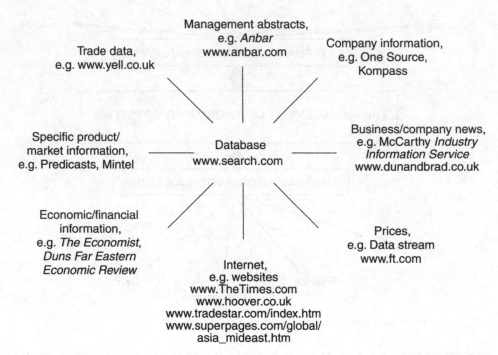

Figure 9.2 Relevant database sources

The benefits of online searching compared to traditional methods may be summarized as follows:

Online features	Benefits
Speed in searching	Time saving
Selectivity in searching	Quality data
Flexibility in searching	Comparative data
Interactive searching	Flexible scope
Data manipulation	Usable statistics
Up to date	Best available data
User-friendly	Will be used
Charge on actual use	Economic access
Professional methodology	Competitive edge

With information of particular importance to the marketer, areas of business database application should include:

o Market research and marketing plans
o Marketing presentations and customer relations/communications
o Market/sales analysis and sales force coordination.

Some final words of warning must be noted regarding computer databases as a panacea for marketing solutions. There is a considerable *learning curve* involved in the effective use of such systems and many commercially available databases are expensive to subscribe for any but the largest company. More crucially the most important information, namely that relating to future plans and developments, is not normally available even on real-time systems.

Similarly there are limitations on the potential of ICT in allowing the marketer to keep in touch with the environment and respond flexibly to the changing product and service demands of the customer. These include:

o The need to balance the need for information against the cost of obtaining it.
o The dangers of information overload on managers and their reliance on experience and intuition rather than cross-referenced reliable knowledge.
o Ultimate dependence on human interpretation/judgement of the information no matter how fully or speedily provided.
o The reality of physical and psychological communication barriers and resistance.

Exam hint

Key skills: improving learning and performance

The most common cause of poor examination performance is the failure to address the question. To prevent this:

o Practise on as many questions as possible
o Conform to the format and context requirement
o Underline the instructions, for example explain/compare/give implications/illustrate/discuss
o Double underline key words that represent the central issue of the question
o Produce a trigger word structural answer plan and compare it to the specimen
o If you have misunderstood, carefully consider why and learn the lesson.

The importance of marketing research

The quality of marketing decisions is normally directly related to the quality of information that underpins them. Key questions for the marketer in terms of 'who are my customers' and 'what are their needs and wants' must be addressed before decisions on product, price, promotion and place can be made. Marketing research is important because it can generate the specific and tailored information required to answer these questions:

- o It is an important marketing tool in terms of the information it generates.
- o It underpins marketing decisions that need to be based on an in-depth understanding of the market in general and the behaviour of the consumer in particular.
- o It systematically collects, researches and analyses information about specific marketing problems or in order to take advantage of marketing opportunities.
- o Examples include calculation of market potential, assessment of market trends, competitor analysis and short-range and long-range forecasting.
- o It is problem orientated and a continuous process in an environment of change.
- o It feeds into the MIS through environmental scanning of the PEST factors and monitoring change in the behaviour of customers and competitors.
- o It improves the ability of the marketer to make timely decisions.

The information benefits of marketing research

These derive from key stages* in the marketing research process which include:

- o Define the research problem
- o Set specific research objectives
- o Design a research plan
- o Determine information needs*
- o Define secondary sources and gather information*
- o Plan quantitative and qualitative data collection*
- o Select research techniques and implement research plan
- o Data analysis, interpretation and reporting of findings*.

Exam hint

Many CIM candidates are providing answers in their 'second language'. Examiners account this – where misinterpretation occurs but given that CIM employ specialists to screen papers for potential language confusions, it is safest, if in doubt, either to answer another question or to explain your interpretation of the question at the outset. The examiner can then make an informed judgement in the light of your justification.

The information benefits that flow from the market research process include the following:

- o Focus on your organization-specific information requirements.
- o Assistance in defining the nature of your marketing problems.
- o Detail that is unavailable from mere scanning of secondary sources.
- o Information tailored to current and future needs of the organization.
- o Information unavailable to competitors and a potential source of competitive advantage.
- o In-depth survey of secondary sources and identification of primary data needs.
- o Adoption of appropriate and cost-effective research approaches to gather primary data.
- o Objective interpretation of timely information that can form the basis of appropriate action.

Question 9.3

Key skills: using information

Can you match up the definitions to the marketing research terms?

- o Exploratory research
- o Observational research
- o Causal research
- o Descriptive research
- o Qualitative research
- o Quantitative research.

    - Test hypotheses regarding cause–effect relationships.
    - Gather primary data by people, behaviour and situations.
    - Gather preliminary data to help define problems or suggest relationships.
    - Collect interview data in sufficient volume to allow statistical analysis.
    - Help describe markets and marketing problems, for example, market potential.
    - Uncover customer motivations, attitudes or buying behaviour using personal or small group techniques.

Much of the value of market research is that it helps to define future marketing potential, and it is to the future and its prediction that we now turn. The future is essentially unknowable in other than general terms and the further forward we attempt to peer, the more uncertain our view becomes. We will first review these problems of forecasting and then consider some of the techniques available to forecast future demand.

Coping with the environmental challenge: the key problems

Since the determinants and resulting shape of the future market for a product may be significantly different from the past, most forecasting techniques that rely on historic information and the projection of past and current trends will tend to be misleading. Even highly sophisticated forecasting based on computer models, as used by the UK Treasury, has been prone to considerable error. One cynic suggested that economists had successfully forecast nine of the last five recessions!

Marketing environment in practice

The British government has predicted that its gambling bill, to allow the establishment of up to 40 'super' casinos, will help regenerate the regions in which they are located and bring much needed revenue flows to local authorities as well as the government. Part of these would be diverted to help with any rise in the incidence of 'problem gamblers'. However, an American study has examined the growing trend for many states to allow slot machines and casinos as a painless means of raising much needed tax revenue. Counties with and without casinos were studied in terms of crime rates, lost productivity, domestic abuse and other social ills. It found that the cost to society of the 3–5 per cent of players who became 'problem gamblers' was equivalent to half of all casino profits. When South Carolina banned slot machines, over two-thirds of its Gamblers Anonymous groups disbanded within 6 months.

The long-awaited green shoots of recovery from the last serious UK recession, for example, took 18 months longer to germinate than predicted and led to the resignation of the Chancellor of the Exchequer. The long-term consequences of the sharp tax rises required and the persistence of the 'feel bad' or at best 'feel insecure' factor that ensued led to a change in government at the following election. Businesses may fare little better. Many have a planning horizon of 5 to 10 years, but to make strategic plans over such a time period implies a reasonable degree of certainty regarding significant environmental trends and developments. However, turbulence frequently undermines predictability making such an approach questionable. Consider Siemens' decision to close its £1.2 billion state-of-the-art semiconductor plant in Tyneside just a year after its opening. Why? Because it had failed to foresee the Asian economic collapse and a fall in chip prices from $55 in 1995 to under $3 at the time of closure. Such are the potential consequences of bad forecasts and any business must address the following problems:

- *Which are the right forecasts?* for example, from a variety of independent economic forecasts.
- *How significant are the different trends?* for example, organic food sales are growing 20 per cent p.a. but only account 2 per cent of total sales.
- *How long before a pattern of events becomes a trend?* Is teleworking a trend yet or not?
- *Where are the turning points?* Failure to anticipate and prepare will result in either lost sales or unsold stock, depending on the error.
- *Which are the discontinuities?* Forecasting is most difficult when the 'rules of the past' no longer apply causing a trend to reverse or disappear, for example, cheap to dear energy in 1973–74 and 2001–04 was a discontinuity. A change in government with a very different economic philosophy can also have this effect. The demise of the nuclear family (2 adults + 2 children) as the norm is another.
- *What is the pace of change?* Knowing the direction of change is one thing, but knowing the speed of its development is the key to an effective response. Who predicted the frightening pace of contraction in the British coal mining industry or the halving, and halving again of EU cod quotas? Suppliers and local traders who failed to anticipate and adjust will also have suffered the consequences. Similarly how rapidly will e-business to business expand in various sectors and will the new 3G videophones take off?

Question 9.4

Key skills: contributing ideas to the strategy process

1. Why must a business forecast?
2. When must a business forecast?
3. What must a business forecast?

Many distinctive trends have reversed or discontinued in recent years. The power and significance of trade unions has declined greatly in many developed economies, share prices and now house prices have fallen, at least temporarily, while inflation in general has decreased to negligible rates not seen for over 25 years. With falling birth rates, youth culture has also given way to an affluent ageing one.

Coping with the challenge of environmental changes: the main techniques

Disagreements over the answers to the key problems outlined above produces very different views of the future with no guarantee as to which will turn out to be the most accurate one. The possible business responses to such forecasting problems are as follows:

○ *Abandon all forecasting pretensions* – This would be a naïve response to such difficulties. Every action involving plans or preparations for tomorrow requires some forecasting to be effective. The essence of managerial decision-making involves forecasting future conditions. Even day-to-day operational decisions, involving a much shorter time horizon than strategic decisions, require a clear view of the future if such matters as stock levels, sales targets or advertising budgets are to be effectively set.

Question 9.5

Key skills: using ICT and the Internet

Identify three strong patterns or trends in a market of your choice that you consider will reverse or discontinue in the next 20 years. Give reasons for your choice.

○ *Concentrate on short-term adaptive planning* – If the further the marketer peers into the future, the murkier the view becomes, then this is a great temptation. Focus on the year ahead but establish a flexible management system that allows rapid adaption to environmental change. This may be possible for some businesses in relatively static markets, but what about a water company, a telecommunications supplier or a pharmaceutical business? A new reservoir must be planned over 10 years ahead, while technological change is so rapid in telecommunications that a reaction strategy, no matter how effective, would come far too late. The drug company must be planning its product life cycles in the knowledge that testing and verification procedures may take a decade. All companies considering acquisition, modernization or diversification must forecast the medium- and longer-term future, if only in broad terms.

○ *Improve the quality of conventional forecasts* – Forecasts normally refer to objective, quantitative techniques which seek to extrapolate or project historical data into the future. Effective forecasting involves the following stages:

- Select the critical environmental variables as future indicators
- Identify relevant sources of information on the variables
- Evaluate forecasting techniques
- Integrate forecast output into strategic plans on a continuous basis
- Monitor and evaluate with particular reference to possible discontinuities.

Exam hint

Improving your performance

Questions are seldom essay style, but will test your communication skills by requiring a brief, presentation or report. *Up to 10 per cent* of the marks *may* be awarded for presentational effectiveness. If a report is required *don't get carried away* with format and forget to answer the question itself which counts for at least *90 per cent of the marks*! Provide a title, introduction, findings and conclusions/recommendations but concentrate on setting the points out clearly and break up the text using lists of short, key statements rather than long sentences.

The problem is not a lack of the necessary statistical techniques but rather the quality and availability of the necessary data. As with computers, the principle of garbage-in garbage-out applies and the resulting projection will only be as good as the data input. Sophisticated statistical methods such as multiple regression, moving averages and exponential smoothing will be of little value if the data collected is suspect. Be warned by the wry response to the question 'Why did God create economists?' – answer, 'To make weather forecasters look good!'

 ## Activity 9.2

Key skills: using information

Match the terms with their correct definitions:

o Demand function
o Depth interview
o Multiple regression
o Moving averages
o Exponential smoothing
o Probability.

- Best estimate of the outcome of each decision alternative.
- Unstructured, usually face to face and intended to elicit meaningful information from a respondent.
- A technique used to calculate the explanatory value of a number of independent variables affecting a dependent one.
- The factors that determine the quantity demanded of a good per period of time.
- Change in the average of, say, sales values over a number of time periods, by adding the most recent value and dropping the earliest in the series.
- When weights used in the averaging process decrease progressively for values further into the past.

o *Use the combined view of experts* (*Delphi technique*) – This is a subjective and qualitative technique relying primarily on human judgement rather than statistical method. They are essentially intuitive techniques, deriving from the expert's blend of knowledge, experience and judgement. The experts may include academics, consultants, relevant stakeholders as well as key directors in marketing, operations, finance and non-executive board members. Each may make an independent forecast of sales, for example, or respond to an initial prediction. These may be fed back for further comment in the light of each expert's contribution. The resulting forecast reflects the collective 'informed view' of those who are in the best position to judge developments. The consensus achieved will 'smooth out' extreme views and should carry credibility with those who use it. Unfortunately it is a time-consuming process and therefore costly in the expert's time. It may also fail to capture the possibility of radical change due to a similar mindset of the experts involved.

  o *Use judgemental analysis to identify a desired future* – We all engage in goal-orientated planning if we wish to progress in life. It is a relatively successful approach so long as the world around us remains relatively stable and predictable. A young boy or girl who decides that becoming a renowned doctor is their goal will plan to get good grades, particularly in maths, so they can progress to secondary school or college level where good results are required in the various sciences if they are to gain entry to a university with a record of excellence and so on towards their goal. The organization may also map out its future towards a desired goal given the current environmental landscape. Lack of perfect foresight, unexpected obstacles and changing conditions might force changes in direction along the way, but the goal is clear and an outline map is better than no map at all! In any event, change for most of us is not all that revolutionary. Taxes, temperatures and sea level may rise a bit, but for the most part things will carry along much as normal.

 Activity 9.3

Key skills: improving your learning and performance

Have you identified your desired future and made a map?

The fact that you are reading this coursebook suggests that you have given some thought to your future, but have you really planned it out?

  o Where do you want to be in 5 years' time? In 10 years time?
  o Where would you like to be at the peak of your career?
  o What do you need to do to ensure that you reach these milestones?
  o What are your personal and intellectual strengths and weaknesses?
  o Are the weaknesses going to inhibit you from achieving your goals?
  o If so, how are you going to remedy them and when?
  o What qualifications, skills and experience will be necessary?
  o Is your job leading somewhere you want to go?

The list could go on, but the important thing is to try to control your own future and not drift along on a hope and a prayer. The environment will change and the unexpected will occur but a future-orientated plan provides a framework for successful adaption.

Mintzberg argues turbulent conditions demand decentralization and devolved responsibility. An evolving or incremental approach is advocated with adjustments made within a broad vision of the organization's future. He also reminds us that every generation believes its environment to be more turbulent than preceding ones and that the best way forward is to avoid over-formal planning processes and to put the emphasis on 'learning and flexibility'.

○ *Use scenarios* – These are alternative views of the future and have been developed by organizations such as Shell to assist prediction in uncertain times. The best way of understanding scenarios is by comparing them with quantitative forecasts:

A scenario	A forecast
A description of the future based on mutually consistent groupings of determinants.	A statistical synthesis of probabilities and expert opinion
Says here are *some* of the key factors you have to take into account and this is the way they could affect your business.	Accounts relevant factors to yield *the best answer* – what is most likely to happen. This tends *to dictate final decisions*
Designed to be considered with other scenarios – it is valueless on its own.	Stands alone
A tool to assist understanding. It forms the backdrop to decision-making, not an integral part of it.	Intended to be regarded as an *authoritative statement*
A means of placing responsibility for planning decisions on the managers concerned.	A means of removing much of the responsibility for the final decision – managers tend to rely on the central forecast
Essentially qualitative.	Fundamentally quantitative

Forecasts are based on the belief that the *future can be measured and controlled*, scenarios suggest it cannot be. Shell warns all corporate planners that the forecasts they know, love and rely on are based on this fallacy. It likens decisions based on them to pursuing a straight line through a minefield, and views much economic and business theory as a 'pretend world' in which people act as if they had knowledge where it cannot exist. Planners seek firm answers and optimum solutions, as if uncertainty and change can be assumed away.

Activity 9.4

Key skills: using information and problem-solving

Identify key variables in the PEST environment and vary your assumptions about them in order to produce two alternative futures for the year 2006. Variables might include such factors as the outcome of the next election, the stage of the economic cycle, demographic trends, trade factors and so forth.

Coping with the challenge of environmental change: the broad approaches

The marketer has a toolbox of techniques and approaches available to assist understanding of a turbulent environment. Forecasting methods have already been considered and form a component among other techniques including external audits, the environmental set, impact analysis, PEST/SWOT analysis and the product life cycle. Other techniques have been described in context, such as competitor analysis, leading indicators and morphological studies. In this section we will consider some of the broader approaches that help to interpret, evaluate and apply the information derived from forecasting techniques.

Environmental audits

Knowledge is power and audits are the means of acquiring this power through the regular identification and collection of relevant information on the current situation.

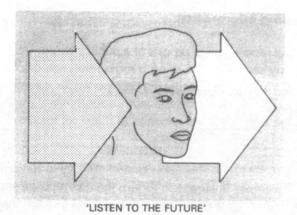

'LISTEN TO THE FUTURE'

Figure 9.3 A marketing logo

Audits are the formalized means of taking stock of the marketing environment. They require the marketer to undertake a detailed examination of external opportunities and threats:

- o Markets, connected stakeholders and competitors
- o The economic environment and key macroeconomic indicators
- o Other external environments.

It enables the organization to systematically understand what is happening in its environment and adapt accordingly. It is a critical input into the strategic planning process and underpins any projected diversification or extension to foreign markets. An external audit would normally be complemented by an internal or marketing audit to assess effectiveness in meeting marketing objectives. To determine how well the marketing activities and actions matched the opportunities and constraints of the environment requires a sound marketing information system. Some organizations use a consultancy firm for objectivity and to independently verify or challenge any critical assumptions the organization had been making. Stakeholder perceptions could also be investigated regarding future trends. Audits, therefore, are a foundation stone in the process of coping with environmental change and provide the necessary inputs to construct the organization's environmental set.

The environmental set

Every organization faces a set of environmental factors over which it may have some influence but seldom any direct control. Small or large, public or private, manufacturer or service organization, they all operate in the context of a shifting set of what are, in effect, potential threats or opportunities. The set that concerns any specific business will, however, be individual to its own particular circumstances and situation. It will also change over time as the elements in the set shift in relative importance and actual impact upon the business.

The board of directors, assisted by the marketers, must ensure that they monitor changes in their set and rank the elements in terms of likely impact on the business. Elements for a manufacturer might include the state of the economy, currency movements, interest rate changes, competitive pressures, wage movements and skill shortages. The set is the starting point for environmental assessment and SWOT analysis providing the basis for formulating a strategic response.

 Activity 9.5

Key skills: collecting and using information

Produce a current environmental set for your own organization.

○ Rank the elements to identify and consider their probable significance now and in 12 months time.

The environmental set concept may be applied to any organization although those for a voluntary or public sector organization would reflect very different concerns to those of the manufacturer. Since most local government funding derives from the centre, political factors will have more significance than economic ones. If revenues are obtained from local taxation or payments for services provided, then the state of the local economy will assume greater importance. Clearly, the more buoyant the local economy and the more households and businesses paying local taxes the better the services that can be provided.

Further sets could be developed to represent the major influences to be accounted for by businesses in financial services, import – export, retailing, construction and so forth. Only the elements will vary and, indeed, a threat for one organization may be an opportunity for another. Private security firms are seizing the opportunities provided in the run-up to Iraqi elections and the privatization of low-security prison facilities.

Impact analysis

This is a simple but applied approach to forecasting and assessing the probable impact of a specific environmental change on an organization or its competitors. In effect it is measuring the sensitivity of key parameters to changes in environmental variables. A number of impact grids may be constructed to provide a more informed view of the implications of environmental change:

Environmental future	Sainsbury's	Tesco	Asda	Kwik Save	Aldi
Edge-of-town planning restrictions tighten	– –	– –	– – –	–	– – –
Food Agency set up	–	–	–	–	0
Serious recession	–	–	0	+	++
Genetically modified foods backlash	– –	– –	++	0	0

Figure 9.4 Competitor impact grid

○ *Competitor impact grid* – Figure 9.4 shows the effect of potential/probable environmental changes on direct competitors in multiple groceries. The effect is rated on a scale ranging from +++ to – – – with 0 representing a neutral situation. A positive score suggests opportunity and improvement in profits, sales or competitive position.

Activity 9.6

Key skills: using information and problem-solving

Either extend the above grid for other potential environmental developments (e.g. takeover of Safeway or, better still, create one for your own industry. Alternatively construct one for your college and consider the prospective impact of educational policies or socio-demographic changes.

○ Competitors vary in their ability to withstand threats or exploit opportunities. In the above example, most are affected by tightening planning regulations, but some more than others. Aldi is a relatively new entrant to the market and is short of sites for expansion. WalMart/Asda is concentrated in the North of England so the regulations may prevent correction of this imbalance. A serious recession tends to advantage the cost-focused retailers at the expense of Sainsbury's and Tesco, while WalMart/Asda with its cost proximity should weather the storm. A boycott on GM foods would advantage those who have publicly declared GM-free zones against those who will merely label ingredients. This analysis enables the marketer to assess the effects of environmental change in advance and adapt accordingly.

○ *Environmental impact grid* – The marketer identifies environmental forces critically impacting on elements of the business and then awards a weighted assessment ranging, say, from 0 (neutral) to 7 (critical impact). Figure 9.5 provides an outline of the technique using the case of cross channel ferries.

○ *Trend impact analysis* – This is a straightforward development of the environmental impact grid. Any trend, in say commodity prices or household composition, is plotted up to date, according to its impact on revenues or costs, and then projected forward to highlight any significant change in impact.

Question 9.6

Key skills: problem-solving

Using your own knowledge and/or common sense, complete Figure 9.5.

○ *Cross impact analysis* – As the title suggests, this approach recognizes that the impact of a change in one variable may cause consequential impacts on other variables producing either positive, that is reinforces initial impact, or negative feedback.

○ *Influence diagrams* – These are designed to provide the marketer with a clearer perception of the critical environmental influences on the business. These can then be closely monitored in order to provide early warning of threats or opportunities. A response to the contingency can then be planned and executed. A positive relationship in the influence diagram means that a change in any direction by the independent environmental variable will bring about a corresponding movement in the same direction by the dependent variable. A negative relationship applies the pressure in the opposite direction. In Figure 9.6, each environmental factor is designated by a box, a direction arrow and a + or – sign. A firm marketing jacuzzis would recognize that sales volumes were influenced by private sector luxury house building, modernization and refurbishment trends and growth in health and fitness facilities. These will in turn be influenced by factors such as consumer confidence, house prices and the numbers moving house. Influences on these factors include interest rates, real incomes, employment and activity levels and so on. A rise in interest rates would therefore depress consumer confidence and in turn the demand for new luxury houses causing demand for jacuzzis to fall.

Environmental factor / Impact on ferries	Duty free removed	High-speed rail link in place	Exchange rate falls sharply	UK joins Euro	Low-cost airlines win Paris landing slots
Car passenger demand					
Foot passengers					
Lorries					
Ferry prices					
Marketing costs					

Figure 9.5 Environmental impact grid

Question 9.7

Key skills: problem-solving

Can you fill in the lower part of the influence diagram relating to environmental influences affecting new health and fitness facilities? These are currently expanding rapidly in Britain causing jacuzzi sales to rise. There are a number of + and – influence movements to identify.

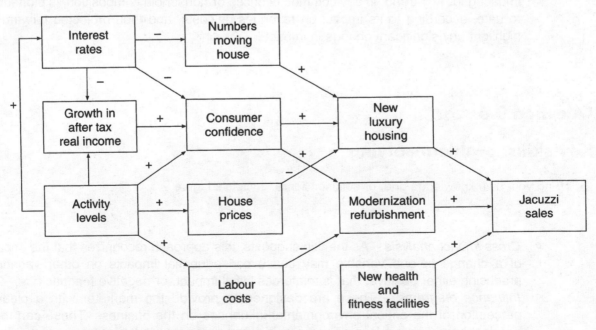

Figure 9.6 Influence diagram for sales of jacuzzis

SWOT analysis

This analysis distils the results of the internal and external audit. When combined with impact analysis, it allows the organization to focus on its critical organizational strengths and weaknesses relative to the threats and opportunities faced in the environment. The whole purpose of the technique is to encourage the marketer to be outward looking. This means they must anticipate and understand important environmental developments and their impact on the business. An opportunity represents an area or development that, with appropriate marketing, would enable the organization to achieve a competitive advantage. Conversely, a threat has been defined as a challenge posed by an unfavourable trend in the environment, which would lead in the absence of marketing action to the erosion of the organization's competitive position. Much of this coursebook has been concerned with the identification and discussion of threats and opportunities associated with the various elements of the marketing environment and will not be repeated here. However, every marketer is confronted with a unique array of such forces and these require some means of differentiation.

SWOT analysis provides a framework for the collection and systematic classification of information. Not all threats demand the same degree of concern and attention since the probability of impact and extent of consequential damage vary. The marketer naturally wishes to focus on the more threatening or potentially costly ones. Similar thinking applies to the range of emerging opportunities to which the organization's resources could be committed. Resources are scarce and have opportunity costs. The marketer requires some means of ranking opportunities according to:

- ○ Potential attractiveness/prospective rate of return.
- ○ Degree of matching with the organization's critical success factors (i.e. its strengths and weaknesses in key areas for exploiting the opportunity relative to competitors).
- ○ Feasibility of alternative courses of action to exploit them.
- ○ Probability of success – based on risk analysis/assessment.

Kotler suggests that if strengths and weaknesses represent where the organization is now, and opportunities and threats represent where it wishes to be at a given time in the future, then the role of the marketer is to supply the creativity to fill the gap between the two.

One classification technique can be seen in Figure 9.7, where opportunities are located in the matrix according to their probability of success and relative attractiveness. The latter is weighed in terms of, for example, potential profitability, projected growth rates and actual/potential competition, while the former is based on assessment of relative strengths. Threats are assessed by judging the likelihood of them happening against the scale of the potential damage if they do.

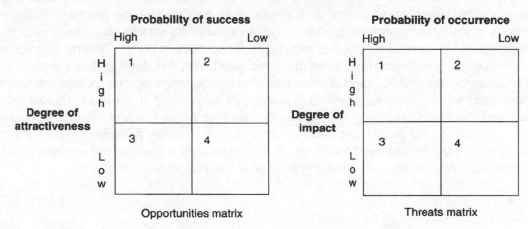

Figure 9.7 Opportunities and threats matrix

Each box in the analysis provides a ranking of significance. Marketers will clearly be more interested in opportunities located in Area 1, since they are both attractive and provide a good fit with organizational strengths. Area 1 threats require more serious consideration than those in Area 4. The analysis can be applied with varying degrees of sophistication through the use of calculated probabilities, weights and so forth. However, at the end of the day the role of the analysis is to concentrate marketing minds on future plans to exploit the 'right' opportunities and/or defuse serious and imminent threats to the continued success of the business.

Exam hint

Key skills: improving learning

Make time to apply all of the techniques discussed in this section to 'fix' each one in your mind. Use them to analyse your organization or college and it will programme the methods into your long-term memory.

Product life cycle (PLC)

This concept will be more familiar to candidates of Marketing Fundamentals than the Marketing Environment. However, there are aspects of this fundamental concept that have value in appreciating the future environment. The PLC is, after all, a trend projection but with a familiar S shape. Individual product PLCs can vary significantly due to the characteristics of the market environment and/or the marketing commitment of the firm.

The concept can be applied to product categories, for example washing machines, or to more short-lived brands. To plan for the future an organization needs to project its revenues and costs for all its product lines. This applies as much to a college or a consultancy as to a fmcg manufacturer. The stage the product has reached needs to be determined along with the profile of future contribution. This will partly depend on micro-environment factors (e.g. strength of rivals/changing consumer tastes), partly on the macro-environment (e.g. substitutes/legislation/demography) and partly on marketing decisions on the costs and benefits of product extension and promotional strategies.

The technological environment is particularly relevant to the PLC since it underpins both product development (Stage 1) and decline (Stage 5). Acceleration in technology, and particularly in the manipulation of information, images and ideas, has meant ever-shortening product design and development cycles. A succession of new generation products is the norm for brands of cars, computers and other lifestyle products as rapidly changing customer tastes, fashions and preferences reinforce this desire for something better. Decline often comes from technological substitution and must be anticipated. Are the days of the personal computer numbered by the development of more powerful and versatile laptops, notebooks and mobiles, more cost-effective workstations and interactive television? If so then marketing action is required. Impending maturity also signals the need for innovation and regeneration as competition intensifies and profits decline. An organization requires a regular audit to assess the portfolio and trigger the need for action. We have already discussed the importance of change agents and intrapreneurs in providing a catalyst for this process.

Marketing information system (MIS) – a summary

A final tool of analysis requires restatement and that is the crucially important MIS. Unless internally and externally generated data are collected, processed, disseminated and promptly acted upon, all other techniques will be of limited benefit to the marketer. Processing data into meaningful information is the critical activity for marketers and might be regarded as an additional P in the marketing mix. An MIS provides the equivalent of the pieces of the jigsaw that depict the ever-changing marketing environment and is an important sub-system within the organization.

As we have seen the knowledge-based society has arrived and the organizations that will succeed in a global information environment will be those that can identify opportunities, create value and develop their in-house knowledge assets. A marketing information system provides the means by which an innovative business can learn, adapt and change. This is a core competency in the electronic age. The need is to create repositories of marketing knowledge (internal, external and informal); improve access and transfer among users and to manage the knowledge as an asset by exploiting customer databases, creating and sharing new knowledge and so on. According to Galagan 'smart companies' would use an MIS to:

o   Generate new knowledge
o   Access knowledge from external sources
o   Represent knowledge in documents, databases, software, promotions, and so on
o   Embed knowledge in new processes, products and services
o   Diffuse existing marketing information throughout an organization
o   Apply accessible knowledge to effective marketing decision-making
o   Facilitate knowledge growth through market research and competitor intelligence
o   Measure the value of marketing knowledge assets and their impact.

It is important that the marketer sets the information agenda rather than the other way round. A clear focus is required so that the data gathered fits the intended purpose. There are large amounts of readily accessible information in the public domain that may be economically mined by the MIS. However, since much of the required environmental data is company specific, so resources need careful targeting. Market research can provide some important specific feedback, but a marketing intelligence gathering system is the main means of identifying emerging trends. A balance has, of course, to be struck between the benefits of additional information and the costs of collecting it. Equally the marketer must weigh the costs of inaccuracy arising from insufficient data, not least because of the constraint imposed on the use of the techniques discussed in this section.

The continuing impact of new information communication technology

This is an appropriate point to review in more depth the concept and development of information communication technology (ICT). This refers to the convergence of information technology and communication advances and represents the key drivers of change in a dynamic information-driven environment. It offers the ability to create more accurate profiling of customer needs and their buying behaviour thereby allowing for precisely targeted communication and feedback systems to support customer relationship management.

The explosion in computer, information and communication technologies, demonstrated most dramatically by the global web of computer networks known to all as the Internet, provides the ultimate information source for marketers. It has seen a dramatic expansion both in terms of websites to access and the spiralling number of users. This process was facilitated by Internet Service Providers (ISPs), such as AOL, offering free or discounted services to potential subscribers. Intense competition also forced telecommunication providers to reduce their phone line access charges but substantial losses in the dot-com crash forced a rationalization that may make 'free' web access a distant memory. Competition and expansion are still set to continue with the development of broadband digital services being provided through satellite, cable and aerials to televisions for armchair e-mail, internet shopping and information searches.

Development is worldwide, but varies in pace with China forging rapid expansion through cable television and the recent introduction of broadband services. E-mail is becoming part of every-day life within the government and increasing numbers of individuals. Internet cafés have been established and most hotels have web access in their business centres. Internet connections are relatively slow in China, however, due to the government control of international gateways and limited numbers of ISPs. Sri Lanka and Malaysia make increasingly heavy use of the internet for communications and e-mail is expanding at exponential rates. In Nigeria, by contrast, the use of the Internet is still very limited. There are a number of ISPs but a poor telecommunication infrastructure makes links relatively unreliable and slow.

New websites open daily throughout the world. Important sites for you to access are those of the Chartered Institute of Marketing (www.cim.co.uk and www.cim.virtualinstitute.com), offering access to new syllabus information, examiner reports, specimen answers, but unfortunately not forthcoming examination questions! Having said this, the CIM has had to take steps to counter the transmission of such questions from one time zone to another. Most organizations now have such a site and while sensitive information may be withheld there is much that may be inferred in intelligence terms from what remains. The technology also means that more research can be desk based and up to date.

The interactiveness of the Internet also means that the marketer can readily build information networks and relationships with stakeholders. Information can be both gathered from and distributed to stakeholders, including employees and customers more quickly, and at a fraction of previous cost levels.

As organizations seek to create and fulfil their vision and mission, the only certainty is that change will occur even faster in future. Indeed, as marketers strive to match business delivery to customer demand, converging information communication technologies are opening up an era of connected customers and stakeholders together with a new age of marketing opportunities.

The world is changing from a physical asset-dominated industrial structure into knowledge and information-based digital societies. Built on continuing and significant advances in ICT, all aspects of doing business are likely to be affected including:

- o Relationships with influential stakeholders can be enhanced through the Internet.
- o A marketing opportunity lies in gathering data arising from two-way interaction with customers and external stakeholders.
- o Virtual organizations have no boundaries in configuring their structure/relationships.
- o Flexibility and competitive advantage can be achieved by creating value added net-works, for example, intranets for automating operational decisions and transactions along the value chain.
- o Business to business electronic commerce is currently the primary driver.
- o Emergence of infomediaries in marketing research/intelligence areas.

Information communication technology is leading to the empowerment not only of buyers, but also of stakeholders in general, creating new dilemmas and new challenges for the organization. Fortunately it is also generating new technologies for dealing with them but marketers must dramatically improve their electronic competencies to emulate best practice.

Summary

In this unit we have seen that:

o It is crucially important for the marketer to monitor change in the marketing environment.
o Information is the critical resource and needs to be organized within the framework of an MIS.
o Marketing research is the foundation stone to effectively anticipating consumer needs.
o There are problems in making accurate forecasts when the environment is turbulent and unpredictable, but scenarios can provide management with useful alternative views of the future.
o Useful techniques exist to classify/analysis the changing environment.
o Frequent audits provide the necessary inputs for impact and SWOT analysis.
o The marketer must be future orientated and be wary of the patterns of the past.
o Issues and environmental challenges should be scanned for continuously with a view to determining the ones that constitute potential threats or opportunities for the organization.
o The continuing potential of the Internet and electronic databases in accessing information.
o A turbulent environment demands adaptability and flexible strategic planning.

Further study and examination preparation

This is the newest element of the syllabus, so questions have arisen frequently on recent papers. This provides a strong probability of a full or at least a part question on this important syllabus area, particularly since it can easily be linked in with other elements. This linkage can be seen in Question 9.2 while 9.1 represents a full question. Part questions occur on both of the specimen cases. Remember that even if you don't prepare a full answer to each question, you should at a minimum prepare an outline plan.

Extending knowledge

Palmer and Hartley, *The Business and Marketing Environment*, McGraw-Hill, 1999 – Chapter 14, Analysing the Marketing Environment, Chapter 5, The Information Environment.

Palmer, A. *The Business Environment*, McGraw-Hill, 2001 – Chapter 13, The Dynamic Business Environment, Chapter 4, The Internet Environment.

See also R.I. Cartwright, *Mastering the Business Environment*, Palgrave, 2001.

Interesting websites include:

www.ecommercetimes.co.uk

www.internetindicators.com

www.e-commerce.research.ml.com

www.pwcglobal.com

www.ecountries.com/africa/

www.lanka.net/chamber

www.asiansources.com

Exam question 9.1

Please see Question 6, June 2004. For specimen answers go to www.cim.co.uk.

Exam question 9.2

Please see Question 5a, December 2003. For specimen answers go to www.cim.co.uk.

Exam question 9.3

Please see Question 1a/b, December 2000. For specimen answers go to www.cim.co.uk/learning zone.

Exam question 9.4

Please see Question 1c, June 2004. For specimen answers go to www.cim.co.uk.

Exam question 9.5

Please see Question 3c, December 2003. For specimen answers go to www.cim.co.uk.

appendix 1
guidance on examination preparation

Preparing for your examination

You are now nearing the final phase of your studies and it is time to start the hard work of exam preparation.

During your period of study you will have become used to absorbing large amounts of information. You will have tried to understand and apply aspects of knowledge that may have been very new to you, while some of the information provided may have been more familiar. You may even have undertaken many of the activities that are positioned frequently throughout your coursebook, which will have enabled you to apply your learning in practical situations. But whatever the state of your knowledge and understanding, do not allow yourself to fall into the trap of thinking that you know enough, that you understand enough, or even worse, that you can just take it as it comes on the day.

Never underestimate the pressure of the CIM examination.

The whole point of preparing this textbook for you is to ensure that you never take the examination for granted, and that you do not go into the exam unprepared for what might come your way for 3 hours at a time.

One thing is for sure: there is no quick fix, no easy route, no waving a magic wand and finding you know it all.

Whether you have studied alone, in a CIM study centre, or through distance learning, you now need to ensure that this final phase of your learning process is tightly managed, highly structured and objective.

As a candidate in the examination, your role will be to convince the Senior Examiner, for this subject, that you have credibility. You need to demonstrate to the examiner that you can be trusted to undertake a range of challenges in the context of marketing and that you are able to capitalize on opportunities and manage your way through threats.

You should prove to the Senior Examiner that you are able to apply knowledge, make decisions, respond to situations and solve problems.

Very shortly we are going to look at a range of revision and exam preparation techniques, and at time management issues, and encourage you towards developing and implementing your own revision plan, but before that, let's look at the role of the Senior Examiner.

A bit about the Senior Examiners!

You might be quite shocked to read this, but while it might appear that the examiners are 'relentless question masters' they actually want you to be able to answer the questions and pass the exams! In fact, they would derive no satisfaction or benefits from failing candidates; quite the contrary, they develop the syllabus and exam papers in order that you can learn and then apply that learning effectively so as to pass your examinations. Many of the examiners have said in the past that it is indeed psychologically more difficult to fail students than pass them.

Many of the hints and tips you find within this appendix have been suggested by the Senior Examiners and authors of the coursebook series. Therefore, you should consider them carefully and resolve to undertake as many of the elements suggested as possible.

The Chartered Institute of Marketing has a range of processes and systems in place within the Examinations Division to ensure that fairness and consistency prevail across the team of examiners, and that the academic and vocational standards that are set and defined are indeed maintained. In doing this, CIM ensures that those who gain the CIM Certificate, Professional Diploma and Postgraduate Diploma are worthy of the qualification and perceived as such in the view of employers, actual and potential.

Part of what you will need to do within the examination is be 'examiner friendly' – that means you have to make sure they get what they ask for. This will make life easier for you and for them.

Hints and tips for 'examiner friendly' actions are as follows:

- Show them that you understand the basis of the question, by answering *precisely* the question asked, and not including just about everything you can remember about the subject area.
- Read their needs – how many points is the question asking you to address?
- Respond to the question appropriately. Is the question asking you to take on a role? If so, take on the role and answer the question in respect of the role. For example, you could be positioned as follows:
- 'You are working as a Marketing Assistant at Nike UK' or 'You are a Marketing Manager for an Engineering Company' or 'As Marketing Manager write a report to the Managing Partner.'

These examples of role-playing requirements are taken from questions in past papers.

- Deliver the answer in the format requested. If the examiner asks for a memo, then provide a memo; likewise, if the examiner asks for a report, then write a report. If you do not do this, in some instances, you will fail to gain the necessary marks required to pass.
- Take a business-like approach to your answers. This enhances your credibility. Badly ordered work, untidy work, lack of structure, headings and subheadings can be off-putting. This would be unacceptable in the work situation, likewise it will be unacceptable in the eyes of the Senior Examiners and their marking teams.
- Ensure the examiner has something to mark: give them substance, relevance, definitions, illustration and demonstration of your knowledge and understanding of the subject area.
- See the examiner as your potential employer or ultimate consumer/customer. The whole purpose and culture of marketing is about meeting customers' needs. Try this approach – it works wonders.

○ Provide a strong sense of enthusiasm and professionalism in your answers; support it with relevant up-to-date examples and apply them where appropriate.

○ Try to do something that will make your exam paper a little bit different – make it stand out in the crowd.

All of these points might seem quite logical to you, but often in the panic of the examination they 'go out of the window'. Therefore, it is beneficial to remind ourselves of the importance of the examiner. He or she is the 'ultimate customer' – and we all know customers hate to be disappointed.

As we move on, some of these points will be revisited and developed further.

About the examination

In all examinations, with the exception of Marketing in Practice at Certificate level and Analysis and Decision at Postgraduate Diploma level, the paper is divided into two parts.

○ Part A – Mini-case study = 40 per cent of the marks

○ Part B – Option choice questions (choice of three questions from seven) = 60 per cent of the marks.

Let's look at the basis of each element.

Part A: The mini-case study

This is based on a mini-case or scenario with one question, possibly subdivided into between two and four points, but totalling 40 per cent of marks overall.

In essence, you, the candidate, are placed in a problem-solving role through the medium of a short scenario. On occasions, the scenario may consist of an article from a journal in relation to a well-known organization: for example, in the past Interflora, EasyJet and Philips, among others, have been used as the basis of the mini-case.

Alternatively, it will be based upon a fictional company, and the examiner will have prepared it in order that the right balance of knowledge, understanding, application and skills is used.

Approaches to the mini-case study

When undertaking the mini-case study there are a number of key areas you should consider.

Structure/content

The mini-case that you will be presented with will vary slightly from paper to paper and, of course, from one examination to the other. Normally, the scenario presented will be 250–400 words long and will centre on a particular organization and its problems or may even relate to a specific industry.

The length of the mini-case study means that usually only a brief outline is provided of the situation, the organization and its marketing problems, and you must therefore learn to cope with analysing information and preparing your answer on the basis of a very limited amount of detail.

Time management

There are many differing views on time management and the approaches you can take to manage your time within the examination. You must find an approach to suit your way of working, but always remember, whatever you do, you must ensure that you allow enough time to complete the examination. Unfinished exams mean lost marks. A typical example of managing time is as follows:

Your paper is designed to assess you over a 3-hour period. With 40 per cent of the marks being allocated to the mini-case, it means that you should dedicate somewhere around 75 minutes of your time to both read and write up the answer on this mini-case. Some students, however, will prefer to allocate nearly half of their time (90 minutes) on the mini-case, so that they can read and fully absorb the case and answer the questions in the context of it. This is also acceptable as long as you ensure that you work extremely 'SMART' for the remaining time in order to finish the examination.

Do not forget that while there is only one question within the mini-case, it can have a number of components. You must answer all the components in that question, which is where the balance of time comes into play.

Knowledge/skills tested

Throughout all the CIM papers, your knowledge, skills and ability to apply those skills will be tested. However, the mini-cases are used particularly to test application, that is your ability to take your knowledge and apply it in a structured way to a given scenario. The examiners will be looking at your decision-making ability, your analytical and communication skills and, depending on the level, your ability as a manager to solve particular marketing problems.

When the examiner is marking your paper, he or she will be looking to see how you differentiate yourself, looking at your own individual 'unique selling points'. The examiner will also want to see if you can personally apply the knowledge or whether you are only able to repeat the textbook materials.

Format of answers

On many occasions, and within all examinations, you will most likely be given a particular communication method to use. If this is the case, you must ensure that you adhere to the requirements of the examiner. This is all part of meeting customer needs.

The likely communication tools you will be expected to use are as follows:

- ○ Memorandum
- ○ Memorandum/report
- ○ Report
- ○ Briefing notes
- ○ Presentation
- ○ Press release
- ○ Advertisement
- ○ Plan.

Make sure that you familiarize yourself with these particular communication tools and practise using them to ensure that, on the day, you will be able to respond confidently to the communication requests of the examiner.

By the same token, while communication methods are important, so is meeting the specific requirements of the question. This means you must understand what is meant by the precise instruction given. *Note the following terms carefully*:

o   *Identify* – select key issues, point out key learning points, establish clearly what the examiner expects you to identify.
o   *Illustrate* – the examiner expects you to provide examples, scenarios and key concepts that illustrate your learning.
o   *Compare and contrast* – look at the range of similarities between the two situations, contexts or even organizations. Then compare them, i.e. ascertain and list how activities, features, etc. agree or disagree. Contrasting means highlighting the differences between the two.
o   *Discuss* – questions that have 'discuss' in them offer a tremendous opportunity for you to debate, argue, justify your approach or understanding of the subject area – caution, it is not an opportunity to waffle.
o   *Briefly explain* – this means being succinct, structured and concise in your explanation, within the answer. Make your points clear, transparent and relevant.
o   *State* – present in a clear, brief format.
o   *Interpret* – expound the meaning of, make clear and explicit what it is you see and understand within the data provided.
o   *Outline* – provide the examiner with the main concepts and features being asked for and avoid minor technical details. Structure will be critical here, or else you could find it difficult to contain your answer.
o   *Relate* – show how different aspects of the syllabus connect together.
o   *Evaluate* – review and reflect upon an area of the syllabus, a particular practice, an article, etc., and consider its overall worth in respect of its use as a tool or a model and its overall effectiveness in the role it plays.

Source: Worsam, Mike, *How to Pass Marketing*, Croner, 1989.

Your approach to mini-cases

There is no one right way to approach and tackle a mini-case study, indeed it will be down to each individual to use their own creativity in tackling the tasks presented. You will have to use your initiative and discretion about how best to approach the mini-case. Having said this, however, there are some basic steps you can take.

o   Ensure that you read through the case study at least twice before making any judgements, starting to analyse the information provided, or indeed writing the answers.
o   On the third occasion read through the mini-case and, using a highlighter, start marking the essential and relevant information critical to the content and context. Then turn your attention to the question again, this time reading slowly and carefully to assess what it is you are expected to do. Note any instructions that the examiner gives you, and then start to plan how you might answer the question. Whatever the question, ensure the answer has a structure: a beginning, a structured central part of the answer and, finally, always a conclusion.
o   Keep the context of the question continually in mind: that is, the specifics of the case and the role which you might be performing.
o   Because there is limited material available, you will sometimes need to make assumptions. Don't be afraid to do this, it will show initiative on your part. Assumptions are an important part of dealing with case studies and can help you to be quite creative with your answer. However, do explain the basis of your assumptions within your answer so that the examiner understands the nature of them, and why you have arrived at your particular outcome. *Always ensure that your assumptions are realistic.*

    o Only now are you approaching the stage where it is time to start writing your answer to the question, tackling the problems, making decisions and recommendations on the case scenario set before you. As mentioned previously, your points will often be best set out in a report or memo type format, particularly if the examiner does not specify a communication method.

    o Ensure that your writing is succinct, avoids waffle and responds directly to the questions asked.

Part B: Option choice questions

Part B at the certificate level is comprised of six or seven more traditional questions, each worth 20 per cent. You will be expected to choose three of those questions, to make up the remaining 60 per cent of available marks.

Realistically, the same principles apply for these questions as in the case study. Communication formats, reading through the questions, structure, role-play, context and so on – everything is the same.

Part B will cover a number of broader issues from within the syllabus and will be taken from any element of it. The examiner makes the choice, and no prior direction is given to students or tutors on what that might be.

As regards time management in this area, if you used about 75 minutes for the mini-case you should have around 105 minutes left. This provides you with around 30 minutes to plan and write a question and 5 minutes per question to review and revise your answers. Keep practising – use a cooker timer, alarm clock or mobile phone alarm as your timer and work hard at answering questions within the timeframe given.

Specimen examination papers and answers

To help you prepare and understand the nature of the paper, go to www.cim.co.uk/learningzone to access Specimen Answers and Senior Examiner's advice for these exam questions. During your study, the author of your coursebook may have on occasions asked you to refer to these papers and answer the questions. You should undertake these exercises and utilize every opportunity to practise meeting examination requirements.

The specimen answers are vital learning tools. They are not always perfect, as they are answers written by students and annotated by the Senior Examiners, but they will give you a good indication of the approaches you could take, and the examiners' annotations suggest how these answers might be improved. Please use them.

Other sources of information are available at www.cim.co.uk/learningzone. The CIM Learning Zone website provides you with links to many useful case studies which will help you to put your learning into context when you are revising.

Key elements of preparation

There are three important elements to think about when preparing for your examination:

- o Learning
- o Memory
- o Revision.

Let's look at each point in turn.

Learning

Quite often students find it difficult to learn properly. You can passively read books, look at some of the materials, perhaps revise a little, and regurgitate it all in the examination. In the main, however, this is rather an unsatisfactory method of learning. It is meaningless, shallow and ultimately of little use in practice.

For learning to be truly effective it must be active and applied. You must involve yourself in the learning process by thinking about what you have read, testing it against your experience by reflecting on how you use particular aspects of marketing, and how you could perhaps improve your own performance by implementing particular aspects of your learning into your everyday life. You should adopt the old adage of 'learning by doing'. If you do, you will find that passive learning has no place in your study life.

Below are some suggestions that have been prepared to assist you with the learning pathway throughout your revision.

- o Always make your own notes, in words you understand, and ensure that you combine all the sources of information and activities within them.
- o Always try to relate your learning back to your own organization.
- o Make sure you define key terms concisely, wherever possible.
- o Do not try to memorize your ideas, but work on the basis of understanding and, most important, applying them.
- o Think about the relevant and topical questions that might be set – use the questions and answers in your coursebooks to identify typical questions that might be asked in the future.
- o Attempt all of the questions within each of your coursebooks since these are vital tests of your active learning and understanding.

Memory

If you are prepared to undertake an active learning programme, then your knowledge will be considerably enhanced, as understanding and application of knowledge does tend to stay in your 'long-term' memory. It is likely that passive learning will only stay in your 'short-term' memory.

Do not try to memorize in parrot fashion; it is not helpful and, even more important, examiners are experienced in identifying various memorizing techniques and therefore will spot them as such.

Having said this, it is quite useful to memorize various acronyms such as SWOT, PEST, PESTLE, STEEPLE, or indeed various models such as Ansoff, GE Matrix, Shell Directional and so on, as in some of the questions you may be required to use illustrations of these to assist your answer.

Revision

The third and final stage to consider is 'revision', which is what we will concentrate on in detail below. Here just a few key tips are offered.

Revision should be an ongoing process rather than a panic measure that you decide to undertake just before the examination. You should be preparing notes throughout your course, with the view to using them as part of your revision process. Therefore, ensure that your notes are sufficiently comprehensive that you can reuse them successfully.

For each concept you learn about, you should identify, through your reading and your own personal experience, at least two or three examples that you could use; this then gives you some scope to broaden your perspective during the examination. It will, of course, help you gain some points for initiative with the examiners.

Knowledge is not something you will gain overnight – as we saw earlier, it is not a quick fix; it involves a process of learning that enables you to lay solid foundations upon which to build your long-term understanding and application. This will benefit you significantly in the future, not just in the examination.

In essence, you should ensure that you do the following in the period before the real intensive revision process begins.

- ○ Keep your study file well organized, updated and full of newspaper and journal cuttings that may help you formulate examples in your mind for use during the examination.
- ○ Practise defining key terms and acronyms from memory.
- ○ Prepare topic outlines and essay answer plans.
- ○ When you start your intensive revision, ensure it is planned and structured in the way described below. And then finally, read your concentrated notes the night before the examination.

Revision planning

You are now on a critical path – although hopefully not too critical at this time – with somewhere in the region of between 4 and 6 weeks to go to the examination. The following hints and tips will help you plan out your revision study.

- ○ You will, as already explained, need to be very organized. Therefore, before doing anything else, put your files, examples, reading material and so on in good order, so that you are able to work with them in the future and, of course, make sense of them.
- ○ Ensure that you have a quiet area within which to work. It is very easy to get distracted when preparing for an examination.
- ○ Take out your file along with your syllabus and make a list of key topic areas that you have studied and which you now need to revise. You could use the basis of this book to do that, by taking each unit a step at a time.
- ○ Plan the use of your time carefully. Ideally, you should start your revision at least 6 weeks prior to the exam, so therefore work out how many spare hours you could give to the revision process and then start to allocate time in your diary, and do not double-book with anything else.

o Give up your social life for a short period of time. As the saying goes 'no pain – no gain'.
o Looking at each of the subject areas in turn, identify which are your strengths and which are your weaknesses. Which areas have you grasped and understood, and which are the areas that you have really struggled with? Split your page in two and make a list on each side. For example:

Planning and control	
Strengths	**Weaknesses**
Audit – PEST, SWOT, models	Ratio analysis
Portfolio analysis	Market sensing
	Productivity analysis
	Trend extrapolation
	Forecasting

o Break down your list again and divide the points of weakness, giving priority in the first instance to your weakest areas and even prioritizing them by giving them a number. This will enable you to master the more difficult areas. Up to 60 per cent of your remaining revision time should be given over to that, as you may find you have to undertake a range of additional reading and also perhaps seeking tutor support, if you are studying at a CIM Accredited Study Centre.
o The rest of the time should be spent reinforcing your knowledge and understanding of the stronger areas, spending time testing yourself on how much you really know.
o Should you be taking two examinations or more at any one time, then the breakdown and managing of your time will be critical.
o Taking a subject at a time, work through your notes and start breaking them down into subsections of learning, and ultimately into key learning points, items that you can refer to time and time again, that are meaningful and that your mind will absorb. You yourself will know how best you remember the key points. Some people try to develop acronyms, flowcharts or matrices, mind maps, fishbone diagrams and so on, or various connection diagrams that help them recall certain aspects of models. You could also develop processes that enable you to remember approaches to various options. (But do remember what we said earlier about regurgitating stuff, parrot fashion.)

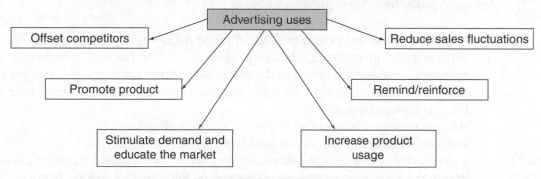

Figure A1.1 Use of a diagram to summarize key components of a concept
Source: Adapted from Dibb, Simkin, Pride and Ferrell, Marketing Concepts and Strategies, 4th edition, Houghton Mifflin, 2001

Figure A1.1 is just a brief example of how you could use a 'bomb-burst' diagram (which, in this case, highlights the uses of advertising) as a very helpful approach to memorizing key elements of learning.

- o Eventually you should reduce your key learning to bullet points. For example: imagine you were looking at the concept of time management – you could eventually reduce your key learning to a bullet list containing the following points in relation to 'effective prioritization':

    - – Organize
    - – Take time
    - – Delegate
    - – Review.

- o Each of these headings would then remind you of the elements you need to discuss associated with the subject area.
- o Avoid getting involved in reading too many textbooks at this stage, as you may start to find that you are getting confused overall.
- o Look at examination questions in previous papers, and start to observe closely the various roles and tasks they expect you to undertake, and importantly, the context in which they are set.
- o Use the specimen exam papers and specimen answers to support your learning and see how you could actually improve upon them.
- o Without exception, find an associated examination question for the areas that you have studied and revised, and undertake it (more than once, if necessary).
- o Without referring to notes or books, try to draft an answer plan with the key concepts, knowledge, models and information that are needed to successfully complete the answer. Then refer to the specimen answer to see how close you are to the actual outline presented. Planning your answer, and ensuring that key components are included, and that the question has a meaningful structure, is one of the most beneficial activities that you can undertake.
- o Now write the answer out in full, time constrained and written by hand, not with the use of IT. (At this stage, you are still expected to be the scribe for the examination and present handwritten work. Many of us find this increasingly difficult as we spend more and more time using our computers to present information. Do your best to be neat. Difficult to read handwriting is often offputting to the examiner.)
- o When writing answers as part of your revision process, also be sure to practise the following essential examination techniques:

    - – *Identify and use the communication method* requested by the examiner.
    - – *Always have three key parts to the answer* An introduction, middle section that develops your answer in full, and a conclusion. Where appropriate, ensure that you have an introduction, main section, summary/conclusion and, if requested or helpful, recommendations.
    - – *Always answer the question in the context or role set*.
    - – *Always comply with the nature and terms of the question*.
    - – *Leave white space* Do not overcrowd your page; leave space between paragraphs, and make sure your sentences do not merge into one blur. (Don't worry – there is always plenty of paper available to use in the examination.)
    - – *Count* how many actions the question asks you to undertake and double-check at the end that you have met the full range of demands of the question.

- *Use examples* to demonstrate your knowledge and understanding of the particular syllabus area. These can be from journals, the Internet, the press, or your own experience.
- *Display your vigour and enthusiasm for marketing* Remember to think of the Senior Examiner as your customer, or future employer, and do your best to deliver what is wanted to satisfy their needs. Impress them and show them how you are a 'cut above the rest'.

o Review all your practice answers critically with the above points in mind.

Practical actions

The critical path is becoming even more critical now as the examination looms. The following are vital points.

o Have you registered with CIM?
o Do you know where you are taking your examination? CIM should let you know approximately 1 month in advance.
o Do you know where your examination centre is? If not, find out, take a drive, time it – whatever you do don't be late!
o Make sure you have all the tools of the examination ready. A dictionary, calculator, pens, pencils, ruler and so on. Try not to use multiple shades of pens, but at the same time make your work look professional. *Avoid using red and green as these are the colours that will be used for marking.*

Summary

Above all, you must remember that you personally have invested a tremendous amount of time, effort and money in studying for this programme and it is therefore imperative that you consider the suggestions given here as they will help to maximize your return on your investment.

Many of the hints and tips offered here are generic and will work across most of the CIM courses. We have tried to select those that will help you most in taking a sensible, planned approach to your study and revision.

The key to your success is being prepared to put in the time and effort required, planning your revision, and equally important, planning and answering your questions in a way that will ensure that you pass your examination on the day.

The advice offered here aims to guide you from a practical perspective. Guidance on syllabus content and developments associated with your learning will become clear to you as you work through this coursebook. The authors of each coursebook have given subject-specific guidance on the approach to the examination and on how to ensure that you meet the content requirements of the kind of question you will face. These considerations are in addition to the structuring issues we have been discussing throughout this appendix.

Each of the authors and Senior Examiners will guide you on their preferred approach to questions and answers as they go. Therefore, where you are presented with an opportunity to be involved in some activity or undertake an examination question either during or at the end of your study units, do take it. It not only prepares you for the examination, but helps you learn in the applied way we discussed above.

Here, then, is a last reminder:

- ○ Ensure you make the most of your learning process throughout.
- ○ Keep structured and orderly notes from which to revise.
- ○ Plan your revision – don't let it just happen.
- ○ Provide examples to enhance your answers.
- ○ Practise your writing skills in order that you present your work well and your writing is readable.
- ○ Take as many opportunities to test your knowledge and measure your progress as possible.
- ○ Plan and structure your answers.
- ○ Always do as the question asks you, especially with regard to context and communication method.
- ○ Do not leave it until the last minute!

The writers would like to take this opportunity to wish you every success in your endeavours to study, to revise and to pass your examinations.

Karen Beamish
Academic Development Advisor

appendix 2
assignment-based assessment

Introduction – the basis to the assignments and the integrative project

Within the CIM qualifications at both Professional Certificate and Professional Diploma levels there are several assessment options available. These are detailed in the outline of modules below. The purpose of an assignment is to provide another format to complete each module for students who want to apply the syllabus concepts from a module to their own or a selected organization. For either qualification there are three modules providing assessment via an assignment and one module assessed via an integrative work-based project. The module assessed via the integrative project is the summative module for each qualification.

	Entry modules	Research & analysis	Planning	Implementation	Management of Marketing
Professional Post Graduate Diploma	Entry module – Professional Post Graduate Diploma	Analysis & Evaluation	Strategic Marketing Decisions	Managing Marketing Performance	Strategic Marketing in Practice
Professional Diploma	Entry module – Professional Diploma	Marketing Research & Information	Marketing Planning	Marketing Communications	Marketing Management in Practice
Professional Certificate		Marketing Environment	Marketing Fundamentals	Customer Communications	Marketing in Practice
Introductory Certificate		Supporting marketing processes (research & analysis, planning & implementation)			

Outline of CIM 'standard' syllabus (© The Chartered Institute of Marketing, September 2003)

The use of assignments does not mean that this route is easier than an examination. Both formats are carefully evaluated to ensure that a grade B in the assessment/integrative project route is the same as a grade B in an examination. However, the use of assignments does allow a student to complete the assessment for a module over a longer period of time than a 3-hour examination. This will inevitably mean work being undertaken over the time-span of a module. For those used to cramming for exams writing an assignment over several weeks which comprises a total of four separate questions will be a very different approach.

Each module within the qualification contains a different assignment written specifically for the module. These are designed to test understanding and provide the opportunity for you to demonstrate your abilities through the application of theory to practice. The format and structure of each module's assignment is identical, although the questions asked will differ and the exact type of assignment varies. The questions within an assignment will relate directly to the syllabus for that particular module, thereby giving the opportunity to demonstrate understanding and application.

The assignment structure

The assignment for each module is broken down into a range of questions. These consist of a core question, a selection of optional questions plus a reflective statement. The core question will always relate to the main aspects of each module's syllabus. Coupled with this are a range of four optional questions which will each draw from a different part of the syllabus. Students are requested to select two optional questions from the four available. In addition, a reflective statement requires a student to evaluate their learning from the module. When put together these form the assessment for the entire module. The overall pass mark for the module is the same as through an examination route, which is set at 50 per cent. In addition, the grade band structure is also identical to that of an examination.

Core question

This is the longest and therefore most important section of your assignment. Covering the major components of the syllabus, the core question is designed to provide a challenging assignment which both tests the theoretical element yet also permits application to a selected organization or situation. The rubric on the front of the assignment will give clear guidance in respect of word limits, therefore pay close attention to them and the overall requirements of CIM in relation to the use of appendices. However, the appendices should be kept to a minimum. Advice here is that they should be no longer than five pages of additional pertinent information.

Optional questions

There are a total of four questions provided for Professional Certificate and Professional Diploma of the syllabus from which a student is asked to select two. Each answer is expected to provide a challenge although the actual task required varies. The rubric on the front of the assignment will give clear guidance in respect of word limits, therefore pay close attention to them and the overall requirements of CIM in relation to the use of appendices.

These are designed to test areas of the syllabus not covered by the core question. As such it is possible to base all of your questions on the same organization although there is significant benefit in using more than one organization as a basis for your assignment. Some of the questions specifically require a different organization to be selected from the one used for the core question. This only occurs where the questions are requiring similar areas to be investigated and will be specified clearly on the question itself.

Within the assignment there are several types of questions that may be asked, including:

- *A report* – the question requires a formal report to be completed, detailing an answer to the specific question set. This will often be reporting on a specific issue to an individual.
- *A briefing paper or notes* – preparing a briefing paper or a series of notes which may be used for a presentation.
- *A presentation* – you may be required either to prepare the presentation only or to deliver the presentation in addition to its preparation. The audience for the presentation should be considered carefully and ICT used where possible.
- *A discussion paper* – the question requires an academic discussion paper to be prepared. You should show a range of sources and concepts within the paper. You may also be required to present the discussion paper as part of a question.
- *A project plan or action plan* – some questions ask for planning techniques to be demonstrated. As such, the plan must be for the timescale given and costs shown where applicable. The use of ICT is recommended here in order to create the plan diagrammatically.
- *Planning a research project* – while market research may be required, questions have often asked for simply a research plan in a given situation. This would normally include timescales, the type(s) of research to be gathered, sampling, planned data collection and analysis.
- *Conducting research* – following on from a research plan, a question can require student(s) to undertake a research gathering exercise. A research question can be either an individual or a group activity depending upon the question. This will usually result in a report of the findings of the exercise plus any recommendations arising from your findings.
- *Gathering of information and reporting* – within many questions information will need gathering. The request for information can form part or all of a question. This may be a background to the organization, the activities contained in the question or external market and environmental information. It is advisable to detail the types of information utilized, their sources and report on any findings. Such a question will often ask for recommendations for the organization – these should be drawn from the data and not simply personal opinion.
- *An advisory document* – a question here will require students to evaluate a situation and present advice and recommendations drawn from findings and theory. Again, any advice should be backed up with evidence and not a personal perspective only.
- *An exercise, either planning and/or delivering the exercise* – at both Professional Certificate and Professional Diploma exercises are offered as optional questions. These provide students with the opportunity to devise an exercise and may also require the delivery of this exercise. Such an activity should be evidenced where possible.
- *A role-play with associated documentation* – several questions have asked students to undertake role-plays in exercises such as team building. These are usually videoed and documentation demonstrating the objectives of the exercise provided.

Each of these questions related directly towards specific issues to be investigated, evaluated and answered. In addition, some of the questions asked present situations to be considered. These provide opportunities for specific answers relating directly to the question asked.

In order to aid students completing the assignment, each question is provided with an outline of marking guidance. This relates to the different categories by which each question is marked. The marker of your assignment will be provided with a detailed marking scheme constructed around the same marking guidance provided to students.

For both the core and optional questions it is important to use referencing where sources have been utilized. This has been a weakness in the past and continues to be an issue. There have been cases of plagiarism identified during marking and moderation, together with a distinct lack of references and bibliography. It is highly recommended that a bibliography be included with each question and sources are cited within the text itself. The type of referencing method used is not important, only that sources are referred to.

The reflective statement

This is the final aspect to each module assignment. The purpose of the reflective statement is for each student to consider how the module has influenced him or her as an individual and reflect upon their practice. A shorter piece of work than for other aspects at 500 words (Professional Certificate) or 750 words (Professional Diploma), it is also more personal in that your answer will often depend upon how you as an individual have applied the learning from the module to your work and other aspects.

A good reflective statement will comprise a number of aspects, including:

o Details of the theoretical aspects that you found beneficial within the module, and their reasons. If you have found particular resources beneficial state this and the reason why.
o How these concepts have affected you as a practitioner with examples of application of concepts from the module to your work and/or other activities.
o How you intend to progress your learning further after completing the module assessment.

When looking at the reflective statement your tutor or an assessor will try to award marks for your demonstration of understanding through the module together with how you have applied the theoretical concepts to practice. They are looking for evidence of learning and application over time, rather than a student simply completing the question because they have a deadline looming. The result of this marking tends to be that students who begin to apply the module concepts early often achieve higher marks overall.

Integrative project structure

The integrative project is designed to provide an in-company approach to assessment rather than having specified assignments. Utilized within the summative module element of each level's syllabus, this offers a student the chance to produce a piece of work which tackles a specific issue. The integrative project can only be completed after undertaking other modules as it will rely on information in each of these as guidance. The integrative project is approximately 5000 words in length and was introduced from September 2002 at the Professional Certificate. It was introduced from September 2003 at Professional Diploma with the commencement of the new syllabus. The integrative project is marked by CIM assessors and not your own tutors.

Assignments – Marketing Environment

Divided into four different elements, the Marketing Environment module covers all the aspects of the business environment. As such, questions can be drawn from a number of different areas. For each of the four elements, a sample question is given together with an evaluation of the type of answer that would be expected at this level.

Element 1 – The nature of the organization and the impact of its environment

This element of the syllabus covers the role of the marketing environment, the mission statement, objectives and potential future environmental issues. A typical question covering this aspect would be:

Taking your own or a selected organization, consider your mission statement and objectives in the light of TWO potentially significant external environmental issues. Evaluate the significance of these events together with potential responses which are available.

This question requires a consideration of both the internal and external marketing environment. In addition, the element draws in aspects of the mission statement and objectives. It is important to select an organization where the ability to foresee potential environmental changes exists. An example answer to this question would be:

- A background to the organization selected, together with information regarding their current marketing environment.
- Detail of the organization's mission statement and objectives. A background to these would also be beneficial. It is important that the scene is set for later consideration of the mission and objectives in the light of potential environmental change.
- The current influences on the setting of objectives within the organization need to be considered. Where an objective has been given, its reason or background would be beneficial at this point.
- The next stage would be to evaluate the marketing environment, both internal and external. The use of marketing environment theory is recommended. In addition, a pictorial or written representation in a table of the organization's marketing environment is the best route here.
- Following from this, the two potentially significant effects should be highlighted. This may be a change in government, a new currency such as the Euro, retirement of the organization's founder and many other aspects. A rationale for their selection over other aspects needs to be given together with an evaluation of the event's significance.
- The final stage of the question relates to recommendations for managing this event, whether internal or external.
- The format of this question should be as a report, using diagrammatic representation where possible.

Element 2 – Micro-environment

This element considers stakeholders and other factors affecting the organization which are within its control. As such a question will usually consider how these elements can be managed for the success of the organization. A typical question covering this element would be:

A new Marketing Assistant has recently joined the department and your manager has asked you to meet with them to discuss the micro-environment in which your organization or an organization of your choice operates. You are required to prepare a discussion paper that you can use as a basis for your meeting that identifies the key stakeholders of the organization, the influence that the organization has over these previously identified stakeholders and that these stakeholders have on the organization.

To develop an effective answer to this question it is important to select an organization where information on the stakeholders and other micro-environmental aspects is readily available. The setting is important as is the context of the question asked. The question requires a discussion paper for a meeting. This does not need to be as formal as a report, but should contain enough information to be easily accessible and understandable by the new marketing assistant as they are the audience for the document. An answer would include:

- o The selection of the organization. A background to the organization and the rationale for its selection is required here.
- o The organization needs considering in detail. This should cover aspects of the organization's stakeholders and their current micro-environment.
- o The micro-environmental aspects should be set in scene with use of theory on the internal environment and stakeholders. This might include diagrammatic representations of both the marketing environment and types of stakeholders.
- o The key stakeholders in the organization should be identified using the theory covered previously. Representation of the stakeholders in a table or diagram is advisable.
- o The relationships between the *key* stakeholders and the organization should be discussed. The level of influence the organization has over these three stakeholders needs to be discussed. Models used here would include stakeholder mapping diagrams.
- o A series of recommendations should follow which assess how these stakeholders could be better managed. Recommendations may centre around improved communication and relationship building together with advice on future monitoring.

Element 3 – Macro-environment

This element builds upon the micro-environmental analysis to expand the marketing audit out to a wider perspective. Drawing in many factors, a question relating to this element would ask for consideration of the external marketing environment, as with the question below:

> *Your Marketing Manager is coordinating a marketing audit and has asked you to carry out a detailed audit of the EXTERNAL factors that are currently affecting your organization or an organization of your choice. You are required to write a report that evaluates the influence of these factors.*

The key component of this question is the consideration of the external marketing environment. An answer to the question would require the selection of an appropriate organization that is affected considerably by the macro-environment:

- o Identify a suitable organization as the basis for the question – give a background and rational for the selection of the organization. In addition, an answer should relate the role of an external environmental audit to the marketing audit as a whole.
- o The next stage would be to undertake secondary research into external environmental information available. This would need to examine all aspects of the external environment affecting the organization. The sources of evidence should be given where known.
- o The third stage is to categorize the information gathered using the 'PESTEL' or a similar model and their relevance to the organization. The use of a table would be advisable here to help represent the information shown. In addition, ranking of the factors is also advisable.
- o The final stage would be to make recommendations to the organization following the macro-environmental analysis. The context of the question is as part of a full marketing audit and therefore advice needs to relate to the marketing audit as a whole.
- o The format requested is as a report. Therefore this should be adhered to and any sources of information used cited within the answer.

Element 4 – Environmental information systems

The final element of this module relates directly to the use of information technology and other information systems as a means for gathering environmental information. Questions from this element will relate to market research as an information-gathering tool, the use of ICT technology and mechanisms for forecasting, together with the example question below:

You have been asked to prepare a presentation on the use of a marketing information system to other members of your organization, mostly from the operations and human resources sections. This presentation is to last approximately 30 minutes and cover the use, benefits and drawbacks of such a system. You will also need to prepare a handout detailing the types of information which form a marketing information system.

The format of this question is important. A presentation is to be prepared, along with supporting information. In addition, an appropriate organizational setting should be selected. A typical answer to the question would consist of the following aspects:

- The presentation should be created using ICT, and provided as part of the handout to the audience. It is important to consider that the audience are non-marketers and therefore are unlikely to have any specific marketing knowledge.
- A background to the organization and the situation should be given. This needs to set the scene for the presentation.
- A definition of marketing information systems is required. In addition, diagrams such as Kotler's may also be used. Typical examples of information which would comprise a marketing information system should be included.
- The presentation should show both benefits and drawbacks, with theory drawn from texts and referenced. Examples may also be used here.
- Finally, issues of implementing a marketing information system into the organization should be considered.
- The handout prepared needs to relate to the information given, and should be submitted along with the presentation.

Assignment regulations

There have been a number of changes to the assignment structure compared with previous years, timed with the introduction of the new syllabi. These have been designed to provide consistency in approach for a student whether they are completing the assessment for a module by examination, assignment or integrative project. The more significant changes include:

- For the current academic year tutors at CIM centres will mark assignments. These are then moderated by CIM assessors. An integrative project is marked by CIM assessors only.
- No resubmission of assignments, as per an examination. In previous years a range of assignments were being submitted. Where a student does not achieve the 50 per cent pass mark, they are requested to retake the assessment for the module through examination or assignment/integrative project.
- Whichever assessment route is selected is fixed rather than having the option to change at the last minute. Past history has shown that students sometimes begin on an assignment route, change to an examination at the last minute due to not meeting a deadline and then score badly in the examination. The paths to an assignment or examination are different and therefore it is inadvisable to switch, which is the reason for the change of rule.

o In the 2002–3 academic year word limits for questions and assignments were introduced due to assignments being submitted which were of a wide variety of lengths. These ranged from under 2000 words to over 25 000 words. Where a student is completing four modules by assignment this would equal over 100 000 words – the equivalent of a medium-sized textbook or novel. As such it became impossible for two assignments to be considered together. Therefore the word limit guidance was introduced in order to provide equality for all students undertaking assessment by assignment.

o Two sets of assignments per year as with the examination route. With this change students are required to complete the assignment aimed at the nearest examination session. Previously students had between 3 months and 9 months to complete an assignment depending upon whether it was given out in September for a June deadline or March for the June deadline. Therefore a decision was made to follow the examination route with the intention of giving all students equal time to complete an assignment.

These summarize the key changes which have occurred due to the introduction of new syllabi with the assignment/integrative project route in order that there is parity of assessment at all levels and using all formats. Some of these changes have been significant, others minor. However, all the changes have been considered thoughtfully and with the best intentions for the student in mind.

Use of case studies

For anyone who is not working or has difficulty accessing information on their or another organization, there are a number of case studies available which allow the completion of a module using a case-based approach rather than basing it upon an organization identified by the student. These case studies are provided on a request-only basis through your accredited CIM centre and should only be used as a last resort. Using a case study as the basis for your assignment will not mean an easier approach to the assignment. However, they do provide an opportunity to undertake assignments when no other alternative exists. Each case study comes with a certain amount of information which can be used specifically for the completion of a question. Additional information may need to be assumed or researched in order to create a comprehensive assignment.

Submission of assignments/integrative project

The following information will aid yourself, your tutor who marks your work and also the CIM assessor who will be moderating your work and moderating the integrative project. In addition the flow diagram represents the process of an assignment/integrative project from start to final mark.

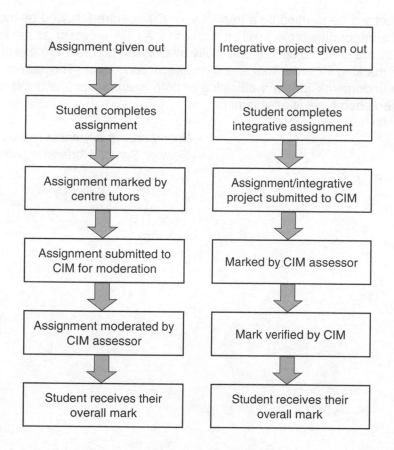

When completing and submitting assignments or the integrative project, refer to the following for guidance:

- Read through each question before starting out. Particularly with the core question there will be a considerable amount of work to undertake. Choose your optional questions wisely.
- Answer the question set and use the mark guidance given regarding the marking scheme.
- Reference each question within the assignment and use a bibliography.
- Complete all documentation thoroughly. This is designed to aid both the CIM and yourself.
- Ensure that the assignment is bound as per instructions given. Currently assignments are requested not to be submitted in plastic wallets or folders as work can become detached or lost. Following the submission instructions provided aids both CIM administrators and the CIM assessor who will be marking (integrative project) or moderating (assignments) your work.
- Complete the candidate declaration sheet showing that you have undertaken this work yourself. *Please note that if you wish the information contained in your assignment to remain confidential you must state this on the front of the assignment.* While CIM assessors will not use any information pertaining to your or another organization, CIM may wish to use the answer to a question as an example.

An assignment will be marked by a tutor at your CIM centre followed by moderation by a CIM assessor. The integrative project will be marked by a CIM assessor as per an examination with moderation by the CIM. To ensure objectivity by CIM assessors there exists a mark-in meeting prior to any marking in order that standardization can occur. The senior assessor for each subject also undertakes further verification of both examinations and assessments to ensure parity between each type of assessment.

Based on the appendix written by David C. Lane,
Former Senior Moderator (Advanced Certificate),
February 2003

appendix 3
answers and debriefings

Unit 1

Debriefing Activity 1.2

- o *Ownership* – Private/public/mutual/cooperative
- o *Legal form* – Limited company/sole proprietor/partnership
- o *Control* – Directors/shareholders/workers/trustees
- o *Sector* – Public/private/voluntary
- o *Objectives* – Profit/public welfare/social responsibility
- o *Accountability* – to shareholders/ministers/customers
- o *Activity* – Agriculture/manufacturing/services/utilities/construction
- o *Size* – Small/SMEs/global.

Debriefing Activity 1.3

5, 4, 6, 1, 2 and 3

Debriefing Activity 1.4

	Public sector	Private sector
Strengths (there are more)	Provide essential but non-profit-making services	Private ownership means initiative
	Avoids wasteful duplication of expensive resources	Strong motivation to use resources well
	Funds are easily raised through taxation	Funds are efficiently/effectively used
	Can overcome failings in the market	Respond quickly to market signals
	Employees are motivated by public service	Employees are paid by results
Weaknesses (again there are more)	Tendency towards political interference/ indecision	May mean ruthless exploitation of the weak
	Monopolies and bureaucracies don't serve public	Outcome of competition = monopoly?
	Over-accountability limits entrepreneurship	Competitive over-investment wasteful
	Unions tend to be powerful/taxpayers weak	Ignore costs that affect/damage society
	Public expectations over level of 'free' services	Question values – everything has a price!

Debriefing Activity 1.5

You should have considered implications from the employment and marketing side. For example, the increasing numbers of working wives is filling the gap left by declining numbers of school-leavers. (Women are expected to account for 46 per cent of the workforce by 2006 and contribute the majority of employment growth, according to the 2000 *Social Trends* report.) This allows flexible staffing using part-time hours but demands changes in personnel policy as a result. Working wives alter the times of peak shopping hours and increase the demand for convenience and frozen foods.

Debriefing Activity 1.6

The vast majority of shareholders have not and will not attend an AGM unless their holding is very substantial. As one share in a portfolio, an AGM held during the working week and often a long way away, and with little or no influence over proceedings, the incentive is small.

Debriefing Activity 1.8

Unless the adoption of a mission statement changes organizational behaviour, it has little value. Yet its absence is like being a traveller without a destination with no way of determining progress. Organizational objectives must therefore be formulated which enables progress towards them to be measured.

A mission statement should differentiate the organization from others and establish its individuality, if not its uniqueness. As such, it defines what the organization 'wishes to be' and provides a unifying concept which both enlarges its view of itself and brings it into focus.

It should be relevant to all the direct stakeholders and motivate their commitment. Accordingly, it needs to excite and inspire, encouraging participation through a shared vision. Do your mission statements meet these criteria?

Debriefing Question 1.2

Management may think twice about making as much profit as possible if:

o It involves taking high risks, for example it may lead to an anti-monopoly investigation.
o It encourages wage demands and rising dividend expectations.
o It is at the expense of sales/market share and attracts new entrants.
o It prejudices customers who link the profit to high prices and will turn to alternatives when available.

Debriefing Activity 1.10

The need to be close to the customer, sensitive to change in the environment and coordinated to ensure quick response throughout the organization would require:

o Marketing representation at main Board/MD level
o A flat decentralized structure
o Delegation of decision to those closest to the customer

    o Open communications internally and externally
    o Profit-centred general manager structure for coordination of all functions
    o Integrated Management Information System (MIS)
    o Customer service philosophy promoted by the organization.

Unit 2

Debriefing Activity 2.1

Consider a resource such as market research, or information generated from loyalty cards. How would you fully exploit the information?

Debriefing Activity 2.4

A funeral director (Low/Low), a computer software manufacturer (H/H), a university (M/M), a biscuit manufacturer (L/M), a pop group (H/L), an advertising agency (M/L).

Debriefing Activity 2.5

Product availability and promotion would be priorities for distributors while innovation, particularly in product and place, would be the probable means of achieving sustainable advantage.

Debriefing Activity 2.6

The following matrix adapted from Mendelon is another useful approach to drawing a stakeholder map since it locates each one according to their degree of interest and power in the organization:

The implications of the matrix for the marketer are to keep Box A stakeholders informed; Box B stakeholders quiet; Box C stakeholders contented and Box D stakeholders satisfied.

Debriefing Activity 2.7

Sectional/interest – Chambers of Commerce, British Medical Association.

Cause/promotional – CAMRA and the Mothers' Union.

Debriefing Question 2.4

Aerosols – CFCs/ozone layer; agriculture – fertilizer runoff; airlines – energy, noise, ozone; chemicals – effluent, spillage; paper – energy, greenhouse effect; refrigeration – CFCs and disposal; tobacco – health, passive smoking; tourism – areas of natural beauty; toxic waste – leaks, accidents, health.

Other industries coming into the firing line might include biotechnology – genetic implications; transport – congestion, safety and accidents; pharmaceuticals – dependency and ethical considerations.

Debriefing Activity 2.8

Potential benefits include enhanced reputation for companies at the leading edge (e.g. Body Shop or Norsk Hydro – the Norwegian chemicals, paper and energy company which was first to use independent environmental auditing); attracting a new market segment of environmentally concerned consumers; cost savings through recycling or improved energy efficiency.

Guidelines for implementation might include:

- o Apply from product conception through to final disposal
- o Responsibility of staff at all levels
- o Build achievement of environmental objectives into the reward structure of the business
- o The business should not knowingly do harm to the environment
- o The business should behave as a custodian of resources for future generations.

Debriefing Question 2.5

Recent examples include McDonald's, Microsoft, Firestone, Equitable Life, KFC, Jarvis.

Unit 3

Debriefing Question 3.1

Health/fitness, restaurants and large sections of fast food, increasing concentration at top/city end and travel lodges on main routes. Factors include need for close personal attention (restaurants), early growth stage (health/fitness), easy entry (fast food).

Debriefing Question 3.2

Examples could include longer opening hours for convenience stores, fast-food deliveries, store-interior formats.

Debriefing Question 3.4

Fragmented is best described by 3, concentrated by 4.

Debriefing Question 3.5

From London substitutes include charter/scheduled flights/Ryanair/EasyJet/Eurostar/car and ferry/hovercraft. Price performance ratios are relatively close with the exception of charter and some scheduled flights. If opportunity cost, duration and timing are of the essence, the director will justify the latter. Change is taking place due to the high oil prices, rail disruption and the curtailment of duty-free sales etc.

Debriefing Activity 3.2

1. Has low/stable returns
2. Has low/risky returns – liable to entry in upturns and periods of windfall profit but firms don't exit as conditions deteriorate
3. Has high/stable returns – very attractive as the unsuccessful leave the industry
4. Has high/risky returns – unsuccessful stay and fight.

Debriefing Question 3.6

Aldi – Thompsons– Toyota (cost leadership); Sainsbury's – Thomas Cook– Ford (diff.); Lidl – Wallace Arnold's – Hyundai (cost focus); Iceland/M&S – Kuoni – BMW/Land Rover.

Debriefing Exam Question 3.1

- o Use examples (catering v banks) and provide a comparison matrix
- o Refer to the context and refer to a number of sources and an information system
- o In (2) refer to the interdependent nature of the industry and the need to monitor closely

Debriefing Exam Question 3.4

- o Divide your answer between explaining the five forces (theory) and the contribution to the marketer's understanding. Set your points in the context of an industry with examples.

Unit 4

Debriefing Activity 4.1

Certainly multinationals wield massive economic power since their turnover often equals that of a relatively large country's GDP. Car-makers, for example, do launch new product developments, often with only cosmetic changes, at regular intervals and then apply pressure on customers to upgrade to the latest model. On the other hand, perhaps the customers are demanding regular change and technological improvement and they drive the process observed. It also suggests that consumers are 'easy' to manipulate by promotional means yet history is scattered with the debris of product offerings that the customer rejected.

Debriefing Activity 4.2

2, 4, 3, 5 and 1

Debriefing Question 4.1

Few examples. Craft industries, personal services (e.g. funerals and nursing homes).

Debriefing Question 4.2

Sales volume by product, product group, region, channel and market segment. Intelligence reports on competitor prices and promotion, strengths and weaknesses. Assessment of own promotional mix effectiveness. Accounts provide data on cost of sales, debtors, overall sales analysis by customer, variances. Purchasing provides assessment of supplier reliability, stock control and availability, service levels. Operations provide order status, completion dates and production capacity.

Debriefing Question 4.3

- o The key to answering this question was to recognize it refers to 'changes' in the natural environment. Identify three or four 'changes', explain their influence and relate to fast food.
- o Adopt a wide definition of the natural environment, for example, vulnerability to BSE/foot and mouth; clearing of rainforests for grazing; use and disposal of natural materials (packaging).

Debriefing Question 4.4

- o Make the case for published and internal methods over primary research bar specific surveys.
- o Be sure to provide 'sources' such as the ONS Census of Population or *Social Trends* and *Regional Trends* for income trends.
- o Provide a brief commentary on why each source would be 'effective' for the purposes of the Fitness Club.

Unit 5

Debriefing Activity 5.1

Browse through the charts and tables in *Social Trends* or its local equivalent.

Debriefing Question 5.1

Those retiring will have state pensions supplemented by private pensions. They will have planned financially for retirement and may have inherited valuable properties in recent years. They will form a market segment with clear ideas regarding their requirements. They will still be fit and active. The mix must reflect this, especially in terms of the product and the financing arrangements. Promotion must address their wants.

Debriefing Question 5.2

- o New technology improved agricultural productivity; industrialization; opened up the lands of the New World; emigration; refrigeration; demographic transition, etc.
- o No unexploited continents; global competition; immigration laws; pollution consequences of modern agriculture. A lot therefore rests on development of sustainable technologies and overseas aid. Population growth does not necessarily mean market opportunities because it tends to correlate with very low or falling income per head.
- o An optimum population allows full advantage to be taken of resources. A growing population can revitalize and bring larger markets and more mobility. Excessive population as seen in parts of Africa and Latin America can unbalance the ecology through overgrazing and deforestation.

Debriefing Question 5.4

Quality, service, value for money and greater durability. Over-45s will be renewing household effects after child-rearing and will look for design, not functionality.

Debriefing Question 5.5

Apart from logistical considerations, lifestyles will be different. Outlying areas poorly served by public transport will have higher car ownership and infrequent, high-spending trips to retailers.

Debriefing Question 5.6

The culture, attitudes and buying habits of these groups differ significantly from the indigenous population. The entrepreneurial abilities of some of these minorities are also outstanding: 17 per cent of the Indian community are self-employed against 11 per cent for all groups. However, the traditional 'open all hours' corner shop is under pressure from multiple super-markets (25 per cent fall in 10 years) and the work ethic of the parents is no longer matched by their aspiring children who are not prepared to put up with long hours of racial abuse.

Debriefing Question 5.7

○ For business the main attraction is flexibility to employ when the labour is required (e.g. retail shopping peaks). Wages tend to be lower and other wage costs are avoided. Exemption from employment legislation and National Insurance also contribute.

○ For employees, especially married women, it may fit well with other responsibilities and needs. It also suits the semi-retired.

○ For government it reduces the overall unemployment rate.

○ Recent legislation has put part-time workers on equal employment status to full-time.

○ A change in work patterns implies changes in buying and shopping patterns. One-stop shopping and convenience purchases are reflections of this trend. It is also more likely that the male is more involved in routine shopping decisions.

Debriefing Activity 5.6

Other trends might include health and fitness; novelty and change; energy and environmental friendliness; value for money; supranational or global orientation.

Unit 6

Debriefing Question 6.1

The only viable solution to this conflict between growth and a pollution-free environment is to pursue *sustainable growth*. Zero growth is not a real option due to concern over rising unemployment in industrial economies and rising populations in less-developed ones. Continued progress towards industrialization is required but using cleaner technologies, renewable energy and recyclable products.

Debriefing Question 6.2

○ The rate of interest. As the rate of interest falls, less is saved and more is invested and vice versa. It will not work quickly because other factors also affect the decision to save (e.g. income, expectations and preferences) and invest (e.g. expected returns, competitive pressures).

○ Where injections = leakages.

Debriefing Question 6.3

○ Multiplier $= 1/t = (0.4) + m = (0.2) + s = (0.1) = 1/0.7 = 1.43$

○ The tax multiplier is smaller because households who receive £3 billion of new disposable income save 0.1 before any spending occurs.

Debriefing Question 6.4

○ *Consumption* – will remain unchanged due to uncertainty and savings as a precaution against unemployment. *Investment* will be unchanged or falling due to idle capacity and 'wait and see' attitudes. *Exports* will be unchanged or falling due to depression in overseas markets. Only *government* can be increased to stimulate activity. This was Keynes' main policy recommendation.

○ No significant effects in the short run due to stickiness in the response. In the longer run costs would fall and business would become more competitive leading to higher activity rates. However, Keynes observed that 'in the long run we are dead' and people want jobs and incomes today.

Debriefing Question 6.5

1. China 7.5 per cent to Sri Lanka's 2.5 per cent
2. No, not automatically – see 'limitations of the data'.

Debriefing Question 6.6

○ *Recovery* – Starts from lower turning point; income, output and expenditure rise at an increasing rate; employment rises/unemployment levels off; caution at employing full-timers; new investment planned as confidence recovers; inflation remains low as increased utilization occurs.

○ *Boom* – Bottlenecks in faster growth sectors; resource prices bid up; passed on in higher prices; fully utilized resources; productivity is the only source of higher output; profit, investment and confidence high; interest rates rising sharply, imports sucked in.

○ *Downturn* – Starts from upper turning point; momentum through multiplier-accelerator; confidence and spending fall; precautionary savings rise; investment becomes unprofitable; business failures rise and cutbacks multiply.

Debriefing Activity 6.1

- ○ *Downturn* – Control stock in line with order slowdown. The psychology is still one of growth with orders up on a year ago. This is the right time to conduct a Pareto analysis to weed out weak products and channel outlets. Recruitment should be halted and no further long-term commitments taken on.
- ○ *Recession* – Sit tight and wait for upturn. Be aware of brighter times ahead so retain skilled core and upgrade. Order capital equipment for installation, 18 months, since prices are at the lowest for all resource contracts.
- ○ *Recovery* – Talk is still of recession but the rate of change in orders is upward. Start building stock and encourage distributors to do likewise. Start hiring and prepare new products for launch.

Debriefing Question 6.7

High and rising unemployment means downward pressure on wages. Businesses can recruit without raising wages to attract labour. With many people chasing each vacancy in Britain managers can pick from the top of the barrel. Workers are likely to work harder to preserve their jobs and also accept technical and other change.

Debriefing Activity 6.2

Policies fall into six groups:

1. *Stimulate demand for labour directly* (e.g. government spending) – higher prices?
2. *Reduce the number of job seekers* (e.g. more in higher education) – inefficient?
3. *Improve the matching of unemployed to vacancies* (e.g. better job centres)
4. *Reduce the real wage* (e.g. pay restraint)
5. *Share out the available work* (e.g. part-time, early retirement) – do workers want to?
6. *Increase domestic at expense of overseas* (e.g. tariff barriers) – inefficient?

For jobs to be *sustainable* they must not be subsidized. Unemployment can only fall if the growth of GDP exceeds the net growth of the working population and its productivity.

Debriefing Question 6.8

Think in terms of technology transfer, value added (wages + demand for local components + local taxes), balance of payments (initial investment + exports), demonstration effect for positives. Competition, remitted profits, power (e.g. avoid taxes) for negatives.

Debriefing Activity 6.3

Activity, growth and unemployment rates

- ○ Volume of retail sales/comparative per capita output.
- ○ Industry surveys of investment intentions/confidence.
- ○ Rates of change in key groups: skilled, young, over-55's, male/female. Inflation and interest rates.
- ○ Cost of living or price index/the underlying rate/main competitor rate.
- ○ Rate of change in earnings/tax changes in the pipeline.
- ○ The growth in the money supply.

Trade figures and exchange rates

○ Balance on current account (symbol of international 'competitiveness')
○ Terms of trade reflects relative movement of import/export prices
○ Share of world trade in manufactures/invisibles reflect longer-term performance.

Debriefing Question 6.9

○ Small firms who tend to rely on bank credit for cash flow
○ Small firms who suffer when large customers delay payment
○ Fast-growing firms
○ Manufacturing firms with higher working capital requirements.

Such firms suffer in three ways – higher interest costs, limited credit and reduced consumer spending power (e.g. small builders).

Debriefing Activity 6.4

1-5-6-2-4-3

Debriefing Exam Question 6.4

○ Illustrate means that a labelled diagram with a trend line is required (see Figure 6.3).
○ Provide 3 or 4 points why understanding is required.
○ Define the upper turning point in b, as boom giving way to recession. Focus on counter-cyclical policies not company policies and develop their significance.

Debriefing Exam Question 6.5

○ This is a question about your understanding of the international environment and information not how to sell abroad.
○ Focus on the four sections and refer to the Study Tip in Unit 1 on mission statements for key success factors.

Unit 7

Debriefing Activity 7.1

6-2-4-3-1

Debriefing Question 7.1

Think about office politics and positioning for promotions and perks. Departmental conflicts arise over resources and priorities. The quality press and periodicals like *The Economist* and *Newsweek*. Trade associations and lobbyists. Also consider websites, for example, lcweb.loc.gov/homepage/lchp.html is the Library of Congress – one of the largest in the world.

Debriefing Question 7.2

Think in terms of product positioning, 'value for voting' and differentiation of manifestos and policies, that is, clear blue water between the parties.

Debriefing Question 7.3

- ○ Do not be rushed – no obligation to give interview there and then – phone back!
- ○ First know why, why you, who's calling, how long and what's wanted?
- ○ Gather your thoughts – take advice – no off-the-record comments.
- ○ Prepare a statement if you are suspicious of their motives.
- ○ Don't answer leading or hypothetical questions.
- ○ Keep it short and to the point. Be polite and positive.

Debriefing Question 7.4

This might include the requirement for public liability insurance, laws governing the use of public transport, road traffic laws, health and safety at work, employment protection law including discrimination, unfair dismissal, sexual harassment and equal pay. If you go shopping then a whole battery of legislation will apply if you feel unreasonably treated.

Debriefing Activity 7.5

1-4-3-2-6-5-7

Debriefing Question 7.5

Excessive, unnecessary and often complicated formalities involved in government regulations.

Debriefing Question 7.6

Many policies were sold to people for whom they were not suitable or really wanted. More and clearer information should be given to potential customers, including the likelihood and cost of early cancellation. Consultation with the industry to ensure workability would probably be advisable. While consumers' awareness of their rights has increased as a result of legislation, considerable ignorance and lethargy still remain. Consumers often have neither the time nor the inclination to exercise fully their existing rights, especially where small-value purchases are concerned. On the other hand, suppliers are more likely to implement the letter of the law rather than risk their reputation or the wrath of the pressure groups and enforcement agencies. The legislation has successfully removed outright dangerous products from the market and outlawed dubious methods such as pyramid selling and mail order trading of unsolicited goods.

Unit 8

Debriefing Question 8.1

- ○ Examples are numerous, for example IT, pharmaceuticals, chemicals, car design, financial services.
- ○ Most have been affected by IT systems. Craft goods and personal services provide possibilities.

Debriefing Question 8.2

None of the information technology-based consumer products and services was available – video cassette recorders, mobiles, airbags, cash dispensers, microwaves, camcorders, sophisticated computer games, etc.

Debriefing Question 8.3

The main threats involve the loss of market share/profitability as a result of technological surprises; when to invest since rapid technological change will make premature investments obsolete; hi-tech may involve highly specialized plant and inflexibility in the face of changing consumer tastes; high cost of investment (e.g. microchip plants currently cost $1 billion); risk and loss of failure (e.g. Sinclair C5 car, Philips videodisc). The main opportunities involve excess profit, competitive advantage, lower costs, faster growth, greater flexibility. See also the benefits of microprocessors.

Debriefing Question 8.4

Example: The *motorist* would be stranded since microprocessors control ignition, steering, braking and in-board control systems on modern cars. Traffic lights would cease to function as would petrol pumps. *The marketing department* relies on 'information systems' defined as the products, services, methods and people used to collect, store, process, transmit and display information. It also relies on the telephone now controlled through digital exchanges not to mention televisions that receive advertisements. Product information derived from barcode scanners would be lost and banking and credit systems would fail.

Debriefing Question 8.5

Clearly, an array of marketing strategies are relevant here including price skimming and penetration. Licensing and franchising are other possibilities to consider in achieving rapid coverage of the national/international markets.

Debriefing Question 8.6

The degree of diffusion varies but only the virtual reality holidays and intelligent motorways appear to be further into the future. According to General Motors within 50 years six biofeed sensors in dashboards will detect incipient slumber and vibrate to wake the driver. The motorist could steer into a 'nap lane', set a course using the car's satellite-guided navigation system, engage the autopilot and go to sleep. Computer chips embedded in the tarmac will 'read' the road. Hydrogen-powered fuel cells will replace petrol engines and a joystick will control all movements including braking and accelerating.

Debriefing Question 8.7

Look for products such as:

- o Books
- o Holidays
- o CD's
- o Pornography
- o Clothing and basic foodstuffs.

As against:

- o Fashions
- o Personal services
- o Furniture
- o Cosmetics and luxuries.

Explanations in terms of these being the subject of leisure or impulse shopping, or requiring personal presence.

Debriefing Question 8.8

Portable computers are already transforming the capability of the salesforce, giving them the opportunity to access the corporate database to answer customer queries regarding product availability, order status, promotions, and so on. They could also enter orders immediately ensuring that stock is allocated. Intelligence regarding competitors could be input into the system. These combine through the power of the computer to offer massive potential to the salesforce of the future. Legislation may limit mobile phone use.

Debriefing Question 8.9

Factors include lack of: competitive pressure, incentive, finance, support from the board, champions, a risk-taking culture, long-term horizons, skills and experience of change, awareness of potential.

Debriefing Question 8.10

Resistance may lead to loss of orders in the extreme, increased returns, more queries and complaints, a rise in errors, and so on.

- o You may have suggested such things as joint consultation over the proposed changes or, more importantly, involving customers in formulating them in the first place. Communications and incentives also have a role to play.

Debriefing Exam Question 8.3

- o 4a provides considerable scope for identifying impacts but only ICT examples. Don't forget to assess the implications of each one for the final customer.
- o In b, relate the factors driving the diffusion process (not the process itself) in this unit to the oligopolistic market structure of the world car industry.

Debriefing Exam Question 8.4

- ○ Be sure to relate the changes in technology to grocery distribution.
- ○ The answer should focus on discussion of technology's influence on the elements of the stem.
- ○ Your answer could adopt a 4 Ps approach or discuss technologies that ensure the right goods–time–price and to the right customer.

Unit 9

Debriefing Activity 9.1

Did you think of scrolling down the index? Did you scan through Unit 8? Did you access the glossary on www.marketingonline.co.uk?

Debriefing Question 9.1

Classify as key elements in the information process: collection (e.g. EDI); processing (e.g. decision support systems); storage (e.g. servers) and transmission (e.g. broadband).

Debriefing Question 9.2

List the types of information on competitors that will not be available in published sources. What other methods are available for obtaining information in the areas you have identified?

Roles are interacting with functional managers to assess their information needs; deriving the needed information from internal records, marketing intelligence or marketing research; processing it into a useful form; distributing it (right time/format) to decision makers. Information on strategies, product developments, planned promotions, future intentions, likely reactions. Methods range from industrial espionage to debriefing former employees to questioning associated stakeholders.

Debriefing Question 9.3

3, 2, 1, 5, 6 and 4

Debriefing Question 9.4

Forecasts are necessary whenever resource decisions affecting the future (e.g. investment in plant and equipment, new product research and development, etc.) require a view to be taken of future supply and demand conditions. Factors affecting supply and demand must be forecast, which in effect means all relevant factors in the micro- and macro-environments.

Debriefing Activity 9.2

4-2-3-5-6-1

appendix 4
learning materials

The Business and Marketing Environment	A. Palmer and B. Hartley	1999, 3rd edition, McGraw-Hill
Business Environment	A. Palmer	2001, McGraw-Hill
The Business Environment	Brooks and Weatherston	Prentice Hall, latest edition
Principles of Marketing	Kotler and Armstrong	9th edition, 2001, Prentice Hall
E-shock, the New Rules	M. de Kare-Silver	Palgrave, 2001
Mastering the Business Environment	R. Cartwright	Palgrave, 2001

www.bookfind-online.com

Referred to
www.cim.co.uk
www.cim.vlib.org.uk/
www.marketingportal.cim.co.uk
www.cimtutors.com (Tutors only)
www.marketingonline.co.uk
www.ft.com

Unit 1

Organizational Behaviour – An Introductory Text	A.A. Huczynski and D.A. Buchanan	Prentice Hall, 1991
The Practice of Management	P.F. Drucker	Butterworth-Heinemann, 1989
Management Theory and Practice	G.A. Cole	Continuum (latest edition)
E-shock, the New Rules	M. de Kare-Silver	Palgrave, 2001

Unit 2

| The Competitive Advantage of Nations | M. Porter | Macmillan, 1990 |
| The Business Environment | I. Brooks and J. Weatherston | Prentice Hall, 1997 |

Unit 3

Which? reports		Consumer Association
In Search of Excellence	T. Peters and R.H. Waterman, Jr	Harper and Row, 1982
Competitive Strategy	M. Porter	The Free Press/Macmillan, 1980
Competitive Advantage	M. Porter	The Free Press/Macmillan, 1985

www.economist.com
www.ebusinessforum.com/
www.ft.com
www.competition-commission.org.uk/reports/report1.htm
www.carol.co.uk/
www.europages.com
www.mra.warc.com
www.keynote.co.uk
www.strategy-business.com

Unit 4

The New Industrial State	J.K. Galbraith	Penguin
Economics and the Public Purpose	J.K. Galbraith	Penguin
Innovation and Entrepreneurship	P.F. Drucker	Butterworth-Heinemann, 1985

www.cnn.com
www.news.bbc.co.uk
www.washingtonpost.com
www.newsnow.co.uk
www.allafrica.com
www.chinapages.com
www.MyMalaysia.net.my
www.lanka.com
www.worldbank.org/data/wdi/environment.htm

Unit 5

The Age of Unreason	C. Handy	Business Books, 1989
Principles of Marketing	Kotler and Armstrong	9th edition, Prentice Hall

www.statistics.gov.uk/
www.gallup.com/
www.nop.co.uk/
www.mori.com/polls

Unit 6

www.worldbank.org/data/countrydata/html
www.tradepartners.gov.uk/about our services
www.un.org/pubs/CyberSchool/Bus/information/e_information.htm

Unit 7

www.parliamentlive.tv.co.uk
www.statistics.gov.uk/onlineproducts/#economy
www.open.gov.uk
www.gold.net/ifl/
www.the-times.co.uk
www.Europa.EU.Int
www.poptel.org.uk/labour-party/index-t.html
www.conservative-Party.org.uk

Unit 8

Future Shock	A. Toffler	Collins, 1975
Business Environment	Palmer, Hartley and Worthington	2001 edition, McGraw-Hill
E-shock, the New Rules	M. de Kare-Silver	Palgrave, 2001
www.wnim.com		

Unit 9

www.ecommercetimes.co.uk
www.internetindicators.com
www.e-commerce.research.ml.com
www.pwcglobal.com
www.asiansources.com
www.nua.ie/surveys/

appendix 5
past examination papers and examiners' reports

The Chartered
Institute of Marketing

Certificate
in Marketing

Marketing Environment

5.23:	**Marketing Environment**
Time:	**14.00-17.00**
Date:	**2nd December, 2003**

3 Hours Duration

This examination is in two sections.

PART A – Is compulsory and worth 40% of total marks.

PART B – Has **SIX** questions; select **THREE**. Each answer will be worth 20% of the total marks.

DO NOT repeat the question in your answer, but show clearly the number of the question attempted on the appropriate pages of the answer book.

Rough workings should be included in the answer book and ruled through after use.

© The Chartered Institute of Marketing

Certificate in Marketing

5.23: Marketing Environment

PART A

Cutting the Fat at McDonald's

McDonald's, the fast food chain, is a global business. Rapid expansion through franchising has made it a recognisable symbol across the world. Since the first outlet opened in 1955, the company has sold over 100 billion burgers. Every day 46 million people eat at McDonald's; a third of all cattle bred for meat in the USA are used by the company, and on average it opens 4.2 new branches every day.

Despite its symbolic reflection of the American dream, analysts suggest the company has over-stretched itself. Following a sharp fall in its share value, McDonald's recorded its first-ever quarterly loss in 2003 and announced its intention to cut back operations in some regions, closing 175 outlets in ten countries. This included Trinidad and Tobago, where, despite heavy marketing, its beef burgers had failed to make headway against the local **cultural preference** for fried chicken. Potential customers associated the outlets with beef burgers and preferred the rival KFC offering, even when McDonald's provided chicken based products.

McDonald's had been obsessed with growth due to the capital intensity of its production operations. To ensure product identity, meat and fries are mass-produced in huge factories and delivered frozen and standardised to every franchise. This approach has underpinned global expansion into three fifths of the world's nations, with 30,000 outlets in total. Despite this expansion, the appetite for 'Big Macs' appears to have levelled out. Its main markets in the USA and the UK are saturated and yet new outlets have been added, cannibalising existing franchises. Expansion into Malaysia has required the creation of a new and costly supply system while success in Moscow's Pushkin Square is more symbolic than commercial.

Worse might be to come, since there appears to be a number of environmental factors causing consumers to turn away from fast food in general and 'Big Macs' in particular. For example:

- European sales fell and have yet to fully recover following outbreaks of the cattle illness BSE and foot-and-mouth disease.

- Middle East sales fell by 25% following September 11th.

- Japanese fears over BSE and an import ban on chicken forced the removal of chicken nuggets from the menu.

- The President of Belarus has declared hamburgers a danger to health and forbidden further outlets.

- President Bush has urged Americans to eat fruit and vegetables instead of junk food, to counter obesity.

- The growth of domestic competition offering 'low calorie' alternatives, e.g. the Subway sandwich chain. McDonald's acknowledge on its web site that a 'Big Mac' represents 500 calories and fries 200 calories.

The company also faces threats on two other fronts. Firstly, the company has become a symbol of American **culture** and therefore attracts adverse publicity and radical protest ranging from fatal bombings in Indonesia to deliberate resistance of many French consumers to the burger concept. Secondly, there is a growing anxiety over the nutritional quality of McDonald's food and the fizzy drinks that accompany it. **According to latest statistics, 61% of Americans are overweight with at least 20% medically obese. Obesity related illnesses are thought to cost the country $117 billion in healthcare and result in 300,000 premature deaths in 2002.** A special tax on 'junk food' is being considered by Congress. More surprisingly, obesity is afflicting people in the less developed world. **Nearly one in five people around the world is clinically obese and rates are rising sharply in countries such as China and Brazil. Even in sub-Saharan Africa, where malnutrition is widespread, obesity is rising, particularly among urban women**.

Fast food chains like McDonald's also appear likely to be the next victims of 'compensation culture'. A lawsuit in New York alleged that McDonald's was responsible for the obesity of two teenagers by failing to warn them or their parents that continued consumption could seriously damage their waistline and consequent health. McDonald's has fought off this charge, but with others bringing similar cases, it underlines how far the culture of individual responsibility and indeed legal principles such as caveat emptor (let the buyer beware – the purchaser buys at his/her own risk), are potentially being undermined. Whether burgers are judged to be as addictive as cigarettes remains to be seen, but these legal cases have much wider implications for marketers, not least when the promotional influence of **McDonald's $600 million plus budget on advertising is considered. In fact the US food industry spends $10 billion each year trying to influence the eating habits of the young. The average child is bombarded with 10,000 food adverts per year of which 95% are for fast food or sugary drinks**. This may yet prove to be as large and powerful a business lobby as that faced by the tobacco industry.

The future for McDonald's is therefore uncertain, particularly in the light of its relative lack of product or service innovation. In a global economy where unlimited choice is the main selling point of its competitors, McDonald's core product philosophy still seems to be 'you'll eat what we think is good for you'.

(The above data has been based on a real life organisation, but details have been changed for assessment purposes, and do not reflect the current management practices. Data is based on excerpts from various newspaper reports and 'The Week' articles).

PART A

Question 1.

a.   The case provides various statistics to support points made in the text. Refer to the statistics presented (in bold) in paragraphs five and six, and suggest what research methods and information sources may have been used to produce them.

(10 marks)

b.   Use the case material to produce an environment impact grid (environmental analysis) for McDonald's. Justify your relative weightings for the **FOUR** factors required in this assessment.

(10 marks)

c.   Assess the changing nature of the legal environment confronting the Food Industry in general and McDonald's in particular.

(10 marks)

d.   The terms 'culture' and 'cultural preference' are both used in this case.

Define the term culture and explain why cultural preferences are so important to the global marketer.

(10 marks)
(40 marks in total)

PART B – Answer THREE Questions Only

Question 2.

a. Produce a short report for your Marketing Manager on the dynamic and complex nature of changes in the marketing environment affecting the Soft Drinks Industry (soft drinks being, for example, orange juice) in a country of your choice.

(12 marks)

b. Attach an appendix to your report outlining implications of these changes for marketing strategy and planning.

(8 marks)
(20 marks in total)

Question 3.

a. What is the nature of the interrelationship between a business college and its customer and employee stakeholders?

(8 marks)

b. What internal sources of information would help the business college understand the nature of this interrelationship with customers and employees?

(6 marks)

c. Suggest **THREE** external sources of information on its potential customers and briefly explain the value of the information obtained.

(6 marks)
(20 marks in total)

Question 4.

West European exporters of environmental protection equipment have to operate to European Union standards. Assess the potential significance of the following challenges to a UK based exporter of environmental protection equipment:

a.   Expansion of the European Union to include Eastern European economies.

(5 marks)

b.   Another World Environment Summit fails to secure global agreement on emission limits.

(5 marks)

c.   Technological breakthroughs in hydrogen fuel offer the early prospect of a cheap, clean and abundant alternative energy source to hydrocarbons.

(5 marks)

d.   China's new 10 year plan puts priority on developing its emergent environmental protection industry.

(5 marks)
(20 marks in total)

Question 5.

a.   Write brief notes on the relevance and application of the following concepts to a marketer working in the public sector:

   i)   Marketing research.

   ii)   Marketing information system.

   iii)   Delphi technique.

(12 marks)

b.   Suggest **ONE** reason why the marketing objectives within the public sector might differ from the private sector and **ONE** reason why they might be similar.

(8 marks)
(20 marks in total)

Question 6.

As a Marketing Executive for a major supermarket chain, briefly explain the probable impact on your company of each of the following developments:

a.   Developments in digital television and online trading facilitate armchair shopping.

(5 marks)

b.   A well resourced North American chain takes over one of your major rivals.

(5 marks)

c.   Farmers succeed in forming a co-operative to co-ordinate supplies and prices.

(5 marks)

d.   The government agency charged with regulating monopoly practices launches an investigation into supermarket pricing and value for money.

(5 marks)
(20 marks in total)

Question 7.

a.   Using an example, explain the difference between the macro and micro environment of a voluntary organisation.

(8 marks)

b.   Selecting the macro environment, prepare a memorandum for your Marketing Manager summarising why an understanding of this environment is important from a marketing perspective.

(12 marks)
(20 marks in total)

Certificate in Marketing - Stage 1

Marketing Environment

December 2003

Examination Papers

Each subject differs slightly from the other, and you need to make sure that you are familiar with the style of question and the requirements of the different examinations.

There are three basic question types:

1. **The mini case or scenario or article**
    Part A of all papers (except Analysis and Decision) has a mini case, scenario or article, with compulsory questions. This represents only part of the paper, but students are required to make marketing decisions based on the information given. Spend time evaluating the material given in the case, but do not rewrite this for the examiners. You will gain credit for the decisions and recommendations you make on the basis of the analysis, but nothing for the analysis itself. This is a compulsory part of the paper designed to evaluate practical marketing skills. Make sure you allocate enough time to it, but do not ignore the other part of the paper.

2. **The straightforward exam question**
    You are expected to make a choice from a number of questions. There is some skill necessary in selecting the questions which you are best prepared to answer. Read the questions through carefully before making your choice. Think about how you will tackle the question. Check you are answering the question in the context it has been set, then make a rough plan before you start writing. Remember that examiners are interested in quality answers.

3. **Analysis and Decision (Diploma)**
    This final paper is an open book examination. The Case Study is sent out 4 weeks before the paper is sat. Students should complete their analysis and preparation before the examination takes place. The questions asked will require marketing decisions and actions in specific response to the questions set. The question paper will include extra information about the case which will have to be used to obtain best marks.

Common Mistakes

Reports from examiners are published regularly and are available to students. Even a casual look through these reveals the same concerns and problems coming up time and time again across all subject areas. Most of these common mistakes are caused by a lack of exam technique and examination practice.

–   **Not answering the question set**
    The examiners are looking for both **relevant content** and its application in an **appropriate context**. You must be able to work flexibly with the material you have studied, answering different questions in different ways, even though the fundamental theory remains the same.

–   **Presentation and style**
    Both of these essential business skills are of great importance to a marketing practitioner. The examiners expect work to be presented in a well-written, professional manner. 'Report' style, using sub-headings and indented numbering for points etc. is not only acceptable, but looks much more commercially credible than academic essays. This approach allows you to break the work up, highlight the key points, and structure your answer in a logical way. Take care with your grammar and use of language; small errors can change the sense considerably.

–   **Timing**
    The scarce resource in an examination is time. You must control the allocation of this resource carefully. Read the instructions to the paper carefully, and identify what has to be done and how the marks are allocated. Spread your time proportionately to the mark allocation, i.e. if the mini case = 40% of marks, allocate 40% of your time to it. Allow a few minutes at the end to read through your work.

    It is no good only completing four questions when you should have done five. It is so much harder for you to pass on just four questions. Have a clock or watch with you and be ruthless in your timekeeping. If you find you are spending too long on an answer, you are probably not answering the question specifically enough.

–   **Theory without application**
    The examiners expect relevant theory to be illustrated with practical examples and illustrations. These can be drawn from your own marketing experience, or observations, or your reading. A theory paper without evidence of practical appreciation is unlikely to be successful.

Special Notice

The Chartered
Institute of Marketing

Certificate
in Marketing

Examiner's Report

23:   Marketing Environment
Date: January 2004

© The Chartered Institute of Marketing

Certificate in Marketing

23:   Marketing Environment – Examiner's Report
Date: January 2004

General Strengths and Weaknesses of Candidates

General Strengths

- Considerable knowledge of many aspects of the marketing environment syllabus.

- More candidates appear to be reviewing past papers and practising examination technique.

- The ability to answer four questions, normally at some length and in some detail. Most candidates generally answered what they wanted to in the three hours. There was little evidence of hurried short notes for the last question attempted.

- The ability to provide relevant and interesting applications and examples, many of which were relatively up-to-date suggesting interest in current environmental developments. This strength has long been evident in many Centres but is increasing.

- Adoption of formally requested formats, particularly in home centres, but with continuing take-up elsewhere.

- Ability to relate to the case material and effectively incorporate it into the answers to section A was quite marked, suggesting that case method had been well covered in many Centres.

- There was some further evidence of understanding in respect to Environmental Information Systems in a number of Centres but worrying gaps remain e.g. large numbers did not understand Delphi or Impact analysis.

- Less evidence of 'theory dumping' although still present with weaker candidates.

- Candidates were generally strong on macro and micro issues.

- There is substantial evidence of reading the Workbooks and CIM Companion but little else.

General Weaknesses

- The wasteful tendency of providing non-required format continues and in some centres has intensified. One centre not only provided unnecessary report format for all questions but also carried section on assumptions and interpretations of the question. This wasted valuable time and resulted in no marks being earned until well into the second page of answer text.

- Despite there being no format requirement in section A, a significant number of candidates still provided it with some so doing for each part of the question. Again this was all at the expense of the actual answer required.

- By comparison, less obvious format requirements were missed by many candidates. For example question 5 required brief notes yet most provided neither heading nor bullet points.

- Too many candidates still ignore context requirements. This was particularly noticeable in question 5a. (the public sector) and 7b. the voluntary organisation.

- The examination concerns Marketing Environment yet too many candidates rely on the Marketing Fundamentals syllabus to answer questions such as 2. On the soft drinks industry.

- The critical weakness remains the inability or unwillingness of some candidates to follow the directions provided and answer the question that is posed. Question 1a. could not have more clearly asked for research methods and information sources, yet significant numbers provided either one or the other or were unclear as to which was which.

- Weaker candidates continue to use questions as 'theory dumps' suggesting that they either don't read or don't understand the question posed. Question 5 clearly asked for brief notes on the relevance and application of marketing research and MkIS for a public sector marketer, yet many answers contained all one ever wanted to know about the concepts themselves and often with no reference at all to a government organisation. Inability at translating knowledge into understanding therefore remains a problem.

- Setting an answer within the required context continues to be a weakness. Most questions will have a required context and high marks depend on answers being related to it. While performance improved in terms of relating section A questions to the McDonald's case, this was not so on the optional questions. For example question 2 focussed on the 'dynamic and complex nature of changes' yet very few candidates even referred to this aspect. Question 3a. should have been a 'banker' question on stakeholders yet most candidates failed to explain 'interrelationships' as the question required. Question 7 was another 'banker' on the macro and micro environment if only candidates had focussed on the 'differences' between them rather than providing applications relevant to a voluntary organisation. Ironically these differences were often introduced in part b.

- Many candidates are extremely verbose in their answers and often write a couple of pages on a point or example where a short paragraph would have sufficed. This is not the best way to impress the Examiner who is looking for concise but justified points not laborious 'blurb'. This weakness was particularly noticeable in the case with page-long, non scoring general introductions or conclusions.

- Candidates should use bullet points with justification/application far more frequently.

Strengths and Weaknesses by Question

PART A

- The compulsory case primarily concerned environmental impacts on McDonald's with particular emphasis on research data and legal/ cultural factors.

- The McDonald's context appeared to provide a level playing field across all centres.

- Questions carried equal marks and were a mixture of research methodology, environmental analysis techniques as well as macro environment topics with marketing implications.

- The health and obesity themes were topical for most centres.

- The emphasis on the Environmental information systems part of the syllabus (accounting two of the four questions) had been specifically flagged following the syllabus review and in the last Examiner's report.

- Some centres struggled with the environmental impact grid (syllabus ref: 4.6) and most provided either a PEST or a less relevant SWOT analysis. Fortunately there was sufficient material in the case to provide up to 4/10 but this question suggested that far too few centres had fully covered this new and important section of the syllabus. There is little point having knowledge of environmental factors if no understanding of how to analyse their impacts is demonstrated.

- Candidates continue to repeat case material verbatim. Case material needed to be processed in the light of syllabus knowledge and understanding for it to be useful in answering questions. One glaring example was question 1a, where many candidates unnecessarily wrote out the highlighted sections of text referred to in the question.

- There were no format marks but it was important that candidates set their answers in the required context. In 1c, it was not always clear whether the candidate was addressing McDonald's or the industry in general, while in 1d, a number of candidates managed answers that made no reference at all to the global marketer.

- The trend for a small but rising proportion of candidates to not answer all four parts of question 1 continued. Part b. in particular tended to be omitted.

- Weaker candidates, sometimes provided little content to mark, choosing instead to concentrate on optional questions. With 40% of the marks at stake this is not a passable strategy.

- A small proportion of candidates did treat their answers to all four questions as a report (as it was in June). Unfortunately, it was not always clearly indicated which part of the case they were addressing making marking quite difficult.

- There is some evidence that candidates do not read the whole paper at the outset in order to make their choices and plan their answers. It was noticeable that very few suggested Delphi (Q5) as part of the answer to 1a.

a.

- The question referred to element 4 of the syllabus (4.4/4.5) and was generally very well done.

- The relevant statistics in the text were highlighted and there was no need to reproduce them in the answer. The use of the term 'refer to' in the question did not mean write out in full.

- Reference was required to them but only in so far as to link the suggested research methods and sources to the case context.

- It was not necessary to consider each paragraph in turn but rather to provide a framework of research methodology linked to the production of the various statistics.

- It would have been desirable to separate the treatment of methods and sources as the question suggested although marks were not lost if this did not happen.

- Some candidates provided a comprehensive analysis of research methods but with no mention of sources or linkage to the case context. It is critical that contextualisation is provided where required.

- A list of generalised information sources such as newspapers, TV, the internet and journals were not what was required although it was valid to quote the source of the case material itself.

- Better candidates linked the statistics in the case to primary and secondary/quantitative and qualitative research methods which were in turn linked to specific sources.

- It was not a question on how to undertake the various methods, nor was it a question on the detailed content of the sources. Similarly it was not concerned with what to research in order to undertake a PEST analysis.

- Better candidates focussed on research methods and information sources linked to the relevant case statistics. Weaker candidates repeated case material and provided narrow or generalised answer. Most candidates, however, earned at least a pass mark.

b.

- This question was very poorly answered. This was despite the Examiners report for June 2003 drawing attention to deficiencies in this area of the syllabus and the likelihood of further questions. This does beg the question as to the breadth of readership of such reports amongst students and, more importantly, tutors.

- The question referred to Element 4: Environmental information systems (4.6) of the syllabus.

- Only better candidates had any conception of impact analysis, let alone representing this in a grid format. It was particularly worrying that so few candidates even attempted to produce a grid of any description. The majority providing an illustration favoured a SWOT or PEST analysis, prompted perhaps by the reference in the question to four required factors and the assist in brackets drawing attention to the fact that an environmental analysis was required.

- Some more Marketing Fundamentals candidate's discussed the 4 P's. It is perhaps fortunate that Porter's analysis has five elements.

- The majority of candidates omitted all reference to weightings although those who did combine a case based PEST analysis with commentary on relative importance did achieve a high mark despite the absence of a grid. One would have expected at least an attempt at explanation of the term even if relative values were not considered.

- In the event most candidates provided an 'environmental analysis' and ignored the rest of the question. Even here a large number considered more than four factors and wrote at excessive length.

- Some of these answers ran into pages of generalised comment on the PEST (or SWOT) environments. Better candidates did select the required four factors by referring to the case material and re-processing the points in a PEST framework.

- A number of candidates considered McDonald's impact on the environment rather then the impact of the wider environment on McDonald's. This was particularly marked where strengths and weaknesses (internal to the business) were concerned.

- Only the best candidates actually justified the weights they allocated to the environmental factors (say on a scale of 0 - 10+/-).

- Overall this question made the lowest impact in terms of candidate competence and the corresponding weighting in the final mark for part A was correspondingly low.

c.

- There had not been an explicit part A question on the legal environment for quite a period of time and this was reflected in the relatively quality of answers received.

- Most candidates were able to make some points but the general standard was low with very few attaining very high marks.

- Weaker candidates were content to repeat case references to legal matters with little or no development.

- Better candidates dealt with legal issues arising from the case and supplemented their assessment with knowledge and understanding of syllabus material.

- Only the best candidates explicitly referred to the 'changing nature' of the legal environment.

- The context was important since it required assessment both in terms of McDonald's and the wider Food Industry.

- Relevant issues for assessment included health and safety; quality assurance; advertising standards; fair trade/competition policies; trade descriptions; compensation culture; health warnings and franchise contracts. Very few candidates picked up on the latter prompt in the case material.

- It was also acceptable to discuss social responsibility, ethics, pressure group activity and different forms of regulation.

- Many answers to this question were overly brief giving the examiner little to credit.

- It appears that some Centres consider the legal environment as one to leave out or cover superficially. This question demonstrates the inadvisability of such a choice.

d.

- This was much better answered overall and provided high marks for the focussed candidate.

- Most candidates had a reasonably good grasp of what culture meant although definitions were often either overly brief, excessively waffling or rather confused.

- There were a number of references to culture in the case and most candidates were able to provide at least a basic definition of the term.

- Weaker candidates were unable to provide the link to the global marketer context.

- Many were content to cite a number of cultural variations based on colour, religion or tastes but drew little of importance from their recognition as far as any type of organisation was concerned.

- Some candidates discussed what McDonald's should do about variations in cultural preferences despite this not being required by the question.

- However, despite these criticisms the overall impression was of candidates with a good general grasp of culture and its importance for the organisation.

Part B - Question 2

- This was a relatively popular question amongst weaker candidates. Questions, such as this, are despite appearances sometimes deceptively difficult. In this case it was avoided by many of the better-prepared candidates.

- The format requirement should have been straightforward and indeed most produced a report format. Unfortunately, some candidates omitted to attach an appendix, preferring instead to head part b. as 'Implications arising'.

- The question was more difficult than it appeared because it referred to 'the dynamic and complex nature of changes'. Unfortunately most candidates ignored this part of the question and produced a relatively static report of the marketing environment.

- The context was also important since failure to base it in a specific country and the soft drinks industry reduced the marks potential significantly. A number of candidates still referred to alcoholic liquids while others chose to answer it despite admitting their country did not grow oranges and they knew little about it.

- Weaker candidates from some centres therefore devoted much of their answer to discussing the vagaries of the weather and the need for irrigation.

- Dynamic changes might have included factors such as increasing competitiveness; globalisation trends; changing consumer tastes; natural environment concerns and social changes e.g. health and fitness trends.

- The marketing environment included the industry/competitive environment but was not a signal to produce a Porter 5 force analysis. The main emphasis should have been on the macro environments and certainly not the internal environment.

- Weaker candidates did one of the following:

- Provided a detailed description of the soft drinks industry and the merits of its various brands.

- Provided a Marketing Fundamentals answer incorporating key aspects of the marketing mix.

- Discussed how to analyse the environment.

- Part b. asked for a series of bullet point (outlining) implications relevant to marketing strategy/planning.

- Very few made any attempt to define marketing strategy/planning but took it for granted.

- Some provided an Ansoff matrix despite the question referring to changes identified in part a.

- Better candidates made points arising out of part a. including the importance of monitoring competitors and the environment; responding to pressure groups; product development; focus/niche opportunities and so on.

Part B - Question 3

- The popularity of this question varied between centres.

- Part a. should have been relatively easy marks provided that the candidate focussed on the term interrelationship. Unfortunately many candidates focussed on how to build relationships rather than the nature of the interrelationships themselves.

- It was also important that the context of a business school was applied throughout.

- Up to 2 marks were available for a definition of stakeholders although most candidates either did not provide one or lapsed into the traditional distinction between internal, connected and external stakeholders.

- Most were able to define who the customer and employee stakeholders were for a business college and better candidates perceived that customers might include parents, sponsoring businesses and potential students.

- Too many candidates extended consideration to other stakeholder groups and often wrote far too much for the 8 marks available.

- Weaker candidates basically ignored interrelationships and listed either the policies of the Business College or the job descriptions/roles of the employees/students. Others explained how to build better relationships with the two stakeholder groups.

- Only better candidates focussed on the two way relationships.

- In b. most candidates struggled since they had not established the interrelationship in a.

- Many did not seem to understand what an internal information source was and concentrated more on what information was required or how it helped the Business College to perform.

- Suggestions such as e-mail, telephone numbers, post codes, billboards, leaflets and memos were rather tenuous whilst meetings, ledgers, records and newsletters needed some further explanation.

- Part c. was much better answered in the main with most candidates restricting themselves to 3 external sources and providing an explanation of the information's value.

- Popular selections were other/competing colleges; the Education Ministry; the Industry Association/CIM; electoral register/census and media coverage of education.

- Better candidates made the link between the source and how it contributed to understanding of the interrelationship.

Part B - Question 4

- This was a relatively popular question in UK centres due presumably to the EU context.

- Some very high marks were achieved where the candidates focussed carefully on the question requirements.

- There was no format requirement although some candidates wasted valuable time in providing one.

- The perspective was that of a UK based exporter of environmental protection equipment. Weaker candidates sometimes looked at it from other perspectives implied in the four challenges.

- A key assumption was that the equipment met EU standards.

- Each challenge required five assessment points to be made for the full marks.

- Part a. was generally well done with expansion of the EU implying an enlarged export market protected by a common external tariff; undeveloped domestic industries; a requirement to apply the standard in theses new member states; scope for partnerships etc.

- Part b. was less well done with some candidates confusing likely consequences. Better candidates referred to uncertainty; restricted market opportunities; cancelled orders; the need to wait and see; the threat from competitors with lower standards etc.

- Part c. was not well done although most recognised the likely reduction in demand for equipment. Better candidates recognised the long lead time for the new fuel especially in less developed markets and the need to re-focus on the laggards segment.

- Part d. was quite well done given the option of discussing alternative possibilities e.g. China becoming a major producer in its own right, suggesting that the exporter should go for long term relationships/partnerships/offer know-how/re-locate to take advantage of low wage costs, or avoid exchange rate risks versus China as a huge undeveloped market with massive export potential.

Part B - Question 5

- This was a popular question but was not particularly well attempted by many candidates.

- The main problem in part a. was a failure to comply with the contextual requirements of the question.

- Most candidates did not write brief notes or signal their intention to do so. Others preferred a memo or report format despite its not being required. This produced a significant amount of irrelevant text.

- Too many 'prepared answers' were in evidence for i) and ii) and applied with no thought for what the question actually required.

- Far too many candidates ignored the public sector context for the marketer and either used none or a private sector example. Some confused public sector with the Plc and some with voluntary organisations. A notable few stated they were relating to the public sector but then suggested without qualification that competitors be monitored and assessed.

- Some used parts i) and ii) as extensive theory dumps for all they knew about marketing research and MkIS. This often included detailed diagrams, as in the case of the latter concept. Unfortunately the question concerned relevance and application of the concepts not their description. Indeed weaker candidates provided all description and no relevance or application.

- Better candidates provided a brief definition of the terms and then focussed on public sector applications.

- Part iii) was often missed out entirely or confused by candidates. Some missed out parts ii) and iii) but still attempted the question.

- It was clear that this forecasting technique had not been brought to the attention of such students. There was also less inclination to find public sector applications for this concept.

- Part b. was relatively well done in most cases as far as differences were concerned but less convincing on similarities.

- Weaker candidates chose not to compare objectives at all but opted for various aspects of legal form of organisation. Also, stating that the private sector made a profit while the public sector did not was not likely to earn all 4 marks on offer.

- The best similarity was to explain the need for customer orientation in both sectors.

Part B - Question 6

- This was a very popular question with certain centres and yielded some high marks for the focussed candidate.

- It also proved possible to misinterpret the perspective and earn relatively low marks.

- The perspective was a major supermarket chain and the requirement was for explanation of 5 probable impacts per development on it (rather than say, the final customer). The first 3 developments represented aspects of Porter 5 force analysis i.e. development of a substitute, new entrant, increased bargaining power of suppliers, while the last represented the regulatory environment.

- In a. too many candidates chose to discuss the meaning of the development and its implications for 'armchair customers' rather than the impact on a supermarket chain. Focus on the latter provided a large number of probable impacts ranging from the need to make investments in various aspects of the new technology to contractions in the physical store side, and even reductions in impulse sales.

- In b. there were clear parallels with the Walmart - Asda take-over for UK centres. Good answers were received mentioning impacts on sales volumes, margins and customer flows.

- In c. there were many good answers, with most recognising the probable impact on higher costs and customer prices but recognising that the impact would be spread across all supermarkets. Better candidates identified possible positives in the shape of economies of scale, cost savings, greater certainty of supply and scope for building relationships.

- Part d. was less well done suggesting limited coverage of this syllabus aspect. However, many used their common sense to differentiate impacts where the industry paticipants were colluding and where they were not.

Part B - Question 7

- This question was answered by most candidates and did appear to be a gift question for many.

- Unfortunately not all candidates read all of the question leading to many marks being needlessly sacrificed for the sake of a minute or two of more careful scrutiny.

- Part a. required an example of a voluntary organisation that many successfully provided. Failure to do so not only lost a mark but potentially undermined the relevance of the answer to part b.

- Part a. also required a brief explanation/definition of a voluntary organisation.

- The question was about 'differences' between the macro and micro environment, not an extensive explanation of the macro and micro environment of the named charity. Macro aspects in any case belonged to part b. yet many candidates ended up repeating themselves or scratching round for content.

- Differences included such points as direct 2 way interaction/indirect longer term impact can control/influence the connected micro but not the external macro environment

- Part b. provided 2 easy format marks and the potential for high marks so long as the context was maintained. The question implied the use of the selected voluntary organisation but examiners would accept any stated context.

- Many candidates found themselves repeating macro content erroneously put into part a. or more seriously, choosing not to.

- Some saw part b. as their opportunity to discuss the business cycle despite this being of limited relevance to a voluntary organisation.

- Many candidates reproduced material already provided in part a. in terms of defining the macro environment. Differences between the macro and micro environments were also belatedly introduced.

- Weaker candidates unfortunately omitted the context altogether and merely discussed the macro environment in very superficial terms.

- Better candidates explained with examples how the various macro environments impacted from a marketing perspective.

The Chartered
Institute of Marketing

Professional Certificate in Marketing

Marketing Environment

23:   **Marketing Environment**

Time: **14.00-17.00**

Date: **8th June, 2004**

3 Hours Duration

This examination is in two sections.

PART A – Is compulsory and worth 40% of total marks.

PART B – Has **SIX** questions; select **THREE**. Each answer will be worth 20% of the total marks.

All questions relate to both CIM Certificate in Marketing old (pre-July 2002) and new (post-July 2002) Syllabi unless otherwise stated.

DO NOT repeat the question in your answer, but show clearly the number of the question attempted on the appropriate pages of the answer book.

Rough workings should be included in the answer book and ruled through after use.

© The Chartered Institute of Marketing

Professional Certificate in Marketing

23: Marketing Environment

PART A

China Defies the Global Gloom

While global stagnation has depressed most of the major economies, China continues to expand at a dramatic rate. As economies such as the USA's and the UK's struggle to adjust to **deflationary forces,** Chinese **economic growth** goes from strength to strength. It has averaged over 9% per annum since the late 1980s while exports rose by a third in 2001 alone. The USA and the UK by contrast are confronted with widening balance of payments deficits and **rising personal and public debt ratios**. China is now the world's fourth largest industrial producer after the US, Japan and Germany. The term 'Made in China' is no longer confined to toys and handicrafts since the country now accounts for production of 50% of the world's cameras, 25% of its steel, 30% of its washing machines, 37% of its hard disk drives and 10% of its computer monitors. No wonder that China is now the largest exporter to the US, pushing Japan into second place.

China's political environment is almost exclusively controlled by the **Communist** party, yet its leadership has successfully transformed the economic environment into one similar to **Capitalism**. Within 15 years, huge sectors of the economy have been opened up to privatised or foreign firms and the Chinese are virtually free to conduct business wherever they please. However, with an economic strategy that bans independent trade unions, limits health, safety and environmental regulations and is strongly pro-business, it is clearly not 'enlightened' capitalism. For example, much of the so-called 'cyber waste' from the US ends up in a vast re-processing plant in South China employing 100,000 people that strips old computers of their valuable parts. Environmental laws are weak, costs are low and residual wastes are dumped locally causing wells to be so polluted that water has to be trucked in. On the other hand, any political challenges to the authority of party are suppressed. This includes the World Wide Web where the government employs 30,000 'Internet police' and pressures companies such as Yahoo and AOL to sign pledges agreeing to co-operate with government censorship.

Unsurprisingly, with only **European Union 'enlargement'** as a potentially attractive alternative, multinational direct investment is flowing into China and much of it is hi-tech in nature. Motorola is planning a $1.3 billion research investment and Microsoft an investment worth $750 million. Unlike in Eastern Europe, the main attraction is the vast pool of labour. Wage rates are around 5% of the level in the US and probably five times cheaper than the likes of Hungary or Poland. With a massive agricultural reserve to draw from it is unlikely these rates will rise sharply in future. Added to this there is a large state educated elite of middle managers and engineers who can oversee quality and performance standards on behalf of multinational companies.

There are some question marks over the sustainability of future growth, not least from political protest among the poor. Notwithstanding the prosperity of its Eastern cities like Beijing and Shanghai, the country as a whole is still one of the poorest in the world. Rural incomes have fallen over the last five years as near-bankrupt state farms have laid off millions of workers. An estimated 270 million are below the $1 a day poverty standard of **the World Bank**. Also, after years of insisting that AIDS is a problem associated with the decadent West, the government has now acknowledged the issue and mobilised one million students to travel through the country warning the population of the danger.

The middle classes, by contrast, are prospering and it is forecast that by 2020 around 100 million Chinese will holiday abroad each year. Bank credit and government budget deficits have financed much of the rapid growth and these could become over-stretched. However, the state still has many assets left to privatise, such as land, oil firms or phone companies, and these could raise billions of dollars.

China's success has become a threat to other global economies. Japan may suffer more than most due to its proximity and already depressed economic state. Chinese imports are putting pressure on margins while adding to its deflation by continuously forcing down the price of consumer durables. The potentially offsetting opportunity of a huge domestic Chinese market is, unfortunately, limited by endemic corruption and an **inadequately developed regulatory regime** that allows considerable copyright infringement.

(Based on excerpts from various newspaper reports and 'The Week' articles).

PART A

Question 1.

a. Compare the meaning of **two** of the following sets of terms that are in bold text in the case:

    i)   Deflationary forces and economic growth.

    ii)   Capitalism and communism.

    iii)   Rising personal and public debt ratios.

    iv)   European Union enlargement and the World Bank.

(12 marks)

b. Brief a marketer from a Chinese travel company on the marketing opportunities presented by a prospering middle class.

(10 marks)

c. Use the case material to produce an outline SWOT analysis of the Chinese economy.

(10 marks)

d. Explain the marketing implications of an 'inadequately developed regulatory regime' for a multinational pharmaceutical company seeking to establish its products in Chinese markets.

(8 marks)
(40 marks in total)

PART B – Answer THREE Questions Only

Question 2.

a.   Explain the meaning of a privatised business.

(4 marks)

b.   Using an example, compare the possible objectives of an organisation before and after privatisation.

(8 marks)

c.   What are main drivers for change from a public sector organisation into a privatised organisation?

(8 marks)
(20 marks in total)

Question 3.

All marketing orientated businesses must, by definition, be open systems.

Demonstrate the truth of this statement by explaining how a road haulage (transportation of goods) company would respond to changing conditions in:

i)   Its competitive environment.

(10 marks)

ii)   Its macro environment.

(10 marks)
(20 marks in total)

Question 4.

You are a Marketing Assistant in a chemical company which operates a number of large chemical plants in sea-port locations producing a range of oil based pesticides for domestic and foreign markets.

Your Marketing Manager has asked you to prepare a report ranking the company's **four** most influential pressure groups and outlining their potential impacts and/or marketing implications. She would also welcome your views as to how the relationship with the pressure groups might be best managed.

(20 marks)

Question 5.

a. Using examples from your own country, distinguish between the social and cultural environment.

(8 marks)

b. Using your understanding of the social or cultural environment, discuss ways in which you might market jewellery to the 35-50 age group.

(12 marks)
(20 marks in total)

Question 6.

You work in an Executive Recruitment Agency where your Manager firmly believes that timely information adds power to the organisation's marketing efforts. Prepare notes for a presentation to marketing trainees that supports this view. Your presentation should consider the following aspects:

a. The importance of 'quality' information.

(5 marks)

b. The need for an information system.

(5 marks)

c. The impact of new information and communication technologies.

(5 marks)

d. Specific applications that enhance marketing effectiveness.

(5 marks)
(20 marks in total)

Question 7.

You work in the marketing department of a vehicle manufacturer.

a. Explain the concerns of **three** of the organisation's stakeholder groups with how your company impacts on the natural environment.

(6 marks)

b. Explain how the organisation might positively respond to these concerns about the natural environment.

(6 marks)

c. How could the marketing department respond positively to these concerns?

(8 marks)
(20 marks in total)

The Chartered
Institute of Marketing

Professional Certificate in Marketing

Marketing Environment

23:     **Marketing Environment**

SENIOR EXAMINER'S REPORT FOR JUNE 2004 EXAMINATION PAPER

© The Chartered Institute of Marketing

SENIOR EXAMINER'S REPORT FOR
JUNE 2004 EXAMINATION PAPER

MODULE NAME: MARKETING ENVIRONMENT

AWARD NAME: CERTIFICATE IN MARKETING

DATE: JULY 18th 2004

1.   General Strengths and Weaknesses of Candidates

- Drew effectively on case material to provide basic support for answers
- General awareness of format requirements
- Providing enough in most cases for examiners to mark
- Clear understanding of SWOT analysis, however, there seems to be :-
  - Clear appreciation of stakeholders, pressure groups and their concerns/impacts
  - Improving grasp of information and information systems in the light of ICT developments
  - An improved overall mark for the case question due to good marks on 1c.
  - Weak appreciation of the meaning of key terms such as deflation, debt and World Bank
  - A general lack of understanding as to the meaning of a ratio
  - An inability to apply SWOT analysis to internal/external factors on the case leading to confusion of internal strengths and weaknesses for external opportunities and threats
- A tendency to use unnecessary or inappropriate format
- An inability to convincingly contextualise answers
- An over-reliance on 'promotion' among the 4/7 P's when giving marketing recommendations
- Non UK candidates seemed largely unaware of EU enlargement
- Poor optional question selection where parts of the chosen question were either ignored or insufficiently addressed

2. Strengths and Weaknesses by Question

Question 1

- Parts i) and ii) were the predominantly favoured choices. Part iv) was least popular.
- Many candidates, answered all 4 sets of terms despite clear guidance in bold to answer just 2.
- Few provided a formal comparison format despite being requested in the question
- Some answers, especially non UK, were far too brief for the 6 marks per set while others were far too long and detailed
- Focus should have been on defining the meaning of the terms and then making comparisons perhaps by alluding to case material. Many wrote about causes or consequences of the stated terms
- Care should be applied in using dictionary definitions e.g. deflation is a collapse through release of air (Oxford)

Question 1ai

- This produced many confused and often contradictory answers suggesting a lack of real understanding of the economic environment
- Many used this question as a vehicle for discussing the business cycle rather than the terms directly
- Focus tended to be on deflation rather than deflationary 'forces'
- Weaker candidates, particularly in non UK centres merely repeated case material
- Better candidates understood deflation as the opposite of inflation and had a grasp of aggregate demand and supply
- Candidates showed better understanding of economic growth, the concept of GDP and its link to improving economic conditions and the standard of living
- Defining economic growth in terms of 'when the economy grows' is unlikely to earn marks
- Many used the example of Chinese growth to good effect

Question 1aii

- There were some very good answers in both political and economic terms, particularly in UK centres. Some non UK candidates were less clear on their understanding of the terms.
- Some candidates digressed wastefully into polemic and political point scoring
- Too many non UK candidates relied on case material for inspiration
- The case of China was used by better candidates as the basis for comparison although for others it produced some confusion

Question 1aiii

- This was more popular with UK candidates where better answers were received although many tended to be woolly

- Few attempted or succeeded in defining a debt ratio, yet this was the key to the question
- There was confusion over public debt with some seeing it as company debt while others saw it as international debt arising out of balance of payments deficits
- There was a better grasp of personal debt and its sources and implications

Question 1aiv

- This was least popular and answers betrayed limited understanding and awareness, particularly in non UK centres
- There was some confusion that the question involved China joining the UK or visa versa
- Even some UK candidates did not appear to be aware that the EU had very recently enlarged
- Others thankfully knew this, the various countries involved and the consequent enlargement in the market potential
- Most candidates showed limited grasp of the World Bank or its role. The main confusions were with a global central bank or the IMF. Non UK candidates were much more aware of its lending role.

Question 1b

- Many candidates seemed uncomfortable with the context of this question
- Few answers were exceptionally good with many candidates failing to relate points to the emerging and prosperous middle classes
- Many were content to repeat obvious RCM points but failed to take up more subtle prompts such as the educated students or multinational company employees
- Too many provided standard marketing points that could equally have applied to any context
- Many seemed unable to appreciate the huge potential of internal/external tourism opportunities in China.
- Some East Asian candidates provided deeper insights into the social and cultural environment

Question 1c

- This question often provided the basis of an overall pass on the case question given average marks of 7/10
- Virtually all candidates knew what SWOT stood for and some made the distinction between internal/external factors
- Relatively few complied with the 'outline' instruction and instead provided a large number of points under each heading. There were only 2 marks available per element (some only gave 1 element under each heading). Better candidates placed these in a grid to gain a mark.
- Many points were RCM but often supplied with no 'processing' or qualification
- The majority failed to differentiate what was an internal and what was an external factor in a China/country SWOT. Consequently many of the factors

325

supplied as opportunities or threats were actually internal e.g. un-exploited privatisation opportunities.

- Most candidates impressed in their ability to search case material for SWOT possibilities

Question 1d
- Far too few candidates seemed to understand the legal/regulatory environment.
- Even candidates who had performed strongly on 1a to 1c seemed to encounter difficulties with only the very best getting beyond copyright problems.
- Few candidates attempted to even define the meaning of an 'inadequately developed regulatory regime'.
- Many candidates missed out the question altogether or provided very brief responses relying on repeated case material and little more.
- Some candidates applied a SLEPT analysis as if the question concerned a country assessment prior to inward investment

Optional Questions

Question 2a.
- Too many candidates were unaware of the difference between a private and privatised business in this popular question
- Better candidates defined the meaning in terms of a transfer of 51% or more of the ownership from a public sector organisation to the private sector
- Full marks however required further 'explanation' of the meaning e.g. continued regulation by the state, accountability to shareholders or greater freedoms to manage

Question 2b
- Most candidates provided an example although some of these were of doubtful relevance e.g. the NHS, schools and even a supermarket
- Most provided a comparison and often in grid format
- Better candidates related their objectives before and after to their chosen organisation while weaker candidates merely listed generic objectives at best
- Many centres seemed to struggle in their understanding of what an objective was
- There was a lot of digression into commentary on pluses and minuses of public v private sector organisations that alluded to objectives but were insufficient relevant to warrant a mark. Other provided a comparison of operating methods.
- Many candidates got the more obvious objectives of public service – maximum profit but struggled beyond that

Question 2c
- There were some very good answers to this part especially from candidates citin, not only relevant drivers such as government funding and shaking up management and organisational efficiency, but also setting these in the chosen organisational context.

- Many non UK centres struggled with the concept of drivers for change although this is specifically mentioned in syllabus element 1.5
- This was the swing question that decided whether a high as against a passable mark was achieved on this question
- Some candidates produced material in c) that should have been in b) and visa versa

Question 3

- A significant proportion candidates went straight into part i) without any attempt to define the statement provided as the focus of the question
- Of those that did provide some definition, the majority focussed on open (and closed) systems without any explanation of a marketing orientated business.
- The majority did however understand the relationship of an open system to the wider environment and most were familiar with the input – conversion – output – feedback model
- The question was not well answered due primarily to the failure to correctly read and understand the question or to set it in the required context
- The context was clear enough – the road haulage industry, while the question referred to 'company responses' to 'changing (environmental) conditions'. Marks were award for identifying such changes (in context) and responses the road haulage company made
- In the event many candidates either discussed 'competition' or Porter's 5 forces in very static terms and often with little reference to actual or even imagined 'changes' in the haulage industry. Others compared different forms of transport or the merits of competing transport companies
- Knowledge of Porter was very impressive but the ability to apply it to 'changing conditions' in a 'selected context' was not. Consequently any responses provided were seldom linked to a change in conditions
- Part ii) was better answered since there was more scope to focus on changing SLEPT factors, but even here weaker candidates proved only a description of each environment in very general terms
- Some non UK candidates seemed to have a very limited knowledge of their own country SLEPT environment as it applies to transport
- Candidates must be tutored more effectively in the 'art' of understanding an examination question

Question 4
- This was a relatively popular question and was generally well answered
- Some scripts tended to have a lower average due to more limited understanding of impacts and less reference to the context of the question
- Most provided a report format but the mark for ranking the pressure groups was not as easily come by
- Better candidates provided a brief definition of pressure groups prior to identifying them
- Many of the better candidates were able to identify 4 specific pressure groups associated with the given context. Other candidates were normally able to

identify 4 groups even if these were generic, fictional or external stakeholder group.

- Better candidates provided separate sections on potential impacts and marketing implication although one or the other was sufficient to earn full marks.
- Weaker candidates tended to get the impact reversed around i.e. either the company impacts on the pressure groups were considered or more commonly the pressure group's impacts on the wider environment as a result of their activities. Others provided a description of the 'concerns'
- Management of the relationship with the pressure groups was generally well done

Question 5a

- This part of the question was generally well answered although candidates were more precise in their understanding of the cultural than the social environment.
- Examples were provided, often at some length, particularly in non UK centres although it was not always clear which related to which environment
- Most provided examples from their own country, although some did not seem to appreciate what constituted an example and what constituted a description

Question 5b

- Despite being popular, this question was surprisingly badly answered
- The question required understanding of the socio-cultural environment applied to a demographic segment with a view to discussing how best to market jewellery
- Many struggled with this task and relevant 'discussions' were few and far between
- Weaker candidates could do little more than make a few elementary observations
- Better marketing discussions were often generic and could have applied to many other products or services
- Beyond the stated 35-50 age group very few social or cultural variables were referred to
- Better scripts were received with marketing points being tied to variables such as gender, marital relationships, class, ethnicity, discretionary income, cultural values, role models and the like.
- Some candidates did manage to introduce the likes of Beckham into their discussion, although whether he is a role model for the 35-50 age group is a moot point.

Question 6

- This was a popular and generally well answered question yielding a relatively high average mark
- Many were able to take advantage of the format marks by preparing notes for a presentation to marketing trainees
- Unfortunately some prepared the presentation itself or did not relate it to the marketing trainees

- Context was very important to achieving a high mark and notes needed to be set against the requirements of an Executive Recruitment Agency(ERA)
- Candidates often failed to refer to the context at all
- The question provided an opportunity to 'theory dump' a large amount of knowledge on marketing information systems and/or ICT developments. Candidates needed to be disciplined given the specific requirements of each question and the limited marks per section

Question 6a
- This question required notes on the meaning of quality information and on their importance to the ERA
- Weaker candidates tended to state why information in general was important and what it was needed for e.g. to understand the environment or formulate a marketing plan
- Better candidates explained why 'quality' information was important in making marketing decisions within the ERA
- Most candidates kept their notes to 4 or 5

Question 6b
- Weaker candidates tended to define what an information system was but not why it was needed
- Far too much detail, often with supporting diagrams from Kotler, were provided
- Too few candidates related the need for the information system to the 'needs' of the ERA and its marketers

Question 6c
- This tended to be well done given that the context was complied with
- The candidate needed to focus on 'impact' on the ERA, its activities or its market
- Weaker candidates tended to focus on a description of ICT, They also tended not to focus on 'new' ICT's as required by the question
- Better candidates planned their answers and avoided overlap or repetition with part d.

Question 6d
- The focus of this part of the question was on specific application of ICT's in the context of the ERA and shown to enhance marketing effectiveness
- Better candidates used applications such as mobile phones to contact applicants, the internet to research companies as potential customers , the teleconference for interviews and job opportunities accessed on-line
- Weaker candidates neglected the link to marketing effectiveness

Question 7

- This question was reasonably popular but was not particularly well answered. Candidates here seemed to find difficulty in relating their answers to the natural environment context.

329

Question 7a

- All candidates displayed excellent understanding of stakeholders although unfortunately this was not the focus of this particular question
- The question required the 'concerns' of 3 stakeholders regarding how the vehicle manufacturer impacted on the natural environment
- Other than a definitional mark there were no marks for explaining what stakeholders were or even identifying the 3 stakeholder groups. The marks were for the 'concerns'.
- Weaker candidates either trotted out the general concerns of stakeholders e.g. shareholders for profit or consumers for value for money, or their attitude towards the natural environment
- Again it is critical that candidates read and re-read the question to determine the key words to focus on

Question 7b

- Weaker candidates tended not to plan their answers resulting in unnecessary overlap with part c. They also tended to under-emphasise the vehicle manufacture context
- Better candidates explained how the business could deploy techniques such as re-design, re-use of materials, recycling and innovation of environmentally friendlier products and components.
- Some candidates specifically responded to each of the concerns identified in a. This was effective in terms of marks but it was important to recognise that only 6 marks were available in total.

Question 7c

- A good answer required a response set in the context of the marketing mix as a whole rather than consideration of promotional responses alone.
- Weaker answers only considered promotional responses letting stakeholders know just how 'green' the company had become
- Better answers looked at product, price and place

Future Themes

- Papers will continue to expect answers within a stated context
- Context is becoming much more important than formal
- All environments, including the regulatory environment, will be examined from time to time
- Apparent weakness in the definition of environmental terms will lead to similar questions in future
- A slight bias towards questions on environmental information systems will continue
- The case will of necessity tend to have global accessibility in terms of content although questions will continue to apply across the whole syllabus

appendix 6
curriculum information and reading list

Aim

The Marketing Environment unit equips students to explain the nature of the marketing environment and its relevance for organizations and marketing practice. It provides knowledge of marketing information and its use in organizations, particularly in its application in the strategy and marketing planning processes. It aims to provide students with a working knowledge of organizations and the various influences of their wider environments.

Related statements of practice

Ab.1 Collect information.
Ab.2 Interpret and present information.
Bb.1 Contribute information and ideas to the strategy process.
Bb.2 Contribute to the production of marketing plans and budgets.

Learning outcomes

Students will be able to:

5.20.1 Distinguish between the types of organization within the public, private and voluntary sectors, and understand their objectives and the influences upon them.

5.20.2 Explain the main elements of an organization's marketing environment and discuss the significance of current and future environmental challenges.

5.20.3 Describe the interactions between the main elements of the marketing environment.

5.20.4 Assess the potential impact on an organization of key trends in the social, technical, economic, environmental, political, legal and ethical environments.

5.20.5 Demonstrate an understanding of an organization's micro-environment.

5.20.6 Explain the process for collecting information about the marketing environment from relevant primary and secondary sources.

5.20.7 Compare and contrast various techniques for collecting information about the marketing environment.

Knowledge and skill requirements

Element 1: The nature of the organization and the impact of its environment (15 per cent)

1.1 Demonstrate a broad appreciation of the internal environment.

1.2 Explain the classification of private, public and voluntary organizations, their legal status and operational characteristics.

1.3 Assess comparative strengths and weaknesses of small/medium and large/global sized organizations.

1.4 State the meaning and importance of an organization's mission and explain the nature and significance of the objectives pursued.

1.5 Identify the internal and external influences on the formulation of objectives and specify the key drivers for organizational change.

1.6 Explain the nature of open systems and the interface between organizations and their marketing environment.

1.7 Represent the organization as an open system responding to changing environmental conditions.

1.8 Demonstrate the dynamic and complex nature of environmental change and its importance to the development of marketing strategy and planning.

1.9 Appreciate the potential significance of emerging environmental challenges to effective marketing in the present and the future.

Element 2: The micro-environment (20 per cent)

2.1 Describe the external and internal stakeholders that constitute the micro-environment within which organizations operate and their importance to the marketing process.

2.2 Explain the nature of the interactions between the organization and its various stakeholders.

2.3 Demonstrate an awareness of key internal and external sources of information on the micro-environment.

2.4 Explain the significance of the range of pressure groups interested in the organization and their potential impacts.

2.5 Specify the role of marketing in managing these pressure groups.

2.6 Explain the importance of monitoring competitors and industries and how the organization assesses the strategic and marketing implications.

2.7 Examine the impact of competition policies on the organization and its marketing environment.

Element 3: The macro-environment (50 per cent)

3.1 Appreciate the importance of the macro-environment to the marketing process.

3.2 Awareness of key sources of information on the macro-environment.

3.3 Explain the social, demographic and cultural environments and, in general terms, their influence on and implications for marketing.

3.4 Explain the economic and international environments and, in general terms, their influence on and implications for marketing.

3.5 Explain the political and legislative environments and, in general terms, their influence on and implications for marketing.

3.6 Explain the natural environment and, in general terms, its influence on and implications for marketing.

3.7 Explain the importance of the technical and information environments and their actual and potential impacts on organizations, employment, marketing and communications.

3.8 Assess the potential significance of environmental challenges to marketing in the future: e.g. globalization; single currency; information communication technology; and environmental decline.

Element 4: Environmental information systems (15 per cent)

4.1 Explain why information is important to organizations.

4.2 Explain the concept of a marketing information system and its key role in effective marketing decision-making.

4.3 Explain the importance of marketing research and the information benefits it can provide.

4.4 Identify key sources of internal and external information.

4.5 Utilise, interpret and present secondary and primary data in identifying environmental trends and estimating current demand.

4.6 Explain the techniques available for forecasting future demand and coping with the challenge of environmental change.

4.7 Explain the importance of information systems and the continuing impact of new technologies.

Related key skills

Key skill	Relevance to unit knowledge and skills
Communication	Synthesize information from different sources
	Write a report summarizing information
Application of number	Interpret numerical data
	Carry out calculations
Information technology	Identify sources of information
	Collect data from various sources
Working with others	Obtain information from others
Improving own learning and performance	Apply planning techniques to agree targets and plan how these will be met (methods, timescales, resources)
	Select and use a variety of methods for learning
	Manage time effectively
	Seek feedback to monitor performance and modify approach
	Review progress and provide evidence of meeting targets
Problem solving	

Assessment

CIM will normally offer two forms of assessment for this unit from which study centres or students may choose: written examination and an assignment. CIM may also recognize, or make joint awards for, units at an equivalent level undertaken with other professional marketing bodies and educational institutions.

Recommended support materials

Core text

Palmer, A. Hartley, B. (2001) *The Business Environment*, 4th edition, Maidenhead: McGraw-Hill.

Syllabus guides

BPP (2005) *Marketing Environment: Study Text*, London: BPP Publishing.

Oldroyd, M. (2005) *Marketing Environment*, Oxford: BH/Elsevier.

Supplementary readings

Brooks, I. and Weatherston, J. (2002) *The Business Environment: Challenges and Changes*, Harlow: Prentice Hall.

Cartwright, R. (2001) *Mastering the Business Environment*, Palgrave.

Kotler, P., Armstrong, G., Saunders, J. and Wong, V. (2004) *Principles of Marketing*, 4th European edition, Harlow: Prentice Hall.

Needle, D. (2004) *Business in Context: An Introduction to Business and its Environment*, 4th edition, London: Thomson Learning.

BPP (2005) *Marketing Environment: Practice and Revision Kit*, London: BPP Publishing.

Marketing Environment: Success Tape, Learning cassettes by BPP Publishing.

BH (2005) CIM Revision Cards: Marketing Environment 05/06, Oxford: BH/Elsevier.

Overview and rationale

Approach

This unit has been designed to provide introductory knowledge and understanding of the organization, its external environment and the implications for the marketing function. While a significant degree of continuity has been maintained from the original syllabus, there has been a rigorous refinement to ensure both horizontal and vertical separation and integration.

Horizontally this has led to a desirable slimming of the syllabus content by removing significant overlaps with Marketing Fundamentals, particularly in the areas of stakeholder theory, relationship marketing and social responsibility. It builds on the foundation provided by Marketing Fundamentals – of the role of marketing in the identification, anticipation and profitable supply of customer needs – to provide the necessary appreciation of the internal and external environment to fulfil this role.

Vertically there is much more focussed integration between Marketing Environment and the Professional Diploma unit, Marketing Research and Information, which will provide the next tier of knowledge and skills in the marketing research process. This will build upon the study of information collection and marketing information systems undertaken in the Marketing Environment.

The importance of the Marketing Environment concept rests on the recognition that the organization is a creature of its environment. Its resources, income, threats, opportunities and very survival are generated and conditioned by an increasingly uncertain, complex and dynamic environment. The purpose of this unit is to recognise the organization as an open system and to understand how the marketer interfaces between the organization interlocked with a challenging environment. Considerable stress is now laid on the means of collecting and mobilising information and feedback from the environment and the scope for proactive inter-action with it.

The rationale for the unit is that it provides the marketer with a breadth of knowledge and understanding of the environmental system and its inter-relationships of which the organization is part. This useful base of environmental information and its interpretation provides valuable and relevant input and contribution to the planning, budgeting and strategic processes within the organization.

Syllabus content

Following the syllabus review much of the original content remains but the balance of weighting between the four elements has changed. Due to the transfer of syllabus content to the other Professional Certificate units, it has been possible to moderate the loading of what was always a challenging syllabus and this is reflected in the change in weighting.

Element 1: The nature of the organization and the impact of its environment

- o This has been re-titled and its weighting increased from 10 to 15 per cent.
- o The content from 1.1 to 1.7 covers similar syllabus points as before but re-expressed as knowledge or skill requirements.
- o While students are expected to appreciate the configuration of the internal environment and the various types of organization, the orientation of knowledge requirements on objectives and open systems are essentially outward looking.
- o Knowledge requirements 1.8 and 1.9 provide the initial bridge between the organization and its wider environment. This should overview the nature of the environment, the challenge posed by the changes taking place and the significance of environmental understanding and knowledge to the marketer.
- o They provide the overview of the marketing and its significance before proceeding to element 2.

Element 2: Micro-environment

- o This element has slimmed down from a 30 to 20 per cent weighting and the focus remains the micro environment.
- o The appreciation of the micro environment still includes an overview of the stakeholder map and the significance of its more important constituents. However, stakeholder analysis and internal marketing are now treated in Marketing Fundamentals and Customer Communications.
- o Social responsibility and societal marketing are relocated to Marketing Fundamentals.
- o The role and significance of pressure groups remains in the syllabus with current emphasis being given to employees, consumerists and environmental groups since these are currently most relevant to the marketer.
- o The competitive environment and competition policies remain important aspects but there will no longer be an expectation of undertaking a 5 force analysis at this stage.

335

Element 3: Macro-environment

o The macro environment remains largely unchanged except for the inclusion of a new 4.8. This provides a more logical and coherent location for this skill outcome which will draw from consideration of all the macro environments considered in this element.

o The weighting for this element has increased from 45 to 50 per cent accordingly.

Element 4: Environmental information systems

o This has been re-titled.

o The knowledge and skill outcomes are primarily concerned with the sources, collection, organization and use of information from within the organization and the environment.

o There will be an emphasis on marketing information systems and the benefits they can provide.

o Techniques for forecasting the future remain in this element, e.g. quantitative and qualitative forecasting techniques including scenarios; auditing the environment; and impact analysis.

o This element will form the platform for development in the Professional Diploma when the marketing research process will be systematically treated.

Delivery approach

o Marketing Environment should preferably be taught following Marketing Fundamentals, which provides the fundamental base of marketing knowledge, including elements of direct relevance to the environment. Assessments continue to be set in the business context and report format is expected, although only a summarized approach.

o Marketing Environment is a challenging syllabus for tutors and students alike given the knowledge and skills it draws from disciplines such as economics, sociology, politics and management.

o The syllabus contains a number of tools and techniques that need to be applied for their full understanding to be achieved. Students should be encouraged to apply these tools to either their own or a suitable case organization.

o The environment is ever changing and both tutors and students must strive to keep abreast of developments. Use should be made of core texts and additional readings where appropriate, supplemented by current affairs media and relevant websites. These should be linked to regular feedback activities.

o Where possible students should be encouraged to develop collaborative partnerships in the collection of relevant information and cases.

o The syllabus will be reviewed annually with changes being triggered through Strategic Marketing in Practice unit of the Professional PG Diploma i.e. spin-off syllabus implications from identified trends and innovations in marketing.

Additional resources (Syllabus – Professional Certificate In Marketing)

Introduction

Texts to support the individual units are listed in the syllabus for each unit. This Appendix shows a list of marketing journals, press and websites that tutors and students may find useful in supporting their studies at Professional Certificate.

Press

Students will be expected to have access to current examples of marketing campaigns and so should be sure to keep up to date with the appropriate marketing and quality daily press, including:

- *Campaign* – Haymarket
- *Internet Business* – Haymarket
- *Marketing* – Haymarket
- *Marketing Business* – Chartered Institute of Marketing
- *Marketing Week* – Centaur
- *Revolution* – Haymarket

Websites

The Chartered Institute of Marketing

www.cim.co.uk	The CIM site with information and access to learning support for students.
www.cim.co.uk/learningzone	Full details of all that is new in CIM's educational offer including specimen answers and Hot Topics.
www.cimeducator.com	The CIM site for tutors only.

Publications on-line

www.revolution.haynet.com	Revolution magazine.
www.marketing.haynet.com	Marketing magazine.
www.FT.com	A wealth of information for cases (now charging).
www.IPA.co.uk	Need to register – communication resources.
www.booksites.net	Financial Times/Prentice Hall Text websites.

Sources of useful information

www.acnielsen.co.uk	AC Nielsen – excellent for research.
http://advertising.utexas.edu/world/	Resources for advertising and marketing professionals, students, and tutors.
www.bized.com	Case studies.
www.corporateinformation.com	Worldwide sources listed by country.
www.esomar.nl	European Body representing Research Organizations – useful for guidelines on research ethics and approaches.
www.dma.org.uk	The Direct Marketing Association.
www.eiu.com	The Economist Intelligence Unit.
www.euromonitor.com	Euromonitor consumer markets.
www.europa.eu.int	The European Commission's extensive range of statistics and reports relating to EU and member countries.
www.managementhelp.org/research/research.htm	Part of the 'Free Management Library' – explaining research methods.
www.marketresearch.org.uk	The MRS site with information and access to learning support for students – useful links on ethics and code of conduct.
www.mmc.gov.uk	Summaries of Competition Commission reports.
www.oecd.org	OECD statistics and other information relating to member nations including main economic indicators.
www.quirks.com	An American source of information on marketing research issues and projects.
www.statistics.gov.uk	UK Government statistics.

www.un.org	United Nations publish statistics on member nations.
www.worldbank.org	World bank economic, social and natural resource indicators for over 200 countries. Includes over 600 indicators covering GNP per capita, growth, economic statistics, etc.

Case sites

www.bluelagoon.co.uk	Case – SME website address.
www.ebay.com	On-line auction – buyer behaviour.
www.glenfiddich.com	Interesting site for case and branding.
www.interflora.co.uk	e-commerce direct ordering.
www.moorcroft.co.uk	Good for relationship marketing.
www.ribena.co.uk	Excellent targeting and history of comms.
www.sothebys.ebay.com	New services offered because of advances in electronic technology.

© CIM 2005

Index

340